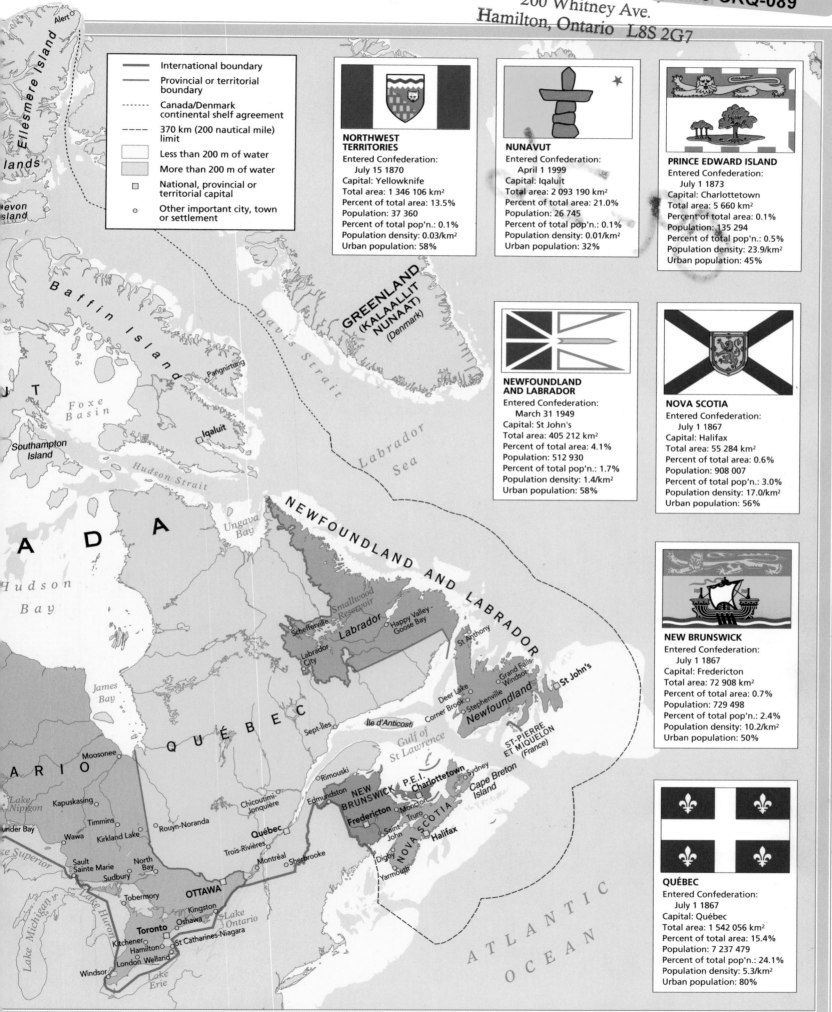

Legend

- International boundary
- Provincial or territorial boundary
- ---- Canada/Denmark continental shelf agreement
- -- 370 km (200 nautical mile) limit
- Less than 200 m of water
- More than 200 m of water
- □ National, provincial or territorial capital
- ○ Other important city, town or settlement

NORTHWEST TERRITORIES
Entered Confederation:
    July 15 1870
Capital: Yellowknife
Total area: 1 346 106 km²
Percent of total area: 13.5%
Population: 37 360
Percent of total pop'n.: 0.1%
Population density: 0.03/km²
Urban population: 58%

NUNAVUT
Entered Confederation:
    April 1 1999
Capital: Iqaluit
Total area: 2 093 190 km²
Percent of total area: 21.0%
Population: 26 745
Percent of total pop'n.: 0.1%
Population density: 0.01/km²
Urban population: 32%

PRINCE EDWARD ISLAND
Entered Confederation:
    July 1 1873
Capital: Charlottetown
Total area: 5 660 km²
Percent of total area: 0.1%
Population: 135 294
Percent of total pop'n.: 0.5%
Population density: 23.9/km²
Urban population: 45%

NEWFOUNDLAND AND LABRADOR
Entered Confederation:
    March 31 1949
Capital: St John's
Total area: 405 212 km²
Percent of total area: 4.1%
Population: 512 930
Percent of total pop'n.: 1.7%
Population density: 1.4/km²
Urban population: 58%

NOVA SCOTIA
Entered Confederation:
    July 1 1867
Capital: Halifax
Total area: 55 284 km²
Percent of total area: 0.6%
Population: 908 007
Percent of total pop'n.: 3.0%
Population density: 17.0/km²
Urban population: 56%

NEW BRUNSWICK
Entered Confederation:
    July 1 1867
Capital: Fredericton
Total area: 72 908 km²
Percent of total area: 0.7%
Population: 729 498
Percent of total pop'n.: 2.4%
Population density: 10.2/km²
Urban population: 50%

QUÉBEC
Entered Confederation:
    July 1 1867
Capital: Québec
Total area: 1 542 056 km²
Percent of total area: 15.4%
Population: 7 237 479
Percent of total pop'n.: 24.1%
Population density: 5.3/km²
Urban population: 80%

Lambert Conformal Conic projection

Pearson
School
Atlas

Robert Morrow

Former Curriculum Co-ordinator
Wentworth County Board of Education

PEARSON

Education
Canada

Toronto

CONTENTS

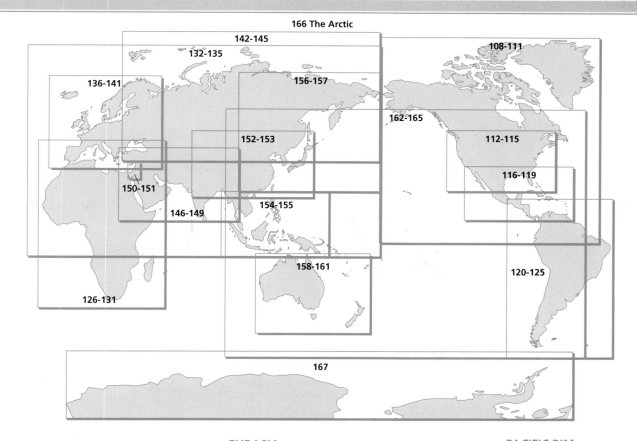

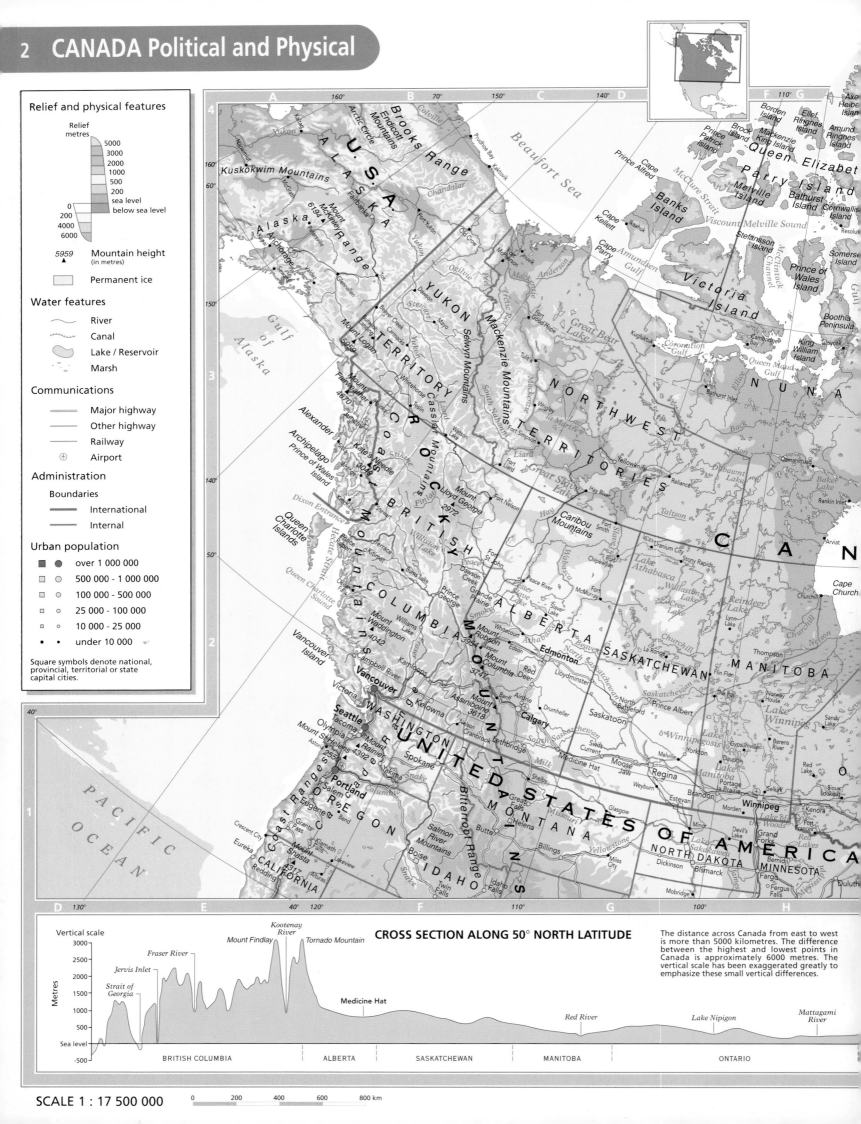

Relief and physical features

Relief
metres
5000
3000
2000
1000
500
200
0 sea level
below sea level
200
4000
6000

5959 ▲ Mountain height
(in metres)

Permanent ice

Water features

~~~ River

~~~ Canal

Lake / Reservoir

Marsh

Communications

Major highway

Other highway

Railway

⊕ Airport

Administration

Boundaries

International

Internal

Urban population

■ ● over 1 000 000

□ ○ 500 000 - 1 000 000

□ ○ 100 000 - 500 000

□ ○ 25 000 - 100 000

□ ○ 10 000 - 25 000

▪ • under 10 000

Square symbols denote national,
provincial, territorial or state
capital cities.

CROSS SECTION ALONG 50° NORTH LATITUDE

The distance across Canada from east to west
is more than 5000 kilometres. The difference
between the highest and lowest points in
Canada is approximately 6000 metres. The
vertical scale has been exaggerated greatly to
emphasize these small vertical differences.

Vertical scale

Metres

3000
2500
2000
1500
1000
500
Sea level
-500

Strait of Georgia
Jervis Inlet
Fraser River
Mount Findlay
Kootenay River
Tornado Mountain
Medicine Hat
Red River
Lake Nipigon
Mattagami River

BRITISH COLUMBIA   ALBERTA   SASKATCHEWAN   MANITOBA   ONTARIO

SCALE 1 : 17 500 000

0   200   400   600   800 km

CROSS SECTION FROM SARNIA TO ST JOHN'S

Lambert Conformal Conic projection

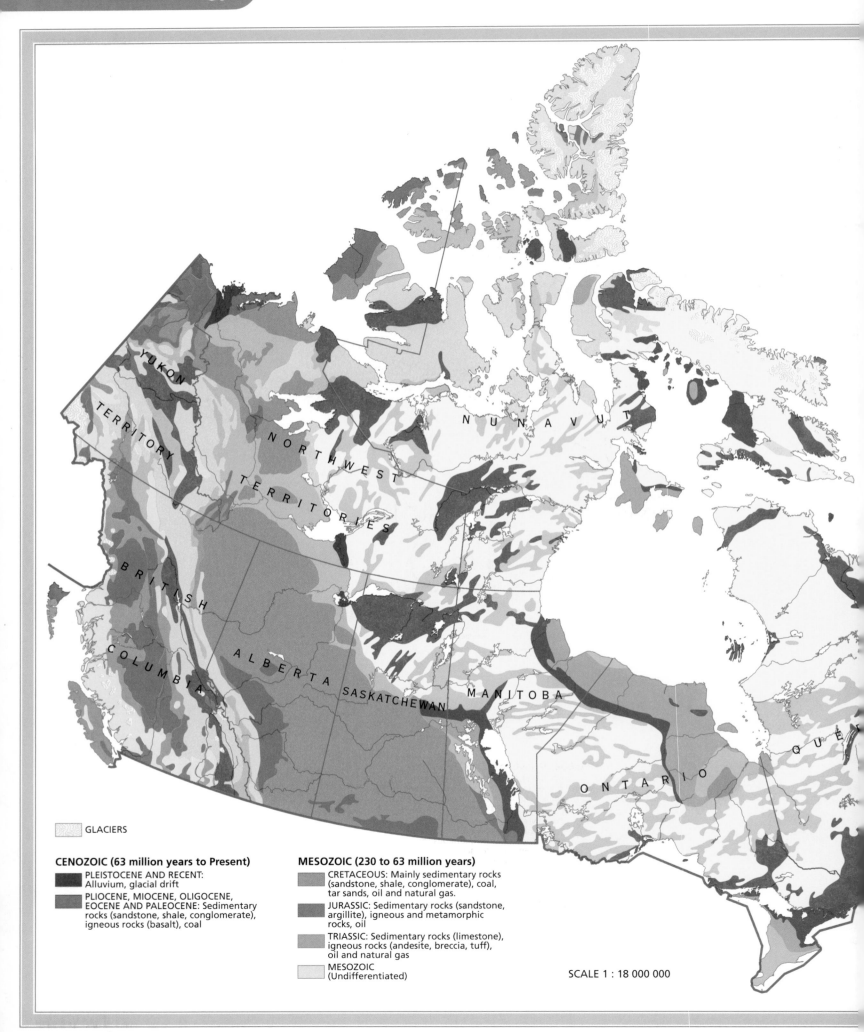

GLACIERS

CENOZOIC (63 million years to Present)

PLEISTOCENE AND RECENT:
Alluvium, glacial drift

PLIOCENE, MIOCENE, OLIGOCENE,
EOCENE AND PALEOCENE: Sedimentary
rocks (sandstone, shale, conglomerate),
igneous rocks (basalt), coal

MESOZOIC (230 to 63 million years)

CRETACEOUS: Mainly sedimentary rocks
(sandstone, shale, conglomerate), coal,
tar sands, oil and natural gas.

JURASSIC: Sedimentary rocks (sandstone,
argillite), igneous and metamorphic
rocks, oil

TRIASSIC: Sedimentary rocks (limestone),
igneous rocks (andesite, breccia, tuff),
oil and natural gas

MESOZOIC
(Undifferentiated)

SCALE 1 : 18 000 000

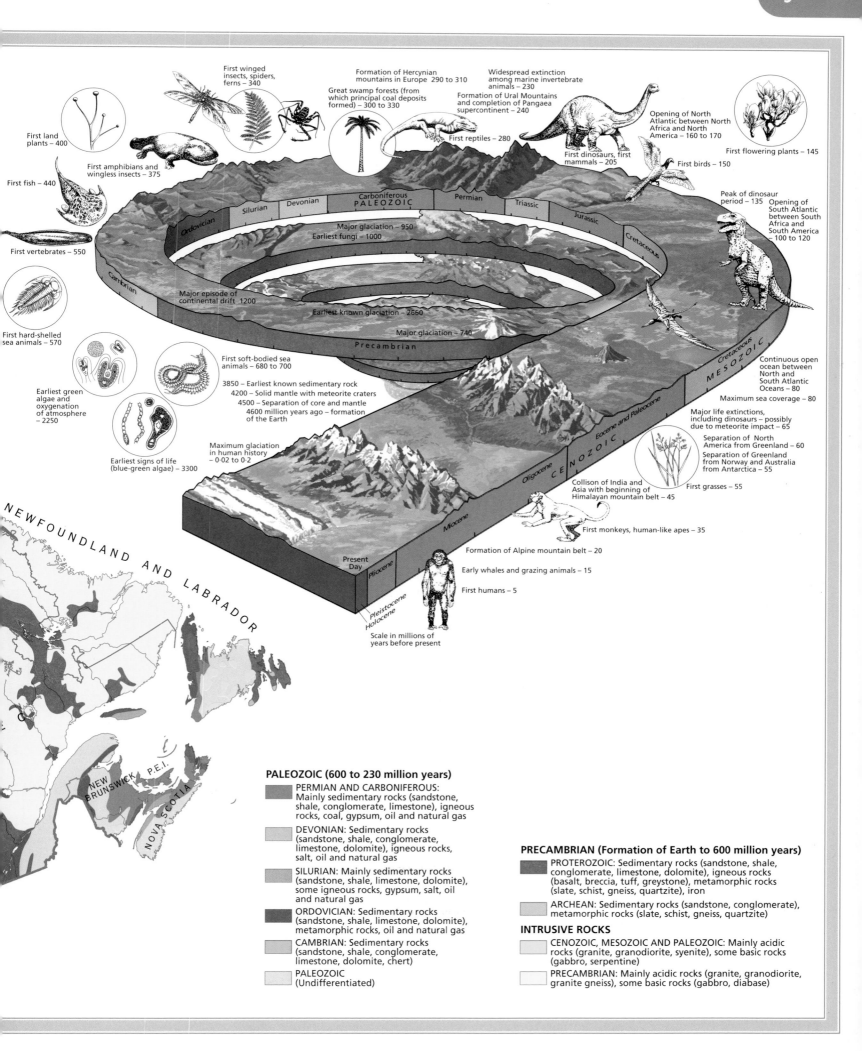

PALEOZOIC (600 to 230 million years)

PERMIAN AND CARBONIFEROUS: Mainly sedimentary rocks (sandstone, shale, conglomerate, limestone), igneous rocks, coal, gypsum, oil and natural gas

DEVONIAN: Sedimentary rocks (sandstone, shale, conglomerate, limestone, dolomite), igneous rocks, salt, oil and natural gas

SILURIAN: Mainly sedimentary rocks (sandstone, shale, limestone, dolomite), some igneous rocks, gypsum, salt, oil and natural gas

ORDOVICIAN: Sedimentary rocks (sandstone, shale, limestone, dolomite), metamorphic rocks, oil and natural gas

CAMBRIAN: Sedimentary rocks (sandstone, shale, conglomerate, limestone, dolomite, chert)

PALEOZOIC (Undifferentiated)

PRECAMBRIAN (Formation of Earth to 600 million years)

PROTEROZOIC: Sedimentary rocks (sandstone, shale, conglomerate, limestone, dolomite), igneous rocks (basalt, breccia, tuff, greystone), metamorphic rocks (slate, schist, gneiss, quartzite), iron

ARCHEAN: Sedimentary rocks (sandstone, conglomerate), metamorphic rocks (slate, schist, gneiss, quartzite)

INTRUSIVE ROCKS

CENOZOIC, MESOZOIC AND PALEOZOIC: Mainly acidic rocks (granite, granodiorite, syenite), some basic rocks (gabbro, serpentine)

PRECAMBRIAN: Mainly acidic rocks (granite, granodiorite, granite gneiss), some basic rocks (gabbro, diabase)

PHYSIOGRAPHIC REGIONS

Innuitian Region
Arctic Lowlands
Cordilleran Region
Interior Plains
The Canadian Shield
Hudson Bay Lowlands
Great Lakes –
St Lawrence Lowlands
Appalachian Region

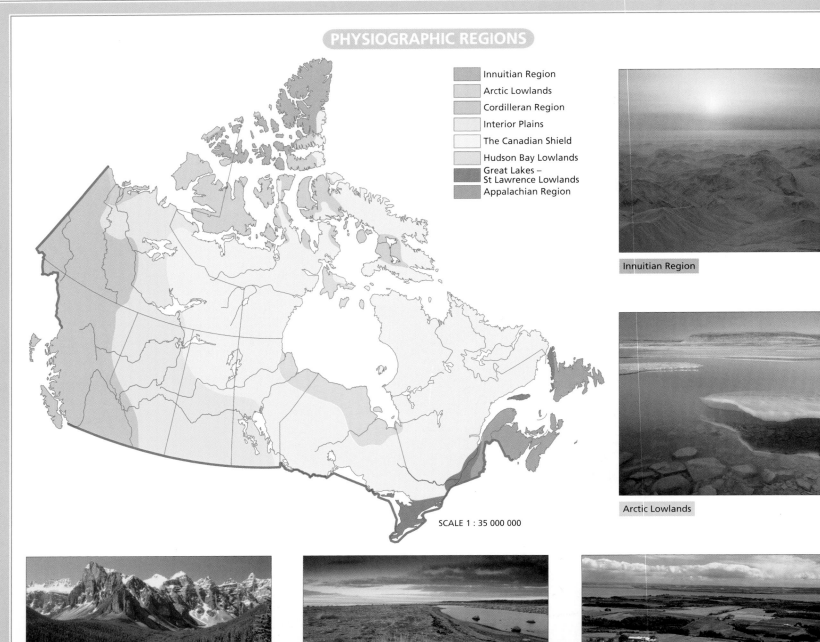

SCALE 1 : 35 000 000

Innuitian Region

Cordilleran Region

Hudson Bay Lowlands

Arctic Lowlands

Appalachian Region

Interior Plains

The Canadian Shield

Great Lakes – St Lawrence Lowlands

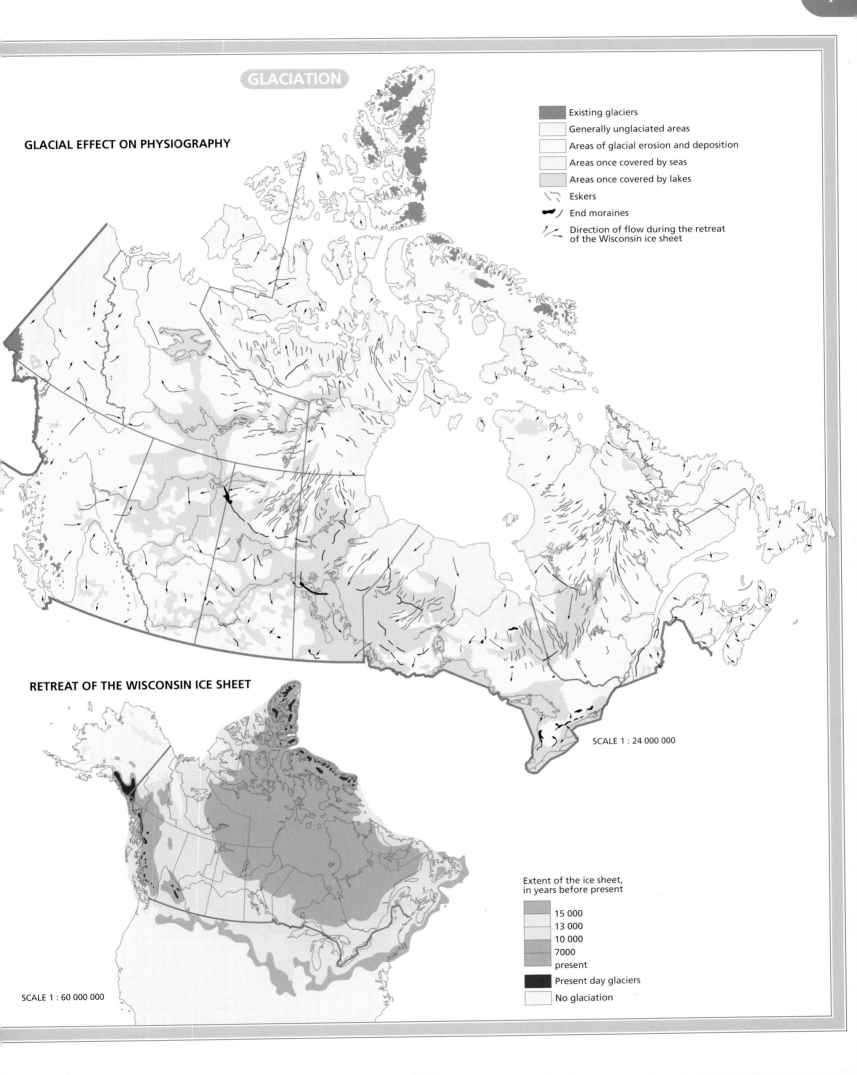

GLACIATION

GLACIAL EFFECT ON PHYSIOGRAPHY

Existing glaciers
Generally unglaciated areas
Areas of glacial erosion and deposition
Areas once covered by seas
Areas once covered by lakes
Eskers
End moraines
Direction of flow during the retreat of the Wisconsin ice sheet

SCALE 1 : 24 000 000

RETREAT OF THE WISCONSIN ICE SHEET

Extent of the ice sheet, in years before present

15 000
13 000
10 000
7000
present
Present day glaciers
No glaciation

SCALE 1 : 60 000 000

AIR MASSES

January

→ Warm ocean current
→ Cold ocean current

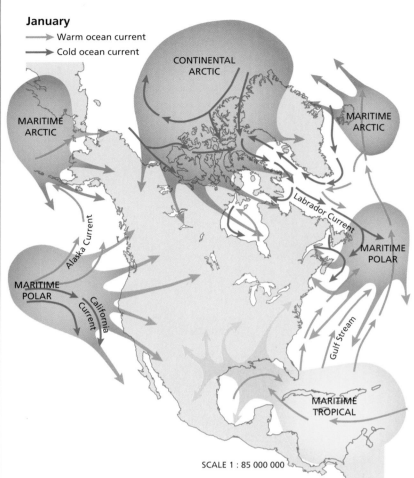

SCALE 1 : 85 000 000

Air masses are large bodies of air in which temperature and moisture conditions are approximately the same throughout the air mass. They take on the characteristics of the areas over which they form. Then, when they move, they take those characteristics to the new areas. Air masses can develop over land or water. In January, the Continental Arctic air mass develops over the northern land and ice-covered areas. It is cold and dry, and brings crisp winter weather further south.

July

→ Warm ocean current
→ Cold ocean current

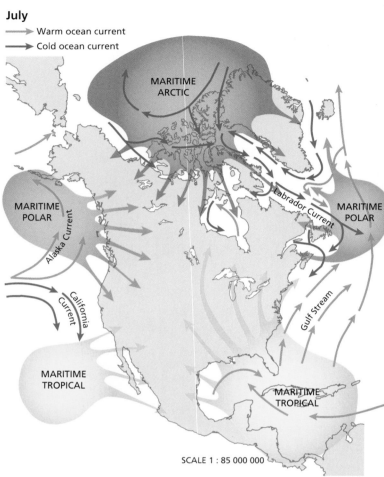

SCALE 1 : 85 000 000

In July, some air masses migrate northward from their January position. The Maritime Tropical air mass becomes much more dominant in eastern Canada, bringing hot, humid weather to areas east of the Rockies. The warm, wet, weather along Canada's west coast is a result of the Maritime Polar air mass moving inland from the Pacific Ocean. However, precipitation is greater in the winter when the Maritime Polar air mass is directly off the west coast.

WEATHER FRONTS

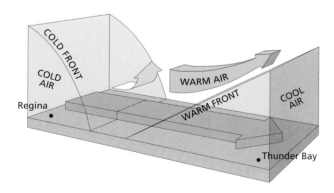

Air masses move in order to equalize atmospheric pressure, moving from high- to low-pressure zones. The line where two masses of air with different characteristics meet is called a *front*. When warm air is moving into an area of cold air, the front is called a warm front. When the reverse is the case, it is called a cold front. Note that cold air burrows *under* warm air, while warm air tends to ride *over* cold air.

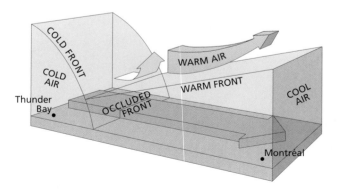

A cold front forces the warm air ahead of it to rise quickly, causing heavy precipitation, often in the form of thunderstorms. In contrast, along a warm front warm air rises slowly over the cold air, creating widespread areas of gentle precipitation. Cold fronts move faster than warm fronts. An occluded front occurs when a cold front catches up to a warm front, forcing all the warm air aloft. In this way, an area may go from cool to cold, without experiencing the warm air.

DAYS WITH PRECIPITATION

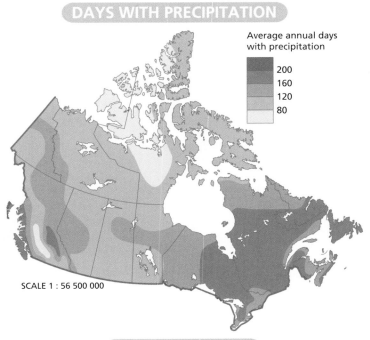

Average annual days with precipitation

- 200
- 160
- 120
- 80

SCALE 1 : 56 500 000

CLOUD COVER

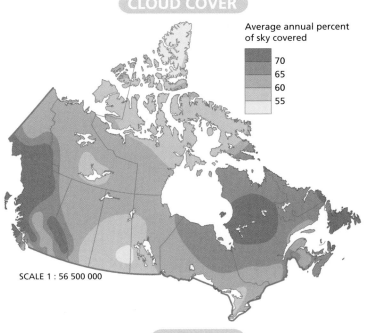

Average annual percent of sky covered

- 70
- 65
- 60
- 55

SCALE 1 : 56 500 000

THUNDERSTORMS

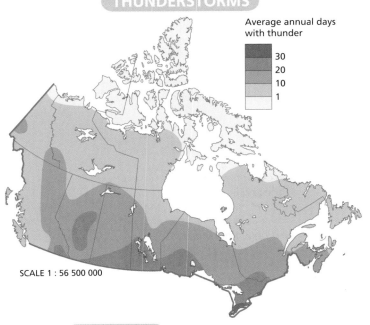

Average annual days with thunder

- 30
- 20
- 10
- 1

SCALE 1 : 56 500 000

UV INDEX

Toronto, 2002

Extreme
High
Moderate
Low
Very Low

UV index

J F M A M J J A S O N D

Time to burn

| days | more than 1 hour | about 30 min | about 20 min | less than 15 min |

HUMIDITY

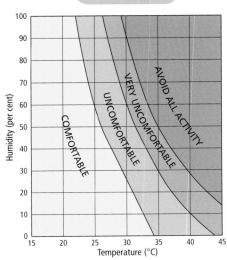

AVOID ALL ACTIVITY
VERY UNCOMFORTABLE
UNCOMFORTABLE
COMFORTABLE

Humidity (per cent)

Temperature (°C)

WIND CHILL

Calculation chart

Wind velocity km/h	Air temperature °C						
	5	0	-10	-20	-30	-40	-50
10	3	-3	-15	-27	-39	-51	-63
20	1	-5	-18	-31	-41	-56	-68
30	0	-7	-20	-33	-46	-59	-72
40	-1	-7	-21	-34	-48	-61	-74
50	-1	-8	-22	-35	-49	-63	-76
60	-2	-9	-23	-37	-50	-64	-78
70	-2	-9	-23	-37	-51	-66	-80
80	-3	-10	-24	-38	-52	-67	-81

Thresholds

Risk of frostbite in prolonged exposure

Frostbite possible in 10 minutes

Frostbite possible in 2 minutes

TEMPERATURE

January

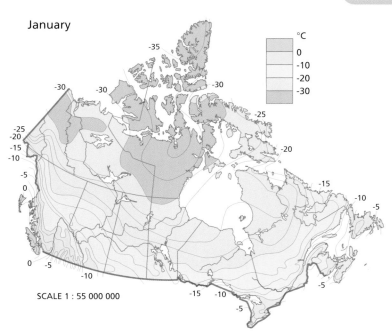

SCALE 1 : 55 000 000

°C
0
-10
-20
-30

Temperatures across Canada are shown on the maps using isotherms – lines joining places with the same temperature. The temperatures in Canada in January are affected by two conditions: latitude and continentality. Differences occur from north to south, showing the effect of latitude. Differences also occur from the coastal regions towards the centre of the continent, showing the effect of the land mass. Places that are north and in the centre of the land mass (e.g., Baker Lake, Cambridge Bay) are very cold in winter.

July

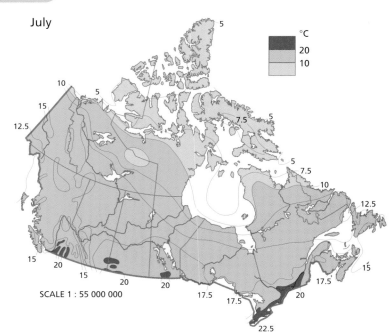

SCALE 1 : 55 000 000

°C
20
10

The temperatures in Canada in July reflect the influence of latitude. This is shown by the general east-west trend of the isotherms. Along the coasts, temperatures are moderated by bodies of water. Interior locations have low winter, but relatively high summer, temperatures. This is a true "continental" climate with a wide range of temperature and low precipitation. Canada's highest summer temperatures are in southern Ontario and the southern parts of British Columbia.

PRECIPITATION

Annual precipitation

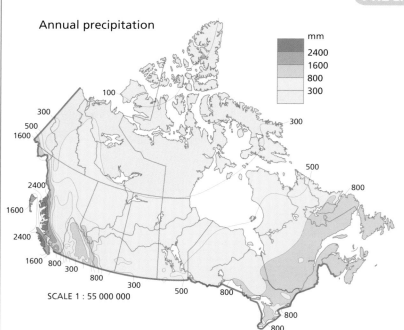

SCALE 1 : 55 000 000

mm
2400
1600
800
300

Precipitation includes all forms of moisture. Several factors influence the pattern of precipitation in Canada: bodies of water, prevailing winds, air masses, and relief. The far northern areas are desert-like, with low precipitation. There is little evaporation associated with the low temperatures and, therefore, little precipitation. Heavy precipitation is concentrated in a narrow area along the west coast by the effect of the mountains.

Annual snowfall

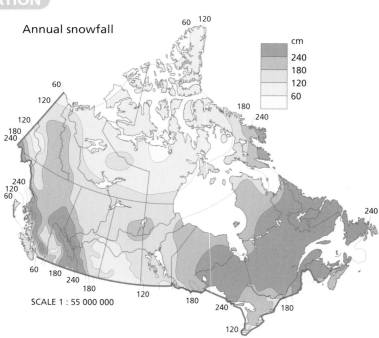

SCALE 1 : 55 000 000

cm
240
180
120
60

Snowfall is included in the annual precipitation totals. The amount of snowfall is converted to water, using a 10:1 snow-to-moisture ratio. The snowfall map shows the influence of the mountains on precipitation. Moisture-laden air from the Gulf of Mexico mixes with the cooler air across northern Ontario and Québec. There is little actual snowfall in much of the far north – very similar to the amounts received in the southern prairies.

SUNSHINE

Solar radiation

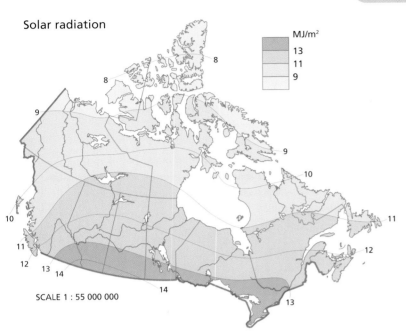

MJ/m²
- 13
- 11
- 9

SCALE 1 : 55 000 000

Solar radiation (infrared, visible, and ultraviolet light) is indispensable for life on Earth. The sun heats up the atmosphere and provides sunlight. However, ultraviolet radiation can be very harmful for humans. UV radiation is responsible for most forms of skin cancer. The pattern of solar radiation reflects the influence of cloud cover, latitude, and the angle of the sun's rays as they enter the atmosphere and penetrate to the earth's surface. Solar radiation is measured in megajoules per square metre (MJ/m²).

Bright sunshine hours

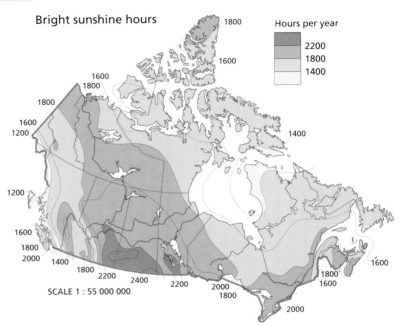

Hours per year
- 2200
- 1800
- 1400

SCALE 1 : 55 000 000

Several factors affect the number of hours of bright sunshine in a given area each year: air masses, cyclonic storms, and number of daylight hours. The southern prairies have the most sunshine hours in a year, reaching more than double the number of hours in some coastal areas of B.C. Estevan, Saskatchewan is Canada's sunshine capital with over 2500 hours of bright sunshine and nearly 3000 hours of clear skies. In contrast, Prince Rupert, B.C. has over 6000 hours of cloudy conditions.

FROST-FREE DAYS

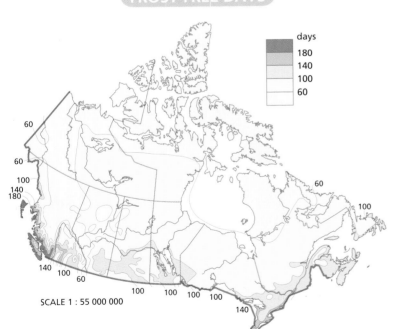

days
- 180
- 140
- 100
- 60

SCALE 1 : 55 000 000

The number of frost-free days is measured from the last frost in the spring to the first frost in the fall. The length of the frost-free period helps to determine planting and harvesting times. However, since these are averages, established over many years of keeping records, the averages cannot be counted upon as a prediction for a specific year. Thompson, Manitoba has the shortest frost-free season in Canada – 64 days.

GROWING SEASON

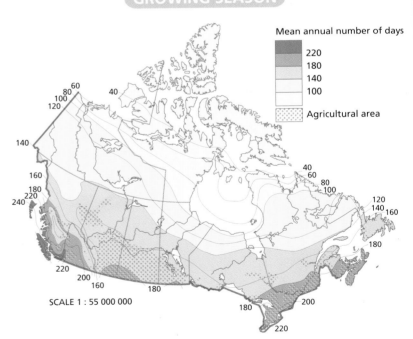

Mean annual number of days
- 220
- 180
- 140
- 100

Agricultural area

SCALE 1 : 55 000 000

The growing season represents the number of days in the growing season when the temperature exceeds 6°C. When temperatures reach this level, plant growth occurs. There may be days when the temperature reaches 6°C and then falls below the freezing point at night. Consequently, the growing season is longer than the frost-free period. The growing season is longest in southern British Columbia and southwestern Ontario.

CLIMATE REGIONS

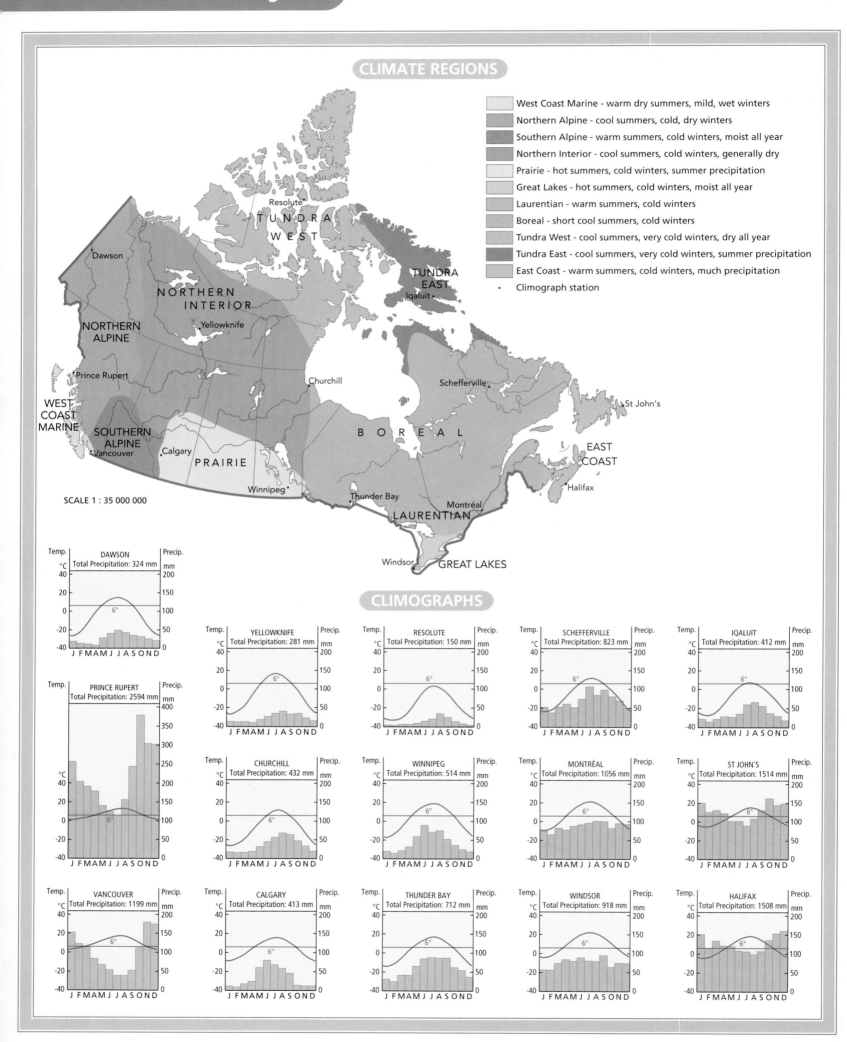

West Coast Marine - warm dry summers, mild, wet winters
Northern Alpine - cool summers, cold, dry winters
Southern Alpine - warm summers, cold winters, moist all year
Northern Interior - cool summers, cold winters, generally dry
Prairie - hot summers, cold winters, summer precipitation
Great Lakes - hot summers, cold winters, moist all year
Laurentian - warm summers, cold winters
Boreal - short cool summers, cold winters
Tundra West - cool summers, very cold winters, dry all year
Tundra East - cool summers, very cold winters, summer precipitation
East Coast - warm summers, cold winters, much precipitation
• Climograph station

SCALE 1 : 35 000 000

CLIMOGRAPHS

DAWSON — Total Precipitation: 324 mm
YELLOWKNIFE — Total Precipitation: 281 mm
RESOLUTE — Total Precipitation: 150 mm
SCHEFFERVILLE — Total Precipitation: 823 mm
IQALUIT — Total Precipitation: 412 mm
PRINCE RUPERT — Total Precipitation: 2594 mm
CHURCHILL — Total Precipitation: 432 mm
WINNIPEG — Total Precipitation: 514 mm
MONTRÉAL — Total Precipitation: 1056 mm
ST JOHN'S — Total Precipitation: 1514 mm
VANCOUVER — Total Precipitation: 1199 mm
CALGARY — Total Precipitation: 413 mm
THUNDER BAY — Total Precipitation: 712 mm
WINDSOR — Total Precipitation: 918 mm
HALIFAX — Total Precipitation: 1508 mm

GREENHOUSE EFFECT

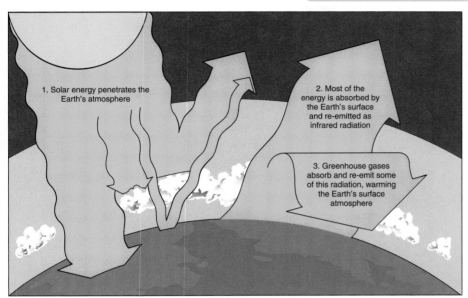

1. Solar energy penetrates the Earth's atmosphere

2. Most of the energy is absorbed by the Earth's surface and re-emitted as infrared radiation

3. Greenhouse gases absorb and re-emit some of this radiation, warming the Earth's surface atmosphere

The atmosphere is more than just "air." The mixture of gases that makes up the atmosphere performs many functions and helps to support life. Just as glass in a greenhouse holds heat in, the atmosphere traps heat and keeps it near Earth's surface. For centuries, the atmosphere changed little in temperature, and the balance of gases was suitable for plant, animal, and human survival. In recent years, however, the balance has been disrupted. Fossil fuels for heating and electrical production, gasoline for cars, and manufacturing have added greenhouse gases to the atmosphere. These gases trap the heat and warm the atmosphere. The main greenhouse gases are water vapour (H_2O), carbon dioxide (CO_2), methane (CH_4), nitrous oxide (N_2O), ozone (O_3), and halocarbons (CFCs, HFCs, etc.).

OZONE

Total ozone, January 1984

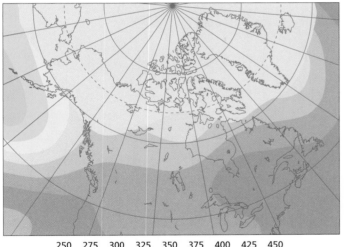

Total ozone, January 2001

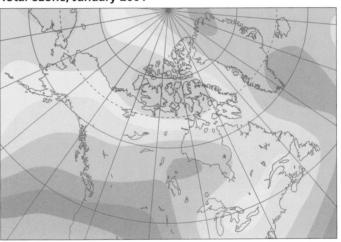

Dobson units   250   275   300   325   350   375   400   425   450   No data

CLIMATE CHANGE IN CANADA

Temperature
Celsius degrees above or below normal

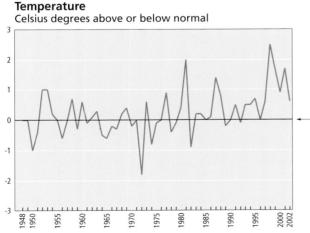

Precipitation
Millimetres above or below normal

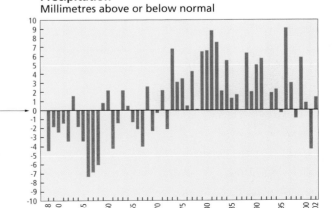

← Normal →

Coastal forest

Parkland

Grassland

VEGETATION AND CHARACTERISTIC FLORA

Tundra		Lichen / heath
		Dwarf shrubs / sedges / lichen / heath
		Alpine sedges / grasses and shrubs
Open woodland		Scattered needleleaf trees / broadleaf shrubs / heath / grass
Bogs		Moss / sedges / strings of needleleaf trees
Boreal forest		Needleleaf trees
		Mostly needleleaf trees with some broadleaf trees
Coastal forest		Large needleleaf trees
Sub-alpine forest		Needleleaf trees
High plateau / Pine forest		Mostly needleleaf trees with some broadleaf trees and grassland
Southeastern mixed forest		Mixture of broadleaf and needleleaf trees
Southern broadleaf forest		Broadleaf trees
Parkland		Broadleaf or needleleaf trees with patches of grassland
Grassland		Low, medium, and tall grasses
		Glaciers and permanent snow (no vegetation)

Tundra

Boreal forest

Southern broadleaf forest

Southeastern mixed forest

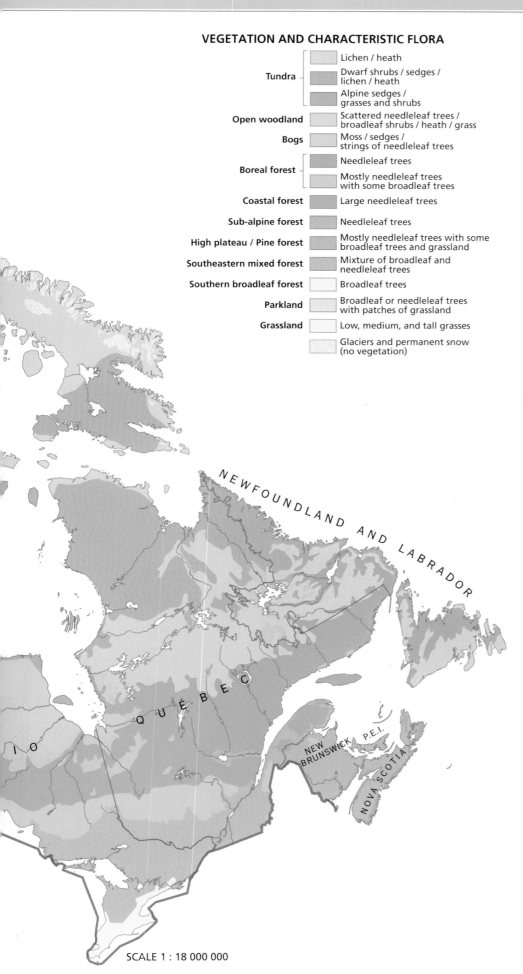

NEWFOUNDLAND AND LABRADOR

QUÉBEC

ONTARIO

NEW BRUNSWICK

P.E.I.

NOVA SCOTIA

SCALE 1 : 18 000 000

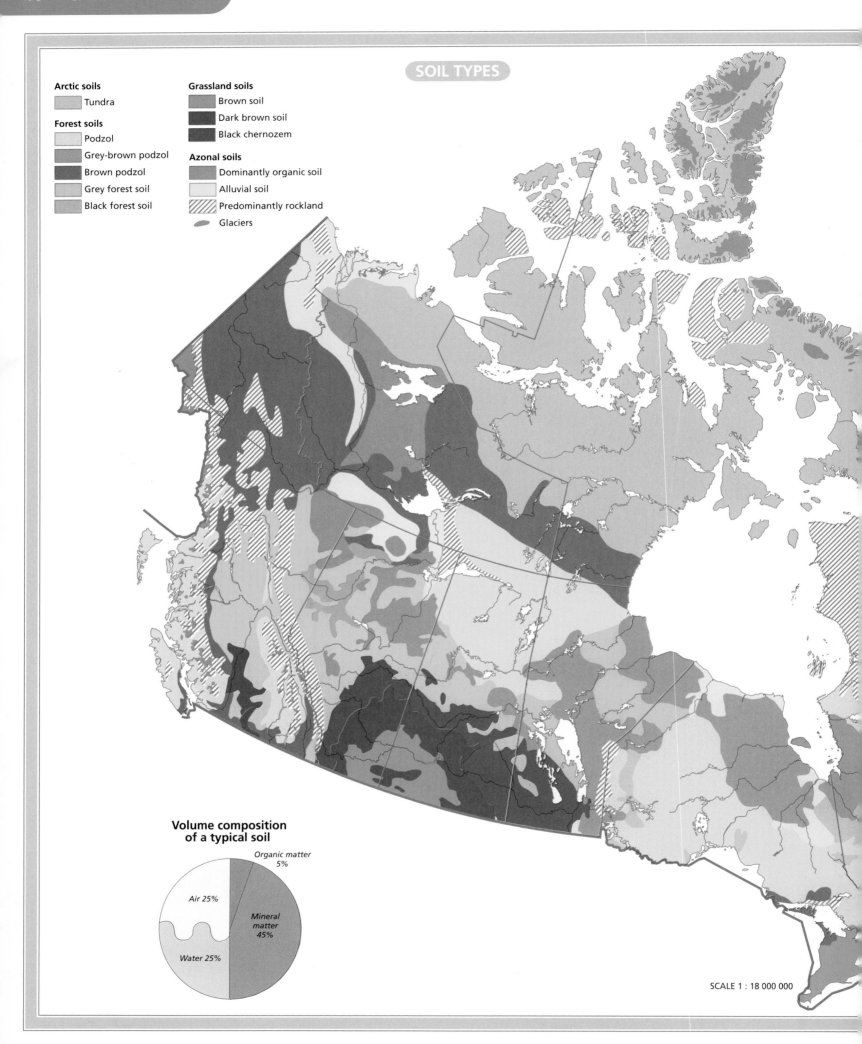

SOIL TYPES

Arctic soils
Tundra

Forest soils
Podzol
Grey-brown podzol
Brown podzol
Grey forest soil
Black forest soil

Grassland soils
Brown soil
Dark brown soil
Black chernozem

Azonal soils
Dominantly organic soil
Alluvial soil
Predominantly rockland
Glaciers

**Volume composition
of a typical soil**

Organic matter
5%

Air 25%

Mineral
matter
45%

Water 25%

SCALE 1 : 18 000 000

SOIL CAPABILITY

Soil capability classes one, two and three

SCALE 1 : 50 000 000

All types of soils can be categorized based on their potential for agriculture – the soil capability. Seven classes are recognized, but only the first three are considered capable of supporting sustained production of commonly cultivated crops. Class one soils have no limitations for capability. Classes two and three have some limitations, ranging from moderate to severe. These limitations may relate to climate, susceptibility to erosion, drainage, or stoniness. The remaining four classes of soil range from those marginal for crops to those completely unsuitable, even as pastureland.

SOIL PROFILES

A typical soil profile

Organic layer

A horizon (topsoil)

B horizon (subsoil)

C horizon

The A horizon is mostly made up of partially decayed organic materials. At the bottom is a modified zone in which water, percolating down, has removed soluble minerals and fine particles.

The B horizon is a combination of mineral and organic material. It contains the soluble minerals and fine particles from the A horizon. It is often possible to identify different layers within this horizon.

The C horizon consists mainly of weathered "parent material," the mineral material from which the soil is made. This can be either bedrock or glacial deposits.

Grey-brown podzol

Grey forest soil

Dark brown soil

Organic soil

Black chernozem

Alluvial soil

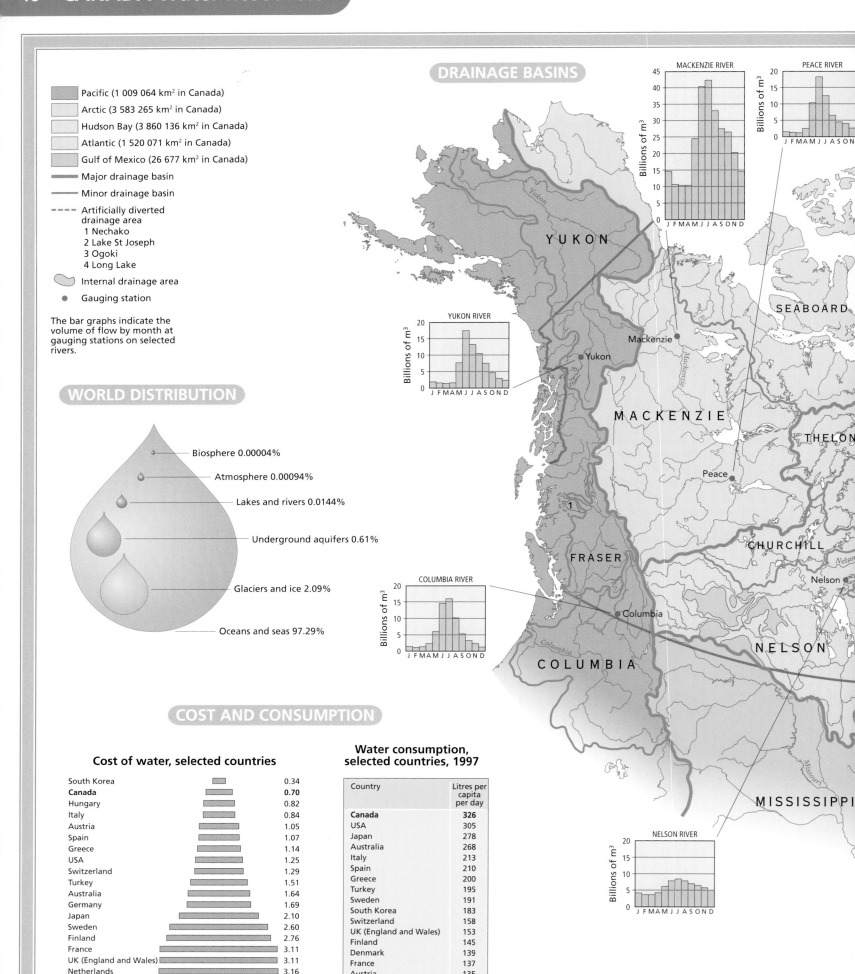

Legend

- Pacific (1 009 064 km² in Canada)
- Arctic (3 583 265 km² in Canada)
- Hudson Bay (3 860 136 km² in Canada)
- Atlantic (1 520 071 km² in Canada)
- Gulf of Mexico (26 677 km² in Canada)

— Major drainage basin

— Minor drainage basin

--- Artificially diverted drainage area
1 Nechako
2 Lake St Joseph
3 Ogoki
4 Long Lake

Internal drainage area

• Gauging station

The bar graphs indicate the volume of flow by month at gauging stations on selected rivers.

WORLD DISTRIBUTION

- Biosphere 0.00004%
- Atmosphere 0.00094%
- Lakes and rivers 0.0144%
- Underground aquifers 0.61%
- Glaciers and ice 2.09%
- Oceans and seas 97.29%

DRAINAGE BASINS

MACKENZIE RIVER

PEACE RIVER

YUKON RIVER

COLUMBIA RIVER

NELSON RIVER

YUKON

MACKENZIE

SEABOARD

THELON

CHURCHILL

FRASER

NELSON

COLUMBIA

MISSISSIPPI

Mackenzie

Yukon

Peace

Columbia

Nelson

COST AND CONSUMPTION

Cost of water, selected countries

Country	US$ per cubic metre, 1994-1998
South Korea	0.34
Canada	**0.70**
Hungary	0.82
Italy	0.84
Austria	1.05
Spain	1.07
Greece	1.14
USA	1.25
Switzerland	1.29
Turkey	1.51
Australia	1.64
Germany	1.69
Japan	2.10
Sweden	2.60
Finland	2.76
France	3.11
UK (England and Wales)	3.11
Netherlands	3.16
Denmark	3.18

US$ per cubic metre, 1994-1998

Water consumption, selected countries, 1997

Country	Litres per capita per day
Canada	**326**
USA	305
Japan	278
Australia	268
Italy	213
Spain	210
Greece	200
Turkey	195
Sweden	191
South Korea	183
Switzerland	158
UK (England and Wales)	153
Finland	145
Denmark	139
France	137
Austria	135
Netherlands	130
Germany	116

Groundwater contamination from a waste disposal site

Recharge area

Residential housing

Waste disposal site

Water table

River

Water supply wells

Contaminated groundwater

SCALE 1 : 24 000 000

MOOSE RIVER
Billions of m³
20
15
10
5
0
J F M A M J J A S O N D

CHURCHILL RIVER
Billions of m³
20
15
10
5
0
J F M A M J J A S O N D

SAINT JOHN RIVER
Billions of m³
20
15
10
5
0
J F M A M J J A S O N D

ST LAWRENCE RIVER
Billions of m³
20
15
10
5
0
J F M A M J J A S O N D

KOKSOAK

Churchill

CHURCHILL

LA GRANDE

AYES

SEVERN

WINISK

ALBANY

Moose

MOOSE

Saint John

St Lawrence

ST LAWRENCE

2

3

4

Provincial populations reliant on groundwater

N.W.T. and Nun.	1%
B.C.	22%
Qué.	22%
Ont.	23%
Man.	24%
Alta.	27%
Nfld. and Lab.	29%
Sask.	45%
N.S.	50%
Y.T.	63%
N.B.	64%
P.E.I.	100%

Water consumption, 2002

Percent not returned to the system
100
90
80
70
60
50
40
30
20
10
0

Agriculture
Electrical power
Manufacturing
Mining
Other industries
Personal and government

Water withdrawal, 2002

Personal and government 8.7 %

Agriculture 10.3%

Other industries 1.9%

Mining 1.5%

Manufacturing 14.2%

Electrical power 63.4%

Water withdrawal: 45 180 000 000 m³

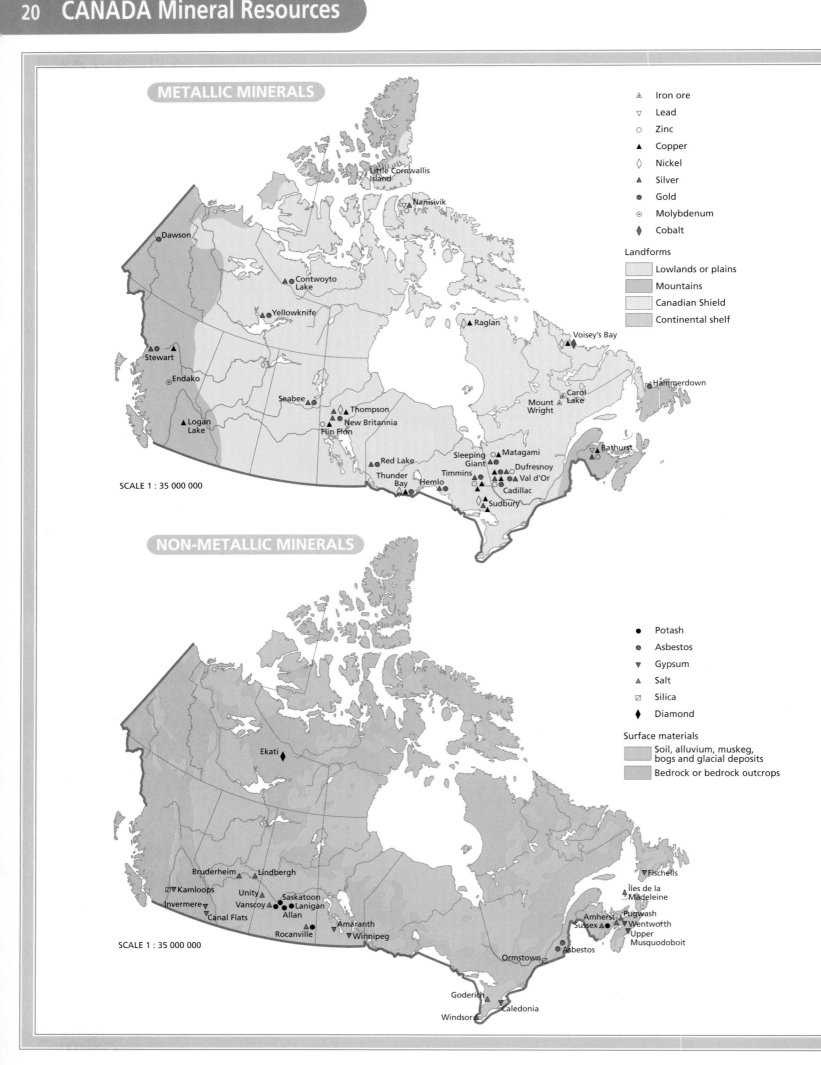

METALLIC MINERALS

Iron ore
Lead
Zinc
Copper
Nickel
Silver
Gold
Molybdenum
Cobalt

Landforms
Lowlands or plains
Mountains
Canadian Shield
Continental shelf

SCALE 1 : 35 000 000

Little Cornwallis Island
Nanisivik
Dawson
Contwoyto Lake
Yellowknife
Raglan
Voisey's Bay
Stewart
Endako
Hammerdown
Seabee
Carol Lake
Mount Wright
Thompson
New Britannia
Flin Flon
Logan Lake
Sleeping Giant
Matagami
Bathurst
Red Lake
Dufresnoy
Timmins
Val d'Or
Thunder Bay
Hemlo
Cadillac
Sudbury

NON-METALLIC MINERALS

Potash
Asbestos
Gypsum
Salt
Silica
Diamond

Surface materials
Soil, alluvium, muskeg, bogs and glacial deposits
Bedrock or bedrock outcrops

Ekati
SCALE 1 : 35 000 000

Bruderheim
Lindbergh
Fischells
Kamloops
Unity
Îles de la Madeleine
Invermere
Vanscoy
Saskatoon
Lanigan
Allan
Amherst
Pugwash
Canal Flats
Amaranth
Sussex
Wentworth
Rocanville
Winnipeg
Upper Musquodoboit
Ormstown
Asbestos
Goderich
Caledonia
Windsor

FUEL MINERALS

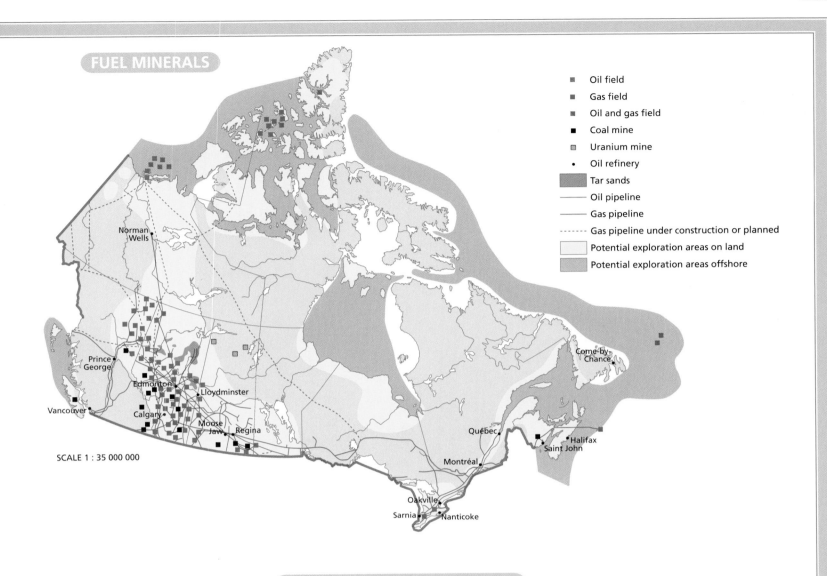

- ■ Oil field
- ■ Gas field
- ■ Oil and gas field
- ■ Coal mine
- ▨ Uranium mine
- • Oil refinery
- Tar sands
- —— Oil pipeline
- —— Gas pipeline
- ----- Gas pipeline under construction or planned
- Potential exploration areas on land
- Potential exploration areas offshore

Norman Wells
Prince George
Vancouver
Edmonton
Lloydminster
Calgary
Moose Jaw
Regina
Québec
Montréal
Come by Chance
Halifax
Saint John
Oakville
Sarnia
Nanticoke

SCALE 1 : 35 000 000

MINERALS : ECONOMIC VALUE

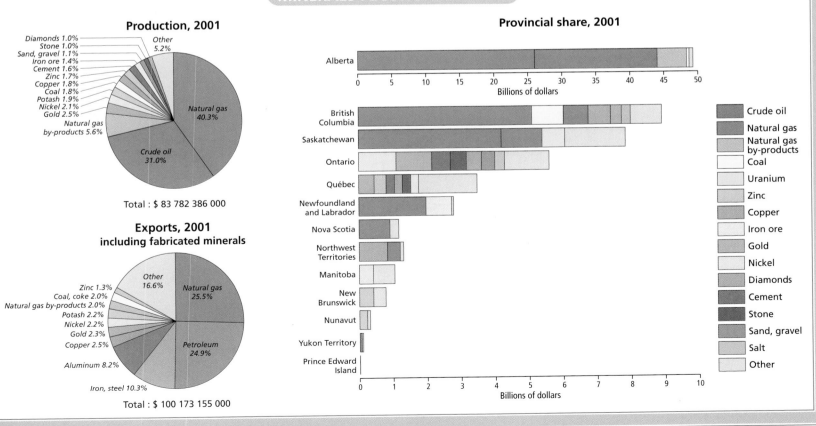

Production, 2001

- Diamonds 1.0%
- Stone 1.0%
- Sand, gravel 1.1%
- Iron ore 1.4%
- Cement 1.6%
- Zinc 1.7%
- Copper 1.8%
- Coal 1.8%
- Potash 1.9%
- Nickel 2.1%
- Gold 2.5%
- Natural gas by-products 5.6%
- Crude oil 31.0%
- Natural gas 40.3%
- Other 5.2%

Total : $ 83 782 386 000

Exports, 2001
including fabricated minerals

- Zinc 1.3%
- Coal, coke 2.0%
- Natural gas by-products 2.0%
- Potash 2.2%
- Nickel 2.2%
- Gold 2.3%
- Copper 2.5%
- Aluminum 8.2%
- Iron, steel 10.3%
- Petroleum 24.9%
- Natural gas 25.5%
- Other 16.6%

Total : $ 100 173 155 000

Provincial share, 2001

Alberta
0 5 10 15 20 25 30 35 40 45 50
Billions of dollars

British Columbia
Saskatchewan
Ontario
Québec
Newfoundland and Labrador
Nova Scotia
Northwest Territories
Manitoba
New Brunswick
Nunavut
Yukon Territory
Prince Edward Island
0 1 2 3 4 5 6 7 8 9 10
Billions of dollars

- Crude oil
- Natural gas
- Natural gas by-products
- Coal
- Uranium
- Zinc
- Copper
- Iron ore
- Gold
- Nickel
- Diamonds
- Cement
- Stone
- Sand, gravel
- Salt
- Other

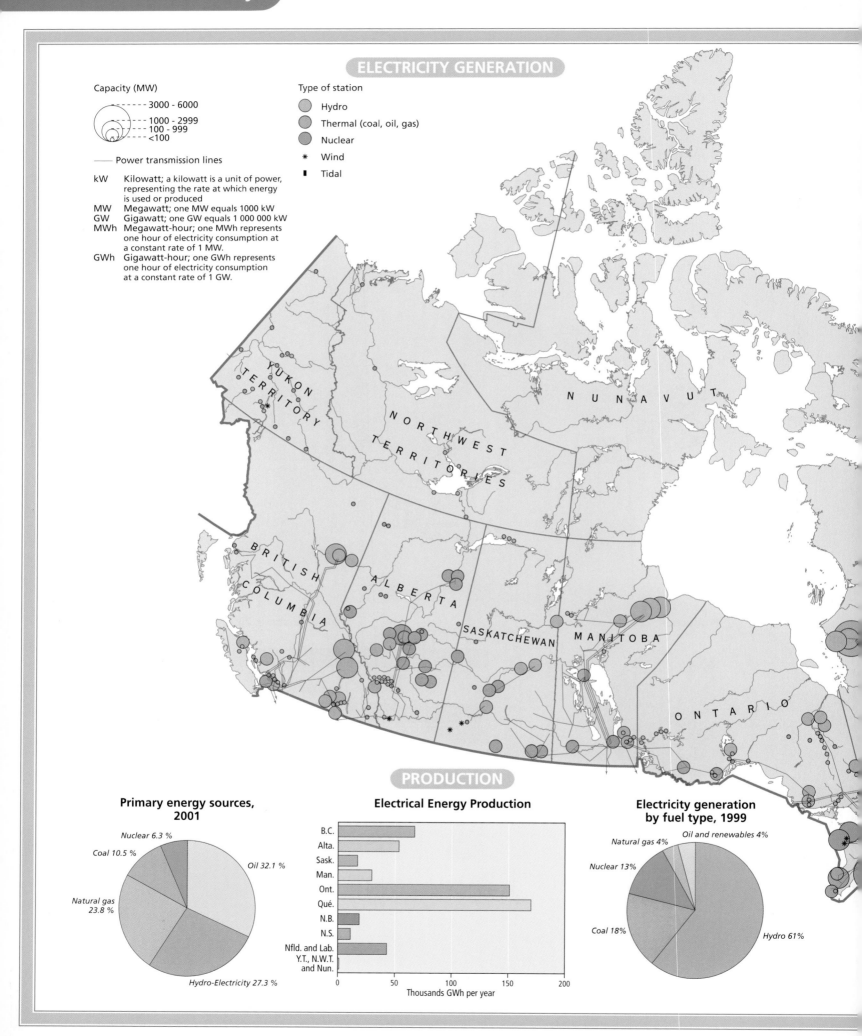

ELECTRICITY GENERATION

Capacity (MW)
- 3000 - 6000
- 1000 - 2999
- 100 - 999
- <100

Power transmission lines

Type of station
- Hydro
- Thermal (coal, oil, gas)
- Nuclear
- ✳ Wind
- ■ Tidal

kW   Kilowatt; a kilowatt is a unit of power, representing the rate at which energy is used or produced
MW Megawatt; one MW equals 1000 kW
GW Gigawatt; one GW equals 1 000 000 kW
MWh Megawatt-hour; one MWh represents one hour of electricity consumption at a constant rate of 1 MW.
GWh Gigawatt-hour; one GWh represents one hour of electricity consumption at a constant rate of 1 GW.

YUKON TERRITORY
NORTHWEST TERRITORIES
NUNAVUT
BRITISH COLUMBIA
ALBERTA
SASKATCHEWAN
MANITOBA
ONTARIO

PRODUCTION

Primary energy sources, 2001

- Nuclear 6.3 %
- Coal 10.5 %
- Natural gas 23.8 %
- Oil 32.1 %
- Hydro-Electricity 27.3 %

Electrical Energy Production

B.C.	
Alta.	
Sask.	
Man.	
Ont.	
Qué.	
N.B.	
N.S.	
Nfld. and Lab.	
Y.T., N.W.T. and Nun.	

0   50   100   150   200
Thousands GWh per year

Electricity generation by fuel type, 1999

- Natural gas 4%
- Oil and renewables 4%
- Nuclear 13%
- Coal 18%
- Hydro 61%

CONSUMPTION

Electricity consumption, 2000

Country	Average annual per capita (kWh)
Iceland	26 220
Norway	25 182
Canada	**16 967**
Kuwait	16 393
Sweden	15 659
Finland	15 285
Luxembourg	15 320
Qatar	14 991
USA	13 843
United Arab Emirates	12 095
Australia	10 052
New Zealand	9 155
Bahrain	8 510
Japan	8 331
Taiwan	8 316
Belgium	8 244
Switzerland	7 843
Singapore	7 467
Brunei	7 437
France	7 302
Austria	7 004
Germany	6 684

Monthly residential electricity costs *

City	Monthly cost in dollars
Winnipeg	98
Montréal	100
Vancouver	101
Ottawa	121
St John's	136
Regina	154
Moncton	154
Halifax	156
Toronto	160
Charlottetown	170
Edmonton	185

* Based on 1000 kWh per month, 2002

Electricity demand, 2001

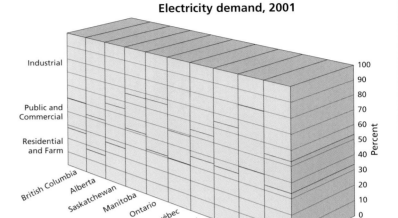

Some energy is lost in the form of heat through transmission lines and transformers.

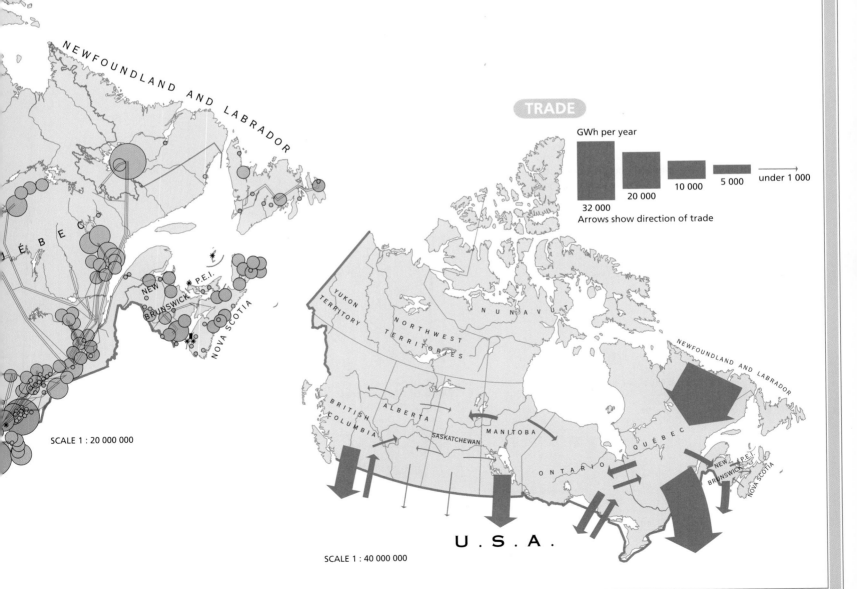

SCALE 1 : 20 000 000

TRADE

GWh per year

32 000 20 000 10 000 5 000 under 1 000

Arrows show direction of trade

U.S.A.

SCALE 1 : 40 000 000

GROWING DEGREE DAYS

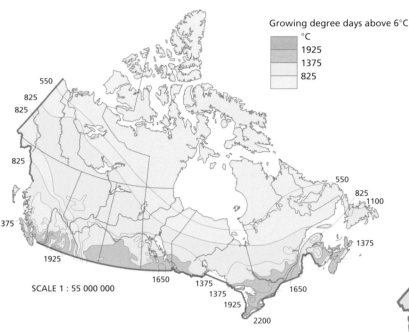

Growing degree days above 6°C

°C
1925
1375
825

550
825
825
825
1375
1925
SCALE 1 : 55 000 000
1650
1375
1375
1925
2200
550
825
1100
1375
1650
1375

Productive Canadian agriculture is focused in the southern part of the prairies and in southern Québec and Ontario. Some products are associated with specific regions – wheat with Saskatchewan – but many areas practise "mixed" farming, involving both crops and livestock. Although there are only 250 000 farms in Canada, they are generally large and mechanized. The average value of a farm in Canada is more than $1 million. Many farmers use sophisticated technology, such as GPS, to assist with efficient and effective production.

Markets have a strong influence on agriculture. Near large urban markets, the diversity of agriculture is increased to meet the demands. Exports are particularly important to Canadian farmers, and account for close to half of all agricultural income.

Environmentally friendly land management practices have gained popularity in recent years and are now used on more than half the land tilled in Canada. Conservation tillage minimizes the number of passes farmers make over their fields. This decreases fuel costs and reduces carbon dioxide emissions.

TYPES OF FARMING

YUKON
TERRITORY

NORTHWEST
TERRITORIES

NU

BRITISH
COLUMBIA

ALBERTA

SASKATCHEWAN

MANI

THE CHANGING FARM

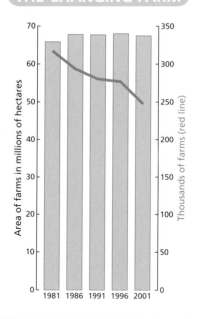

Area of farms in millions of hectares

Thousands of farms (red line)

70 — 350
60 — 300
50 — 250
40 — 200
30 — 150
20 — 100
10 — 50
0 — 0

1981 1986 1991 1996 2001

IMPORTS AND EXPORTS

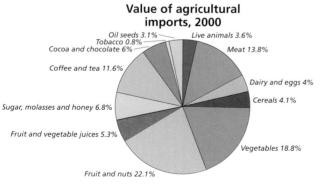

Value of agricultural imports, 2000

Oil seeds 3.1%
Tobacco 0.8%
Cocoa and chocolate 6%
Coffee and tea 11.6%
Sugar, molasses and honey 6.8%
Fruit and vegetable juices 5.3%
Fruit and nuts 22.1%
Live animals 3.6%
Meat 13.8%
Dairy and eggs 4%
Cereals 4.1%
Vegetables 18.8%

Total : $ 7 239 815 000

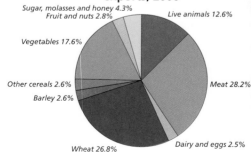

Value of agricultural exports, 2000

Sugar, molasses and honey 4.3%
Fruit and nuts 2.8%
Vegetables 17.6%
Other cereals 2.6%
Barley 2.6%
Wheat 26.8%
Live animals 12.6%
Meat 28.2%
Dairy and eggs 2.5%

Total : $ 9 259 308 000

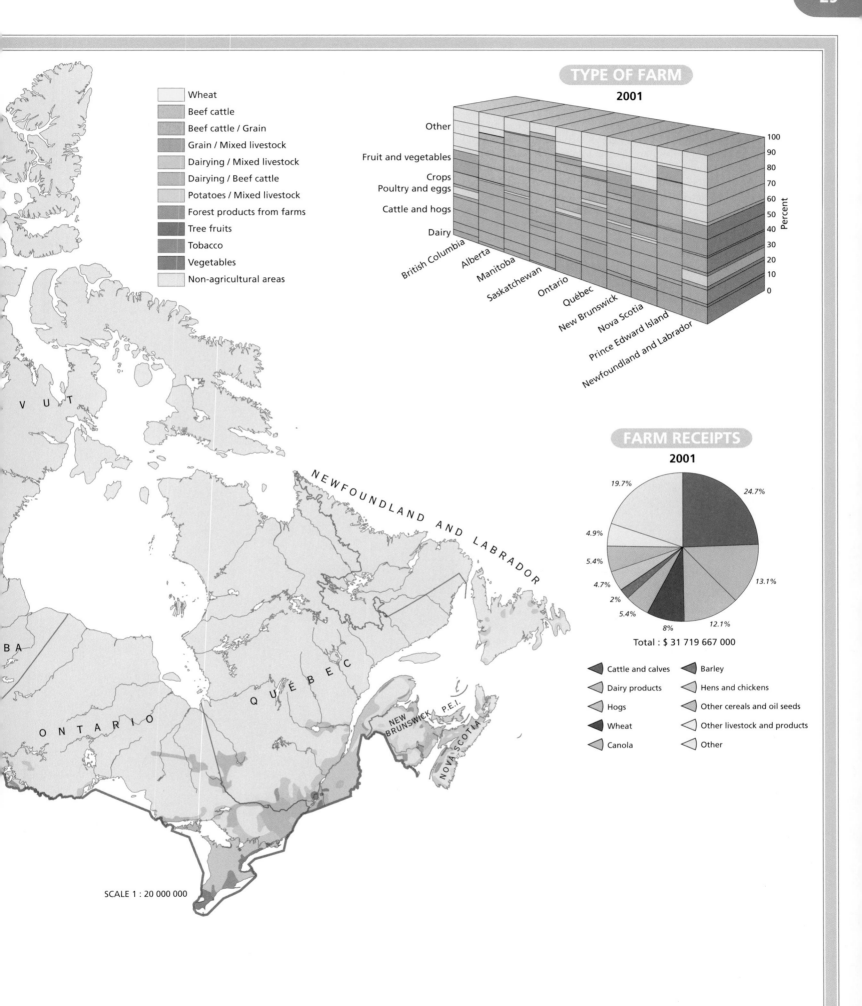

Legend (map)

- Wheat
- Beef cattle
- Beef cattle / Grain
- Grain / Mixed livestock
- Dairying / Mixed livestock
- Dairying / Beef cattle
- Potatoes / Mixed livestock
- Forest products from farms
- Tree fruits
- Tobacco
- Vegetables
- Non-agricultural areas

TYPE OF FARM

2001

(Categories: Other, Fruit and vegetables, Crops, Poultry and eggs, Cattle and hogs, Dairy)

Provinces: British Columbia, Alberta, Manitoba, Saskatchewan, Ontario, Québec, New Brunswick, Nova Scotia, Prince Edward Island, Newfoundland and Labrador

Percent: 0, 10, 20, 30, 40, 50, 60, 70, 80, 90, 100

FARM RECEIPTS

2001

- 24.7%
- 13.1%
- 12.1%
- 8%
- 5.4%
- 2%
- 4.7%
- 5.4%
- 4.9%
- 19.7%

Total : $ 31 719 667 000

- Cattle and calves
- Dairy products
- Hogs
- Wheat
- Canola
- Barley
- Hens and chickens
- Other cereals and oil seeds
- Other livestock and products
- Other

V U T

B A

O N T A R I O

QUÉBEC

NEWFOUNDLAND AND LABRADOR

NEW BRUNSWICK

P.E.I.

NOVA SCOTIA

SCALE 1 : 20 000 000

Surrounded by oceans on three sides, and home to the Great Lakes, it is not surprising that Canada has one of the world's most valuable commercial fishing industries, worth almost $5 billion a year. Canada is a major exporter of seafood and seafood products. Approximately 500 000 tonnes with a value of $4 billion are exported annually. The United States, Japan, and Europe are the most important markets. In the Pacific fishery, top catches are hake, Pacific herring (harvested for roe), rockfish and salmon. Value leaders are clams, halibut, shrimp, rockfish, and salmon. Aquaculture has become a significant element in the west coast fishery, with a value of more than $500 million in recent years. Aquaculture accounts for 10 percent of the total Canadian production of fish and shellfish. Canada is one of the world's main suppliers of farmed salmon (Atlantic, Chinook, and Coho). Trout, steelhead, and Arctic char are also raised. The east coast fishery has focused on cod and other groundfish. However, in recent years, top catches were herring (harvested for its roe), shrimp, snow crab, scallops, cod, and lobster. The value leaders are crab, shrimp, and cod. Lobster continues to be Canada's most valuable seafood product, worth over $500 million.

Unfortunately, pollution in inland waters and in coastal areas has resulted in declines in the fish population and has raised health concerns. The destruction of spawning beds and the construction of dams has affected fish habitats. Weather, ocean conditions, and overharvesting by other nations just outside Canada's territorial waters have added to the problems faced by the fishing industry. In 2003, the northern cod fishery was closed down due to overfishing of the stock and habitat destruction. This has resulted in unemployment in this industry, affecting the economy of provinces such as Newfoundland and Labrador.

SCALE 1 : 13 000 000

FISH HABITATS : WEST COAST

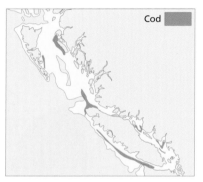
Cod

Salmon

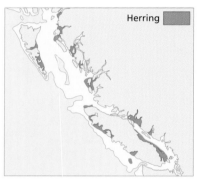
Herring

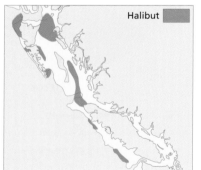
Halibut

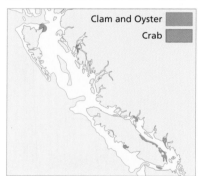
Clam and Oyster
Crab

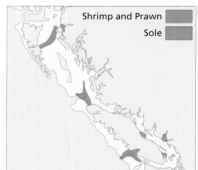
Shrimp and Prawn
Sole

VOLUME AND VALUE OF CATCH

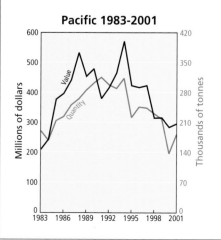
Pacific 1983-2001

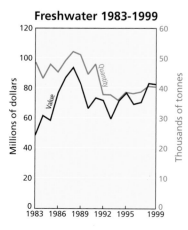
Freshwater 1983-1999

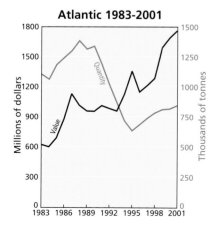
Atlantic 1983-2001

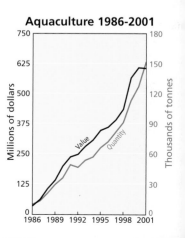
Aquaculture 1986-2001

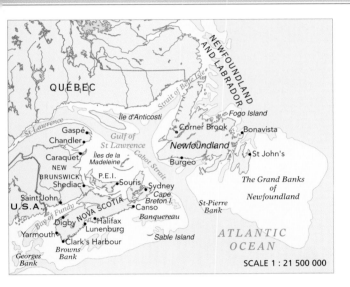

SCALE 1 : 21 500 000

WORLD COMPARISON

Major fishing countries, 2000

Country	Fish production tonnes	Country	Fish production tonnes
1 China	43 069 240	16 Denmark	1 577 698
2 Peru	10 665 420	17 Malaysia	1 441 018
3 Japan	5 752 178	18 Mexico	1 368 021
4 India	5 689 468	19 Spain	1 289 081
5 USA	5 173 583	20 Myanmar	1 168 638
6 Indonesia	4 928 545	21 Canada	1 116 902
7 Chile	4 691 747	22 Argentina	919 509
8 Russian Fed.	4 047 659	23 United Kingdom	898 776
9 Thailand	3 630 578	24 Morocco	898 467
10 Norway	3 191 335	25 France	864 673
11 Philippines	2 280 512	26 Brazil	847 268
12 South Korea	2 146 393	27 Egypt	724 407
13 Iceland	1 986 145	28 Ecuador	654 658
14 Vietnam	1 952 145	29 South Africa	647 763
15 Bangladesh	1 661 385	30 New Zealand	646 964

Total world fish production : 130 433 800 tonnes

FISH HABITATS : EAST COAST

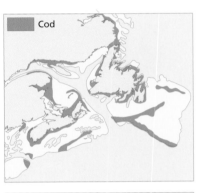

Cod

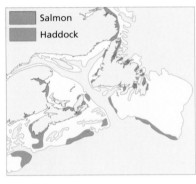

Salmon
Haddock

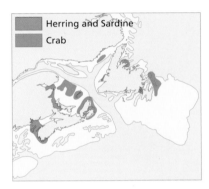

Herring and Sardine
Crab

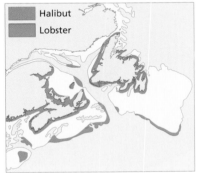

Halibut
Lobster

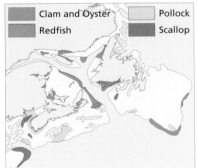

Clam and Oyster   Pollock
Redfish   Scallop

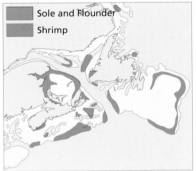

Sole and Flounder
Shrimp

EMPLOYMENT

Number employed

VOLUME AND VALUE

Volume 2001: 1 030 666 tonnes

Landed value 2001: $ 2 056 977 000

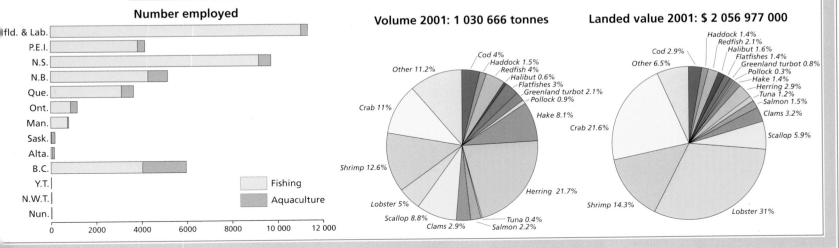

Forest regions and principal tree species

Non-productive forest
- Boreal–forest and barren ground — Black Spruce, White Spruce, Tamarack
- Boreal–forest and grassland — Trembling Aspen, Willow, Bur Oak

Productive forest
- Boreal–predominantly forest — Black Spruce, White Spruce, Balsam Fir, Jack Pine, White Birch, Trembling Aspen
- Subalpine — Alpine Fir, Engelmann Spruce, Lodgepole Pine
- Montane — Douglas Fir, Lodgepole Pine, Ponderosa Pine, Trembling Aspen
- Coast — Western Red Cedar, Western Hemlock, Douglas Fir, Sitka Spruce
- Columbia — Western Red Cedar, Western Hemlock, Douglas Fir
- Deciduous — Beech, Maple, Black Walnut, Hickory, Oak
- Great Lakes-St Lawrence — Eastern White Pine, Eastern Hemlock, Red Pine, Yellow Birch, Maple, Oak
- Acadian — Red Spruce, Balsam Fir, Maple, Yellow Birch

Non-forested land — No major tree species

▲▲▲ Each symbol represents one pulp and paper mill with a production capacity of 300 t (tonnes) or more per day

Forest tenures granted to private companies

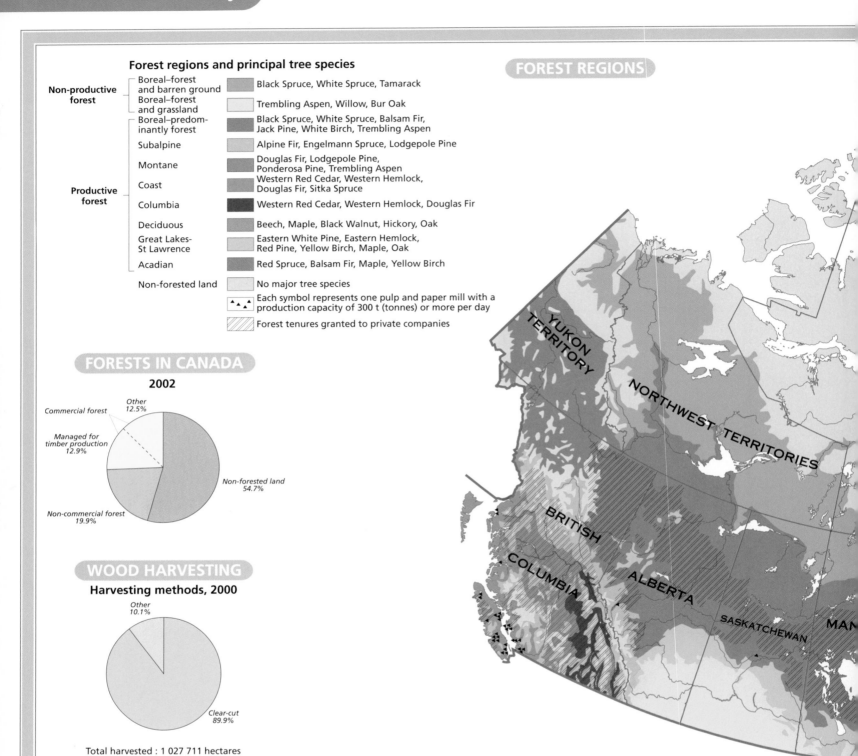

FOREST REGIONS

YUKON TERRITORY
NORTHWEST TERRITORIES
BRITISH COLUMBIA
ALBERTA
SASKATCHEWAN
MAN

FORESTS IN CANADA

2002

- Other 12.5%
- Commercial forest
- Managed for timber production 12.9%
- Non-commercial forest 19.9%
- Non-forested land 54.7%

WOOD HARVESTING

Harvesting methods, 2000

- Other 10.1%
- Clear-cut 89.9%

Total harvested : 1 027 711 hectares

FORESTED LAND

Provincial share, 2002

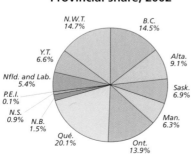

- N.W.T. 14.7%
- B.C. 14.5%
- Y.T. 6.6%
- Alta. 9.1%
- Nfld. and Lab. 5.4%
- P.E.I. 0.1%
- N.S. 0.9%
- N.B. 1.5%
- Qué. 20.1%
- Ont. 13.9%
- Man. 6.3%
- Sask. 6.9%

Total : 417 600 000 hectares

FOREST LOSS

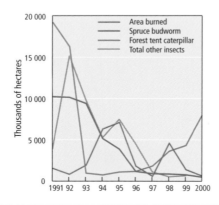

- Area burned
- Spruce budworm
- Forest tent caterpillar
- Total other insects

Thousands of hectares

20 000
15 000
10 000
5 000
0

1991 92 93 94 95 96 97 98 99 2000

WORLD EXPORTS

Export of forest products, 2001

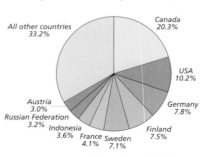

- All other countries 33.2%
- Canada 20.3%
- USA 10.2%
- Germany 7.8%
- Finland 7.5%
- Sweden 7.1%
- France 4.1%
- Indonesia 3.6%
- Russian Federation 3.2%
- Austria 3.0%

Total : US$ 141 489 359 000

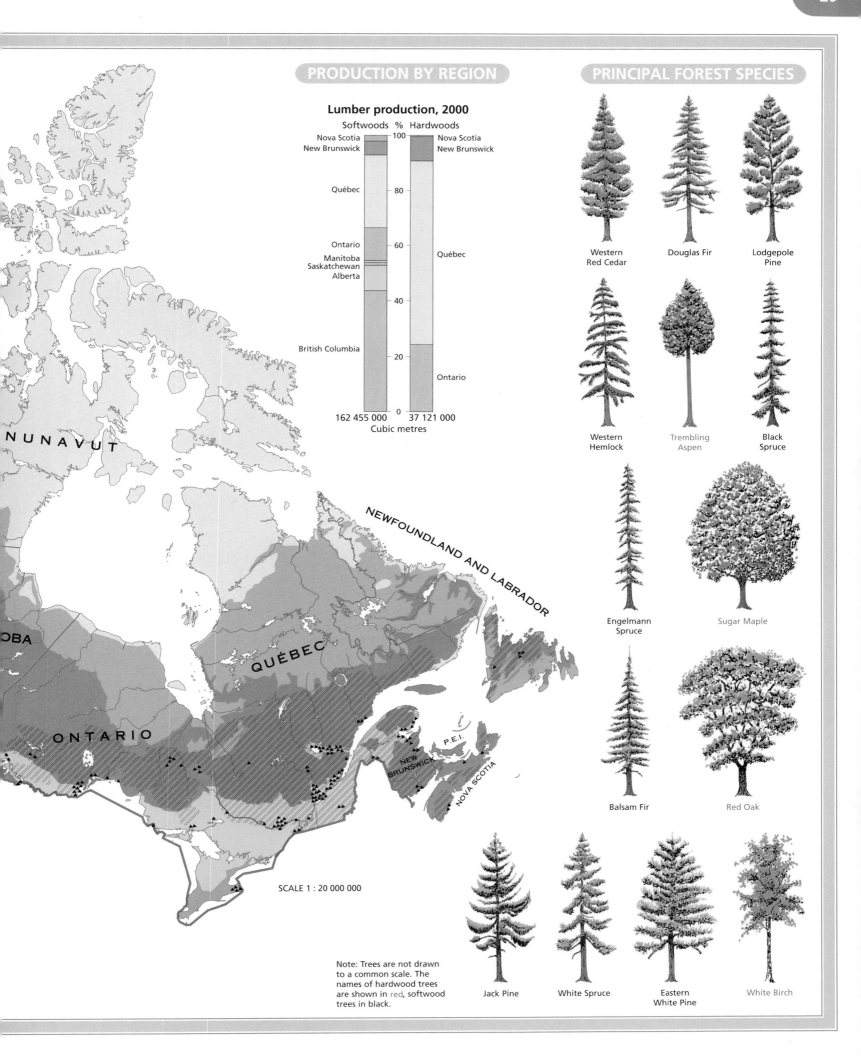

PRODUCTION BY REGION

PRINCIPAL FOREST SPECIES

Lumber production, 2000

Softwoods   %   Hardwoods

Nova Scotia — 100 — Nova Scotia
New Brunswick — New Brunswick

Québec — 80

Ontario — 60
Manitoba
Saskatchewan
Alberta — Québec

— 40

British Columbia — 20

— Ontario

— 0

162 455 000   37 121 000

Cubic metres

Western
Red Cedar

Douglas Fir

Lodgepole
Pine

Western
Hemlock

Trembling
Aspen

Black
Spruce

Engelmann
Spruce

Sugar Maple

Balsam Fir

Red Oak

Jack Pine

White Spruce

Eastern
White Pine

White Birch

NUNAVUT

NEWFOUNDLAND AND LABRADOR

QUÉBEC

ONTARIO

...OBA

P.E.I.

NEW
BRUNSWICK

NOVA SCOTIA

SCALE 1 : 20 000 000

Note: Trees are not drawn
to a common scale. The
names of hardwood trees
are shown in red, softwood
trees in black.

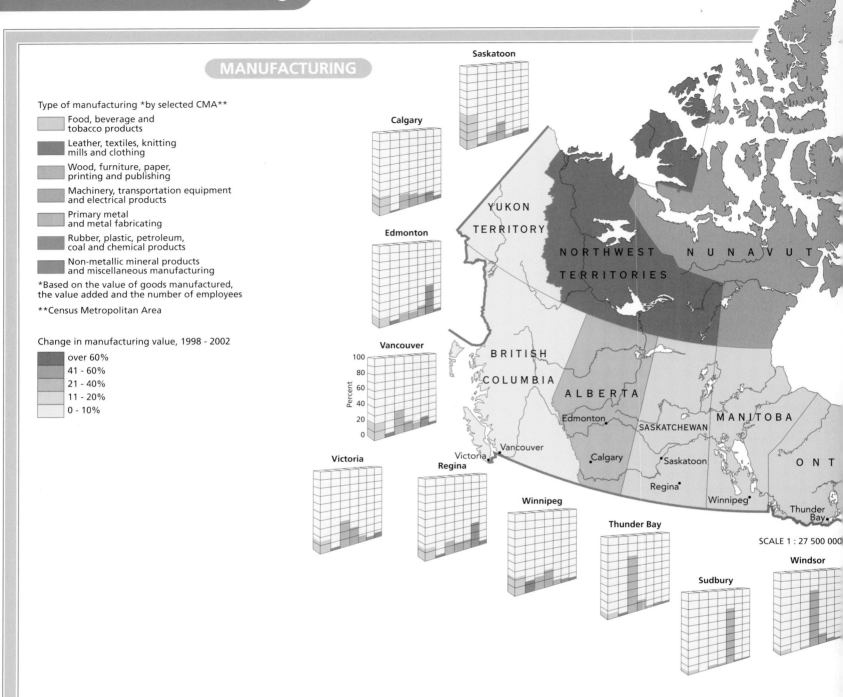

MANUFACTURING

Type of manufacturing *by selected CMA**

- Food, beverage and tobacco products
- Leather, textiles, knitting mills and clothing
- Wood, furniture, paper, printing and publishing
- Machinery, transportation equipment and electrical products
- Primary metal and metal fabricating
- Rubber, plastic, petroleum, coal and chemical products
- Non-metallic mineral products and miscellaneous manufacturing

*Based on the value of goods manufactured, the value added and the number of employees

**Census Metropolitan Area

Change in manufacturing value, 1998 - 2002

- over 60%
- 41 - 60%
- 21 - 40%
- 11 - 20%
- 0 - 10%

SCALE 1 : 27 500 000

MANUFACTURING SHIPMENTS

Value by province, 2002

- Newfoundland and Labrador 0.4%
- Prince Edward Island 0.3%
- Nova Scotia 1.7%
- New Brunswick 2.4%
- British Columbia 6.6%
- Alberta 7.9%
- Saskatchewan 1.4%
- Manitoba 2.2%
- Québec 23.6%
- Ontario 53.5%

Total : $ 518 504 900 000

Value, 1990 - 2002

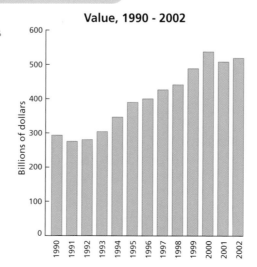

Billions of dollars

1990 1991 1992 1993 1994 1995 1996 1997 1998 1999 2000 2001 2002

EXPORTS

Manufactured goods, 2002

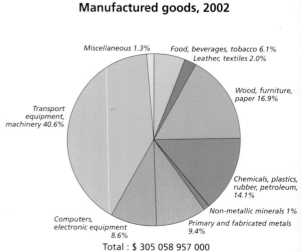

- Miscellaneous 1.3%
- Food, beverages, tobacco 6.1%
- Leather, textiles 2.0%
- Wood, furniture, paper 16.9%
- Transport equipment, machinery 40.6%
- Chemicals, plastics, rubber, petroleum, 14.1%
- Non-metallic minerals 1%
- Primary and fabricated metals 9.4%
- Computers, electronic equipment 8.6%

Total : $ 305 058 957 000

ESTABLISHMENTS AND EMPLOYEES

Type of manufacturing	Number of establishments	Number of employees per establishment
Food Manufacturing	3 467	63
Beverage and Tobacco Products	227	154
Textile Mills	374	71
Textile Product Mills	422	42
Clothing Manufacturing	1 342	63
Leather and Allied Products	176	62
Wood Products	2 144	68
Paper Manufacturing	663	156
Printing and Related Support Activities	2 623	31
Petroleum and Coal Products	204	63
Chemical Manufacturing	1 274	73
Plastics and Rubber Products	1 436	80
Non-Metallic Mineral Products	1 354	34
Primary Metal Manufacturing	478	196
Fabricated Metal Products	4 283	39
Machinery Manufacturing	2 653	50
Computer and Electronic Products	956	101
Electrical Equipment, Appliance and Component Manufacturing	605	87
Transportation Equipment	1 332	182
Furniture and Related Products	1 748	49
Miscellaneous Manufacturing	2 061	25
All Manufacturing	**29 822**	**64**

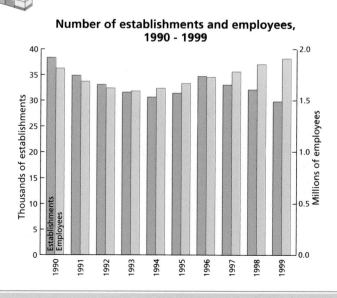

Number of establishments and employees, 1990 - 1999

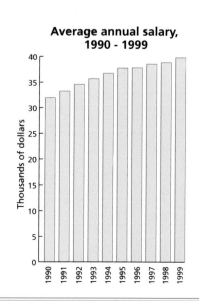

Average annual salary, 1990 - 1999

GROSS DOMESTIC PRODUCT BY REGION

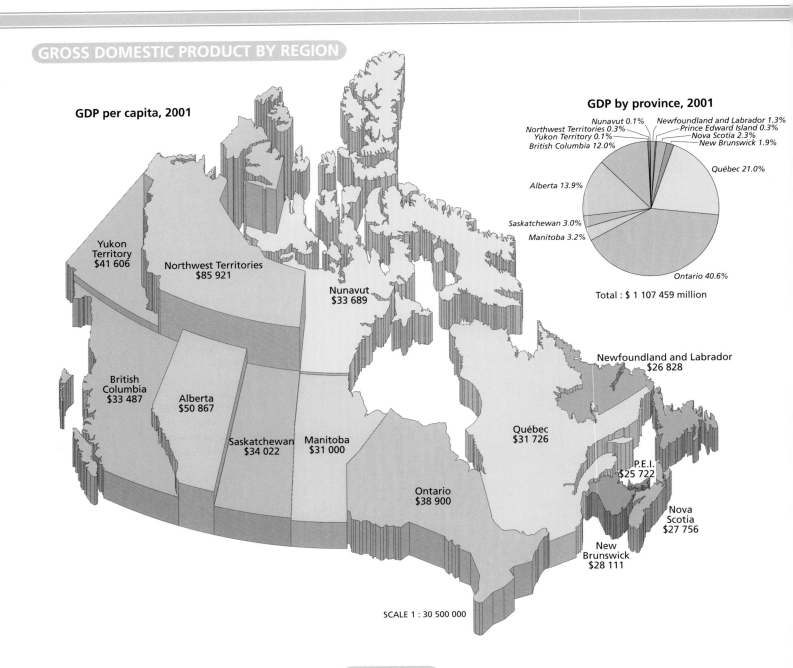

GDP per capita, 2001

Yukon Territory $41 606
Northwest Territories $85 921
Nunavut $33 689
British Columbia $33 487
Alberta $50 867
Saskatchewan $34 022
Manitoba $31 000
Ontario $38 900
Québec $31 726
Newfoundland and Labrador $26 828
P.E.I. $25 722
Nova Scotia $27 756
New Brunswick $28 111

SCALE 1 : 30 500 000

GDP by province, 2001

Nunavut 0.1%
Northwest Territories 0.3%
Yukon Territory 0.1%
British Columbia 12.0%
Newfoundland and Labrador 1.3%
Prince Edward Island 0.3%
Nova Scotia 2.3%
New Brunswick 1.9%
Québec 21.0%
Alberta 13.9%
Saskatchewan 3.0%
Manitoba 3.2%
Ontario 40.6%

Total : $ 1 107 459 million

EARNINGS

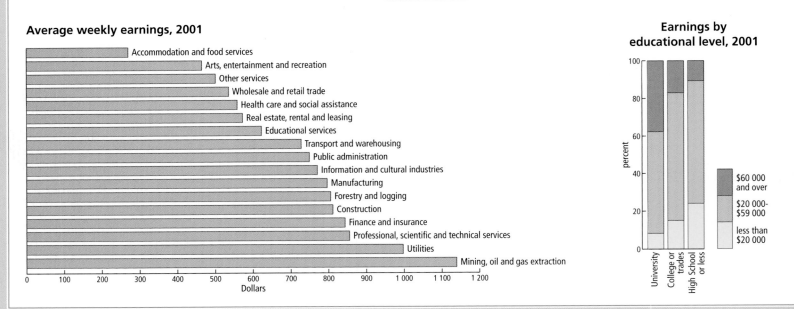

Average weekly earnings, 2001

Accommodation and food services
Arts, entertainment and recreation
Other services
Wholesale and retail trade
Health care and social assistance
Real estate, rental and leasing
Educational services
Transport and warehousing
Public administration
Information and cultural industries
Manufacturing
Forestry and logging
Construction
Finance and insurance
Professional, scientific and technical services
Utilities
Mining, oil and gas extraction

0   100   200   300   400   500   600   700   800   900   1 000   1 100   1 200
Dollars

Earnings by educational level, 2001

percent

University
College or trades
High School or less

$60 000 and over
$20 000-$59 000
less than $20 000

GROSS DOMESTIC PRODUCT BY INDUSTRY

2001

- Primary Industry
- Manufacturing
- Construction
- Transportation and utilities
- Trade
- Health, education, food and accomodation
- Other services
- Public administration

EMPLOYMENT

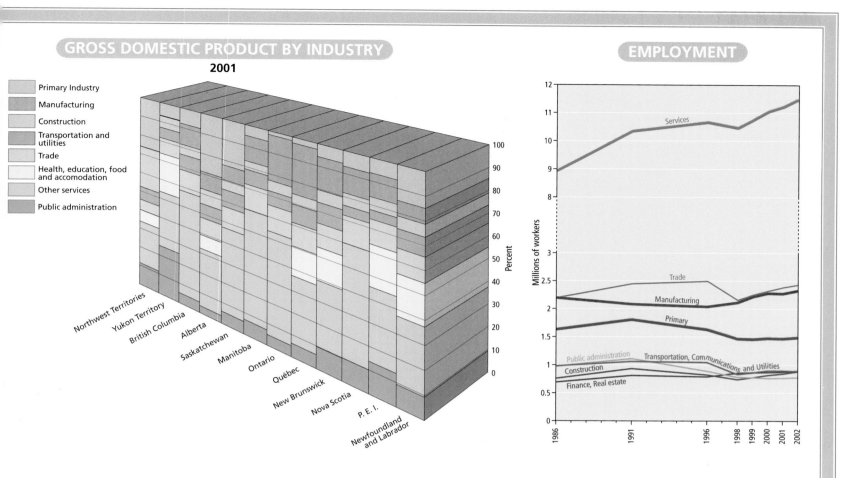

LABOUR FORCE

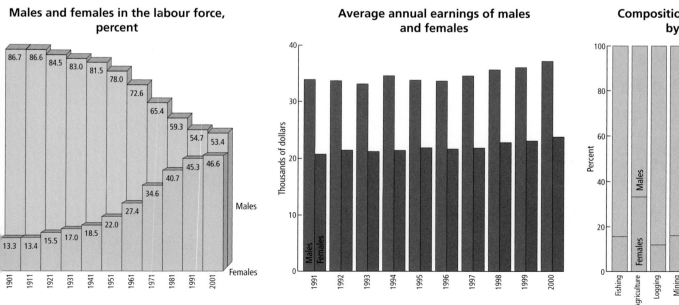

Males and females in the labour force, percent

1901	1911	1921	1931	1941	1951	1961	1971	1981	1991	2001
86.7	86.6	84.5	83.0	81.5	78.0	72.6	65.4	59.3	54.7	53.4
13.3	13.4	15.5	17.0	18.5	22.0	27.4	34.6	40.7	45.3	46.6

Males / Females

Average annual earnings of males and females

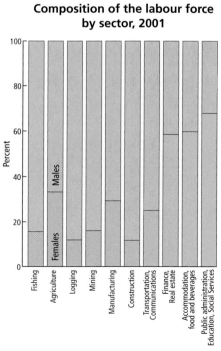

Composition of the labour force by sector, 2001

POPULATION DISTRIBUTION

Population distribution 2001

∴ One dot represents 200 people

YUKON TERRITORY

NORTHWEST TERRITORIES

NUNAVUT

BRITISH COLUMBIA

ALBERTA

SASKATCHEWAN

MANITOBA

ONTA

Population distribution 1871

∴ One dot represents 200 people

SCALE 1 : 50 000 000

Population distribution 1911

∴ One dot represents 200 people

SCALE 1 : 50 000 000

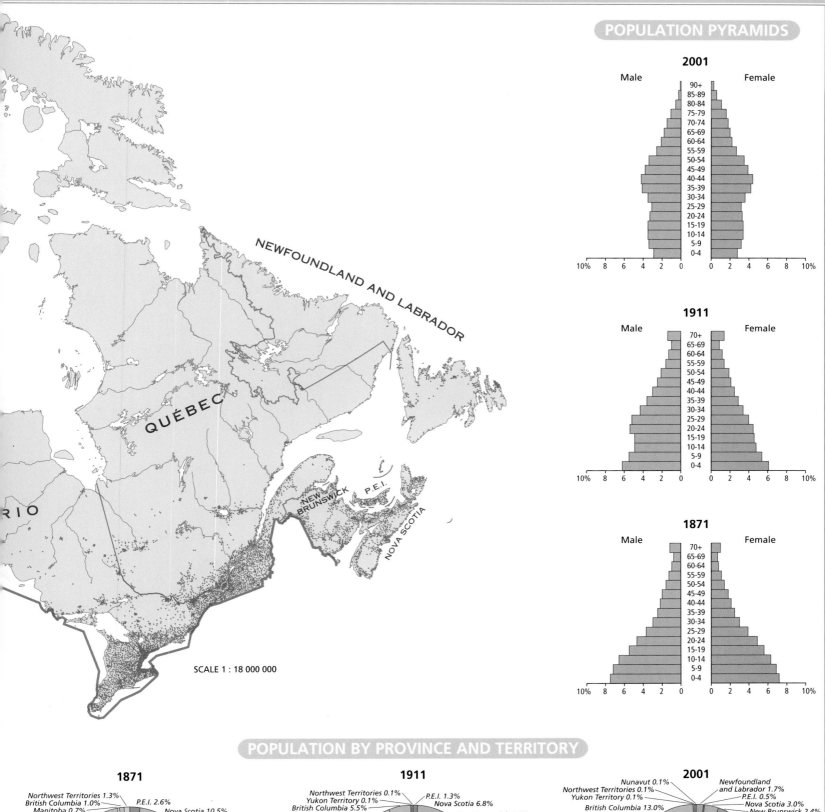

2001

Male — Female

90+, 85-89, 80-84, 75-79, 70-74, 65-69, 60-64, 55-59, 50-54, 45-49, 40-44, 35-39, 30-34, 25-29, 20-24, 15-19, 10-14, 5-9, 0-4

10% 8 6 4 2 0 0 2 4 6 8 10%

1911

Male — Female

70+, 65-69, 60-64, 55-59, 50-54, 45-49, 40-44, 35-39, 30-34, 25-29, 20-24, 15-19, 10-14, 5-9, 0-4

10% 8 6 4 2 0 0 2 4 6 8 10%

1871

Male — Female

70+, 65-69, 60-64, 55-59, 50-54, 45-49, 40-44, 35-39, 30-34, 25-29, 20-24, 15-19, 10-14, 5-9, 0-4

10% 8 6 4 2 0 0 2 4 6 8 10%

SCALE 1 : 18 000 000

POPULATION BY PROVINCE AND TERRITORY

1871
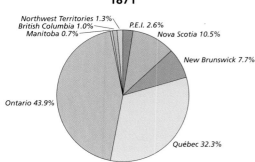

Northwest Territories 1.3%
British Columbia 1.0%
Manitoba 0.7%
P.E.I. 2.6%
Nova Scotia 10.5%
New Brunswick 7.7%
Ontario 43.9%
Québec 32.3%

Total : 3 689 257

1911
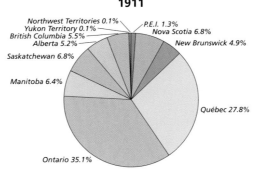

Northwest Territories 0.1%
Yukon Territory 0.1%
British Columbia 5.5%
Alberta 5.2%
Saskatchewan 6.8%
Manitoba 6.4%
P.E.I. 1.3%
Nova Scotia 6.8%
New Brunswick 4.9%
Québec 27.8%
Ontario 35.1%

Total : 7 206 643

2001
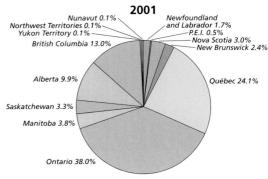

Nunavut 0.1%
Northwest Territories 0.1%
Yukon Territory 0.1%
British Columbia 13.0%
Alberta 9.9%
Saskatchewan 3.3%
Manitoba 3.8%
Ontario 38.0%
Newfoundland and Labrador 1.7%
P.E.I. 0.5%
Nova Scotia 3.0%
New Brunswick 2.4%
Québec 24.1%

Total : 30 007 094

FIRST NATIONS IN MAJOR CITIES

Populations, 2001

City	Total population	First Nations population	Métis population
Toronto	4 682 897	13 780	5 100
Montréal	3 426 350	6 100	3 670
Vancouver	1 986 965	22 700	12 505
Ottawa-Hull	1 063 664	7 555	4 690
Calgary	951 395	10 155	10 580
Edmonton	937 845	18 260	21 060
Quebéc	682 757	3 020	875
Winnipeg	671 274	22 955	31 390
Hamilton	662 401	5 605	1 185
London	432 451	4 415	980
Kitchener	414 284	2 115	865
St Cath.-Niagara	377 009	3 370	1 335
Halifax	359 183	2 350	800
Saskatoon	225 927	11 290	8 305
Regina	192 800	9 200	5 995
Fredericton	81 346	2 225	270

LANGUAGE AND DISTRIBUTION

Population with Aboriginal origins

∴ One dot represents 100 First Nations people

∴ One dot represents 100 Inuit

Language groups
(spellings may vary)

- Algonquian
  Ojibwa, Cree
- Athapaskan
  Dogrib, Sarcee
- Haidan
  Haida
- Iroquoian
  Mohawk, Oneida
- Kutenaian
  Kutenai
- Salishan
  Bella Coola, Comox
- Siouan
  Dakota
- Tlingit
  Inland Tlingit
- Tsimshian
  Nass-Gitksan
- Wakashan
  Haisla, Nootka
- Inuktitut
  Inuktitut

ABORIGINAL PEOPLES BY PROVINCE AND TERRITORY

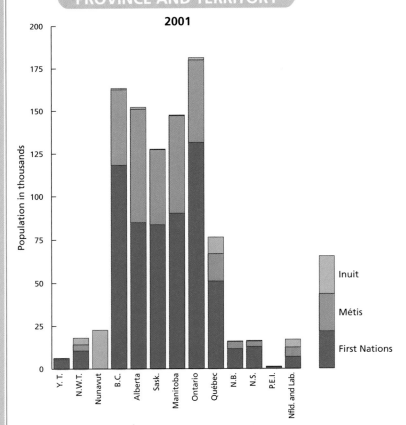

2001

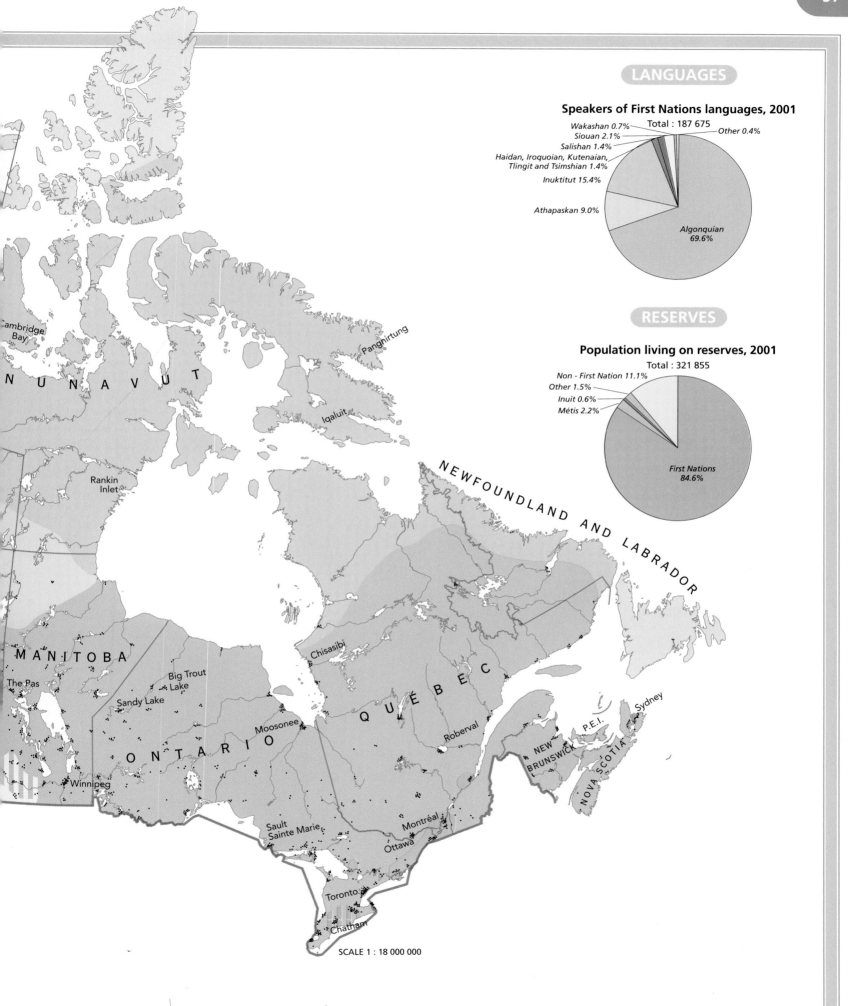

Speakers of First Nations languages, 2001

Total : 187 675

Wakashan 0.7%
Siouan 2.1%
Salishan 1.4%
Haidan, Iroquoian, Kutenaian,
Tlingit and Tsimshian 1.4%
Inuktitut 15.4%
Athapaskan 9.0%
Algonquian 69.6%
Other 0.4%

Population living on reserves, 2001

Total : 321 855

Non - First Nation 11.1%
Other 1.5%
Inuit 0.6%
Métis 2.2%
First Nations 84.6%

Cambridge Bay

Pangnirtung

N U N A V U T

Iqaluit

Rankin Inlet

NEWFOUNDLAND AND LABRADOR

M A N I T O B A

The Pas

Big Trout Lake

Sandy Lake

Chisasibi

Q U É B E C

O N T A R I O

Moosonee

Roberval

Sydney

P.E.I.

NEW BRUNSWICK

NOVA SCOTIA

Winnipeg

Sault Sainte Marie

Montréal

Ottawa

Toronto

Chatham

SCALE 1 : 18 000 000

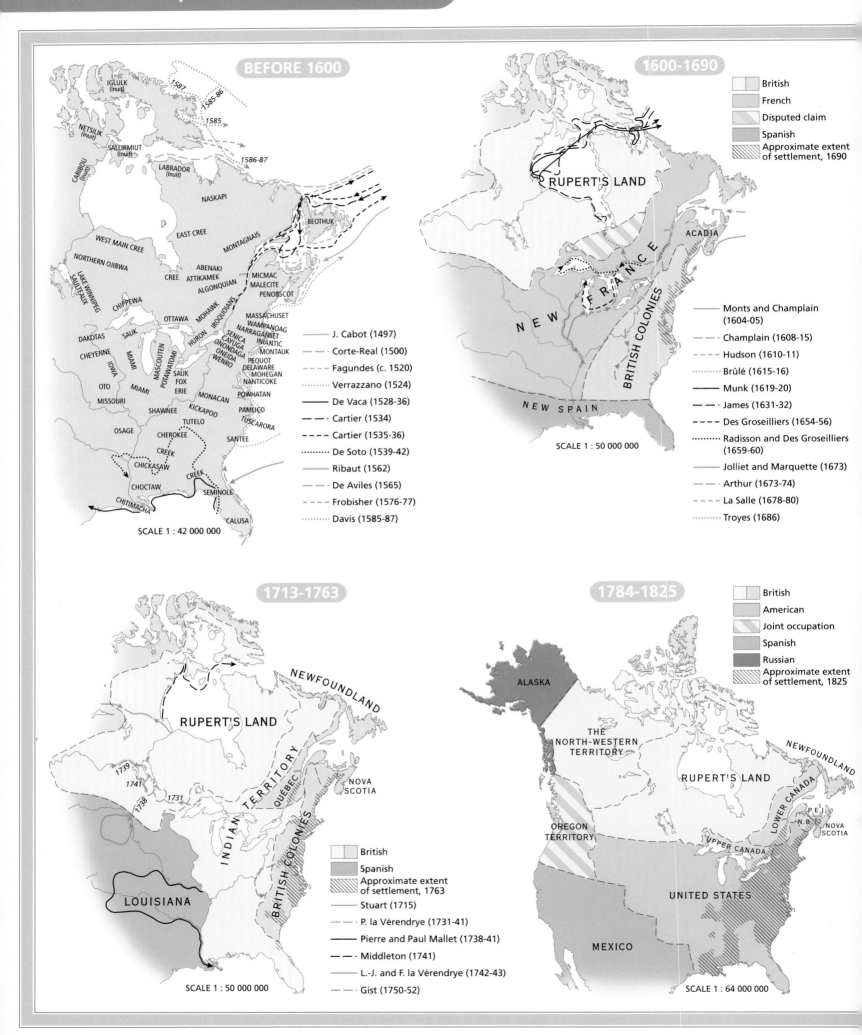

BEFORE 1600

IGLULK (Inuit)

NETSILIK (Inuit)

CARIBOU (Inuit)

SALLIRMIUT (Inuit)

LABRADOR (Inuit)

NASKAPI

EAST CREE

WEST MAIN CREE

NORTHERN OJIBWA

LAKE WINNIPEG SAULTEAUX

CHIPPEWA

DAKOTAS

SAUK

CHEYENNE

IOWA

MIAMI

OTO

MISSOURI

OSAGE

SHAWNEE

CHEROKEE

CREEK

CHICKASAW

CHOCTAW

CHITIMACHA

CALUSA

SEMINOLE

MONTAGNAIS

BEOTHUK

ABENAKI

CREE ATTIKAMEK

ALGONQUIAN

MICMAC

MALECITE

PENOBSCOT

MOHAWK

OTTAWA

HURON

IROQUOIANS

MASSACHUSET

WAMPANOAG

NARRAGANSET

SENICA CAYUGA ONONDAGA ONEIDA WENRO

NIANTIC

MONTAUK

PEQUOT

DELAWARE

MOHEGAN

NANTICOKE

POWHATAN

MONACAN

PAMLICO

TUSCARORA

SANTEE

TUTELO

MASCOUTEN POTAWATOMI

SAUK FOX ERIE

KICKAPOO

MIAMI

- J. Cabot (1497)
- Corte-Real (1500)
- Fagundes (c. 1520)
- Verrazzano (1524)
- De Vaca (1528-36)
- Cartier (1534)
- Cartier (1535-36)
- De Soto (1539-42)
- Ribaut (1562)
- De Aviles (1565)
- Frobisher (1576-77)
- Davis (1585-87)

1587

1585-86

1585

1586-87

SCALE 1 : 42 000 000

1600-1690

- British
- French
- Disputed claim
- Spanish
- Approximate extent of settlement, 1690

RUPERT'S LAND

NEW FRANCE

ACADIA

BRITISH COLONIES

NEW SPAIN

- Monts and Champlain (1604-05)
- Champlain (1608-15)
- Hudson (1610-11)
- Brûlé (1615-16)
- Munk (1619-20)
- James (1631-32)
- Des Groseilliers (1654-56)
- Radisson and Des Groseilliers (1659-60)
- Jolliet and Marquette (1673)
- Arthur (1673-74)
- La Salle (1678-80)
- Troyes (1686)

SCALE 1 : 50 000 000

1713-1763

NEWFOUNDLAND

RUPERT'S LAND

INDIAN TERRITORY

QUEBEC

NOVA SCOTIA

BRITISH COLONIES

LOUISIANA

1739

1741

1738

1731

- British
- Spanish
- Approximate extent of settlement, 1763
- Stuart (1715)
- P. la Vérendrye (1731-41)
- Pierre and Paul Mallet (1738-41)
- Middleton (1741)
- L.-J. and F. la Vérendrye (1742-43)
- Gist (1750-52)

SCALE 1 : 50 000 000

1784-1825

- British
- American
- Joint occupation
- Spanish
- Russian
- Approximate extent of settlement, 1825

ALASKA

THE NORTH-WESTERN TERRITORY

RUPERT'S LAND

NEWFOUNDLAND

OREGON TERRITORY

LOWER CANADA

UPPER CANADA

P.E.I.

N.B.

NOVA SCOTIA

UNITED STATES

MEXICO

SCALE 1 : 64 000 000

ARCTIC EXPLORATION

—————— Davis (1585, 1586, 1587)

— · — · Baffin and Bylot (1616)

— — — Parry (1819-20, 1821-22)

—————— Franklin (1819-22, 1845-47)

— — — Franklin and Richardson (1825-27)

·········· Back (1833-34)

- - - - M'Clure (1850-54)

—————— Sverdrup (1898-1902)

— — Peary (1898-1902, 1905-06, 1908-09)

·········· Amundsen (1903-06)

- - - - Stefansson (1913-18)

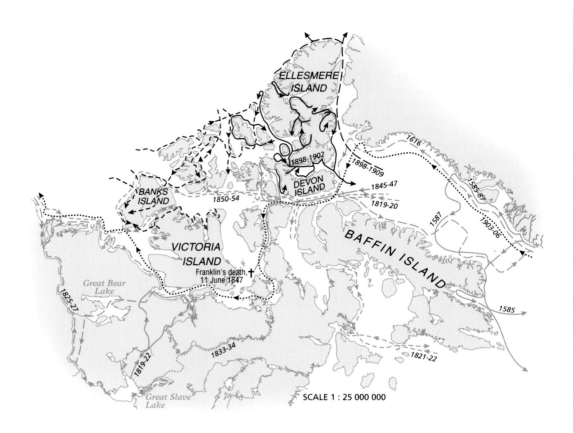

SCALE 1 : 25 000 000

WESTERN EXPLORATION

—————— Bering (1741)

— · — · Henday (1754-55)

·········· Hearne (1770, 1771, 1772)

- - - - Perez (1774)

—————— Cook (1778-79)

— · — · Mackenzie (1789, 1793)

·········· Vancouver (1792, 1793, 1794)

- - - - Thompson (1792-1812)

—————— Fraser (1806, 1808)

— — Simpson (1824-25, 1841)

·········· Campbell (1840, 1843, 1851)

- - - - Tyrrell (1892-94, 1898)

SCALE 1 : 25 000 000

This series of maps illustrates the evolution of the provincial, territorial, and international boundaries of Canada. The series begins in 1866, before Confederation (below) and then proceeds in chronological sequence, working from top to bottom of the four columns of Canadian maps. At Confederation, New Brunswick and Nova Scotia joined with Upper and Lower Canada (renamed Ontario and Québec) to create the Dominion of Canada. Based on a promise to provide a railway link with the east, British Columbia joined Confederation in 1871. Prince Edward Island was added in 1873. Territories were changed to provinces as settlement expanded westward in the early part of the 20th century. By 1912, the country had developed a "look" which is quite similar to that of the current map except for the boundary between Quebec and Labrador, which was established by the Imperial Privy Council in 1927. However, it was not until 1949 that the tenth province – known then as Newfoundland and now as Newfoundland and Labrador – joined Confederation.

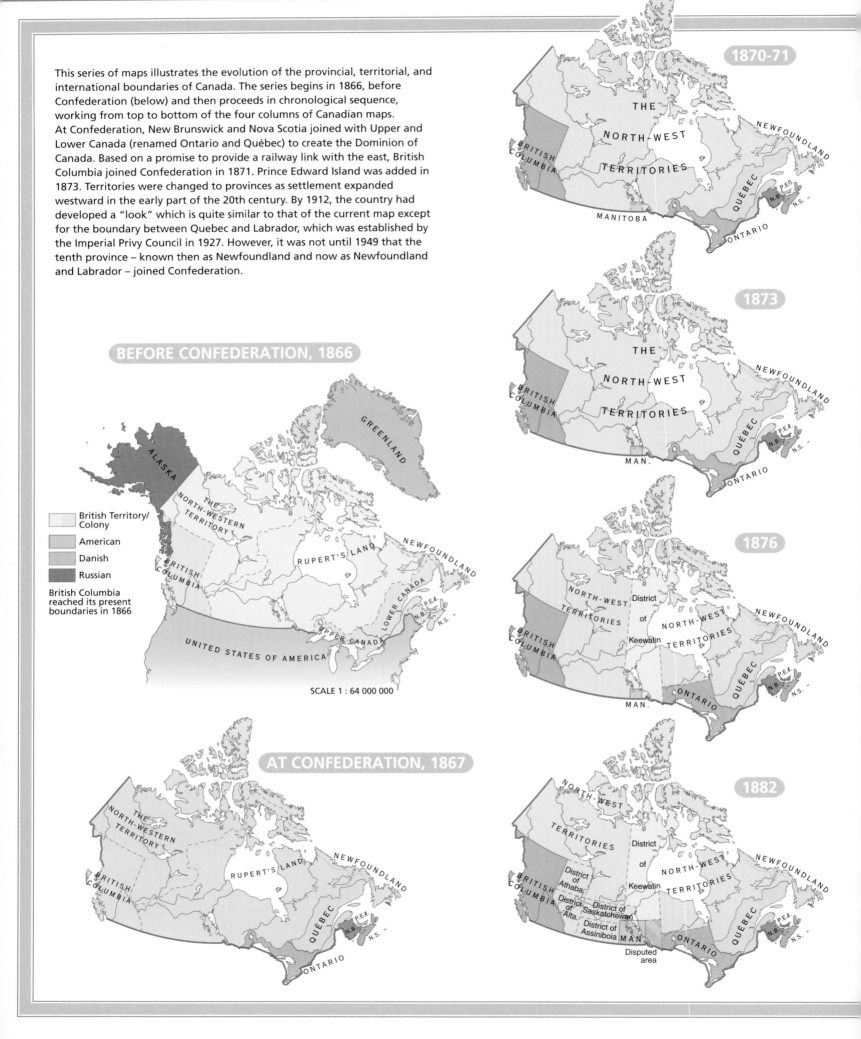

1870-71

1873

1876

1882

BEFORE CONFEDERATION, 1866

Legend:
- British Territory/Colony
- American
- Danish
- Russian

British Columbia reached its present boundaries in 1866

SCALE 1 : 64 000 000

AT CONFEDERATION, 1867

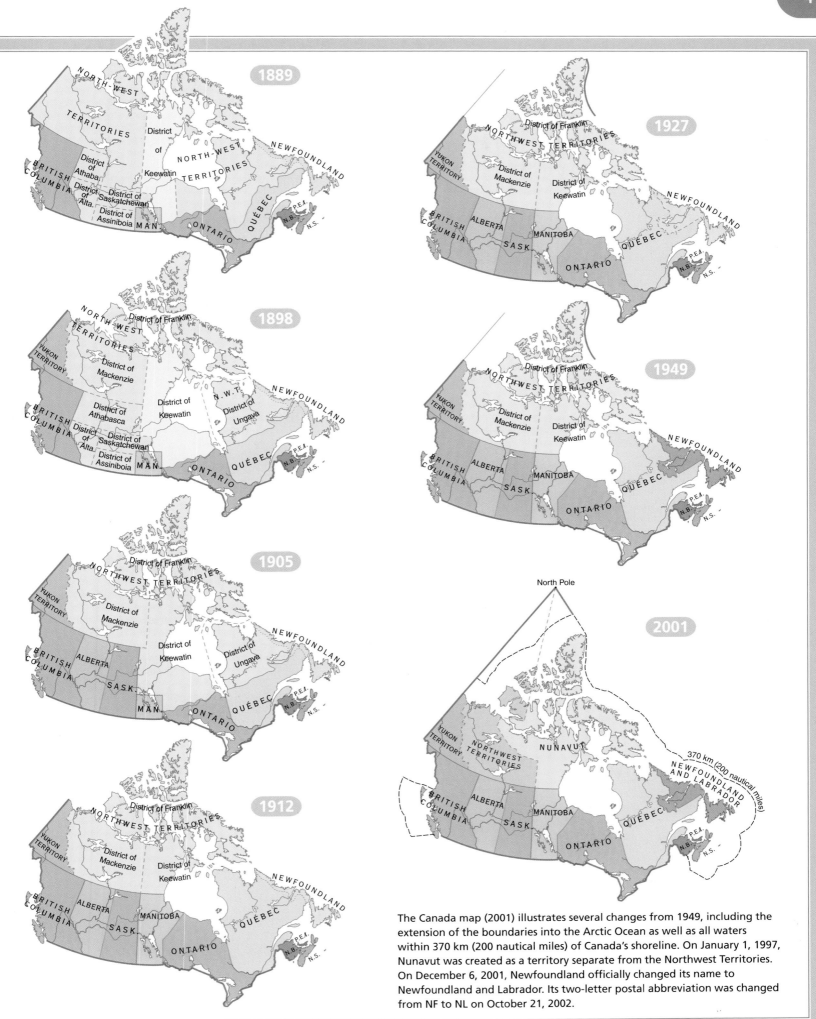

1889

1898

1905

1912

1927

1949

2001

North Pole

370 km (200 nautical miles)

The Canada map (2001) illustrates several changes from 1949, including the extension of the boundaries into the Arctic Ocean as well as all waters within 370 km (200 nautical miles) of Canada's shoreline. On January 1, 1997, Nunavut was created as a territory separate from the Northwest Territories. On December 6, 2001, Newfoundland officially changed its name to Newfoundland and Labrador. Its two-letter postal abbreviation was changed from NF to NL on October 21, 2002.

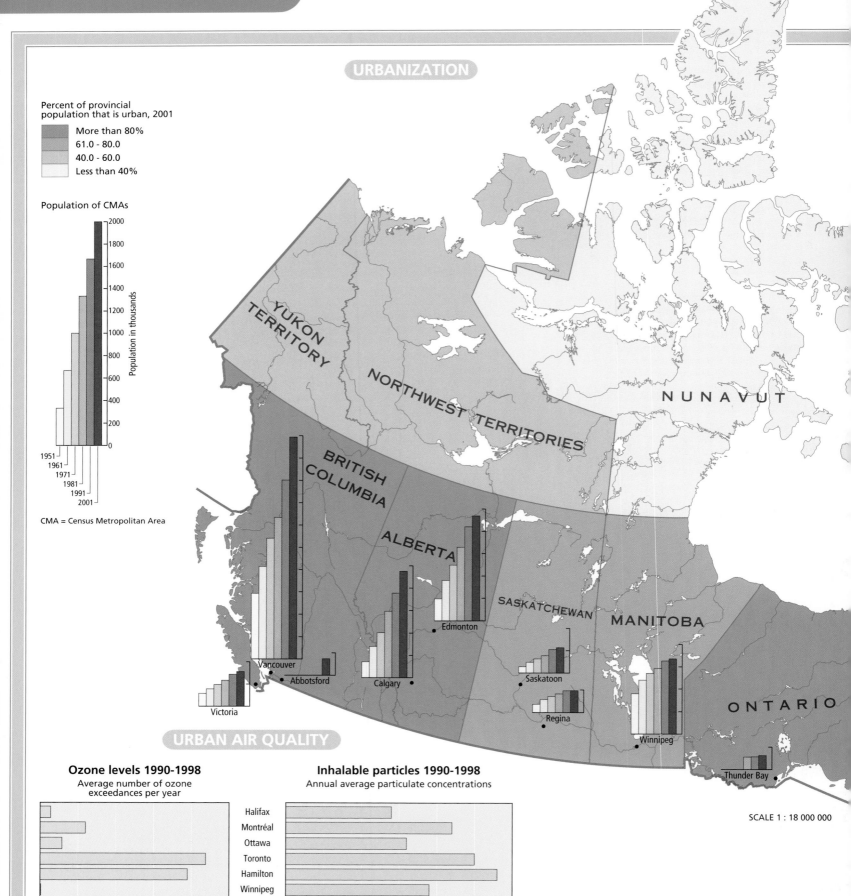

URBANIZATION

Percent of provincial
population that is urban, 2001

- More than 80%
- 61.0 - 80.0
- 40.0 - 60.0
- Less than 40%

Population of CMAs

2000
1800
1600
1400
1200
1000
800
600
400
200
0

Population in thousands

1951
1961
1971
1981
1991
2001

CMA = Census Metropolitan Area

YUKON TERRITORY

NORTHWEST TERRITORIES

NUNAVUT

BRITISH COLUMBIA

ALBERTA

SASKATCHEWAN

MANITOBA

ONTARIO

Vancouver
Abbotsford
Victoria
Edmonton
Calgary
Saskatoon
Regina
Winnipeg
Thunder Bay

SCALE 1 : 18 000 000

URBAN AIR QUALITY

Ozone levels 1990-1998
Average number of ozone
exceedances per year

Inhalable particles 1990-1998
Annual average particulate concentrations

Halifax
Montréal
Ottawa
Toronto
Hamilton
Winnipeg
Regina
Saskatoon
*Edmonton
*Calgary
Vancouver

0   5   10   15   20   25
Number of one-hour values greater than 0.062ppm
* Figures for 1990 – 2000

0   5   10   15   20   25   30
Concentration (ug/m³)
* Figures for 1990 – 2000

URBAN AND RURAL POPULATION

Urban and rural population

[bar chart showing Percent (0–100) vs years 1871, 1881, 1891, 1901, 1911, 1921, 1931, 1941, 1951, 1961, 1971, 1981, 1991, 2001, with Urban and Rural areas]

Urban population comparisons, 2000

Country	Percent urban population
Singapore	100
Kuwait	98
Belgium	97
Qatar	93
Iceland	93
Luxembourg	92
Bahrain	92
Uruguay	91
Malta	91
Israel	91
United Kingdom	90
Lebanon	90
Netherlands	89
The Bahamas	89
Argentina	89
Libya	88
Germany	88
Venezuela	87
New Zealand	87
United Arab Emirates	86
Saudi Arabia	86

Urban population changes

Urban centre	1996 population	2001 population	Percent change
Calgary (Alta.)	821 628	951 395	15.8
Oshawa (Ont.)	268 773	296 298	10.2
Toronto (Ont.)	4 263 759	4 682 897	9.8
Edmonton (Alta.)	862 597	937 845	8.7
Vancouver (B.C.)	1 831 665	1 986 965	8.5
Kitchener (Ont.)	382 940	414 284	8.2
Abbotsford (B.C.)	136 480	147 370	8.0
Windsor (Ont.)	286 811	307 877	7.3
Ottawa-Hull (Ont./Qué.)	998 718	1 063 664	6.5
Hamilton (Ont.)	624 360	662 401	6.1
Halifax (N.S.)	342 966	359 183	4.7
London (Ont.)	416 546	432 451	3.8
Saskatoon (Sask.)	219 056	225 927	3.1
Montréal (Qué.)	3 326 447	3 426 350	3.0
Sherbrooke (Qué.)	149 569	153 811	2.8
Victoria (B.C.)	304 287	311 902	2.5
Kingston (Ont.)	144 528	146 838	1.6
Québec (Qué.)	671 889	682 757	1.6
St Catharines-Niagara (Ont.)	372 406	377 009	1.2
Winnipeg (Man.)	667 093	671 274	0.6
Regina (Sask.)	193 652	192 800	-0.4
St John's (Nfld. and Lab.)	174 051	172 918	-0.7
Trois-Rivières (Qué.)	139 956	137 507	-1.7
Saint John (N.B.)	125 705	122 678	-2.4
Chicoutimi-Jonquière (Qué.)	160 454	154 938	-3.4
Thunder Bay (Ont.)	126 643	121 986	-3.7
Greater Sudbury (Ont.)	165 618	155 601	-6.0

SEWAGE TREATMENT

Cities use a variety of methods to treat sewage. Primary treatment is a physical process that involves screening and settling, and removes approximately 60 percent of solids and 40 percent of organic materials. Sludge is "skimmed" off and disposed of in a variety of ways. Secondary treatment is a biological treatment, using bacteria to break down almost 90 percent of the dissolved organics in the waste. A few urban centres use filters and chemical processes to remove organics, inorganics, and heavy metals in the tertiary treatment stage of sewage treatment.

[map of Eastern Canada with labels: NEWFOUNDLAND AND LABRADOR, QUÉBEC, St John's, Chicoutimi-Jonquière, NEW BRUNSWICK, P.E.I., Saint John, Halifax, Québec, Trois-Rivières, NOVA SCOTIA, Montréal, Sherbrooke, Greater Sudbury, Toronto, Kingston, Oshawa, St Catharines-Niagara, London, Ottawa-Hull, Windsor, Hamilton, Kitchener]

Municipal sewage treatment, selected cities, 1999

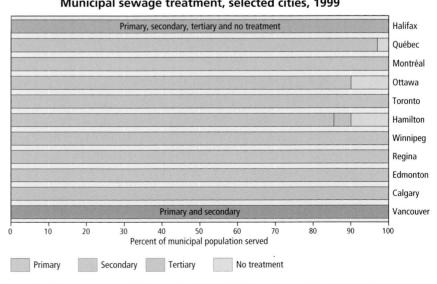

Primary, secondary, tertiary and no treatment — Halifax, Québec, Montréal, Ottawa, Toronto, Hamilton, Winnipeg, Regina, Edmonton, Calgary

Primary and secondary — Vancouver

Percent of municipal population served (0 10 20 30 40 50 60 70 80 90 100)

Primary   Secondary   Tertiary   No treatment

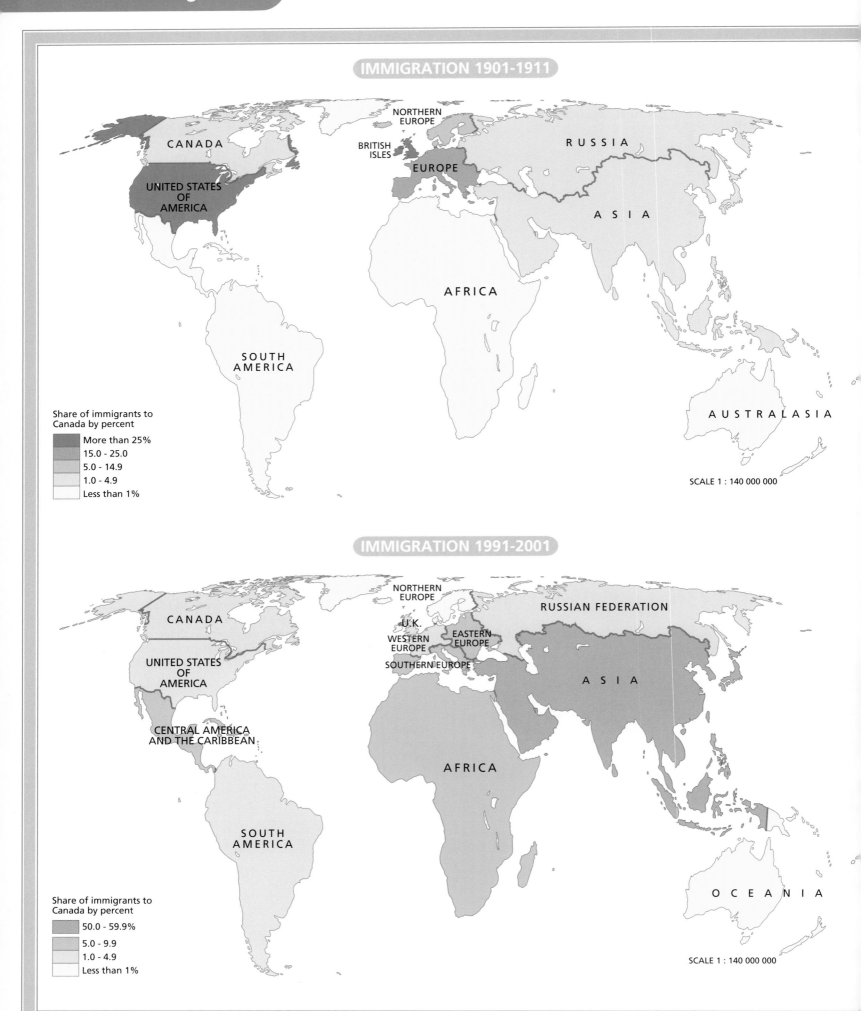

IMMIGRATION 1901-1911

NORTHERN EUROPE

BRITISH ISLES

CANADA

RUSSIA

EUROPE

UNITED STATES OF AMERICA

ASIA

AFRICA

SOUTH AMERICA

AUSTRALASIA

Share of immigrants to Canada by percent

More than 25%
15.0 - 25.0
5.0 - 14.9
1.0 - 4.9
Less than 1%

SCALE 1 : 140 000 000

IMMIGRATION 1991-2001

NORTHERN EUROPE

CANADA

RUSSIAN FEDERATION

U.K.
WESTERN EUROPE

EASTERN EUROPE

UNITED STATES OF AMERICA

SOUTHERN EUROPE

ASIA

CENTRAL AMERICA AND THE CARIBBEAN

AFRICA

SOUTH AMERICA

OCEANIA

Share of immigrants to Canada by percent

50.0 - 59.9%
5.0 - 9.9
1.0 - 4.9
Less than 1%

SCALE 1 : 140 000 000

DESTINATIONS OF IMMIGRANTS

Percent of immigrants
by province/territory, 2001

- More than 20%
- 10.0 - 20.0
- 5.0 - 9.9
- 1.0 - 4.9%

Immigrants as a proportion of
the population of major cities,
2001

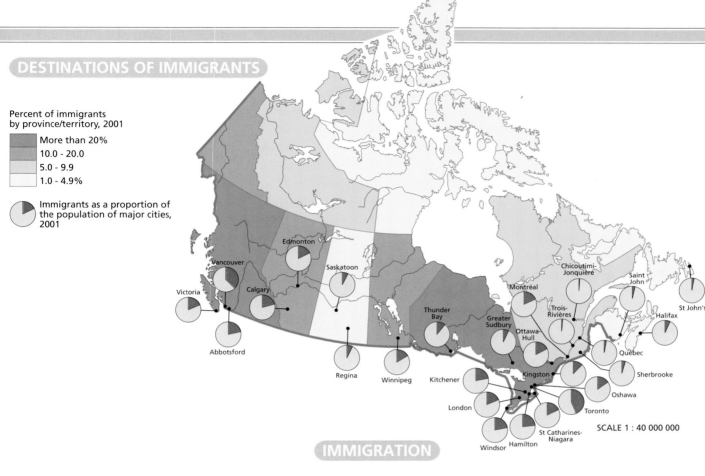

SCALE 1 : 40 000 000

IMMIGRATION

Annual immigration, 1870-2001

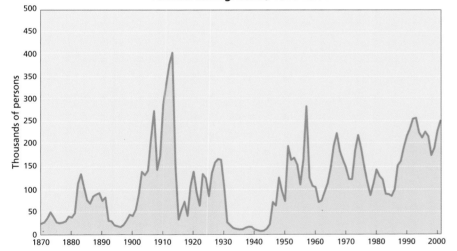

Thousands of persons

Origin of immigrants, 1971-2001

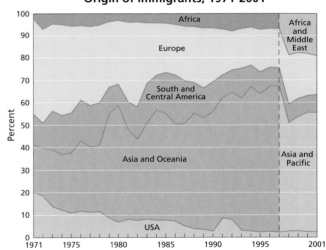

Percent

MIGRATION

Inter-provincial migration 1996-2001

Destination of migrants	Source of migrants												
	N. & L.	P.E.I.	N.S.	N.B.	QUÉ.	ONT.	MAN.	SASK.	ALTA.	B.C.	Y.T.	N.W.T.	NUN.
Newfoundland & Labrador	-	300	2 680	900	860	6 555	365	215	2 175	1 590	85	200	145
Prince Edward Island	910	-	1 740	1 110	395	2 350	90	105	570	495	0	110	20
Nova Scotia	6 745	1 855	-	8 140	3 340	18 220	1 720	990	5 305	6 055	155	270	205
New Brunswick	2 215	1 085	6 925	-	5 630	9 945	910	410	2 785	2 335	150	115	135
Québec	1 005	260	3 035	6 220	-	36 690	1 940	965	3 960	7 745	145	145	310
Ontario	17 555	2 375	22 135	14 080	80 505	-	15 225	8 850	32 275	46 955	775	1 205	565
Manitoba	720	85	1 520	980	1 860	12 800	-	6 850	8 755	8 260	140	425	205
Saskatchewan	790	80	890	550	965	5 290	7 275	-	16 260	9 540	270	585	110
Alberta	13 755	1 305	9 900	6 605	11 820	44 045	20 780	37 645	-	89 685	2 130	4 105	450
British Columbia	2 370	375	4 825	2 220	13 705	52 830	12 280	10 820	48 335	-	2 450	1 260	255
Yukon Territory	125	0	110	30	170	565	95	230	580	1 605	-	190	35
Northwest Territories	550	25	300	125	225	770	325	355	1 600	900	145	-	415
Nunavut	370	20	230	90	280	545	185	95	210	165	25	300	-

ETHNICITY

Ethnic composition of Canada, 2001

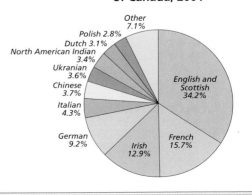

- Other 7.1%
- Polish 2.8%
- Dutch 3.1%
- North American Indian 3.4%
- Ukranian 3.6%
- Chinese 3.7%
- Italian 4.3%
- German 9.2%
- Irish 12.9%
- French 15.7%
- English and Scottish 34.2%

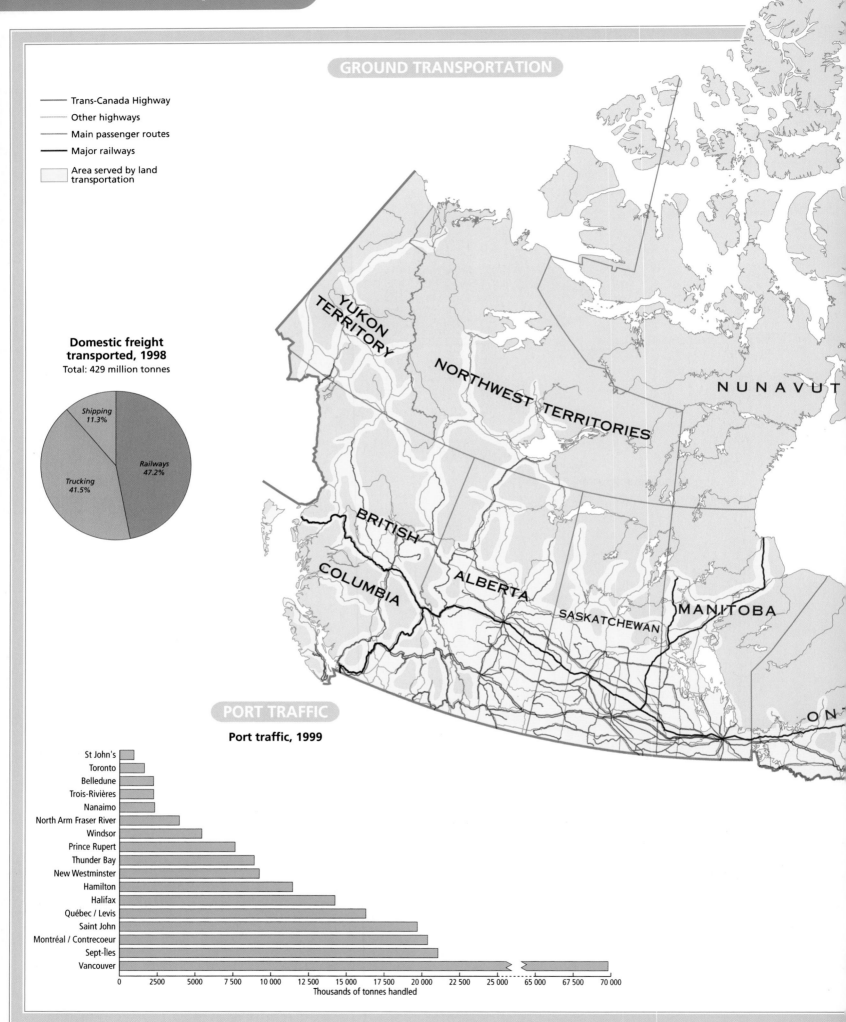

Trans-Canada Highway
Other highways
Main passenger routes
Major railways
Area served by land transportation

Domestic freight transported, 1998
Total: 429 million tonnes

Shipping 11.3%

Railways 47.2%

Trucking 41.5%

YUKON TERRITORY

NORTHWEST TERRITORIES

NUNAVUT

BRITISH COLUMBIA

ALBERTA

SASKATCHEWAN

MANITOBA

ONT

PORT TRAFFIC

Port traffic, 1999

St John's
Toronto
Belledune
Trois-Rivières
Nanaimo
North Arm Fraser River
Windsor
Prince Rupert
Thunder Bay
New Westminster
Hamilton
Halifax
Québec / Levis
Saint John
Montréal / Contrecoeur
Sept-Îles
Vancouver

0   2500   5000   7 500   10 000   12 500   15 000   17 500   20 000   22 500   25 000   65 000   67 500   70 000
Thousands of tonnes handled

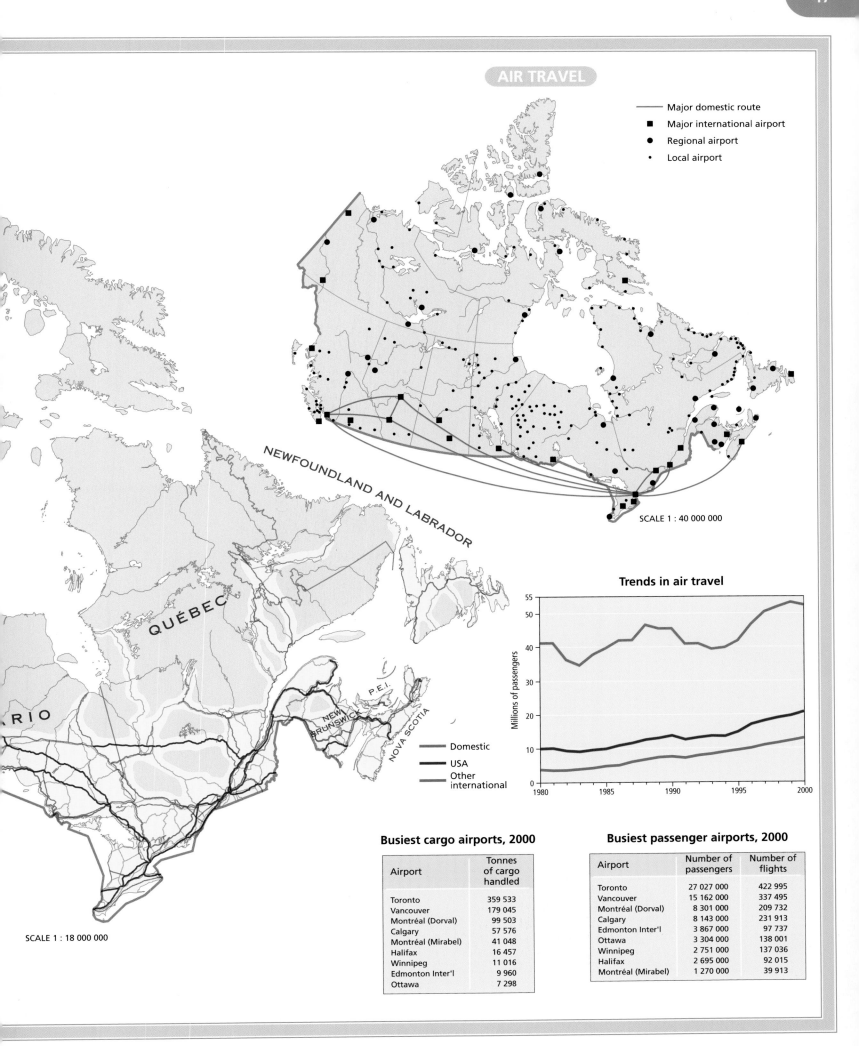

AIR TRAVEL

Major domestic route
■ Major international airport
● Regional airport
· Local airport

SCALE 1 : 40 000 000

NEWFOUNDLAND AND LABRADOR

QUÉBEC

ARIO

NEW BRUNSWICK

P.E.I.

NOVA SCOTIA

SCALE 1 : 18 000 000

Trends in air travel

Millions of passengers

55
50
40
30
20
10
0

1980   1985   1990   1995   2000

Domestic
USA
Other international

Busiest cargo airports, 2000

Airport	Tonnes of cargo handled
Toronto	359 533
Vancouver	179 045
Montréal (Dorval)	99 503
Calgary	57 576
Montréal (Mirabel)	41 048
Halifax	16 457
Winnipeg	11 016
Edmonton Inter'l	9 960
Ottawa	7 298

Busiest passenger airports, 2000

Airport	Number of passengers	Number of flights
Toronto	27 027 000	422 995
Vancouver	15 162 000	337 495
Montréal (Dorval)	8 301 000	209 732
Calgary	8 143 000	231 913
Edmonton Inter'l	3 867 000	97 737
Ottawa	3 304 000	138 001
Winnipeg	2 751 000	137 036
Halifax	2 695 000	92 015
Montréal (Mirabel)	1 270 000	39 913

INTERNATIONAL DESTINATIONS

Numbers of visits
by Canadians, 2001

- 13 527 000
- 750 000
- 500 000
- 250 000
- 100 000
- 0

SCALE 1 : 140 000 000

TRENDS IN TRAVEL

Overnight Person Trips by Canadians

Year	Foreign	Domestic	Total
2001	19 697 000	73 859 000	93 556 000
2000	19 663 000	83 438 000	103 101 000
1999	19 367 000	85 862 000	105 229 000
1998	18 828 000	83 961 000	102 789 000
1997	17 636 000	65 727 000	83 363 000
1996	17 285 000	80 885 000	98 170 000
1995	16 932 000	-	-
1994	15 972 000	76 599 000	92 571 000
1993	15 105 000	-	-
1992	14 741 000	84 043 000	98 784 000
1991	14 912 000	-	-
1990	15 210 000	78 326 000	93 536 000
1989	15 111 000	-	-
1988	15 485 000	79 460 000	94 945 000

International Tourist Arrivals in Canada

Year	United States of America	Overseas tourists					Total overseas	Total arrivals
		UK	Japan	France	Germany	Other countries		
2001	15 590 000	826 000	410 000	356 000	337 000	2 105 000	4 034 000	19 624 000
2000	15 225 000	866 000	500 000	404 000	385 000	2 238 000	4 393 000	19 618 000
1999	15 180 000	780 000	516 000	414 000	393 000	2 084 000	4 187 000	19 367 000
1998	14 893 000	747 000	484 000	402 000	379 000	1 923 000	3 935 000	18 828 000
1997	13 401 000	734 000	566 000	439 000	398 000	2 097 000	4 234 000	17 636 000
1996	12 909 000	691 000	648 000	460 000	447 000	2 131 000	4 377 000	17 285 000
1995	13 005 000	641 000	589 000	430 000	421 000	1 846 000	3 927 000	16 932 000
1994	12 542 000	577 000	481 000	410 000	367 000	1 594 000	3 429 000	15 972 000
1993	12 024 000	562 000	408 000	361 000	339 000	1 411 000	3 081 000	15 105 000
1992	11 819 000	536 000	392 000	310 000	290 000	1 394 000	2 922 000	14 741 000
1991	12 003 000	530 000	393 000	307 000	273 000	1 406 000	2 909 000	14 912 000
1990	12 252 000	553 000	411 000	259 000	253 000	1 482 000	2 958 000	15 210 000
1989	12 184 000	561 000	387 000	243 000	263 000	1 473 000	2 927 000	15 111 000
1988	12 763 000	527 000	324 000	230 000	263 000	1 378 000	2 722 000	15 485 000

INTERNATIONAL VISITORS

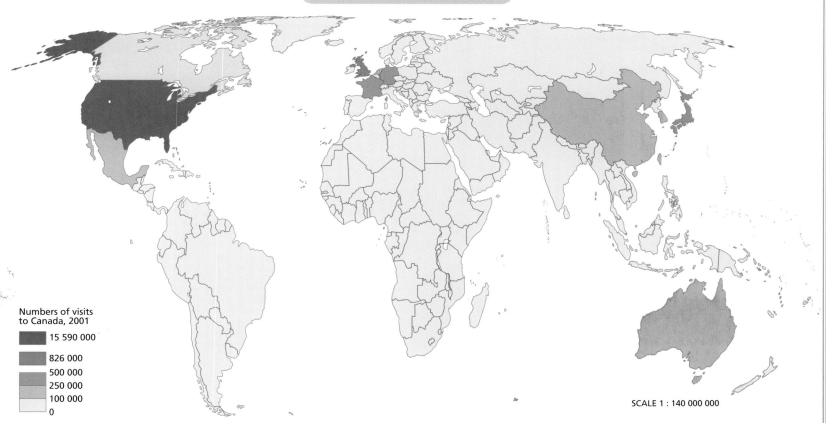

Numbers of visits
to Canada, 2001

- 15 590 000
- 826 000
- 500 000
- 250 000
- 100 000
- 0

SCALE 1 : 140 000 000

TOP INTERNATIONAL DESTINATIONS AND EARNERS

World's Top 15 Tourism Destinations, 2001

Rank 2001	Country	International tourist arrivals (thousands)		Percent change 2001/2000	Market share (percent) 2001
		2000	2001		
1	France	75 600	76 600	1.2	11.0
2	Spain	49 700	49 500	3.4	7.1
3	USA	50 900	45 500	-10.7	6.6
4	Italy	41 200	39 100	-5.2	5.6
5	China	31 200	33 200	6.2	4.8
6	United Kingdom	25 200	22 800	-9.4	3.3
7	Russian Federation	21 200	-	-	-
8	Mexico	20 600	19 800	-4.0	2.9
9	**Canada**	**19 700**	**19 700**	**0.2**	**2.8**
10	Austria	18 000	18 200	1.1	2.6
11	Germany	19 000	17 900	-5.9	2.6
12	Hungary	15 600	15 300	-1.5	2.2
13	Poland	17 400	15 000	-13.8	2.2
14	Hong Kong (China)	13 100	13 700	5.1	2.0
15	Greece	13 100	-	-	-

World's Top 15 Tourism Earners, 2001

Rank 2001	Country	International tourist receipts (US$ millions)		Percent change 2001/2000	Market share (percent) 2001
		2000	2001		
1	USA	82 000	72 300	-11.9	15.6
2	Spain	31 500	32 900	4.5	7.1
3	France	30 800	30 000	-2.5	6.5
4	Italy	27 500	25 800	-6.2	5.6
5	China	16 200	17 800	9.7	3.8
6	Germany	18 500	17 200	-6.8	3.7
7	United Kingdom	19 500	16 300	-16.7	3.5
8	**Canada**	**10 700**	**10 800**	**0.7**	**2.3**
9	Austria	9 900	10 100	1.9	2.2
10	Greece	9 200	-	-	-
11	Turkey	7 600	8 900	17.0	1.9
12	Mexico	8 300	8 400	1.3	1.8
13	Hong Kong (China)	7 900	8 200	4.5	1.8
14	Australia	8 500	7 600	-9.8	1.6
15	Switzerland	7 500	7 600	1.6	1.6

DOMESTIC TRAVEL

		2001	2000	Percent change
Intraprovincial	Same day	67 266 000	75 148 000	-10.5
	Overnight	58 284 000	66 441 000	-12.3
Interprovincial	Same day	3 078 000	3 520 000	-12.6
	Overnight	15 575 000	16 997 000	-8.4
Total	Same day	70 344 000	78 668 000	-10.6
	Overnight	73 859 000	83 438 000	-11.5
Grand total		144 203 000	162 106 000	-11.0

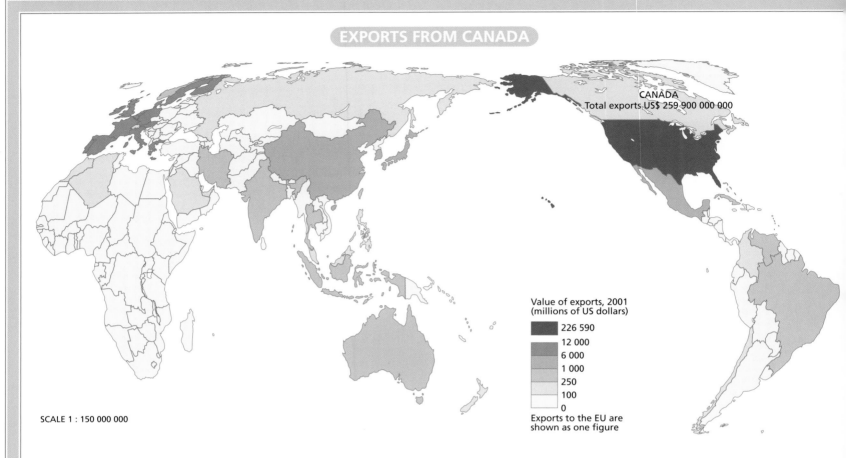

EXPORTS FROM CANADA

CANADA
Total exports US$ 259 900 000 000

Value of exports, 2001
(millions of US dollars)

226 590
12 000
6 000
1 000
250
100
0

Exports to the EU are
shown as one figure

SCALE 1 : 150 000 000

Highest Trade Partners (Exports), 2001

Country	Millions of US dollars
USA	226 590
European Union	11 800
Japan	5 280
China	3 370
Mexico	1 750
South Korea	1 280
Australia	690
Taiwan	640
Norway	640
Brazil	590

Types of Exports, Main Trading Partners, 2001

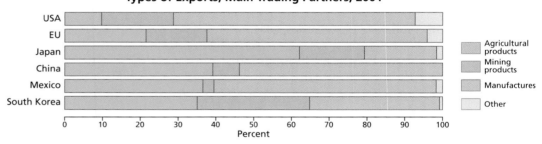

USA
EU
Japan
China
Mexico
South Korea

0 10 20 30 40 50 60 70 80 90 100
Percent

Agricultural products

Mining products

Manufactures

Other

WORLD EXPORTS

Exports by Type, Selected Countries (% of Total Share), 2001

Country	Food, beverages and tobacco		Crude materials		Fuels		Animal and vegetable oils		Chemicals		Manufactured goods		Machinery and transport		Miscellaneous manufactured goods		Other	
	1990	2001	1990	2001	1990	2001	1990	2001	1990	2001	1990	2001	1990	2001	1990	2001	1990	2001
Australia	20.1	20.0	27.0	20.1	19.3	21.5	0.3	0.3	2.6	4.6	12.6	11.7	8.3	11.7	2.6	3.8	7.2	6.3
Canada	7.8	6.8	13.8	7.4	10.0	14.1	0.1	0.2	5.3	5.8	16.0	14.4	37.2	38.2	3.7	6.5	6.1	6.6
China [1]	6.5	3.7	2.5	1.4	2.8	1.9	0.1	0.1	5.4	4.9	17.8	15.4	22.4	37.4	41.8	34.8	0.7	0.4
Egypt [2]	7.9	9.5	8.8	6.7	39.2	40.5	0.1	0.3	4.6	7.7	30.1	18.4	0.5	1.3	8.8	8.5	0.0	7.1
France	15.0	10.5	3.4	1.8	2.3	2.5	0.2	0.2	13.5	15.9	17.3	13.9	37.3	45.0	10.6	10.1	0.4	0.1
Italy	5.9	5.9	1.1	1.0	2.3	1.9	0.4	0.4	6.6	9.7	21.8	20.5	37.5	37.7	23.2	21.2	1.2	1.7
Japan	0.6	0.7	0.7	0.8	0.4	0.4	0.1	0.1	5.5	7.6	11.9	10.2	70.7	67.2	8.5	8.8	1.6	4.2
Mexico [3]	11.4	4.9	4.2	1.1	37.4	9.7	0.1	0.1	6.7	3.2	11.3	8.3	25.1	59.0	3.4	13.6	0.4	0.1
Norway	8.0	6.1	3.5	1.3	39.8	61.6	0.2	0.1	7.3	2.8	21.2	9.6	16.3	11.2	3.6	2.7	0.1	4.6
Saudi Arabia [4]	0.6	0.5	0.2	0.2	91.7	88.8	0.1	0.1	5.0	7.1	1.2	1.6	0.9	1.3	0.3	0.3	0.0	0.1
UK	7.0	4.8	2.2	1.2	5.2	7.8	0.1	0.1	13.1	14.1	15.8	12.9	41.9	47.4	13.9	11.4	0.8	0.3
USA	9.5	6.4	6.9	3.8	3.1	1.8	0.3	0.2	10.1	11.3	8.6	9.1	46.5	51.3	11.0	12.1	4.0	4.0

1 China - 1992 data   2 Egypt - 1994 data   3 Mexico - 2000 data   4 Saudi Arabia - 1991 data

IMPORTS TO CANADA

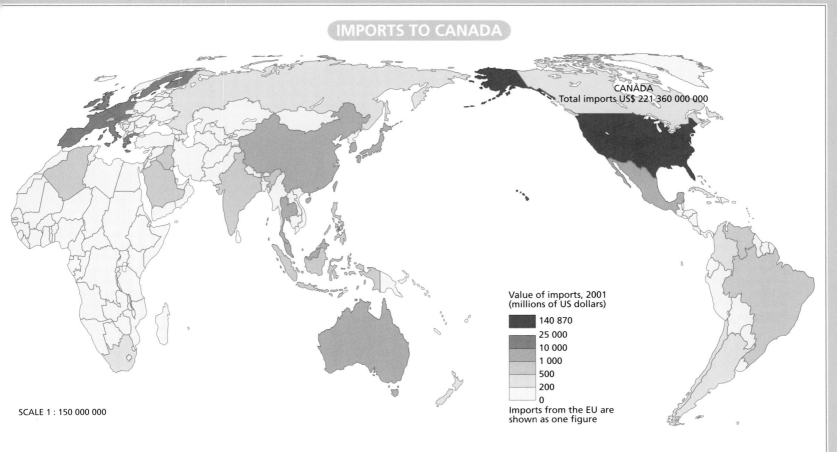

CANADA
Total imports US$ 221 360 000 000

Value of imports, 2001
(millions of US dollars)

- 140 870
- 25 000
- 10 000
- 1 000
- 500
- 200
- 0

Imports from the EU are
shown as one figure

SCALE 1 : 150 000 000

Highest Trade Partners (Imports), 2001

Country	Millions of US dollars
USA	140 870
European Union	24 750
Japan	9 450
China	9 000
Mexico	7 820
South Korea	2 970
Taiwan	2 850
Malaysia	1 220
Thailand	1 090
Australia	1 040

Types of Imports, Main Trading Partners, 2001

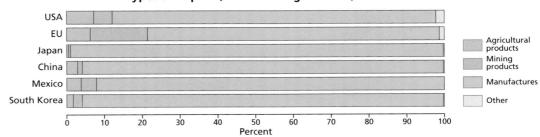

- Agricultural products
- Mining products
- Manufactures
- Other

WORLD IMPORTS

Imports by Type, Selected Countries (% of Total Share), 2001

Country	Food, beverages and tobacco		Crude materials		Fuels		Animal and vegetable oils		Chemicals		Manufactured goods		Machinery and transport		Miscellaneous manufactured goods		Other	
	1990	2001	1990	2001	1990	2001	1990	2001	1990	2001	1990	2001	1990	2001	1990	2001	1990	2001
Australia	4.7	4.6	2.8	1.5	5.7	8.5	0.3	0.2	10.3	12.4	15.4	11.9	45.1	44.5	13.9	14.5	1.8	1.9
Canada	5.9	5.4	3.4	2.8	6.3	5.6	0.1	0.1	6.6	9.3	12.6	12.6	50.2	49.7	12.0	12.1	2.9	2.4
China [1]	5.5	3.1	4.0	5.6	2.9	4.8	0.3	0.3	9.6	9.8	22.2	16.7	33.9	43.8	19.2	15.3	2.4	0.6
Egypt [2]	25.1	23.8	7.5	7.6	1.4	5.0	2.0	1.4	12.2	12.1	18.9	16.4	29.1	22.0	3.8	4.5	0.0	7.2
France	9.3	7.8	4.0	2.6	9.6	9.5	0.3	0.3	10.7	12.7	17.7	14.3	34.1	38.6	14.0	14.1	0.3	0.1
Italy	11.1	8.0	7.7	5.3	10.5	9.2	0.7	0.5	11.1	12.3	16.4	15.2	30.1	33.2	7.9	10.5	4.5	5.8
Japan	13.5	12.4	12.7	6.5	24.2	20.1	0.1	0.2	6.5	7.2	12.6	8.7	15.4	27.3	12.4	15.9	2.6	1.7
Mexico [3]	12.3	3.8	6.4	2.5	3.8	2.9	1.2	0.3	10.3	8.2	13.1	17.5	33.4	50.3	8.6	11.9	10.9	2.6
Norway	5.4	6.4	7.3	7.0	3.7	4.1	0.2	0.4	8.5	9.3	17.9	14.7	40.9	42.1	16.0	15.2	0.1	0.8
Saudi Arabia [4]	12.3	14.7	1.8	2.0	0.3	0.2	0.4	0.5	8.6	9.8	19.6	16.6	40.4	42.0	11.4	11.3	5.2	2.9
UK	9.9	7.5	4.6	2.7	4.7	4.3	0.3	0.2	8.8	9.9	17.8	14.9	38.3	45.0	15.0	15.1	0.6	0.4
USA	5.6	4.3	3.1	1.9	13.3	10.9	0.2	0.1	4.5	6.9	12.2	11.0	41.4	43.1	16.5	17.5	3.2	4.3

1 China - 1992 data   2 Egypt - 1994 data   3 Mexico - 2000 data   4 Saudi Arabia - 1991 data

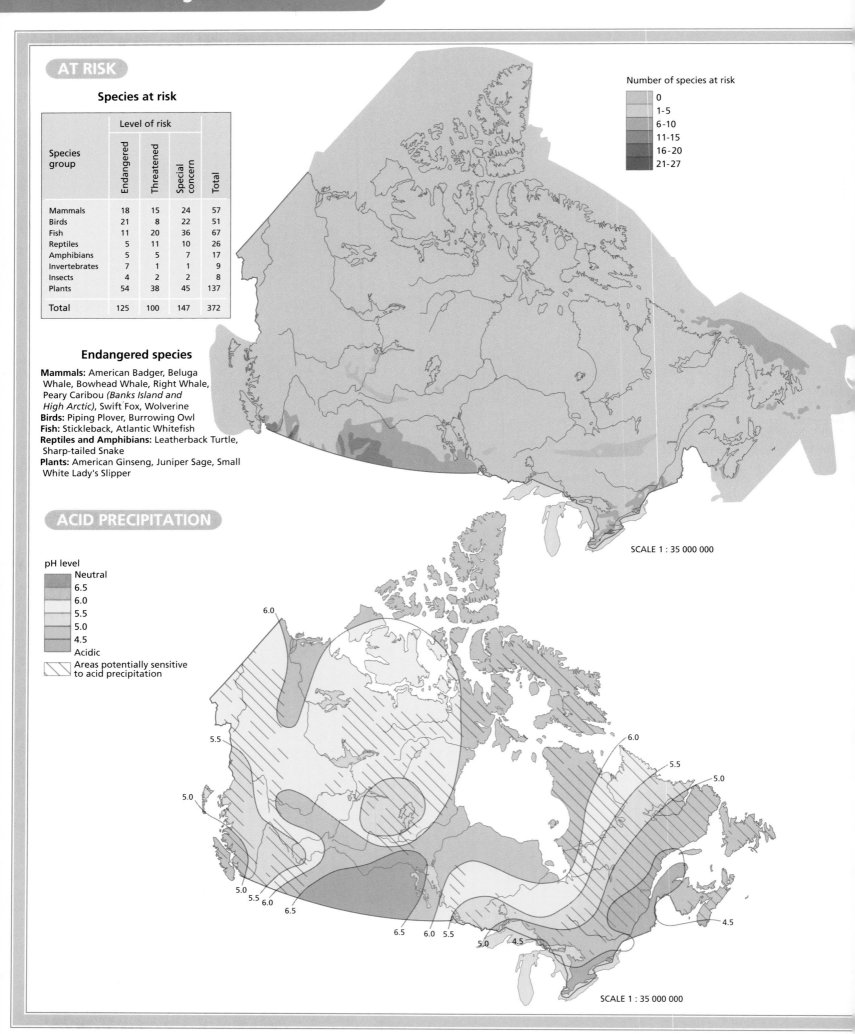

AT RISK

Species at risk

Species group	Level of risk			
	Endangered	Threatened	Special concern	Total
Mammals	18	15	24	57
Birds	21	8	22	51
Fish	11	20	36	67
Reptiles	5	11	10	26
Amphibians	5	5	7	17
Invertebrates	7	1	1	9
Insects	4	2	2	8
Plants	54	38	45	137
Total	125	100	147	372

Endangered species

Mammals: American Badger, Beluga Whale, Bowhead Whale, Right Whale, Peary Caribou *(Banks Island and High Arctic)*, Swift Fox, Wolverine
Birds: Piping Plover, Burrowing Owl
Fish: Stickleback, Atlantic Whitefish
Reptiles and Amphibians: Leatherback Turtle, Sharp-tailed Snake
Plants: American Ginseng, Juniper Sage, Small White Lady's Slipper

Number of species at risk
- 0
- 1-5
- 6-10
- 11-15
- 16-20
- 21-27

SCALE 1 : 35 000 000

ACID PRECIPITATION

pH level
- Neutral
- 6.5
- 6.0
- 5.5
- 5.0
- 4.5
- Acidic
- Areas potentially sensitive to acid precipitation

SCALE 1 : 35 000 000

GREENHOUSE GAS EMISSIONS

**Canada
(692 Mt)**

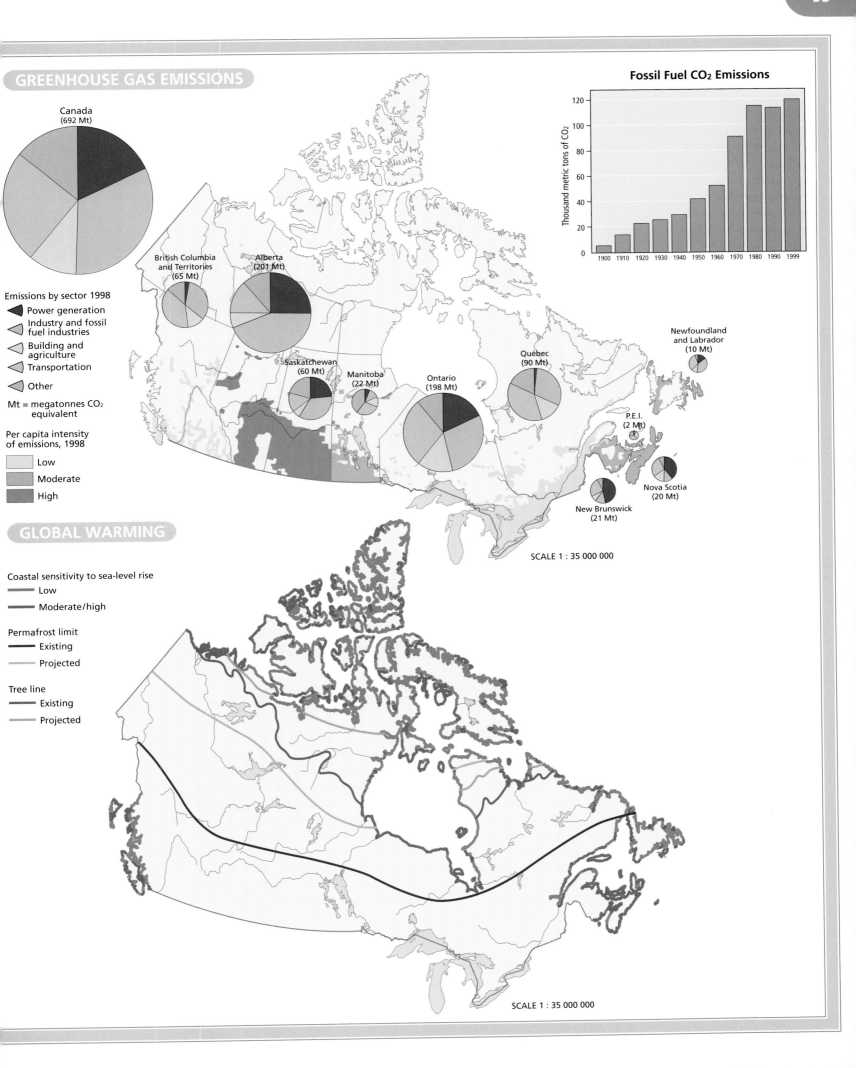

Emissions by sector 1998

- Power generation
- Industry and fossil fuel industries
- Building and agriculture
- Transportation
- Other

Mt = megatonnes CO$_2$ equivalent

Per capita intensity of emissions, 1998

- Low
- Moderate
- High

GLOBAL WARMING

Coastal sensitivity to sea-level rise

- Low
- Moderate/high

Permafrost limit

- Existing
- Projected

Tree line

- Existing
- Projected

Fossil Fuel CO$_2$ Emissions

Thousand metric tons of CO$_2$

1900 1910 1920 1930 1940 1950 1960 1970 1980 1990 1999

British Columbia and Territories
(65 Mt)

Alberta
(201 Mt)

Saskatchewan
(60 Mt)

Manitoba
(22 Mt)

Ontario
(198 Mt)

Québec
(90 Mt)

Newfoundland and Labrador
(10 Mt)

P.E.I.
(2 Mt)

Nova Scotia
(20 Mt)

New Brunswick
(21 Mt)

SCALE 1 : 35 000 000

SCALE 1 : 35 000 000

ECOZONES

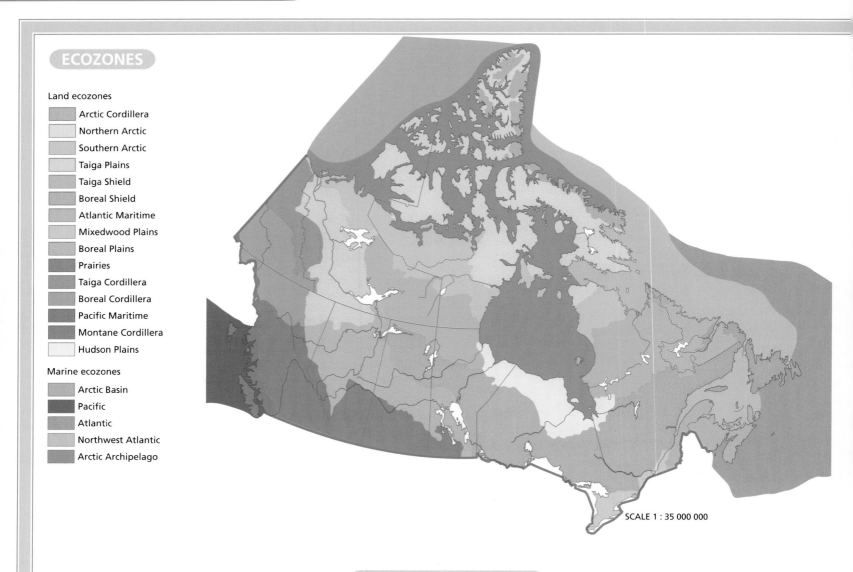

Land ecozones

- Arctic Cordillera
- Northern Arctic
- Southern Arctic
- Taiga Plains
- Taiga Shield
- Boreal Shield
- Atlantic Maritime
- Mixedwood Plains
- Boreal Plains
- Prairies
- Taiga Cordillera
- Boreal Cordillera
- Pacific Maritime
- Montane Cordillera
- Hudson Plains

Marine ecozones

- Arctic Basin
- Pacific
- Atlantic
- Northwest Atlantic
- Arctic Archipelago

SCALE 1 : 35 000 000

EFFECTS ON THE LAND

Major influences on forest ecosystems

ECOZONE	Fire	Insects, Disease	Harvesting	Change to other use	Transport corridors	Pollution
Boreal Cordillera	✓			✓	✓	
Pacific Maritime		✓	✓	✓	✓	✓
Montane Cordillera	✓	✓	✓	✓	✓	
Boreal Plains	✓		✓	✓	✓	
Taiga Plains	✓				✓	
Taiga Shield	✓					
Boreal Shield	✓	✓	✓	✓		✓
Mixedwood Plains		✓		✓		✓
Atlantic Maritime	✓	✓	✓	✓		✓

Major influences on farmland

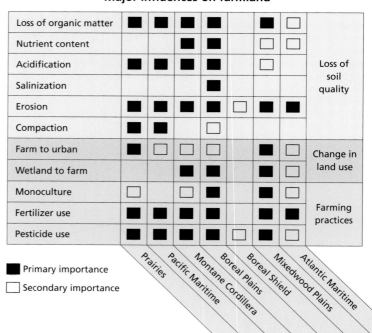

	Prairies	Pacific Maritime	Montane Cordillera	Boreal Plains	Boreal Shield	Mixedwood Plains	Atlantic Maritime	
Loss of organic matter	■	■	■	■		■	□	Loss of soil quality
Nutrient content			■	■		□	□	
Acidification	■	■	■	■		□		
Salinization				■				
Erosion	■	■	■	■	□	■	■	
Compaction	■	■		□				
Farm to urban	■	□	□	□		■	□	Change in land use
Wetland to farm			■	■		■	□	
Monoculture	□		□	■		■	□	Farming practices
Fertilizer use	■	■	■	■		■	■	
Pesticide use	■	■	■	■	□	■	□	

■ Primary importance

□ Secondary importance

PROTECTING THE ENVIRONMENT

- 🌫️ ○ National Park
- ● World Heritage Site
- ○ World Biosphere Reserve

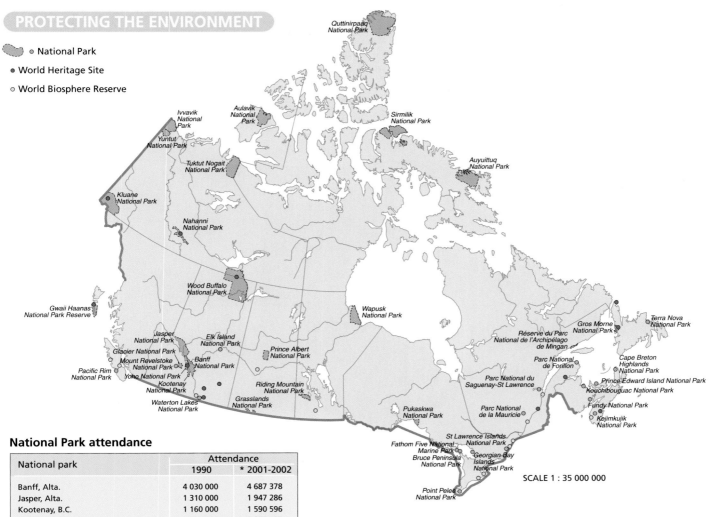

SCALE 1 : 35 000 000

National Park attendance

National park	Attendance	
	1990	* 2001-2002
Banff, Alta.	4 030 000	4 687 378
Jasper, Alta.	1 310 000	1 947 286
Kootenay, B.C.	1 160 000	1 590 596
Yoho, B.C.	680 000	1 371 105
Prince Edward Island, P.E.I.	810 000	927 625
Pacific Rim, B.C.	600 000	644 841
Glacier, B.C.	160 000	} 566 679
Mount Revelstoke, B.C.	160 000	
Saguenay - St Lawrence, Qué.	no data	442 182
Fathom Five, Ont.	no data	435 794
Waterton Lakes, Alta.	350 000	413 515
Riding Mountain, Man.	390 000	411 267
Cape Breton Highlands, N.S.	570 000	366 617
Point Pelee, Ont.	460 000	331 244
Fundy, N.B.	230 000	249 314
Terra Nova, Nfld.	170 000	248 746
Kouchibouguac, N.B.	180 000	242 388
Prince Albert, Sask.	190 000	230 530
Bruce Peninsula, Ont.	3 500	212 457
Elk Island, Alta.	300 000	211 547
La Mauricie, Qué.	280 000	196 786
Forillon, Qué.	210 000	180 320
Gros Morne, Nfld.	98 000	118 071
Georgian Bay Islands, Ont.	49 000	91 331
Kejimkujik, N.S.	170 000	66 472
St Lawrence Islands, Ont.	85 000	65 603
Kluane, Y.T.	69 000	59 517
Archipélago de Mingan, Qué.	25 000	32 269
Pukaskwa, Ont.	15 000	8 488
Nahanni, N.W.T.	1 300	6 918
Grasslands, Sask.	no data	6 773
Gwaii Haanas Reserve, B.C.	no data	2 331
Wood Buffalo, Alta. - N.W.T.	6 600	1 305
Auyuittuq, Nun.	350	413
Quttinirpaaq (Ellesmere Island), Nun.	230	192
Ivvavik, Y.T.	99	165
Aulavik, N.W.T.	no data	88
Wapusk, Man.	no data	no data
Tuktut Nogait, N.W.T.	no data	no data
Sirmilik, Nun.	no data	no data
Yuntut, Y.T.	no data	no data

* Fiscal year

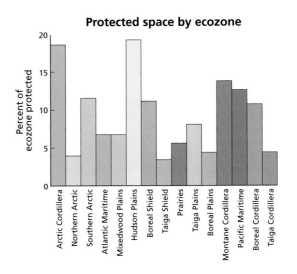

Protected space by ecozone

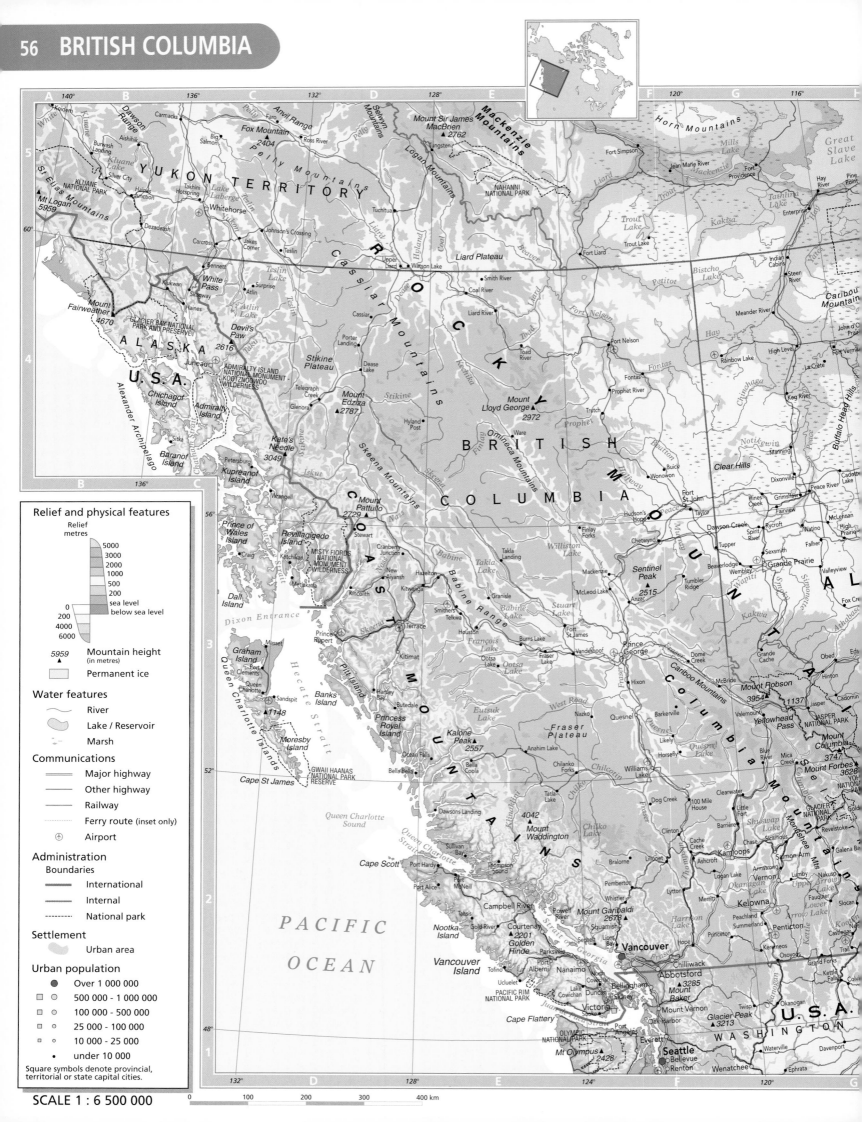

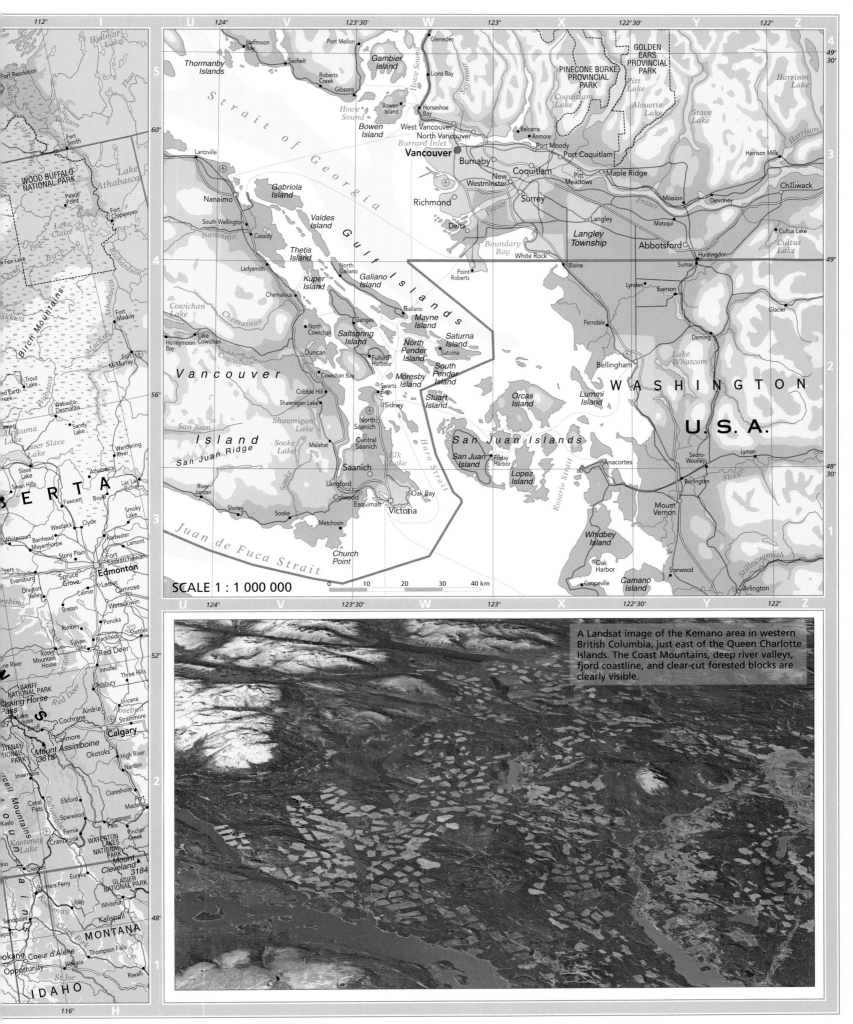

SCALE 1 : 1 000 000

0   10   20   30   40 km

A Landsat image of the Kemano area in western British Columbia, just east of the Queen Charlotte Islands. The Coast Mountains, deep river valleys, fjord coastline, and clear-cut forested blocks are clearly visible.

SCALE 1 : 50 000   Contour Interval : 40 metres

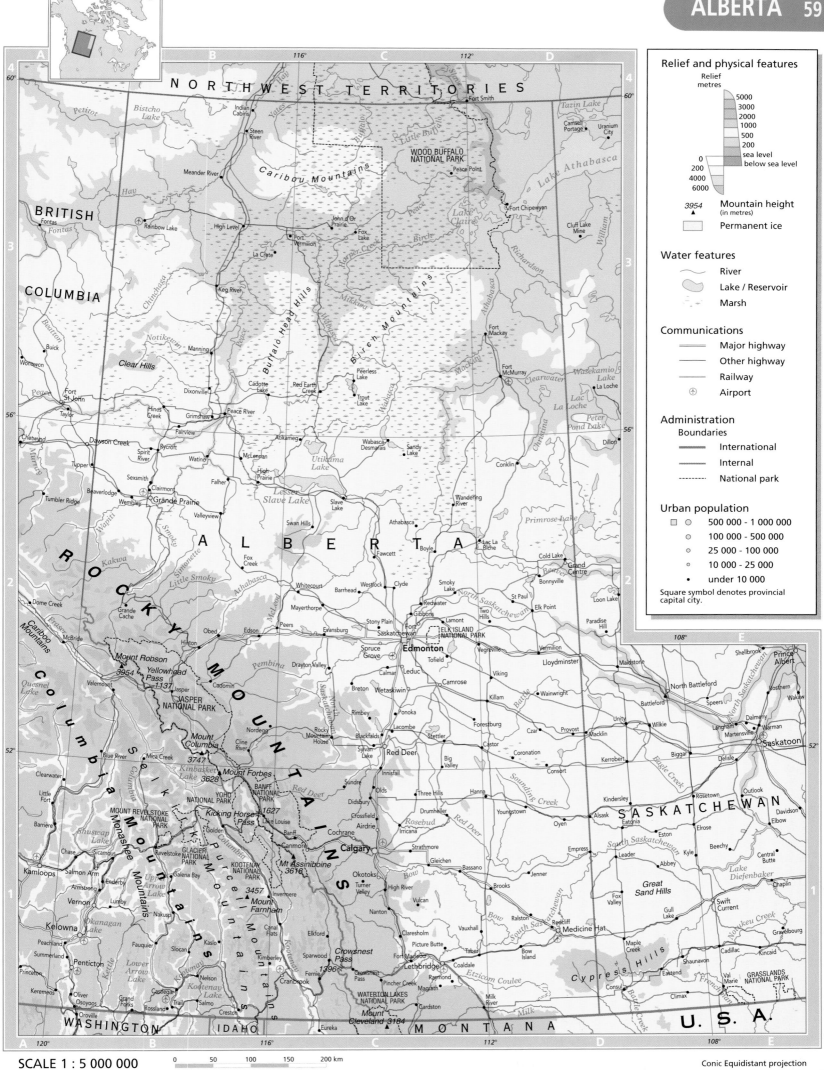

Relief and physical features

Relief metres

5000
3000
2000
1000
500
200
sea level
0
200
4000
6000
below sea level

3954 ▲ Mountain height (in metres)

Permanent ice

Water features

River

Lake / Reservoir

Marsh

Communications

Major highway

Other highway

Railway

⊕ Airport

Administration

Boundaries

International

Internal

National park

Urban population

☐ ◯ 500 000 - 1 000 000

◯ 100 000 - 500 000

◦ 25 000 - 100 000

∘ 10 000 - 25 000

• under 10 000

Square symbol denotes provincial capital city.

NORTHWEST TERRITORIES

BRITISH COLUMBIA

ALBERTA

SASKATCHEWAN

ROCKY MOUNTAINS

WASHINGTON   IDAHO   MONTANA   U.S.A.

WOOD BUFFALO NATIONAL PARK

Caribou Mountains

Buffalo Head Hills

Birch Mountains

Clear Hills

Lake Athabasca

Lake Claire

Edmonton

Calgary

Saskatoon

Mount Robson 3954
Yellowhead Pass 1137

Jasper National Park

Mount Columbia 3747

Mount Forbes 3628

Banff National Park

Yoho National Park

Kicking Horse Pass 1627

Kootenay National Park

Mt Assiniboine 3616

Glacier National Park

Mount Revelstoke National Park

Mount Farnham 3457

Crowsnest Pass 1396

Waterton Lakes National Park

Mount Cleveland 3184

Elk Island National Park

Grasslands National Park

SCALE 1 : 5 000 000

0   50   100   150   200 km

Conic Equidistant projection

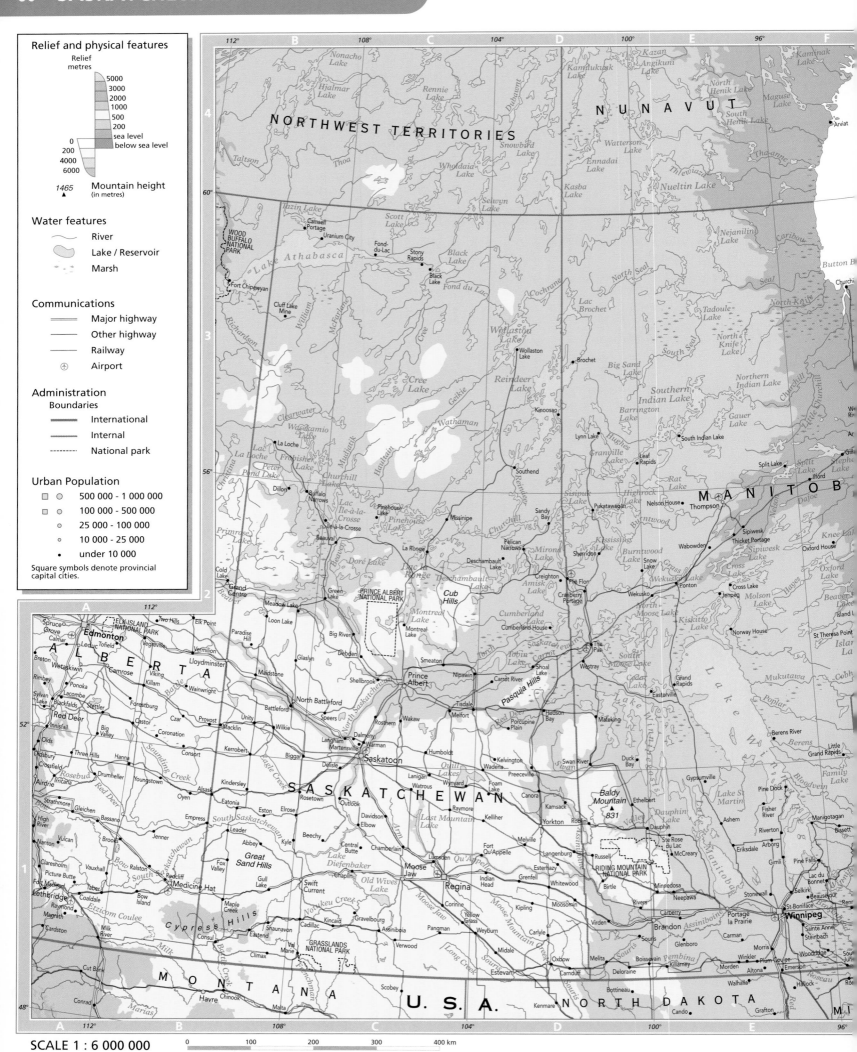

Relief and physical features

Relief
metres

5000
3000
2000
1000
500
200
0 sea level
200
4000 below sea level
6000

▲ 1465 Mountain height
(in metres)

Water features

〜 River

◯ Lake / Reservoir

  Marsh

Communications

═══ Major highway

─── Other highway

─── Railway

⊕ Airport

Administration

Boundaries

═══ International

─── Internal

------ National park

Urban Population

▢ ◯ 500 000 - 1 000 000

▢ ◯ 100 000 - 500 000

◯ 25 000 - 100 000

◦ 10 000 - 25 000

• under 10 000

Square symbols denote provincial capital cities.

SCALE 1 : 6 000 000

0   100   200   300   400 km

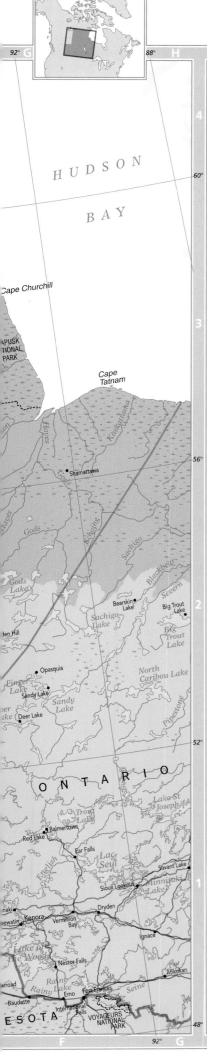

HUDSON

BAY

Cape Churchill

Cape
Tatnam

Shamattawa

Bearskin
Lake

Big Trout
Lake

Big
Trout
Lake

North
Caribou Lake

Opasquia

Sandy Lake

Sandy
Lake

Deer Lake

Gods
Lake

Finger
Lake

Pipestone

ONTARIO

Lake St
Joseph

Trout
Lake

Balmertown

Red Lake

Ear Falls

Lac
Seul

Savant Lake

Sioux Lookout

Minnitaki
Lake

Dryden

Ignace

Kenora

Vermillion
Bay

Lake of
the Woods

Nestor Falls

Rainy
Lake

Emo

Fort Frances

Seine

Baudette

International
Falls

VOYAGEURS
NATIONAL
PARK

ESOTA

This is a "seasonal image" near Altona, Manitoba, combining data collected by space shuttle Endeavour in April and October. Red represents April data; green represents October data, and blue shows the ratio between the two data sets. This rich farmland is important for wheat, barley, canola, corn, sunflowers, and sugar beets.

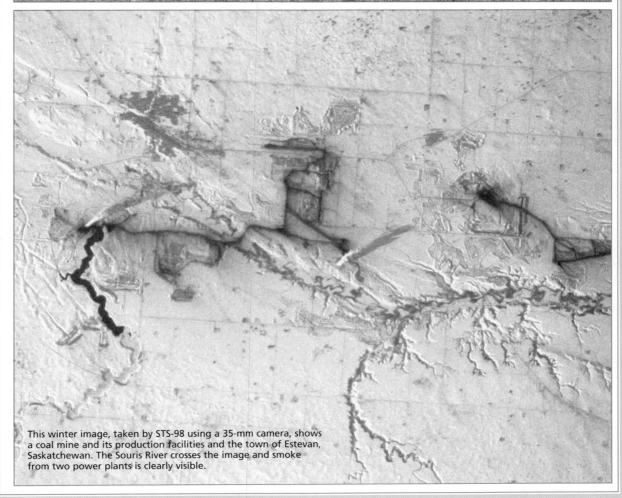

This winter image, taken by STS-98 using a 35-mm camera, shows a coal mine and its production facilities and the town of Estevan, Saskatchewan. The Souris River crosses the image and smoke from two power plants is clearly visible.

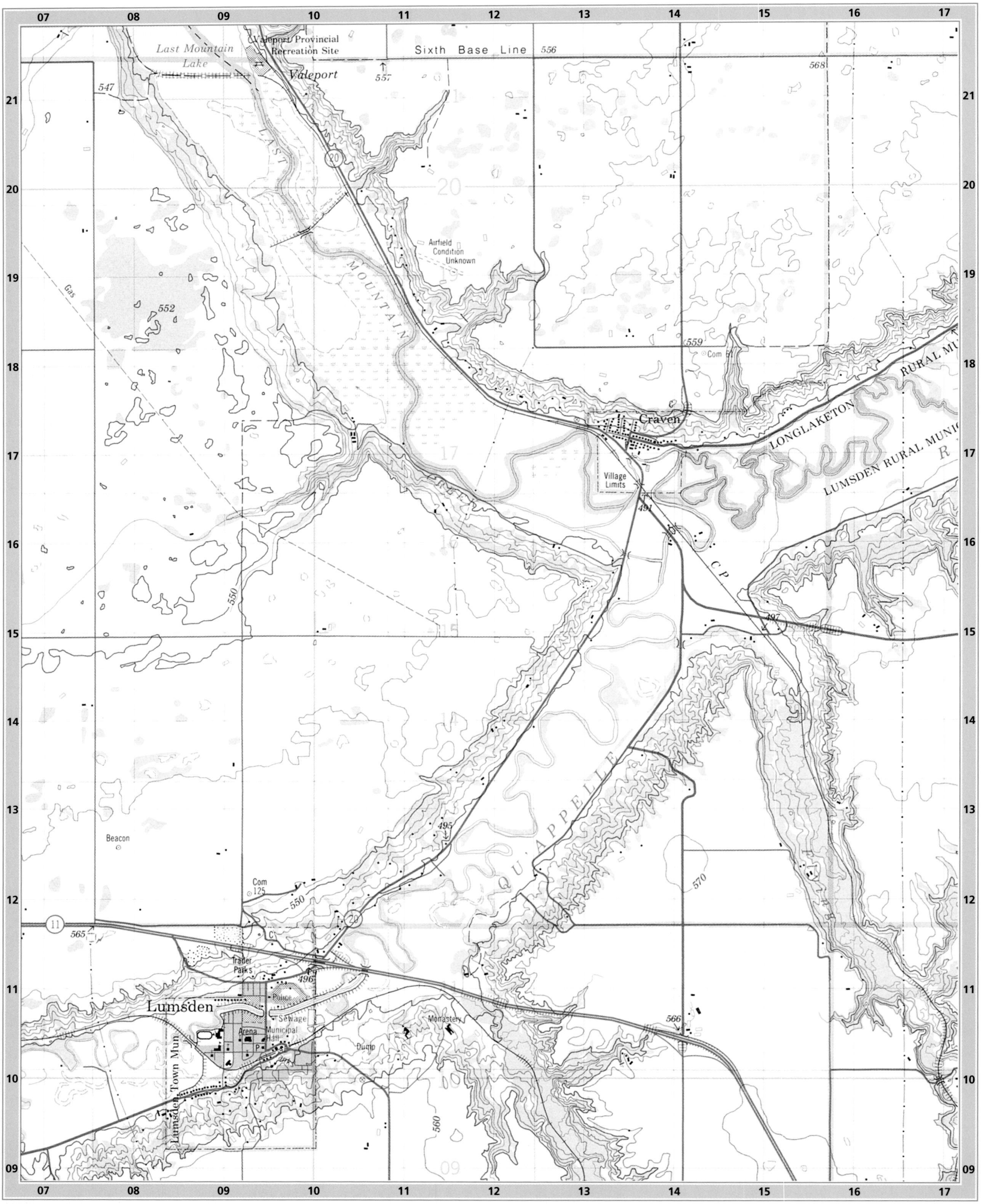

Last Mountain Lake

Valeport Provincial Recreation Site

Sixth Base Line 556

Valeport

557

547

552

550

Gas

MOUNTAIN

Airfield Condition Unknown

20

559

Com

Craven

RURAL MU

LONGLAKETON

Village Limits

491

LUMSDEN RURAL MUNI

R

CP

497

550

495

QU APPELLE

570

Beacon

Com 125

550

565

11

496

20

Trailer Parks

Police

Sewage

Lumsden

Arena

Municipal Hall

Monastery

Dump

566

560

Lumsden Town Mun

SCALE 1 : 50 000   Contour Interval : 10 metres

15   16   17   18   19   20   21   22   23   24   25

15   16   17   18   19   20   21   22   23   24   25

775

70   70

Creek

Morris
Dam

330

69   69

Sewage   (246)

Dump   Communications: 350

C

775   775

787   MORRIS RURAL

775   MONTCALM RURAL

Creek   68   68

775   775   785

Municipal
Hall   Arena
Tanks   788

Senior Citizens
Home
Tanks   H   Police   *R* 67   67

E   Horseshoe
Lake

Morris   Auto
Wreckers   Plant   Mobile
Home
Park   *E*

Town Limits   *D*

66   66
Airfield
Condition Unknown

779   65   65

750

775   *Clubb*   *Coulee*

64   64

775   64

Canadian   *Drain*

776

523   63   63

62   62

772   *Drain*

61   61

750

778   60   60

780

59   *River*   59

75   Tanks
Sewage

Senior
Citizens
Home   Arena
Fire   Tanks

779   (246)   (217)

ALITY   58   58
Convent

15   16   17   18   19   20   21   22   23   24   25

SCALE 1 : 50 000   Contour Interval : 25 feet

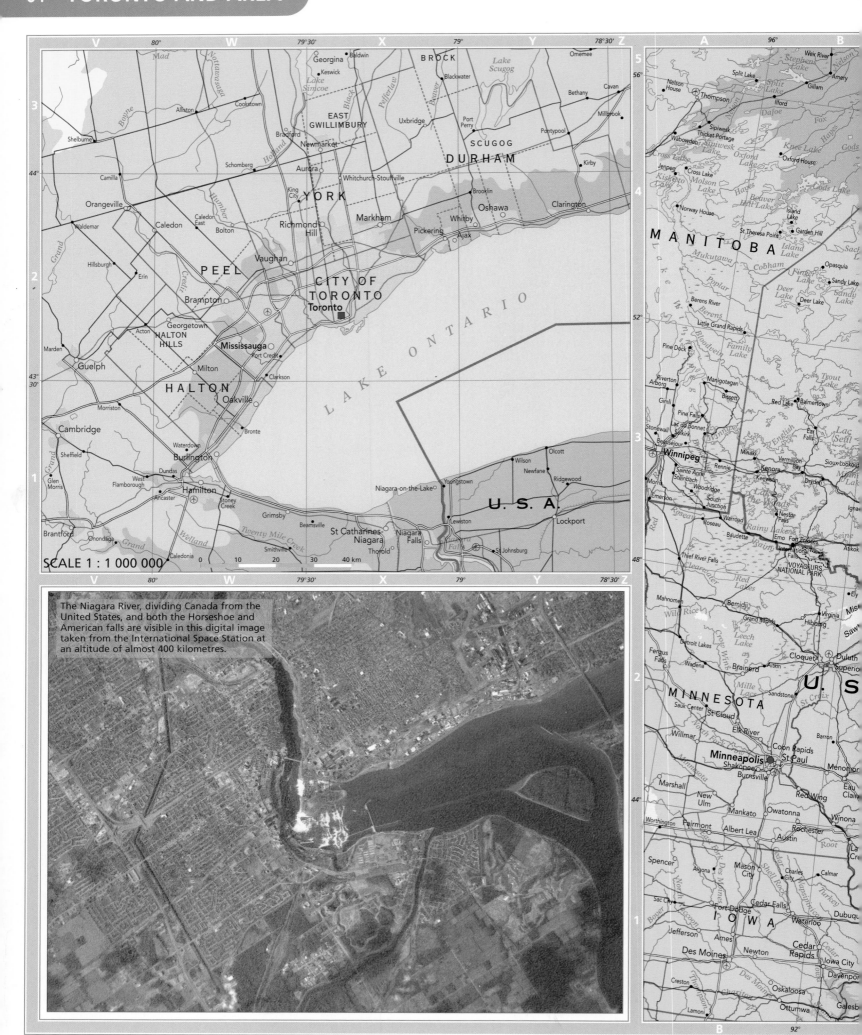

SCALE 1 : 1 000 000

0   10   20   30   40 km

The Niagara River, dividing Canada from the United States, and both the Horseshoe and American falls are visible in this digital image taken from the International Space Station at an altitude of almost 400 kilometres.

Conic Equidistant projection

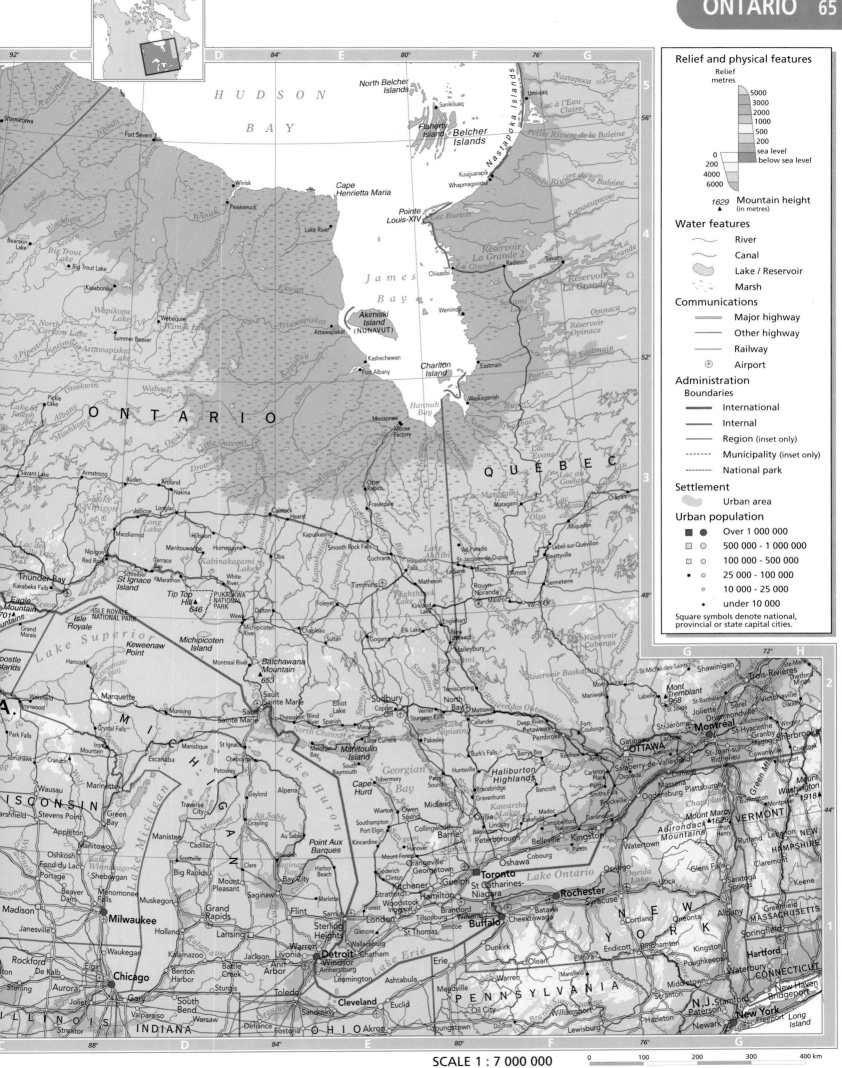

Relief and physical features

Relief metres

5000	
3000	
2000	
1000	
500	
200	
0	sea level
200	below sea level
4000	
6000	

1629 ▲ Mountain height (in metres)

Water features

- River
- Canal
- Lake / Reservoir
- Marsh

Communications

- Major highway
- Other highway
- Railway
- ✈ Airport

Administration

Boundaries

- International
- Internal
- Region (inset only)
- Municipality (inset only)
- National park

Settlement

Urban area

Urban population

■ ●	Over 1 000 000
□ ○	500 000 - 1 000 000
□ ○	100 000 - 500 000
■ ○	25 000 - 100 000
○	10 000 - 25 000
●	under 10 000

Square symbols denote national, provincial or state capital cities.

SCALE 1 : 7 000 000

0   100   200   300   400 km

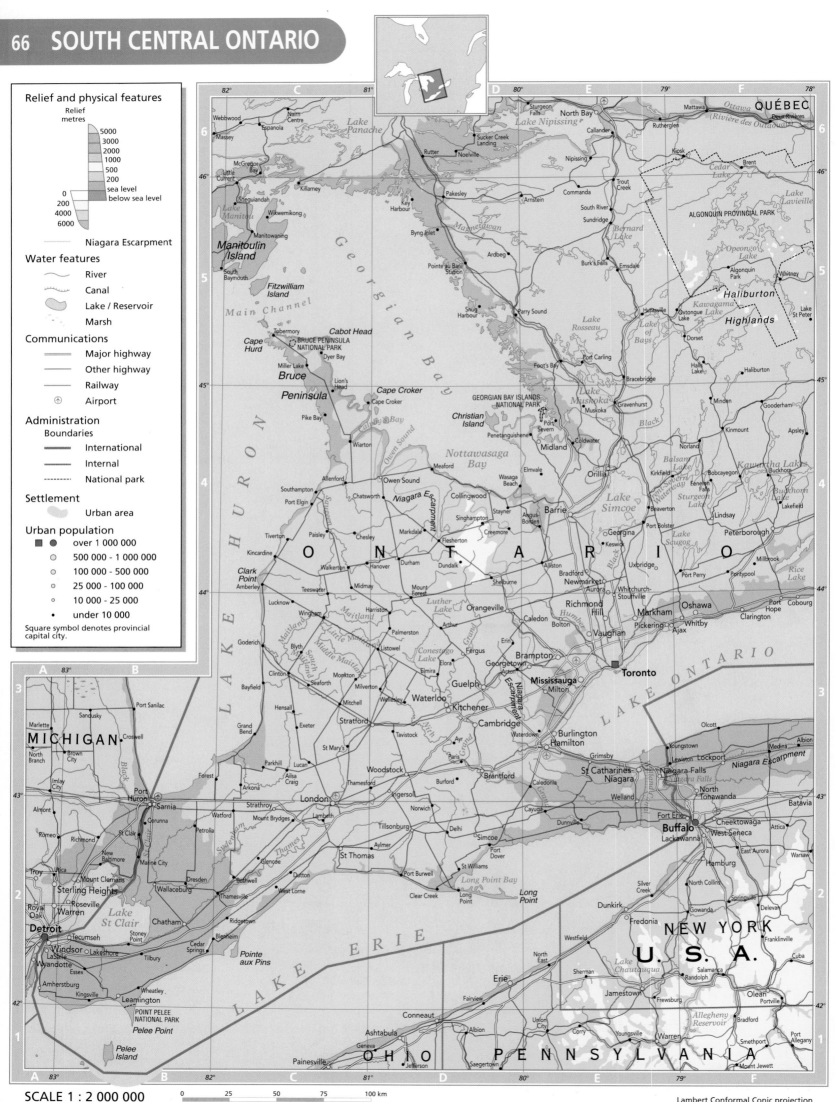

Relief and physical features

Relief
metres

5000
3000
2000
1000
500
200
0 sea level
200
4000 below sea level
6000

Niagara Escarpment

Water features

～～ River

Canal

Lake / Reservoir

Marsh

Communications

Major highway

Other highway

Railway

⊕ Airport

Administration

Boundaries

International

Internal

National park

Settlement

Urban area

Urban population

■ ● over 1 000 000

○ 500 000 - 1 000 000

○ 100 000 - 500 000

○ 25 000 - 100 000

○ 10 000 - 25 000

• under 10 000

Square symbol denotes provincial
capital city.

SCALE 1 : 2 000 000

0   25   50   75   100 km

Lambert Conformal Conic projection

25　26　27　28　29　30　31　32　33　34　35

Craigenputtock
Hookery Three
Island Picnic Pt
Devil's Gulch
Lalla Rookh Sister
Island Bluffs Bivouac Island
71

Muldrew Lake

Middle Lake Landing
Auto Wrecker
70

Dump
Beaver
Klueys Bay
69
Marina Rose
Marina
Dori
226.9
Prospect Pt
Burnt
Stenson
Island
68
240
68
Gordon Point
Lumber Yard
Good Luck I
Long Point
Kilworthy
Fire
Com'72'
Sopher's Landing
67
219.3
67
Cranberry Island
River Point
McLean Bay
Kahshe Lake
Marina
Portlock Channel
240
Motel
66
240
66
Ellison Point
Joseph Pt
Marina
Marie Island
240
Iron City Pt
McCormick Island
Goose Rock
Carl I
Evans
Paul Island
65
John I
Margaret Island
65
Snake
Indian Island
I
Channel Island
Grandview
High Island
Pt
Sparrow Lake
64
Long Island
64
SPARROW
212±
LAKE
Camp
224
63
Duck Bay
237.4
63
Ernest Island
Camp
Speer Island
62
Sparrow Lake
Marina
Monahan Pt
Sewage
62
Lauderdale Point
Sewage
Welsh Bay
61
Port Stanton
61
Sewage
Fairground
Beaver Lake
Severn Bridge
60
230
217.9
60
Hamlet
MUSKOKA DISTRICT MUNICIPALITY
Marina
SEVER

25　26　27　28　29　30　31　32　33　34　35

SCALE 1 : 50 000　　　Contour Interval : 10 metres

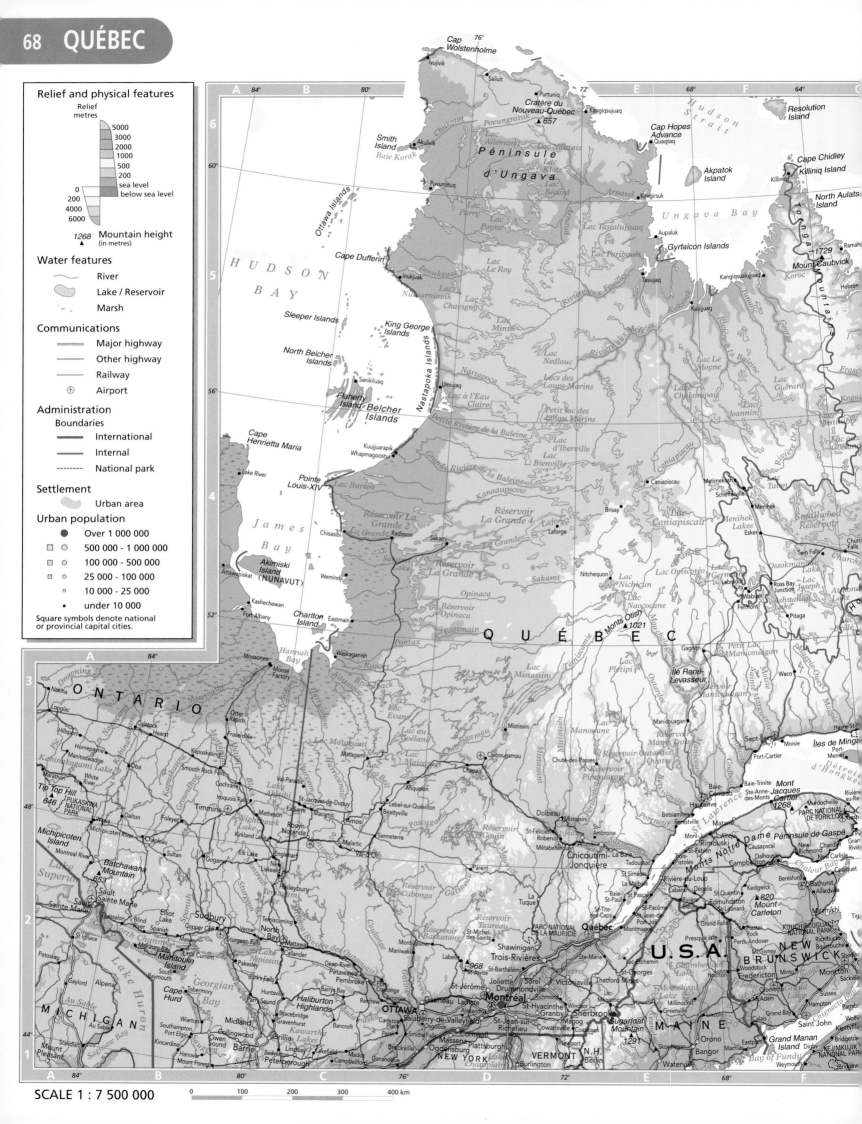

Relief and physical features

Relief metres
5000
3000
2000
1000
500
200
0 sea level
200 below sea level
4000
6000

▲ 1268 Mountain height (in metres)

Water features
River
Lake / Reservoir
Marsh

Communications
Major highway
Other highway
Railway
⊕ Airport

Administration
Boundaries
International
Internal
National park

Settlement
Urban area

Urban population
● Over 1 000 000
⊡ ◎ 500 000 - 1 000 000
⊡ ◦ 100 000 - 500 000
⊡ ◦ 25 000 - 100 000
◦ 10 000 - 25 000
• under 10 000

Square symbols denote national or provincial capital cities.

SCALE 1 : 7 500 000

0   100   200   300   400 km

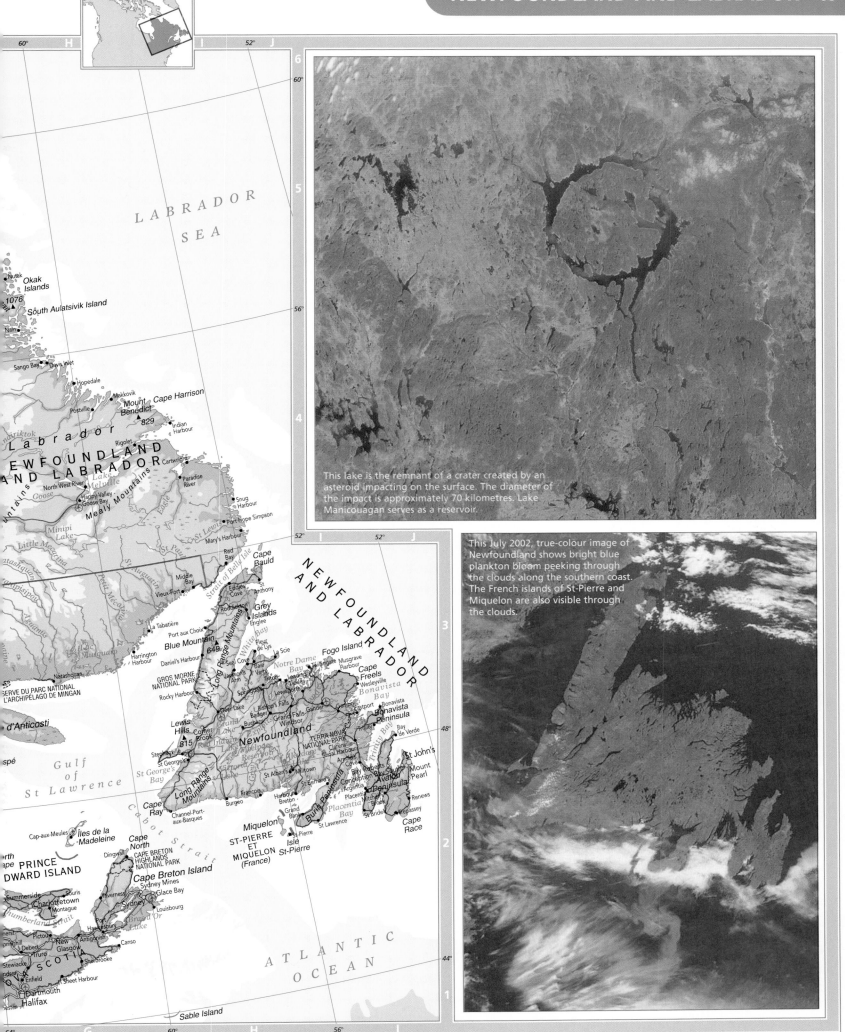

This lake is the remnant of a crater created by an asteroid impacting on the surface. The diameter of the impact is approximately 70 kilometres. Lake Manicouagan serves as a reservoir.

This July 2002, true-colour image of Newfoundland shows bright blue plankton bloom peeking through the clouds along the southern coast. The French islands of St-Pierre and Miquelon are also visible through the clouds.

Conic Equidistant projection

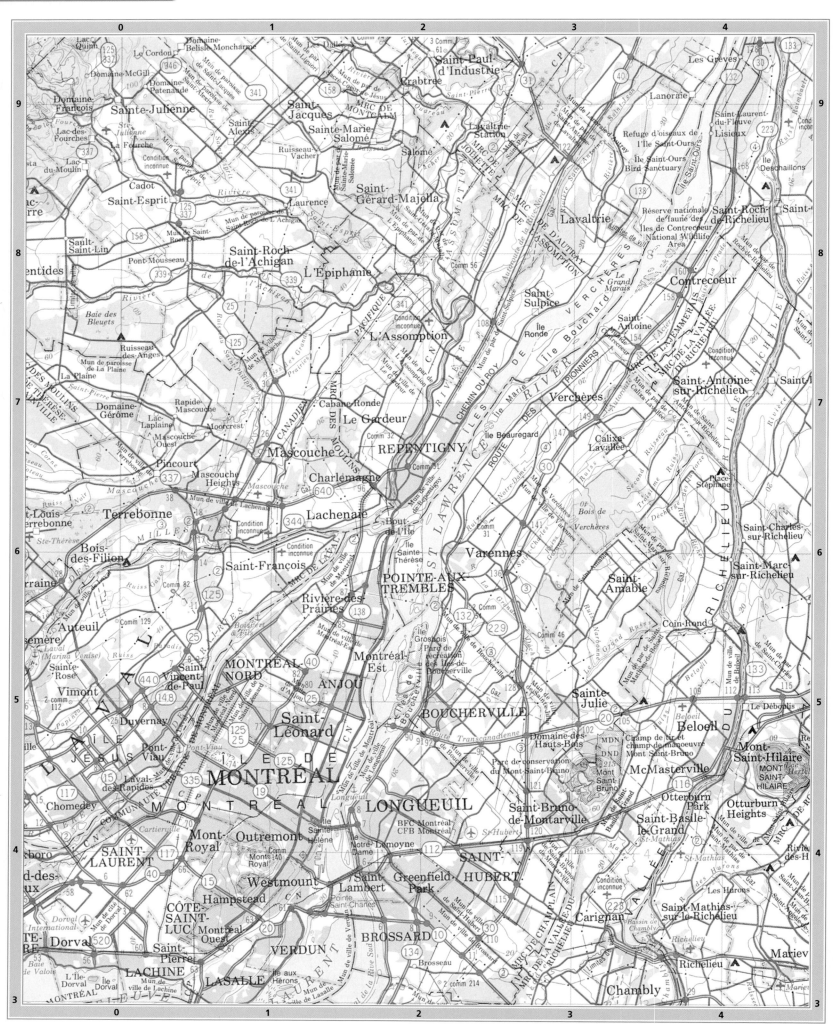

SCALE 1 : 250 000   Contour Interval : 20 metres

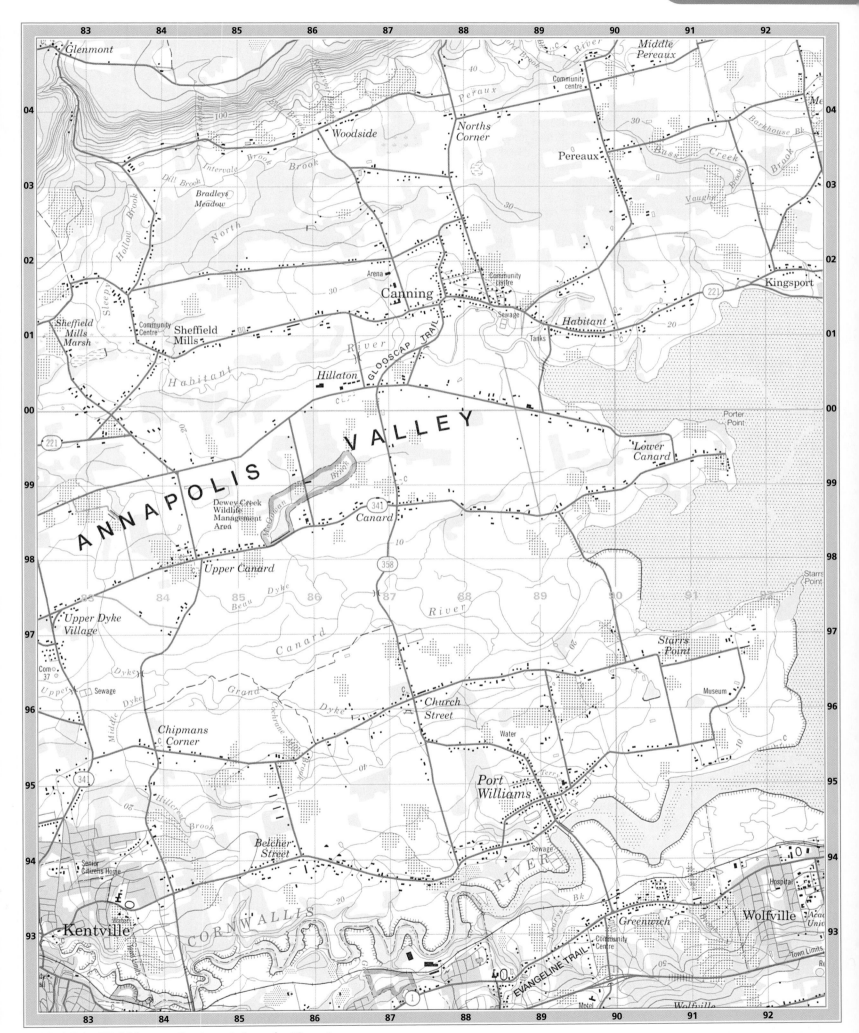

SCALE 1 : 50 000   Contour Interval : 10 metres

Relief and physical features

Relief
metres
5000
3000
2000
1000
500
200
0 sea level
200 below sea level
4000
6000

1606 ▲ Mountain height (in metres)

⋄ Historic site

Water features

River

Lake / Reservoir

Marsh

Urban population

□ ○ 100 000 - 500 000

□ ○ 25 000 - 100 000

○ 10 000 - 25 000

▪ • under 10 000

Square symbols denote provincial capital cities.

Communications

Major highway

Other highway

Railway

Ferry route

⊕ Airport

Administration
Boundaries

International

Internal

National park

SCALE 1 : 3 750 000

0   40   80   120   160 km

This false-colour image taken in March 2001, shows much of New Brunswick. The vegetation is shown in red; old growth forest appears as dark red, and sediment in the Bay of Fundy in green. Ice on rivers and frozen lakes appear in blue tones or white.

N

G 56° **H** 52° **I**

ATLANTIC OCEAN

NEWFOUNDLAND AND LABRADOR

Henley Harbour
Belle Isle
L'Anse aux Meadows National Historic Site
Cape Bauld
Quirpon
St Anthony
Red Bay
Middle Bay
L'Anse-au-Loup
Jeux-Port
Strait of Belle Isle
St Barbe
Hare Bay
Main Brook
St Julien's
Groais Island
Roddickton
Grey Islands
Englee
Bell Island
St John Bay
Ten Mile Lake
Port aux Choix
River of Ponds
Blue Mountain 649
Horse Islands
Daniel's Harbour
Portland Creek Pond
Fleur de Lys
Cape St John
GROS MORNE NATIONAL PARK
Jackson's Arm
Baie Verte
La Scie
Rocky Harbour
Seal Cove
Fogo Island
Gros Morne 806
Hampden
Middle Arm
Springdale
Triton
Notre Dame Bay
Durrell
Twillingate
Shoal Bay
Musgrave Harbour
New World Island
Summerford
Hamilton Sound
Leading Tickles
Germanville
Cape Freels
Deer Lake
Howley
Badger
South Twin Lake
North Twin Lake
Lewisporte
Botwood
Wesleyville
Doe Lake
Grand Lake
Buchans Junction
Bishop's Falls
Norris Arm
Gander
Hare Bay
Bonavista Bay
Corner Brook
Buchans
Red Indian Lake
Grand Falls-Windsor
Gander Lake
Gambo
Glovertown
Bonavista
Eastport
Catalina
Newfoundland
Victoria Lake
Meelpaeg Reservoir
Crooked Lake
Upper Salmon Reservoir
Deer Pond
TERRA NOVA NATIONAL PARK
Musgravetown
Port Rexton
Trinity
Bonavista Peninsula
Granite Lake
Jedoore Lake
Port Blandford
Clarenville
Shoal Harbour
Bay de Verde
White Bear
Trinity Bay
Gisborne Lake
St Alban's
Milltown
Arnold's Cove
Carbonear
Harbour Grace
Heart's Content
Pouch Cove
Torbay
St John's
Burgeo
François
Hermitage-Sandyville
English Harbour East
Long Island
Bay Roberts
Conception Bay South
Mount Pearl
Bay Bulls
Harbour Breton
St Bernard's
Marasheen Island
Long Harbour
Conception Bay
Witless Bay
Ramea Islands
Ramea
Brunette Island
Fortune Bay
Garnish
Argentia
Dunville
Placentia
Avalon Peninsula
Renews
Miquelon
ST-PIERRE ET MIQUELON (France)
Grand Bank
Burin Peninsula
Marystown
Burin
Placentia Bay
Mitchell's Brook
Fortune
St Lawrence
St Bride's
St Mary's Bay
Isle St-Pierre
St-Pierre
Lamaline
Trepassey
Cape Pine
Cape Race

ATLANTIC OCEAN

Conic Equidistant projection

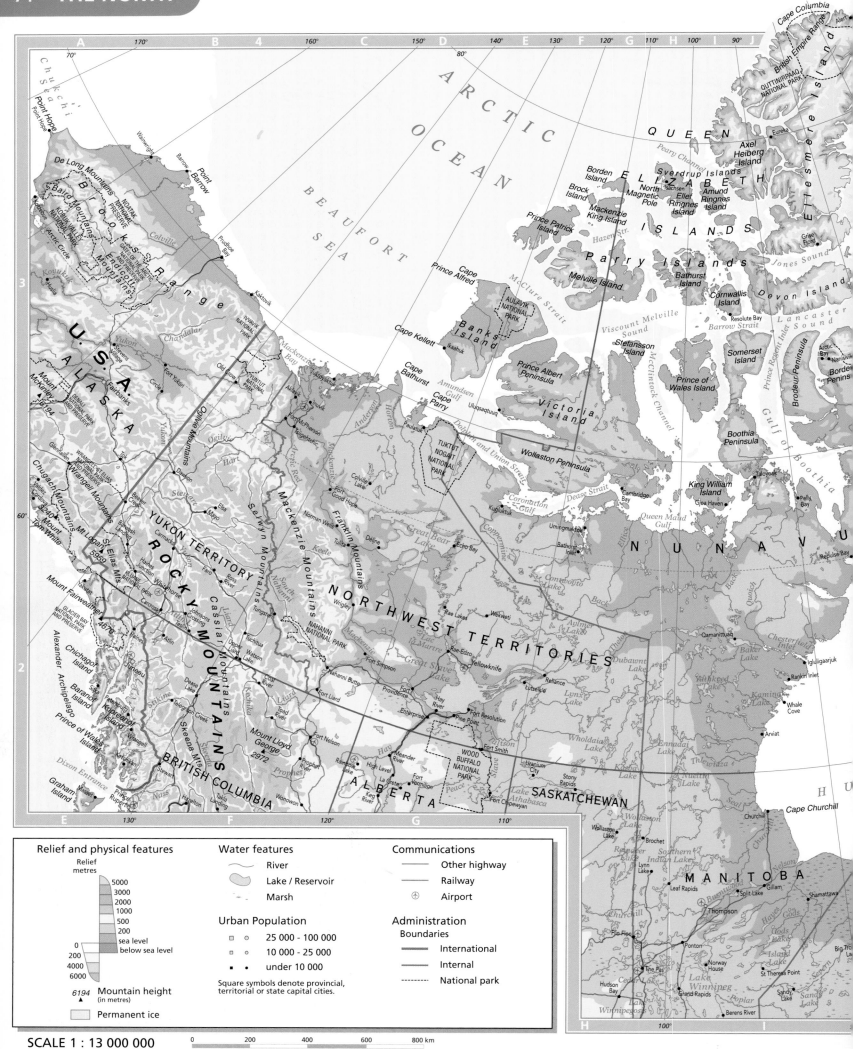

Relief and physical features

Relief metres

5000
3000
2000
1000
500
200
0 sea level
200 below sea level
4000
6000

6194 ▲ Mountain height (in metres)

Permanent ice

Water features

~ River

Lake / Reservoir

Marsh

Urban Population

□ ○ 25 000 - 100 000
□ ○ 10 000 - 25 000
■ • under 10 000

Square symbols denote provincial, territorial or state capital cities.

Communications

— Other highway

— Railway

⊕ Airport

Administration

Boundaries

— International

— Internal

--- National park

SCALE 1 : 13 000 000

0   200   400   600   800 km

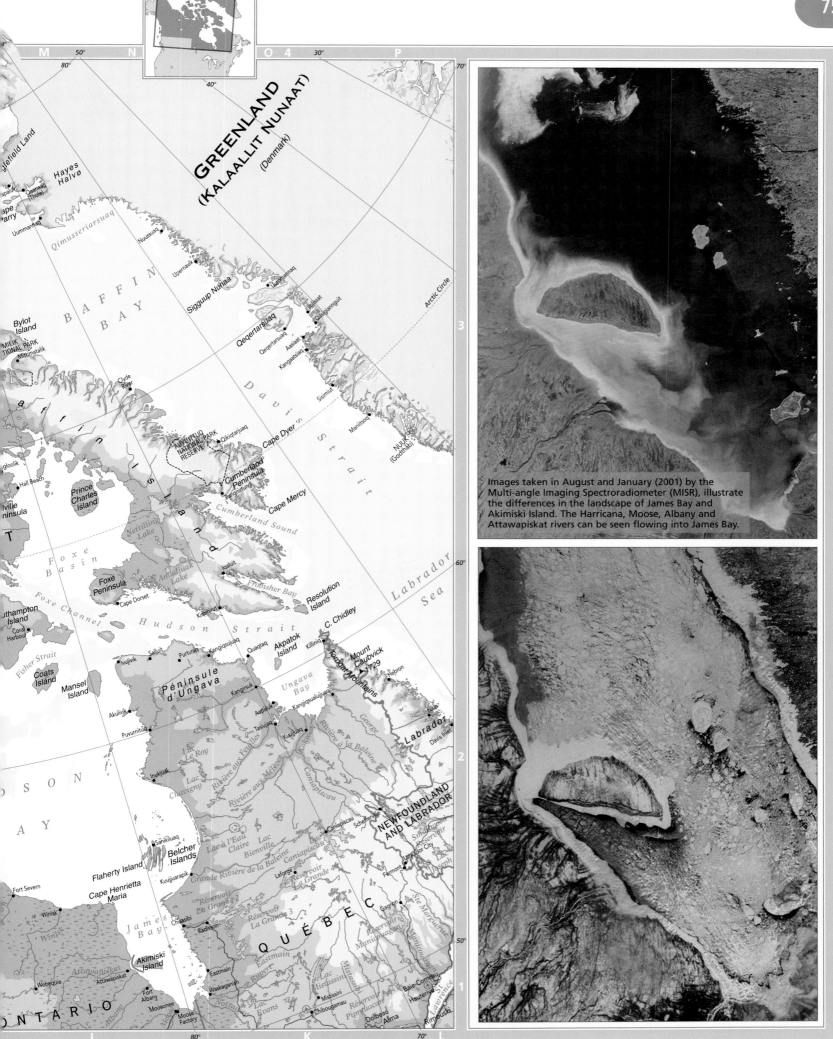

GREENLAND
(KALAALLIT NUNAAT)
(Denmark)

Hayes
Halvø

Gjelfield Land

Qaanaaq
Thule

Cape
arry

Uummannaq

Qimusseriarsuaq

Nuussuaq

Upernavik

Siggup Nunaa

Uummannaq

Ilulissat
Qasigiannguit

B A F F I N
B A Y

Bylot
Island

MILIK
TIONAL PARK

Mittimatalik

Qeqertarsuaq

Qeqertarsuaq

Aasiaat

Kangaatsiaq

Sisimiut

Arctic Circle

Clyde
River

D
a
v
i
s

S
t
r
a
i
t

Maniitsoq

gloolik

Hall Beach

Prince
Charles
Island

AUYUITTUQ
NATIONAL PARK
RESERVE

Qikiqtarjuaq

Cape Dyer

Cumberland
Peninsula

Pangnirtung

NUUK
(Godthåb)

Iville
ninsula

Nettilling
Lake

Cumberland Sound

Cape Mercy

T

Foxe
Basin

Amadjuak
Lake

Foxe
Peninsula

Iqaluit

Frobisher Bay

60°

uthampton
Island

Cape Dorset

Kimmirut

Resolution
Island

L a b r a d o r

Coral
Harbour

Fisher Strait

Coats
Island

Mansel
Island

H u d s o n   S t r a i t

Salluit

Purtuniq

Kangiqsujuaq

Quaqtaq

C. Chidley

Akpatok
Island

Killiniq

S e a

Ivujivik

Péninsule
d'Ungava

Kangirsuk

Mount
Caubvick
1729

Torngat Mountains

Hebron

Akulivik

Aupaluk

Ungava
Bay

Kangiqsualujjuaq

Nain

Labrador

Puvurnituq

Tasiujaq

Davis Inlet

Lac
Le Roy

Rivière aux Feuilles

George

Rivière à la Baleine

Inukjuak

Lac
Chavigny

Rivière aux Mélèzes

Koksoak

Caniapiscau

2

S O N

A Y

Sanikiluaq

Belcher
Islands

Lac à l'Eau
Claire

Lac
Bienville

Rivière de la Baleine

Caniapiscau

NEWFOUNDLAND
AND LABRADOR

Smallwood
Reservoir

Caniapiscau

Schefferville

Flaherty Island

Kuujjuarapik

Grande Rivière de la Baleine

Laforge

Réservoir
La Grande

Labrador City

Fermont

St Joseph

Fort Severn

Cape Henrietta
Maria

Réservoir
La Grande 2

Reservoir
La Grande 3

Rivière
La Grande

Gagnon

Ste Marguerite

Winisk

J a m e s
B a y

Chisasibi

Radisson

Réservoir
Pipmuacan

Q U É B E C

50°

Winisk

Akimiski
Island

Eastmain

Eastmain

Rupert

Réservoir
Manicouagan

Baie Comeau

O N T A R I O

Attawapiskat

Webequie

Attawapiskat

Eastmain

Waskaganish

Lac
Mistassini

Mistassini

Nottaway

Lac
Evans

Chibougamau

Dolbeau

Hauterive

Rimouski

Fort Albany

Moosonee

Moose
Factory

Alma

Images taken in August and January (2001) by the
Multi-angle Imaging Spectroradiometer (MISR), illustrate
the differences in the landscape of James Bay and
Akimiski Island. The Harricana, Moose, Albany and
Attawapiskat rivers can be seen flowing into James Bay.

Lambert Conformal Conic projection

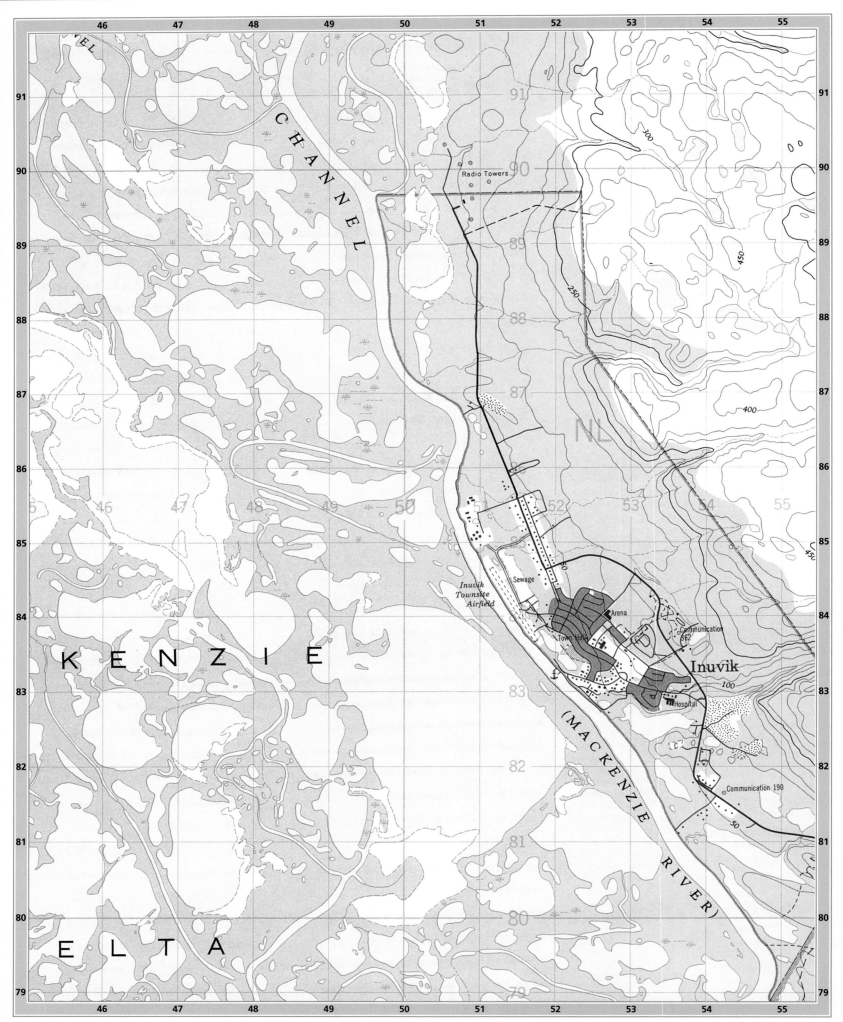

SCALE 1 : 50 000   Contour Interval : 50 feet

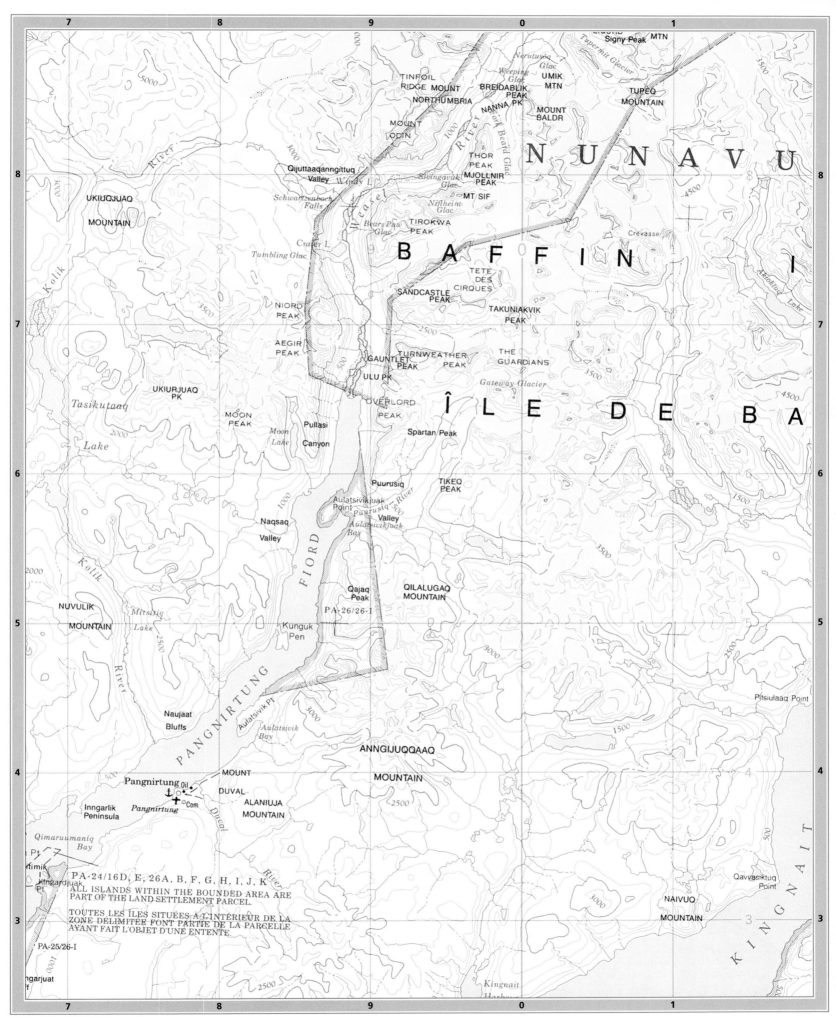

SCALE 1 : 250 000   Contour Interval : 500 feet

PLATE TECTONICS

EURASIAN PLATE

IRANIAN PLATE

ARABIAN PLATE

AFRICAN PLATE

SOMALI PLATE

African Rift System

Carlsberg Ridge

Central Indian Ridge

Himalaya

Japan Trench

Marianas Trench

PHILIPPINE PLATE

Philippine Fault

New Hebrides Trench

PACIFIC PLATE

JUAN DE FUCA PLATE

San Andreas Fault

NORTH AMERICAN PLATE

Mid Atlantic Ridge

COCOS PLATE

CARIBBEAN PLATE

SOUTH AMERICAN PLATE

East Pacific Ridge

NAZCA PLATE

Mid Atlantic Ridge

INDO-AUSTRALIAN PLATE

Southwest Indian Ridge

Southeast Indian Ridge

ANTARCTIC PLATE

SCOTIA PLATE

〰〰 **Subduction Zone** - the downward movements of an oceanic plate along converging continental or oceanic plate boundaries.

—— **Collision Zone** - the upward movement of the earth's crust into fold mountains in response to converging continental plates.

—— **Oceanic Ridges** - produced when plates separate, allowing volcanic material to rise and cool.

- - - **Line of plate boundary uncertain**

⑥ **Rate of plate movement (cm per year)**

← **Direction of plate movement**

EARTHQUAKES AND VOLCANOES

Grimsvotn

Laki

Stromboli

Etna

Erta Ale

Mt Cameroon

Nyiragongo

Réunion

MacDonald I.

Klíuchevskí

Karymsky

Bezymianny

Korovin

Okmok

Akutan

Amukta

Okushiri I. (7.8)

Kuril I. (8.3)

Mt St Helens

Unzen

Xijang (7.9)

Sakura Jima

Mt Pinatubo

Mayon

Kilauea

Guam (8.3)

Mt Peuet

Merapi

Manam

Rabaul

Papandayan

Yasur

Monowai

Ruapehu

Popocatepetl

Soufrière Hills

Pacaya

Arenal

Galeros

Villarrica

El Llaima

▭ **Earthquake* and volcano zone**

*Earthquake force is measured on the Richter scale

• **Major earthquake since 1990 (6.0 to 7.7*)**

Guam (8.3) • **Great earthquake since 1990 (over 7.8*)**

△ **Active volcano**

Rabaul △ **Active volcano with eruption since 1990**

▪ **Major tsunami since 1990**

SCALE 1 : 150 000 000

0   2000   4000   6000   8000 km

Times projection

THE EARTH'S CORE

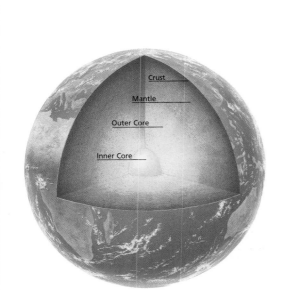

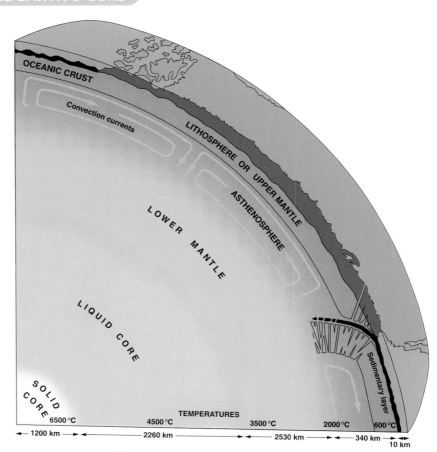

Crust

Mantle

Outer Core

Inner Core

OCEANIC CRUST

Convection currents

LITHOSPHERE OR UPPER MANTLE

ASTHENOSPHERE

LOWER MANTLE

LIQUID CORE

SOLID CORE

Sedimentary layer

TEMPERATURES

6500 °C   4500 °C   3500 °C   2000 °C   600 °C

← 1200 km → ← 2260 km → ← 2530 km → ← 340 km →

10 km

CONTINENTAL DRIFT

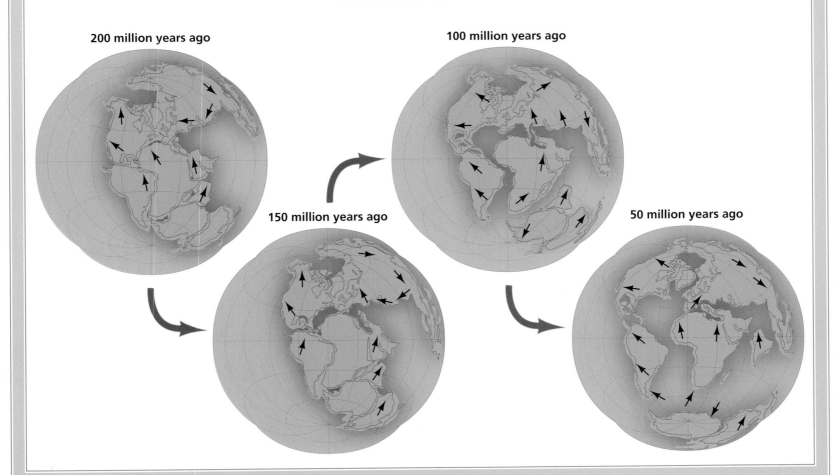

200 million years ago

150 million years ago

100 million years ago

50 million years ago

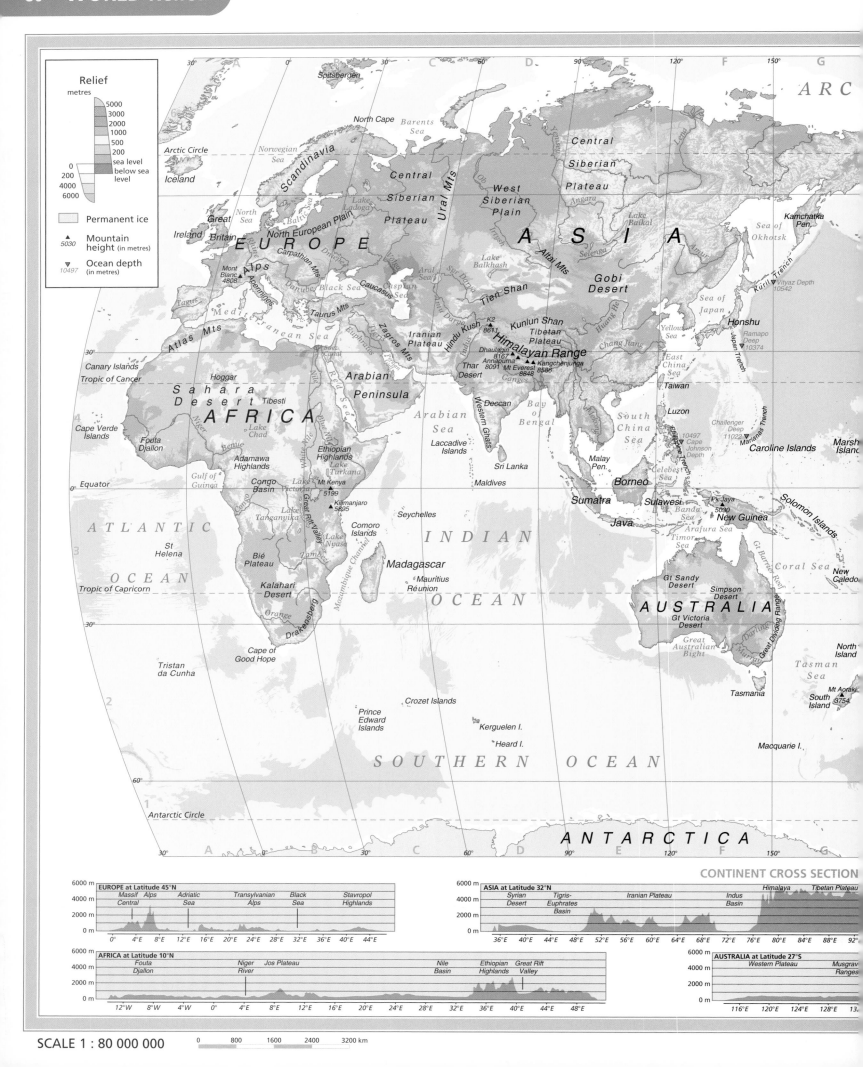

Relief

metres
- 5000
- 3000
- 2000
- 1000
- 500
- 200
- 0 sea level
- 200 below sea level
- 4000
- 6000

Permanent ice

▲ 5030 Mountain height (in metres)

▼ 10497 Ocean depth (in metres)

ARCTIC

Spitsbergen

North Cape *Barents Sea*

Norwegian Sea

Scandinavia

Central Siberian Plateau

Kamchatka Pen.

Sea of Okhotsk

Arctic Circle

Iceland

Great North Sea *Baltic Sea* Lake Ladoga

Ural Mts

West Siberian Plain

Ob

Sea of Japan

Ireland Britain

North European Plain

A S I A

Lake Baikal

EUROPE

Central Siberian Plateau

Yenisey

Lena

Carpathian Mts Dnieper

Irtysh

Angara

Selenga

Amur

Mont Blanc 4808 Alps

Apennines

Volga

Aral Sea

Syr Darya

Altai Mts

Honshu

Ramapo Deep ▼10374

Danube Black Sea Caucasus *Caspian Sea*

Tien Shan

Gobi Desert

Kuril Trench ▼ Vityaz Depth 10542

Tagus

Mediterranean Sea

Taurus Mts

Amu Darya

Euphrates

Zagros Mts

Iranian Plateau

Hindu Kush

K2 8611

Kunlun Shan

Huang He

Yellow Sea

East China Sea

Honshu

Japan Trench

Atlas Mts

Tigris

Himalayan Range

Chang Jiang

Taiwan

Canary Islands

Tropic of Cancer

Suez Canal

Arabian Peninsula

Dhaulagiri 8167 ▲ Annapurna 8091 ▲ Mt Everest 8848 ▲ Kangchenjunga 8586

Tibetan Plateau

Hoggar

Sahara Desert Tibesti

Red Sea

Nile

Thar Desert

Ganges

S a h a r a D e s e r t

AFRICA

Lake Chad

Niger

Blue Nile

Arabian Sea

Western Ghats

Deccan

Bay of Bengal

South China Sea

Luzon

Challenger Deep 11022 ▼ ◄ Marianas Trench

Cape Verde Islands

Benue

Adamawa Highlands

Ethiopian Highlands

Laccadive Islands

10497 ▼ Cape Johnson Depth

Philippine Trench

Caroline Islands

Marsh Island

Fouta Djallon

Gulf of Guinea

Congo Basin

Congo

Lake Turkana

Sri Lanka

Malay Pen.

Celebes Sea

Equator

Equator

Mt Kenya 5199 ▲

Maldives

Borneo

Sumatra

Banda Sea

Sulawesi

Pk Jaya 5030 ▲

New Guinea

Solomon Islands

A T L A N T I C

St Helena

Lake Victoria

Kilimanjaro 5895 ▲

Great Rift Valley

Lake Tanganyika

Seychelles

I N D I A N

Java

Arafura Sea

Timor Sea

O C E A N

Bié Plateau

Lake Nyasa

Zambezi

Comoro Islands

Madagascar

Mauritius

Coral Sea

New Caledo

Mozambique Channel

O C E A N

Tropic of Capricorn

Kalahari Desert

Réunion

Gt Sandy Desert

Simpson Desert

Darling

Great Dividing Range

Orange

Drakensberg

Gt Victoria Desert

AUSTRALIA

North Island

Tristan da Cunha

Cape of Good Hope

Great Australian Bight

Murray

Tasman Sea

Crozet Islands

Prince Edward Islands

Kerguelen I.

Tasmania

Mt Aoraki 3754 ▲

South Island

Heard I.

Macquarie I.

S O U T H E R N   O C E A N

Antarctic Circle

A N T A R C T I C A

CONTINENT CROSS SECTION

EUROPE at Latitude 45°N

| Massif | Alps | Adriatic Sea | Transylvanian Alps | Black Sea | Stavropol Highlands |
| Central | | | | | |

6000 m / 4000 m / 2000 m / 0 m

0° 4°E 8°E 12°E 16°E 20°E 24°E 28°E 32°E 36°E 40°E 44°E

ASIA at Latitude 32°N

| Syrian Desert | Tigris-Euphrates Basin | Iranian Plateau | Indus Basin | Himalaya | Tibetan Plateau |

6000 m / 4000 m / 2000 m / 0 m

36°E 40°E 44°E 48°E 52°E 56°E 60°E 64°E 68°E 72°E 76°E 80°E 84°E 88°E 92°

AFRICA at Latitude 10°N

| Fouta Djallon | Niger River | Jos Plateau | Nile Basin | Ethiopian Highlands | Great Rift Valley |

6000 m / 4000 m / 2000 m / 0 m

12°W 8°W 4°W 0° 4°E 8°E 12°E 16°E 20°E 24°E 28°E 32°E 36°E 40°E 44°E 48°E

AUSTRALIA at Latitude 27°S

| Western Plateau | Musgrave Ranges |

6000 m / 4000 m / 2000 m / 0 m

116°E 120°E 124°E 128°E 13

SCALE 1 : 80 000 000

0 800 1600 2400 3200 km

CONTINENTS	km²
Asia	45 036 492
Africa	30 343 578
North America	24 680 331
South America	17 815 420
Antarctica	12 093 000
Europe	9 908 599
Australia	7 682 300

OCEANS	km²
Pacific Ocean	166 624 000
Atlantic Ocean	86 557 000
Indian Ocean	73 427 000
Arctic Ocean	9 485 000

ISLANDS	km²
Greenland	2 175 600
New Guinea	808 510
Borneo	745 561
Madagascar	587 040
Baffin Island	507 451
Sumatra	473 606
Honshu	227 414
Great Britain	218 476
Victoria Island	217 291
Ellesmere Island	196 236

MOUNTAINS	metres
Mt Everest (Nepal/China)	8848
K2 (Jammu & Kashmir/China)	8611
Kangchenjunga (Nepal/China)	8586
Dhaulagiri (Nepal)	8167
Annapurna (Nepal)	8091
Aconcagua (Argentina)	6960
Ojos del Salado (Argentina/Chile)	6908
Chimborazo (Ecuador)	6310
Mt McKinley (USA)	6194
Mt Logan (Canada)	5959

RIVERS	km
Nile (Africa)	6695
Amazon (S. America)	6516
Chang Jiang (Asia)	6380
Mississippi-Missouri (N. America)	5969
Ob-Irtysh (Asia)	5568
Yenisey-Angara-Selenga (Asia)	5500
Huang-He (Asia)	5464
Congo (Africa)	4667
Río de la Plata-Paraná (S. America)	4500
Mekong (Asia)	4425

LAKES	km²
Caspian Sea (Asia)	371 000
Lake Superior (Canada/USA)	82 100
Lake Victoria (Africa)	68 800
Lake Huron (Canada/USA)	59 600
Lake Michigan (USA)	57 800
Lake Tanganyika (Africa)	32 900
Great Bear Lake (Canada)	31 328
Lake Baikal (Asia)	30 500
Lake Nyasa (Africa)	30 044

Horizontal scale 1 cm to 500 km, Vertical scale in metres, Vertical exaggeration = 105)

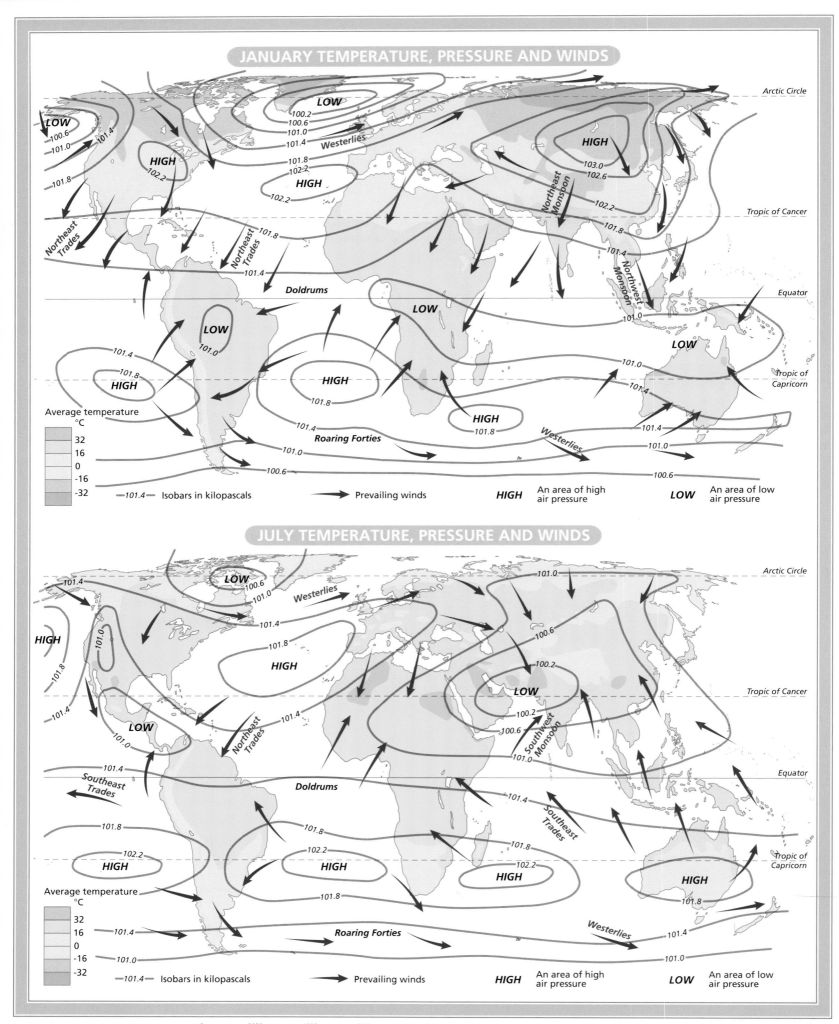

JANUARY TEMPERATURE, PRESSURE AND WINDS

Arctic Circle

LOW
100.2
100.6
101.0
101.4
Westerlies

LOW
100.6
101.4
101.0
101.8

HIGH
102.2

HIGH
102.2

HIGH
103.0
102.6

Northeast Monsoon

Tropic of Cancer

Northeast Trades

Northeast Trades

101.8

102.2

101.4

Northwest Monsoon

101.8

101.4

Doldrums

LOW

Equator

101.0

LOW

101.4

101.0

LOW

Tropic of Capricorn

LOW
101.0

101.4

101.8

HIGH

101.4

HIGH

101.0

101.4

Average temperature
°C

HIGH
101.8

HIGH
101.8

Roaring Forties

101.0

Westerlies

101.0

101.4

| 32 |
| 16 |
| 0 |
| -16 |
| -32 |

100.6

100.6

—101.4— Isobars in kilopascals   ⟶ Prevailing winds   **HIGH** An area of high air pressure   **LOW** An area of low air pressure

JULY TEMPERATURE, PRESSURE AND WINDS

Arctic Circle

LOW
100.6
101.0

Westerlies

101.0

101.4

HIGH

101.8

HIGH

101.4

100.6

100.2

101.4

LOW

102.2

HIGH

101.8

LOW
100.2
100.6

Southwest Monsoon

Tropic of Cancer

101.0

101.4

Northeast Trades

LOW
101.0

101.4

Southeast Trades

Doldrums

101.4

Equator

101.8

101.8

102.2

HIGH

102.2

HIGH

101.8

101.8

Southeast Trades

102.2

HIGH

101.8

Tropic of Capricorn

HIGH

101.8

Average temperature
°C

| 32 |
| 16 |
| 0 |
| -16 |
| -32 |

101.4

101.0

Roaring Forties

Westerlies

101.4

101.0

—101.4— Isobars in kilopascals   ⟶ Prevailing winds   **HIGH** An area of high air pressure   **LOW** An area of low air pressure

SCALE 1 : 140 000 000   0   2000   4000   6000   8000 km   Eckert IV projection

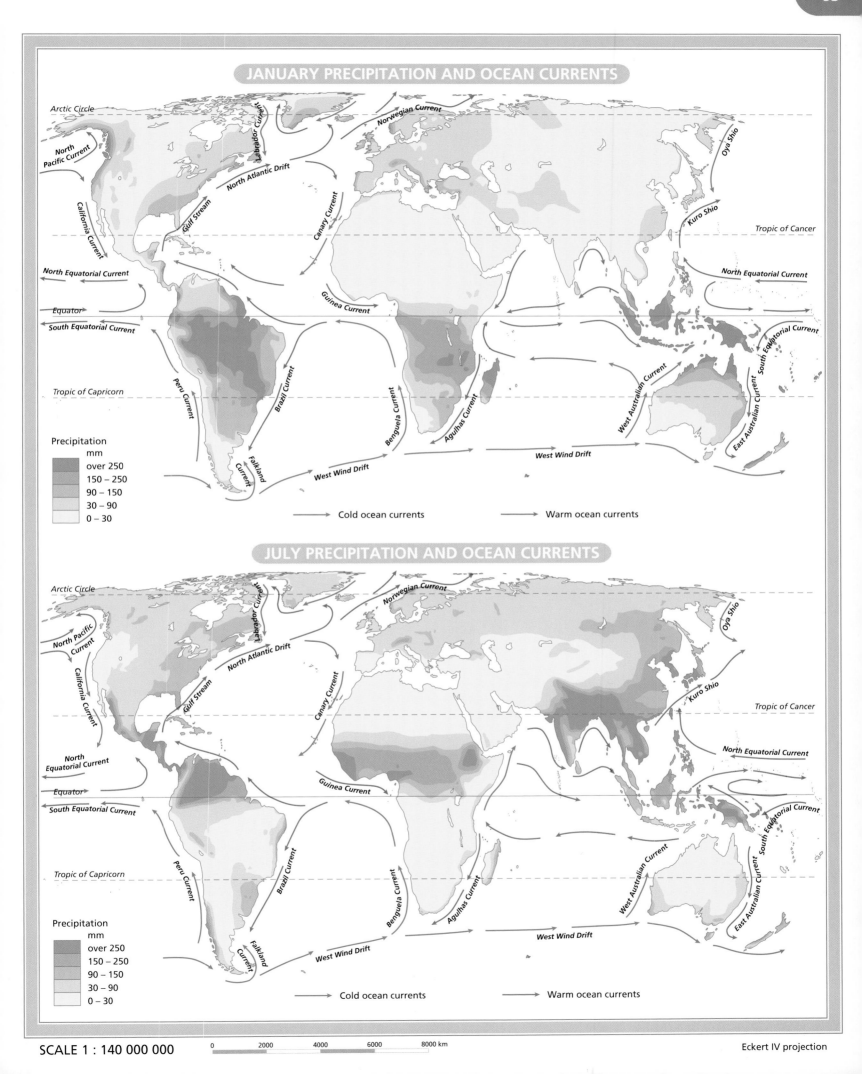

JANUARY PRECIPITATION AND OCEAN CURRENTS

Arctic Circle

North Pacific Current

California Current

North Equatorial Current

Equator

South Equatorial Current

Tropic of Capricorn

Labrador Current

North Atlantic Drift

Gulf Stream

Canary Current

Guinea Current

Peru Current

Brazil Current

Falkland Current

West Wind Drift

Benguela Current

Agulhas Current

West Wind Drift

Norwegian Current

Oya Shio

Kuro Shio

Tropic of Cancer

North Equatorial Current

South Equatorial Current

West Australian Current

East Australian Current

Precipitation
mm
over 250
150 – 250
90 – 150
30 – 90
0 – 30

⟶ Cold ocean currents   ⟶ Warm ocean currents

JULY PRECIPITATION AND OCEAN CURRENTS

Arctic Circle

North Pacific Current

California Current

North Equatorial Current

Equator

South Equatorial Current

Tropic of Capricorn

Labrador Current

North Atlantic Drift

Gulf Stream

Canary Current

Guinea Current

Peru Current

Brazil Current

Falkland Current

West Wind Drift

Benguela Current

Agulhas Current

West Wind Drift

Norwegian Current

Oya Shio

Kuro Shio

Tropic of Cancer

North Equatorial Current

South Equatorial Current

West Australian Current

East Australian Current

Precipitation
mm
over 250
150 – 250
90 – 150
30 – 90
0 – 30

⟶ Cold ocean currents   ⟶ Warm ocean currents

SCALE 1 : 140 000 000

0   2000   4000   6000   8000 km

Eckert IV projection

AIR MASSES

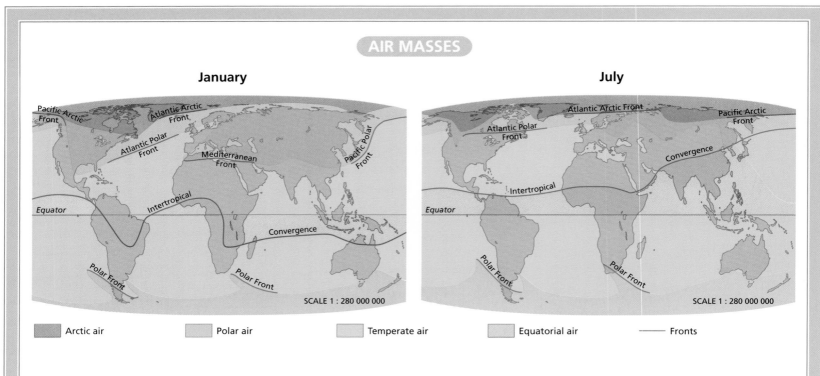

January

July

Arctic air ▢ Polar air ▢ Temperate air ▢ Equatorial air ▢ —— Fronts

Four types of air masses are identified above. The temperature and humidity characteristics of these air masses stay relatively constant over large distances. They remain relatively stationary over an area for a number of days. Fronts separate air masses in the temperate regions. The Intertropical Convergence Zone has low atmospheric pressure and ascending air located at or near the equator.

Air masses and fronts migrate with the apparent movement of the overhead sun (seasons). The movement of the Intertropical Convergence Zone is most obvious. It pushes south of the equator in January, and "fronts" north of the equator in July, moving as far north as central China. Much of Canada is influenced by polar air in January, and temperate air in July.

STORMS

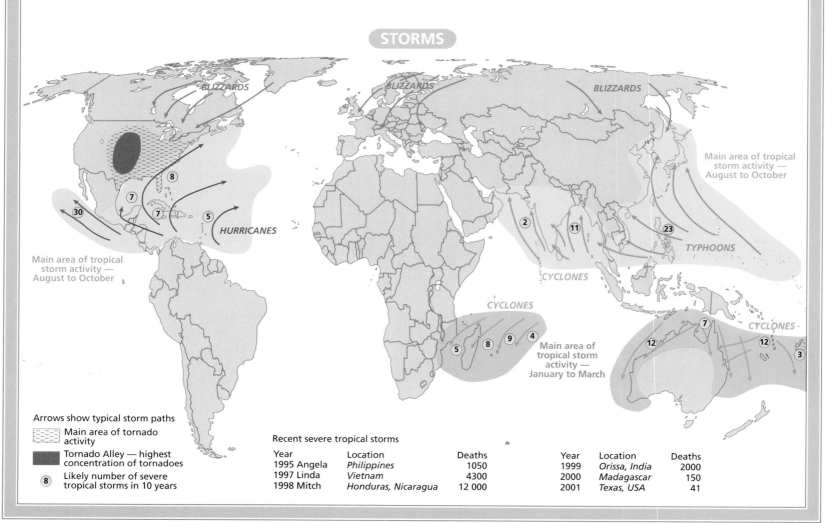

Arrows show typical storm paths

▦ Main area of tornado activity

◼ Tornado Alley — highest concentration of tornadoes

⑧ Likely number of severe tropical storms in 10 years

Recent severe tropical storms

Year	Location	Deaths	Year	Location	Deaths
1995 Angela	Philippines	1050	1999	Orissa, India	2000
1997 Linda	Vietnam	4300	2000	Madagascar	150
1998 Mitch	Honduras, Nicaragua	12 000	2001	Texas, USA	41

SCALE 1 : 140 000 000

0   2000   4000   6000   8000 km

Eckert IV projection

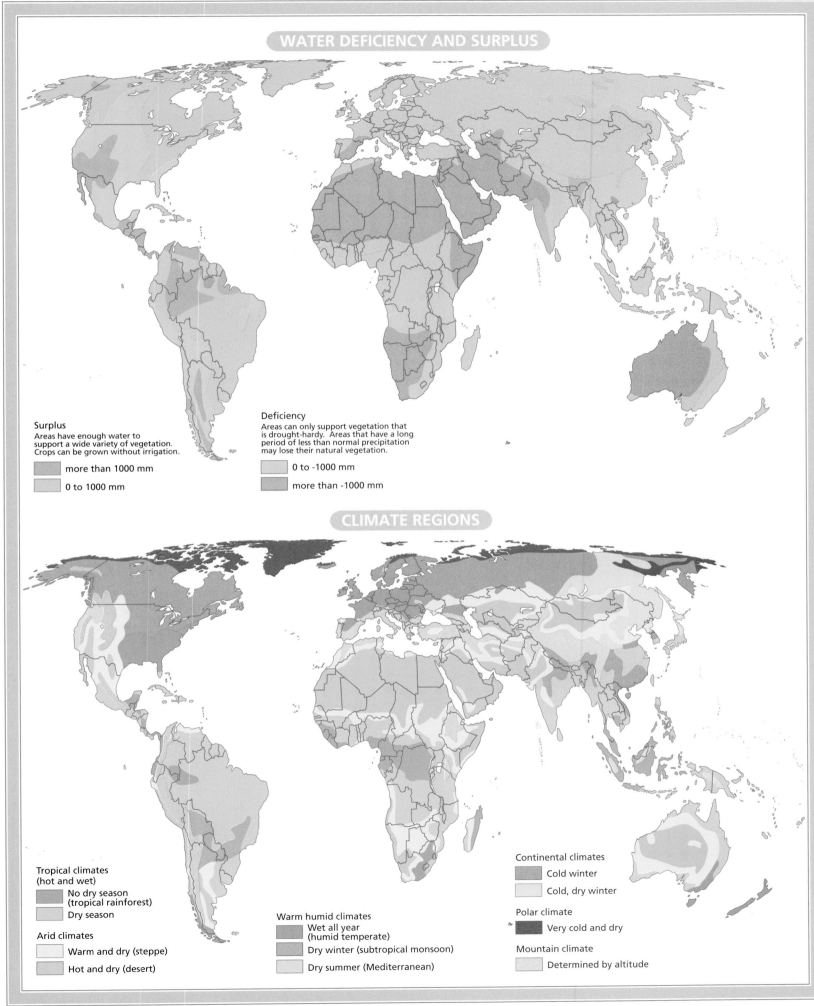

WATER DEFICIENCY AND SURPLUS

Surplus
Areas have enough water to support a wide variety of vegetation. Crops can be grown without irrigation.

more than 1000 mm

0 to 1000 mm

Deficiency
Areas can only support vegetation that is drought-hardy. Areas that have a long period of less than normal precipitation may lose their natural vegetation.

0 to -1000 mm

more than -1000 mm

CLIMATE REGIONS

Tropical climates (hot and wet)

No dry season (tropical rainforest)

Dry season

Arid climates

Warm and dry (steppe)

Hot and dry (desert)

Warm humid climates

Wet all year (humid temperate)

Dry winter (subtropical monsoon)

Dry summer (Mediterranean)

Continental climates

Cold winter

Cold, dry winter

Polar climate

Very cold and dry

Mountain climate

Determined by altitude

SCALE 1 : 140 000 000

0   2000   4000   6000   8000 km

Eckert IV projection

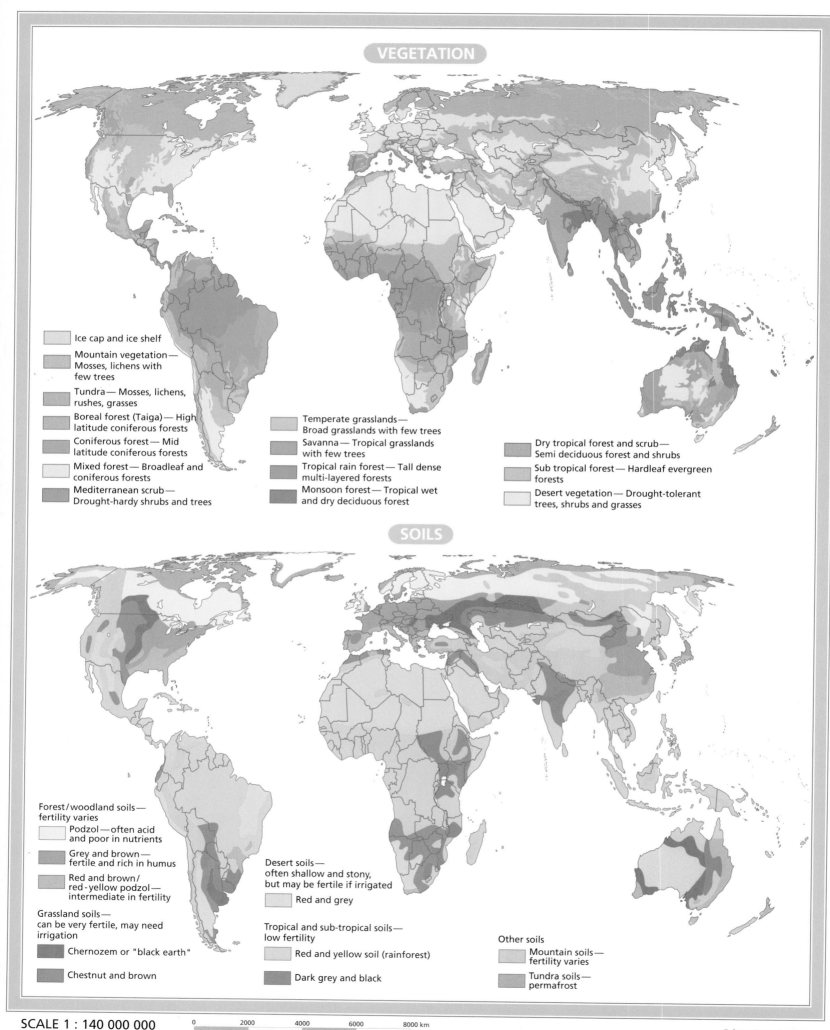

VEGETATION

Ice cap and ice shelf

Mountain vegetation—
Mosses, lichens with
few trees

Tundra— Mosses, lichens,
rushes, grasses

Boreal forest (Taiga)— High
latitude coniferous forests

Coniferous forest— Mid
latitude coniferous forests

Mixed forest— Broadleaf and
coniferous forests

Mediterranean scrub—
Drought-hardy shrubs and trees

Temperate grasslands—
Broad grasslands with few trees

Savanna— Tropical grasslands
with few trees

Tropical rain forest— Tall dense
multi-layered forests

Monsoon forest— Tropical wet
and dry deciduous forest

Dry tropical forest and scrub—
Semi deciduous forest and shrubs

Sub tropical forest— Hardleaf evergreen
forests

Desert vegetation— Drought-tolerant
trees, shrubs and grasses

SOILS

Forest/woodland soils—
fertility varies

Podzol—often acid
and poor in nutrients

Grey and brown—
fertile and rich in humus

Red and brown/
red-yellow podzol—
intermediate in fertility

Grassland soils—
can be very fertile, may need
irrigation

Chernozem or "black earth"

Chestnut and brown

Desert soils—
often shallow and stony,
but may be fertile if irrigated

Red and grey

Tropical and sub-tropical soils—
low fertility

Red and yellow soil (rainforest)

Dark grey and black

Other soils

Mountain soils—
fertility varies

Tundra soils—
permafrost

SCALE 1 : 140 000 000

0   2000   4000   6000   8000 km

Eckert IV projection

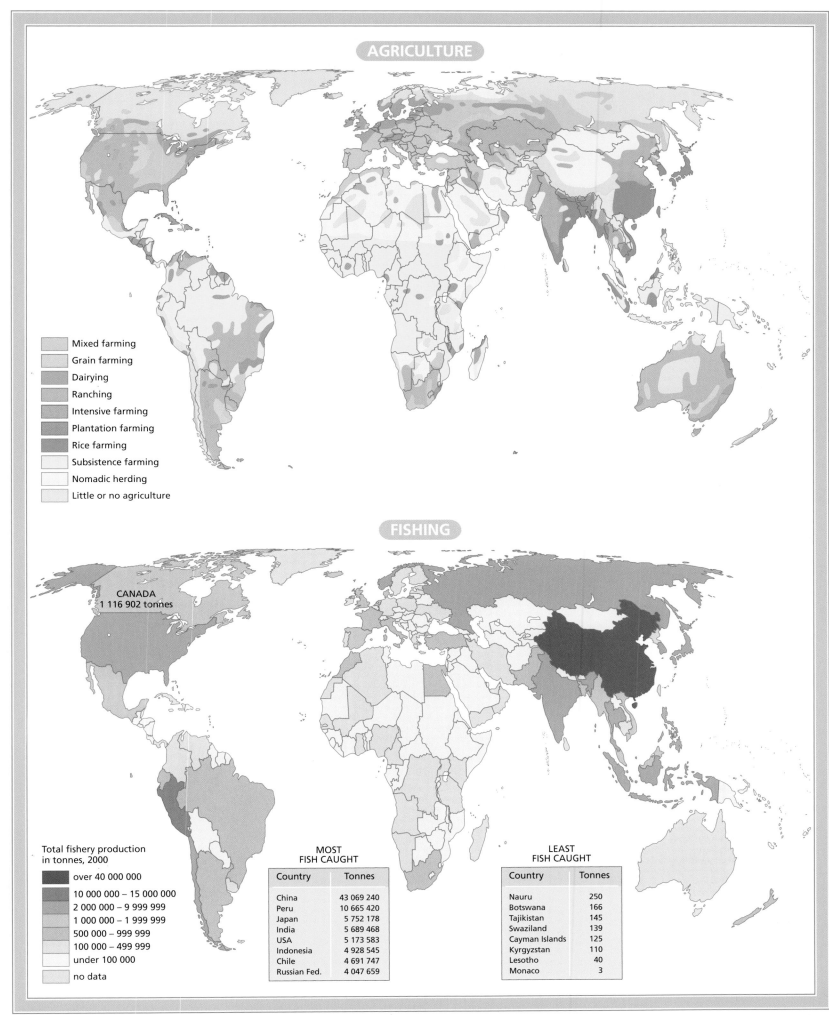

AGRICULTURE

Mixed farming
Grain farming
Dairying
Ranching
Intensive farming
Plantation farming
Rice farming
Subsistence farming
Nomadic herding
Little or no agriculture

FISHING

CANADA
1 116 902 tonnes

Total fishery production
in tonnes, 2000

over 40 000 000
10 000 000 – 15 000 000
2 000 000 – 9 999 999
1 000 000 – 1 999 999
500 000 – 999 999
100 000 – 499 999
under 100 000
no data

MOST FISH CAUGHT	
Country	Tonnes
China	43 069 240
Peru	10 665 420
Japan	5 752 178
India	5 689 468
USA	5 173 583
Indonesia	4 928 545
Chile	4 691 747
Russian Fed.	4 047 659

LEAST FISH CAUGHT	
Country	Tonnes
Nauru	250
Botswana	166
Tajikistan	145
Swaziland	139
Cayman Islands	125
Kyrgyzstan	110
Lesotho	40
Monaco	3

SCALE 1 : 140 000 000

0   2000   4000   6000   8000 km

Eckert IV projection

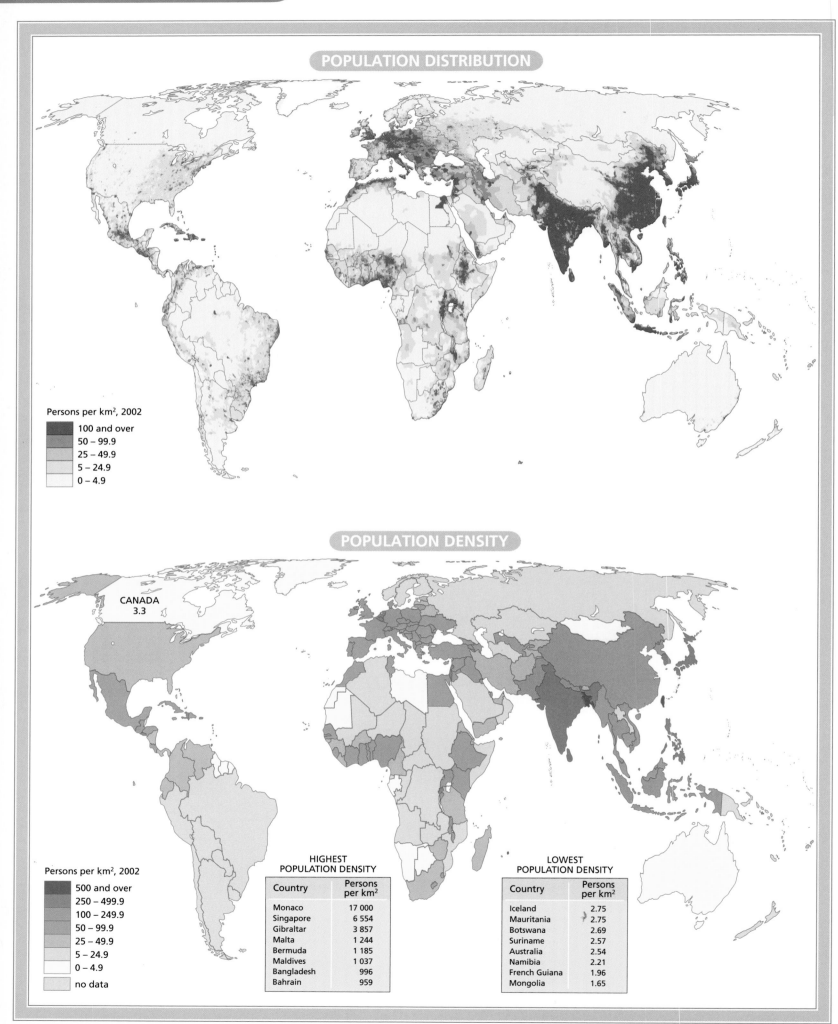

POPULATION DISTRIBUTION

Persons per km², 2002

- 100 and over
- 50 – 99.9
- 25 – 49.9
- 5 – 24.9
- 0 – 4.9

POPULATION DENSITY

CANADA
3.3

Persons per km², 2002

- 500 and over
- 250 – 499.9
- 100 – 249.9
- 50 – 99.9
- 25 – 49.9
- 5 – 24.9
- 0 – 4.9
- no data

HIGHEST POPULATION DENSITY

Country	Persons per km²
Monaco	17 000
Singapore	6 554
Gibraltar	3 857
Malta	1 244
Bermuda	1 185
Maldives	1 037
Bangladesh	996
Bahrain	959

LOWEST POPULATION DENSITY

Country	Persons per km²
Iceland	2.75
Mauritania	2.75
Botswana	2.69
Suriname	2.57
Australia	2.54
Namibia	2.21
French Guiana	1.96
Mongolia	1.65

SCALE 1 : 140 000 000

0   2000   4000   6000   8000 km

Eckert IV projection

LIFE EXPECTANCY

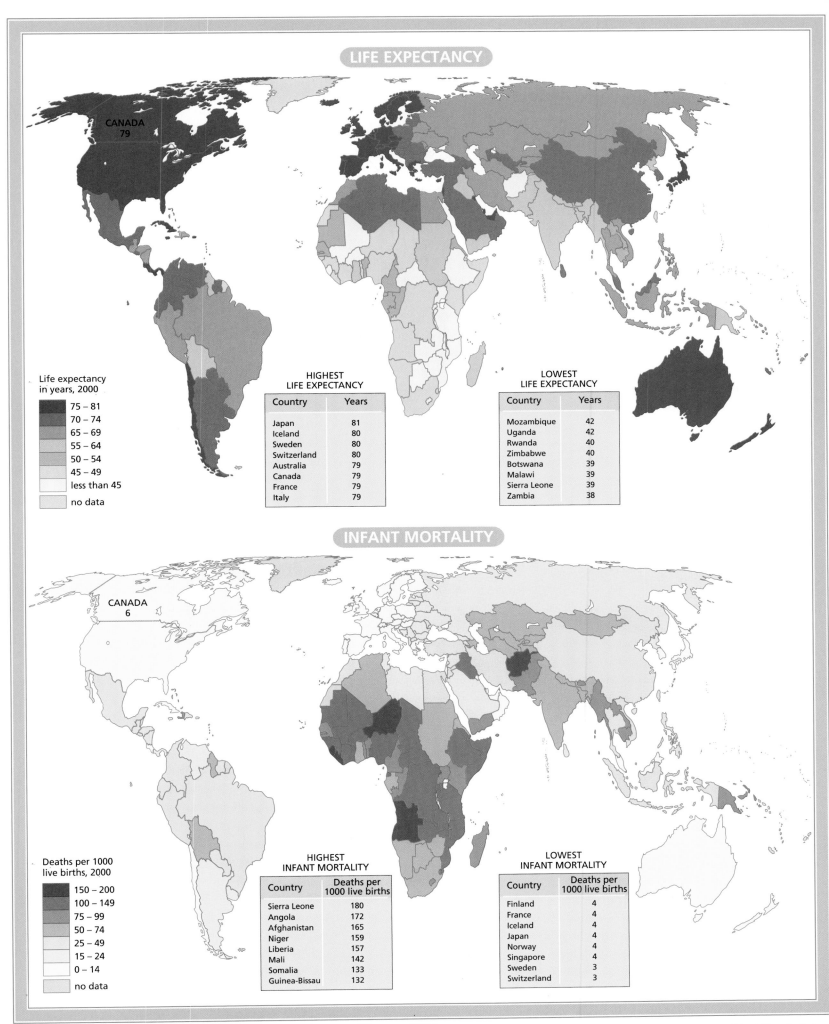

CANADA
79

Life expectancy in years, 2000

- 75 – 81
- 70 – 74
- 65 – 69
- 55 – 64
- 50 – 54
- 45 – 49
- less than 45
- no data

HIGHEST LIFE EXPECTANCY

Country	Years
Japan	81
Iceland	80
Sweden	80
Switzerland	80
Australia	79
Canada	79
France	79
Italy	79

LOWEST LIFE EXPECTANCY

Country	Years
Mozambique	42
Uganda	42
Rwanda	40
Zimbabwe	40
Botswana	39
Malawi	39
Sierra Leone	39
Zambia	38

INFANT MORTALITY

CANADA
6

Deaths per 1000 live births, 2000

- 150 – 200
- 100 – 149
- 75 – 99
- 50 – 74
- 25 – 49
- 15 – 24
- 0 – 14
- no data

HIGHEST INFANT MORTALITY

Country	Deaths per 1000 live births
Sierra Leone	180
Angola	172
Afghanistan	165
Niger	159
Liberia	157
Mali	142
Somalia	133
Guinea-Bissau	132

LOWEST INFANT MORTALITY

Country	Deaths per 1000 live births
Finland	4
France	4
Iceland	4
Japan	4
Norway	4
Singapore	4
Sweden	3
Switzerland	3

SCALE 1 : 140 000 000

0   2000   4000   6000   8000 km

Eckert IV projection

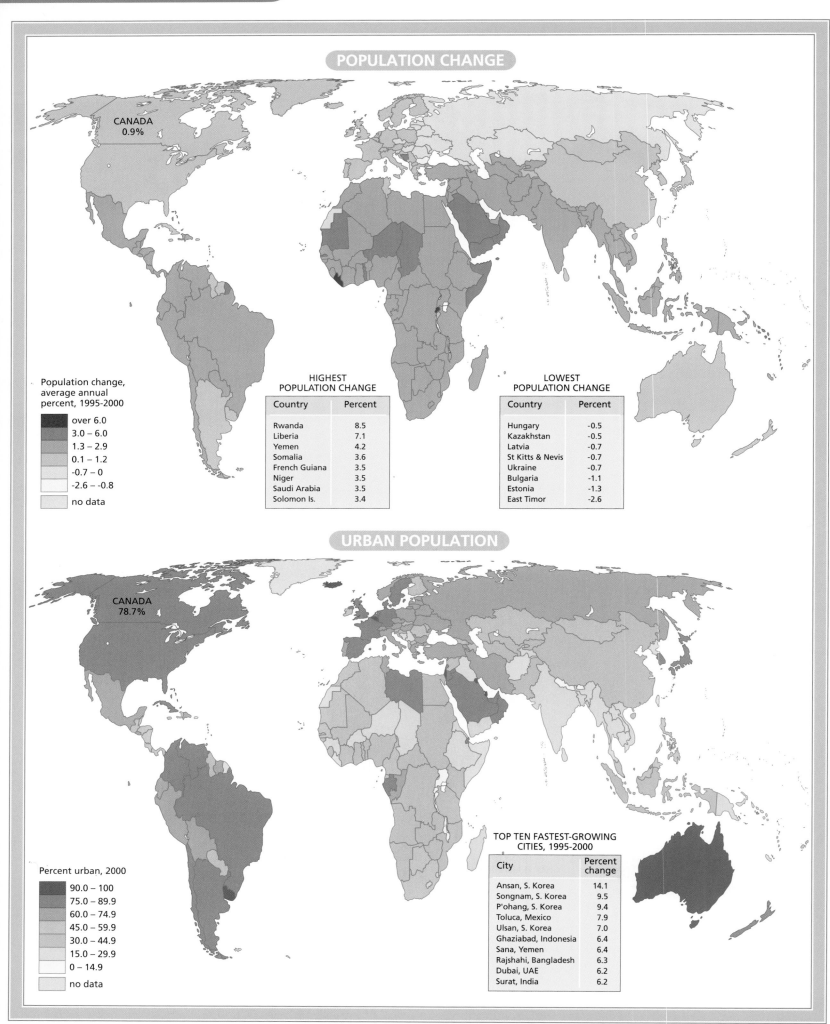

POPULATION CHANGE

CANADA
0.9%

Population change,
average annual
percent, 1995-2000

- over 6.0
- 3.0 – 6.0
- 1.3 – 2.9
- 0.1 – 1.2
- -0.7 – 0
- -2.6 – -0.8
- no data

HIGHEST POPULATION CHANGE

Country	Percent
Rwanda	8.5
Liberia	7.1
Yemen	4.2
Somalia	3.6
French Guiana	3.5
Niger	3.5
Saudi Arabia	3.5
Solomon Is.	3.4

LOWEST POPULATION CHANGE

Country	Percent
Hungary	-0.5
Kazakhstan	-0.5
Latvia	-0.7
St Kitts & Nevis	-0.7
Ukraine	-0.7
Bulgaria	-1.1
Estonia	-1.3
East Timor	-2.6

URBAN POPULATION

CANADA
78.7%

Percent urban, 2000

- 90.0 – 100
- 75.0 – 89.9
- 60.0 – 74.9
- 45.0 – 59.9
- 30.0 – 44.9
- 15.0 – 29.9
- 0 – 14.9
- no data

TOP TEN FASTEST-GROWING CITIES, 1995-2000

City	Percent change
Ansan, S. Korea	14.1
Songnam, S. Korea	9.5
P'ohang, S. Korea	9.4
Toluca, Mexico	7.9
Ulsan, S. Korea	7.0
Ghaziabad, Indonesia	6.4
Sana, Yemen	6.4
Rajshahi, Bangladesh	6.3
Dubai, UAE	6.2
Surat, India	6.2

SCALE 1 : 140 000 000

0   2000   4000   6000   8000 km

Eckert IV projection

MILLION CITIES

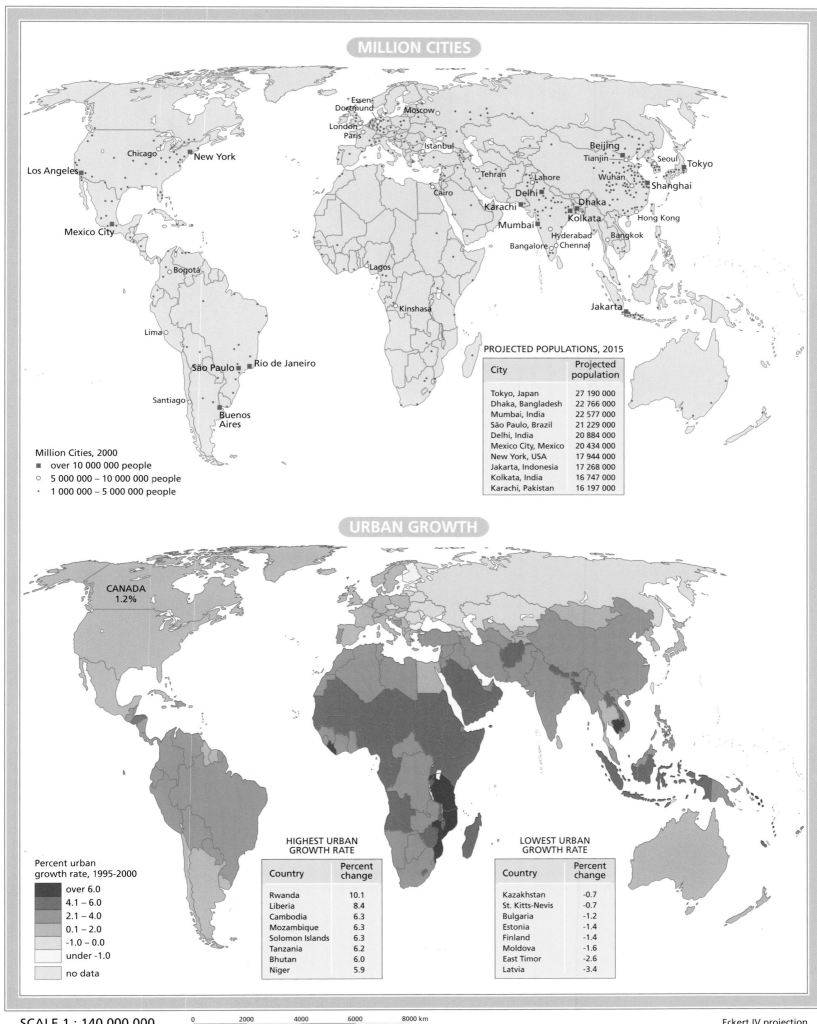

Million Cities, 2000

- ■ over 10 000 000 people
- ○ 5 000 000 – 10 000 000 people
- · 1 000 000 – 5 000 000 people

PROJECTED POPULATIONS, 2015

City	Projected population
Tokyo, Japan	27 190 000
Dhaka, Bangladesh	22 766 000
Mumbai, India	22 577 000
São Paulo, Brazil	21 229 000
Delhi, India	20 884 000
Mexico City, Mexico	20 434 000
New York, USA	17 944 000
Jakarta, Indonesia	17 268 000
Kolkata, India	16 747 000
Karachi, Pakistan	16 197 000

URBAN GROWTH

CANADA 1.2%

Percent urban growth rate, 1995-2000

- over 6.0
- 4.1 – 6.0
- 2.1 – 4.0
- 0.1 – 2.0
- -1.0 – 0.0
- under -1.0
- no data

HIGHEST URBAN GROWTH RATE

Country	Percent change
Rwanda	10.1
Liberia	8.4
Cambodia	6.3
Mozambique	6.3
Solomon Islands	6.3
Tanzania	6.2
Bhutan	6.0
Niger	5.9

LOWEST URBAN GROWTH RATE

Country	Percent change
Kazakhstan	-0.7
St. Kitts-Nevis	-0.7
Bulgaria	-1.2
Estonia	-1.4
Finland	-1.4
Moldova	-1.6
East Timor	-2.6
Latvia	-3.4

SCALE 1 : 140 000 000

0   2000   4000   6000   8000 km

Eckert IV projection

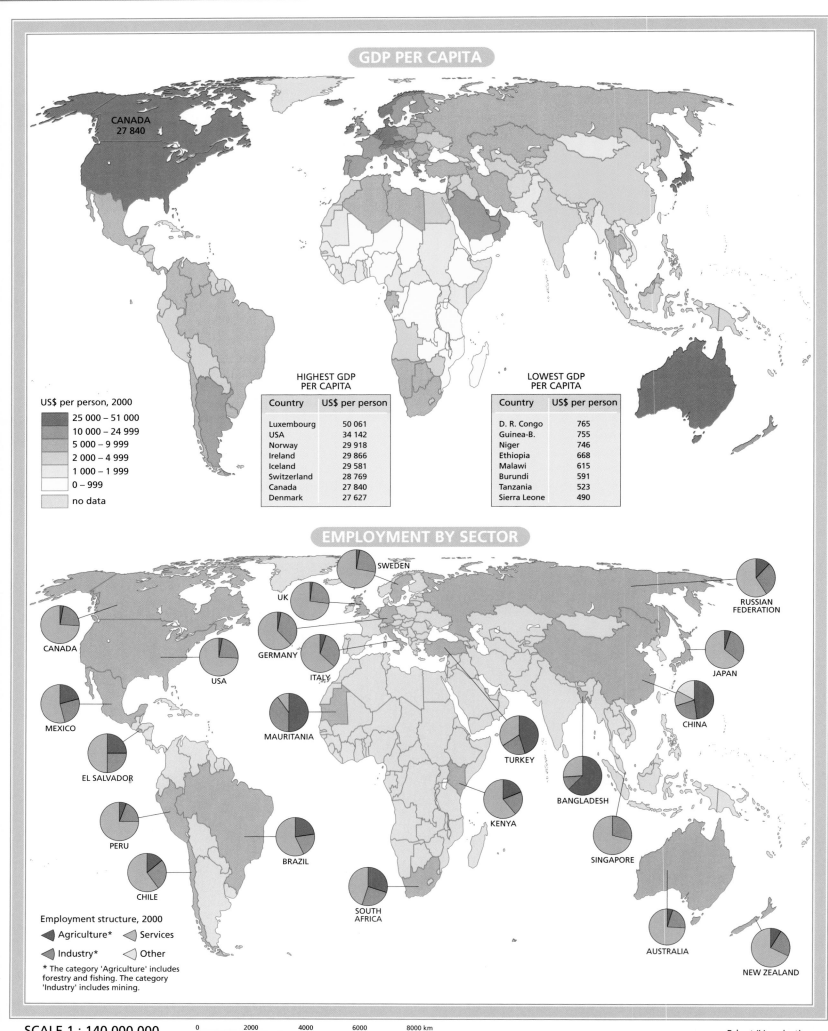

GDP PER CAPITA

US$ per person, 2000

- 25 000 – 51 000
- 10 000 – 24 999
- 5 000 – 9 999
- 2 000 – 4 999
- 1 000 – 1 999
- 0 – 999
- no data

CANADA 27 840

HIGHEST GDP PER CAPITA

Country	US$ per person
Luxembourg	50 061
USA	34 142
Norway	29 918
Ireland	29 866
Iceland	29 581
Switzerland	28 769
Canada	27 840
Denmark	27 627

LOWEST GDP PER CAPITA

Country	US$ per person
D. R. Congo	765
Guinea-B.	755
Niger	746
Ethiopia	668
Malawi	615
Burundi	591
Tanzania	523
Sierra Leone	490

EMPLOYMENT BY SECTOR

SWEDEN
UK
GERMANY
ITALY
RUSSIAN FEDERATION
CANADA
USA
JAPAN
MEXICO
MAURITANIA
CHINA
EL SALVADOR
TURKEY
PERU
BANGLADESH
KENYA
BRAZIL
SINGAPORE
CHILE
SOUTH AFRICA
AUSTRALIA
NEW ZEALAND

Employment structure, 2000

- Agriculture*
- Services
- Industry*
- Other

* The category 'Agriculture' includes forestry and fishing. The category 'Industry' includes mining.

SCALE 1 : 140 000 000

0   2000   4000   6000   8000 km

Eckert IV projection

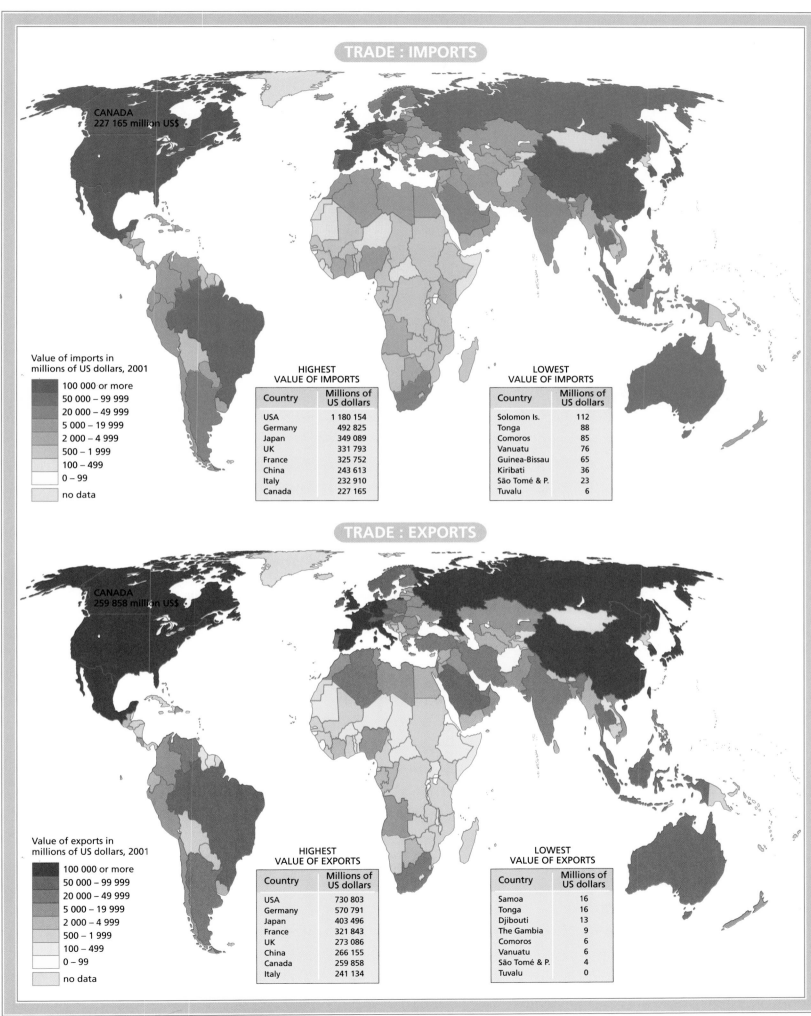

TRADE : IMPORTS

CANADA
227 165 million US$

Value of imports in
millions of US dollars, 2001

- 100 000 or more
- 50 000 – 99 999
- 20 000 – 49 999
- 5 000 – 19 999
- 2 000 – 4 999
- 500 – 1 999
- 100 – 499
- 0 – 99
- no data

HIGHEST VALUE OF IMPORTS

Country	Millions of US dollars
USA	1 180 154
Germany	492 825
Japan	349 089
UK	331 793
France	325 752
China	243 613
Italy	232 910
Canada	227 165

LOWEST VALUE OF IMPORTS

Country	Millions of US dollars
Solomon Is.	112
Tonga	88
Comoros	85
Vanuatu	76
Guinea-Bissau	65
Kiribati	36
São Tomé & P.	23
Tuvalu	6

TRADE : EXPORTS

CANADA
259 858 million US$

Value of exports in
millions of US dollars, 2001

- 100 000 or more
- 50 000 – 99 999
- 20 000 – 49 999
- 5 000 – 19 999
- 2 000 – 4 999
- 500 – 1 999
- 100 – 499
- 0 – 99
- no data

HIGHEST VALUE OF EXPORTS

Country	Millions of US dollars
USA	730 803
Germany	570 791
Japan	403 496
France	321 843
UK	273 086
China	266 155
Canada	259 858
Italy	241 134

LOWEST VALUE OF EXPORTS

Country	Millions of US dollars
Samoa	16
Tonga	16
Djibouti	13
The Gambia	9
Comoros	6
Vanuatu	6
São Tomé & P.	4
Tuvalu	0

SCALE 1 : 140 000 000

0   2000   4000   6000   8000 km

Eckert IV projection

ENERGY PRODUCTION

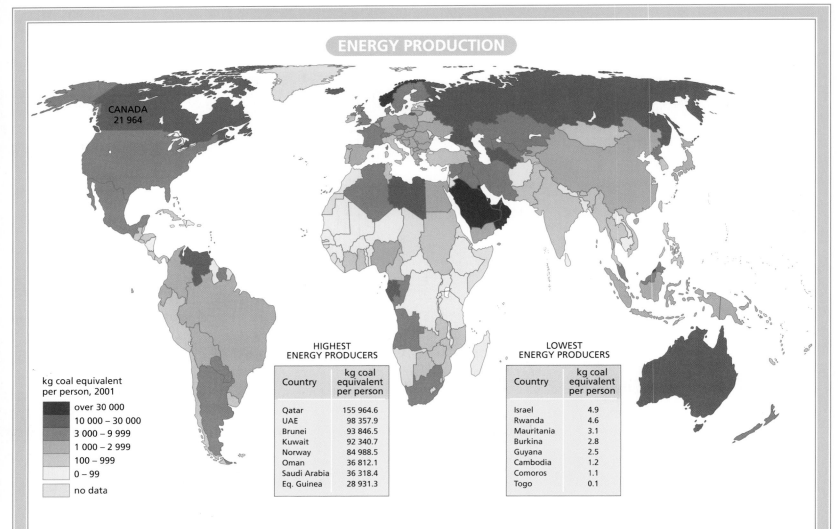

CANADA
21 964

kg coal equivalent
per person, 2001

- over 30 000
- 10 000 – 30 000
- 3 000 – 9 999
- 1 000 – 2 999
- 100 – 999
- 0 – 99
- no data

HIGHEST ENERGY PRODUCERS

Country	kg coal equivalent per person
Qatar	155 964.6
UAE	98 357.9
Brunei	93 846.5
Kuwait	92 340.7
Norway	84 988.5
Oman	36 812.1
Saudi Arabia	36 318.4
Eq. Guinea	28 931.3

LOWEST ENERGY PRODUCERS

Country	kg coal equivalent per person
Israel	4.9
Rwanda	4.6
Mauritania	3.1
Burkina	2.8
Guyana	2.5
Cambodia	1.2
Comoros	1.1
Togo	0.1

ENERGY PRODUCTION AND CONSUMPTION

Percent of World Energy Production, 2000

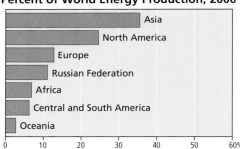

Asia
North America
Europe
Russian Federation
Africa
Central and South America
Oceania

0   10   20   30   40   50   60%

Percent of World Energy Consumption, 2000

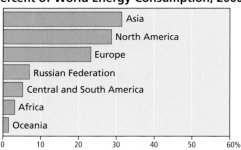

Asia
North America
Europe
Russian Federation
Central and South America
Africa
Oceania

0   10   20   30   40   50   60%

OTHER ENERGY SOURCES

Top Hydro Electric Power Producers, 2000

Country	Percent of world total
Canada	13.2
Brazil	11.3
USA	10.2
China	8.2
Russian Federation	6.1
Norway	5.2
Japan	3.6
Sweden	2.9
India	2.7
France	2.7

Top Nuclear Power Producers, 2000

Country	Percent of world total
USA	30.9
France	16.0
Japan	12.4
Germany	6.6
Russian Federation	5.1
South Korea	4.2
United Kingdom	3.3
Ukraine	3.0
Canada	2.8
Spain	2.4

Top Fuelwood Producers, 2001

Country	Percent of world total
India	15.5
China	10.7
Brazil	7.5
Ethiopia	5.0
Indonesia	4.8
USA	4.1
D.R. Congo	3.7
Nigeria	3.3
Russian Federation	2.5
Philippines	2.3

Top Alternative* Energy Producers, 2001

Country	Percent of world total
USA	34.0
Germany	9.0
Japan	7.6
Brazil	5.8
Philippines	4.8
Spain	3.6
Italy	3.1
Canada	2.8

* Geothermal, solar, wind, wood, and waste

SCALE 1 : 140 000 000

0   2000   4000   6000   8000 km

Eckert IV projection

ENERGY CONSUMPTION

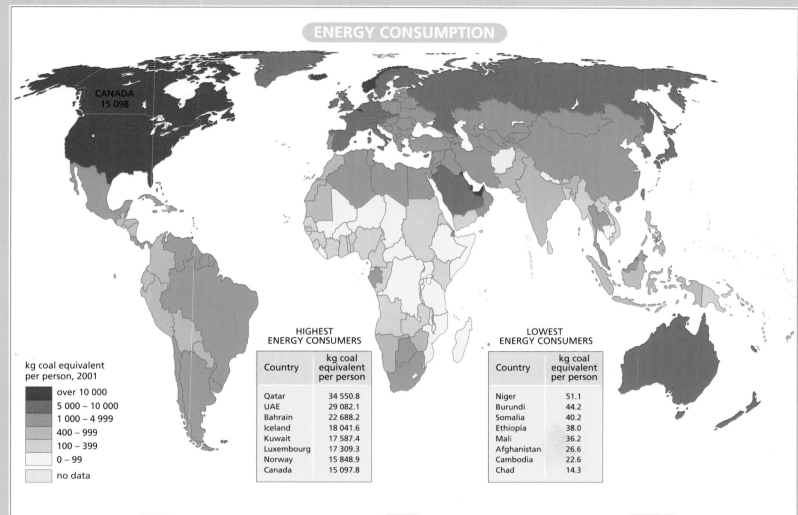

CANADA
15 098

kg coal equivalent
per person, 2001

- over 10 000
- 5 000 – 10 000
- 1 000 – 4 999
- 400 – 999
- 100 – 399
- 0 – 99
- no data

HIGHEST ENERGY CONSUMERS

Country	kg coal equivalent per person
Qatar	34 550.8
UAE	29 082.1
Bahrain	22 688.2
Iceland	18 041.6
Kuwait	17 587.4
Luxembourg	17 309.3
Norway	15 848.9
Canada	15 097.8

LOWEST ENERGY CONSUMERS

Country	kg coal equivalent per person
Niger	51.1
Burundi	44.2
Somalia	40.2
Ethiopia	38.0
Mali	36.2
Afghanistan	26.6
Cambodia	22.6
Chad	14.3

OIL

Reserves, 2001

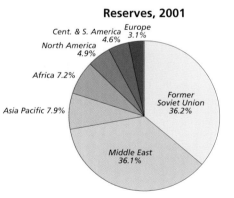

Europe 1.8%
Asia Pacific 4.2%
North America 6.1%
Former Soviet Union 6.2%
Africa 7.3%
Central & South America 9.1%
Middle East 65.3%

Total Reserves : 1 050 thousand million barrels

Top Oil Producers, 2001

Country	Percent of world total
Saudi Arabia	11.8
USA	9.8
Russian Federation	9.7
Iran	5.1
Mexico	4.9
Venezuela	4.9
China	4.6
Norway	4.5
Canada	3.6
Iraq	3.3

GAS

Reserves, 2001

Cent. & S. America 4.6%
Europe 3.1%
North America 4.9%
Africa 7.2%
Asia Pacific 7.9%
Former Soviet Union 36.2%
Middle East 36.1%

Total Reserves : 155 trillion cubic metres

Top Gas Producers, 2001

Country	Percent of world total
USA	22.5
Russian Federation	22.0
Canada	7.0
United Kingdom	4.3
Algeria	3.2
Indonesia	2.6
Netherlands	2.5
Iran	2.5
Norway	2.3
Saudi Arabia	2.2

COAL

Reserves, 2001

Cent. & S. America 2.2%
Africa & Middle East 5.8%
Europe 12.7%
Former Soviet Union 23.4%
Asia Pacific 29.7%
North America 26.2%

Total Reserves : 984 453 million tonnes

Top Coal Producers, 2001

Country	Percent of world total
USA	26.3
China	24.4
Australia	7.5
India	7.2
South Africa	5.6
Russian Federation	5.4
Poland	3.2
Indonesia	2.5
Germany	2.4
Ukraine	1.9

SCALE 1 : 140 000 000

0   2000   4000   6000   8000 km

Eckert IV projection

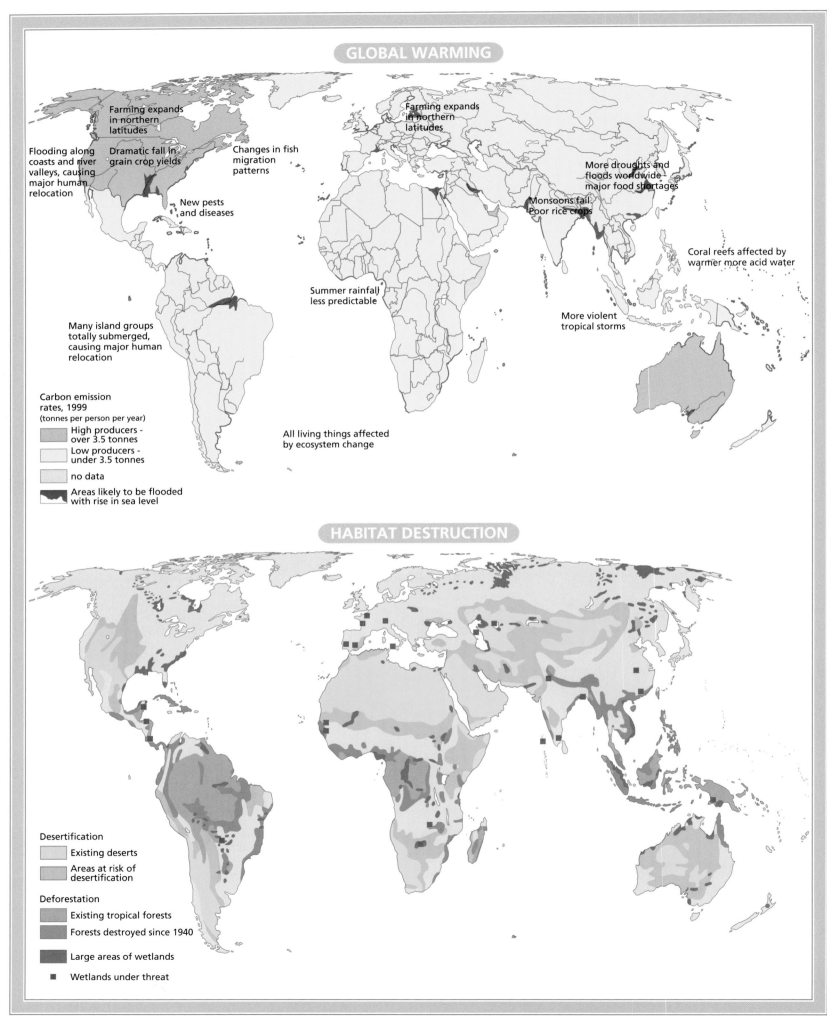

GLOBAL WARMING

Farming expands in northern latitudes

Farming expands in northern latitudes

Flooding along coasts and river valleys, causing major human relocation

Dramatic fall in grain crop yields

Changes in fish migration patterns

More droughts and floods worldwide - major food shortages

New pests and diseases

Monsoons fail. Poor rice crops

Coral reefs affected by warmer more acid water

Many island groups totally submerged, causing major human relocation

Summer rainfall less predictable

More violent tropical storms

Carbon emission rates, 1999
(tonnes per person per year)

High producers - over 3.5 tonnes

Low producers - under 3.5 tonnes

no data

Areas likely to be flooded with rise in sea level

All living things affected by ecosystem change

HABITAT DESTRUCTION

Desertification

Existing deserts

Areas at risk of desertification

Deforestation

Existing tropical forests

Forests destroyed since 1940

Large areas of wetlands

■ Wetlands under threat

SCALE 1 : 140 000 000

0   2000   4000   6000   8000 km

Eckert IV projection

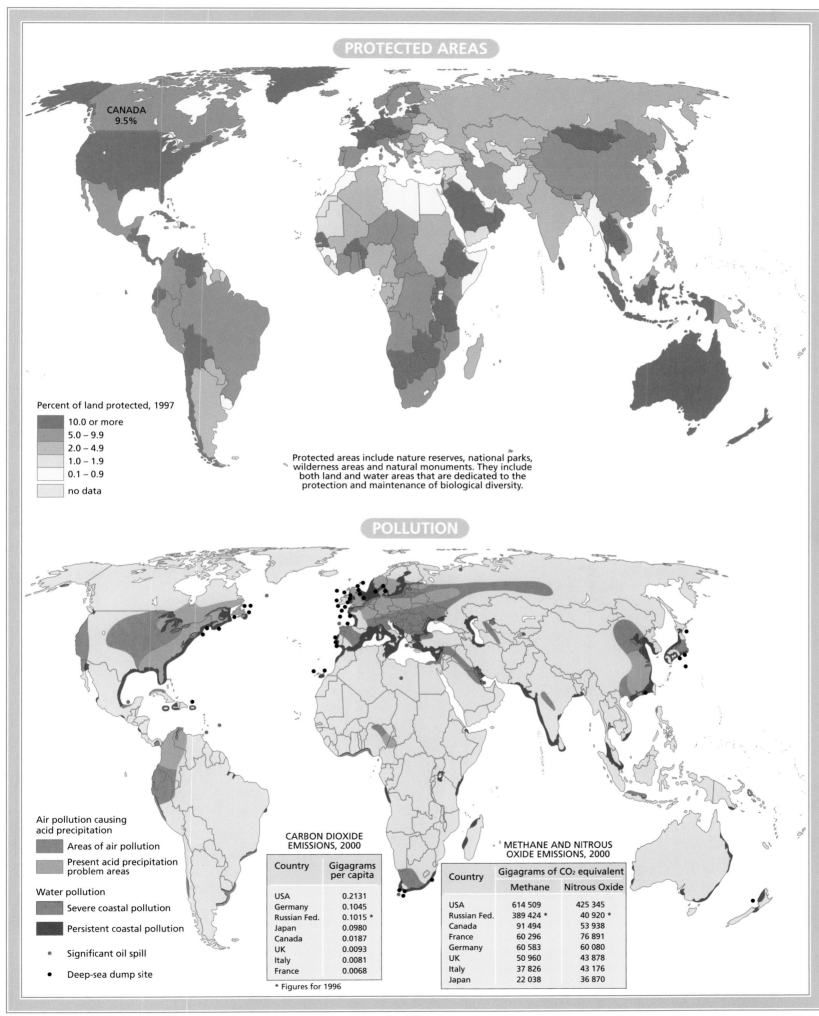

PROTECTED AREAS

CANADA
9.5%

Percent of land protected, 1997

- 10.0 or more
- 5.0 – 9.9
- 2.0 – 4.9
- 1.0 – 1.9
- 0.1 – 0.9
- no data

Protected areas include nature reserves, national parks,
wilderness areas and natural monuments. They include
both land and water areas that are dedicated to the
protection and maintenance of biological diversity.

POLLUTION

**Air pollution causing
acid precipitation**

- Areas of air pollution
- Present acid precipitation
  problem areas

Water pollution

- Severe coastal pollution
- Persistent coastal pollution

- • Significant oil spill
- • Deep-sea dump site

CARBON DIOXIDE EMISSIONS, 2000

Country	Gigagrams per capita
USA	0.2131
Germany	0.1045
Russian Fed.	0.1015 *
Japan	0.0980
Canada	0.0187
UK	0.0093
Italy	0.0081
France	0.0068

* Figures for 1996

METHANE AND NITROUS OXIDE EMISSIONS, 2000

Country	Gigagrams of CO₂ equivalent	
	Methane	Nitrous Oxide
USA	614 509	425 345
Russian Fed.	389 424 *	40 920 *
Canada	91 494	53 938
France	60 296	76 891
Germany	60 583	60 080
UK	50 960	43 878
Italy	37 826	43 176
Japan	22 038	36 870

SCALE 1 : 140 000 000

0   2000   4000   6000   8000 km

Eckert IV projection

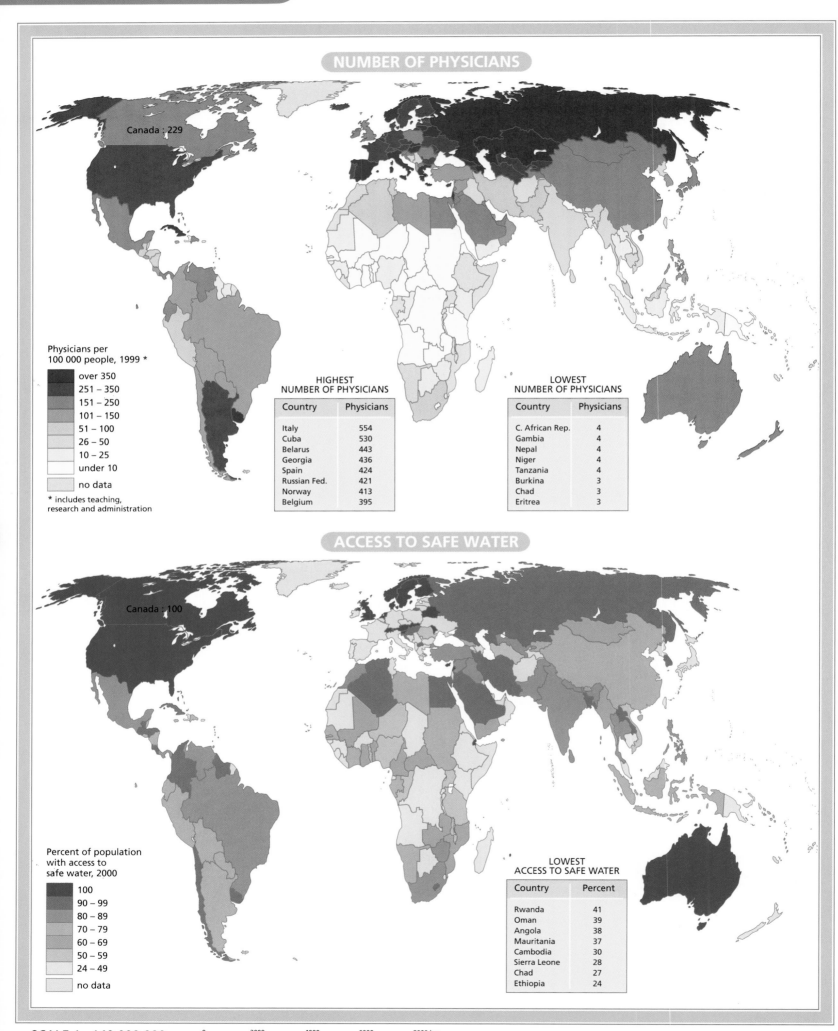

NUMBER OF PHYSICIANS

Canada : 229

Physicians per
100 000 people, 1999 *

- over 350
- 251 – 350
- 151 – 250
- 101 – 150
- 51 – 100
- 26 – 50
- 10 – 25
- under 10
- no data

* includes teaching,
research and administration

HIGHEST NUMBER OF PHYSICIANS

Country	Physicians
Italy	554
Cuba	530
Belarus	443
Georgia	436
Spain	424
Russian Fed.	421
Norway	413
Belgium	395

LOWEST NUMBER OF PHYSICIANS

Country	Physicians
C. African Rep.	4
Gambia	4
Nepal	4
Niger	4
Tanzania	4
Burkina	3
Chad	3
Eritrea	3

ACCESS TO SAFE WATER

Canada : 100

Percent of population
with access to
safe water, 2000

- 100
- 90 – 99
- 80 – 89
- 70 – 79
- 60 – 69
- 50 – 59
- 24 – 49
- no data

LOWEST ACCESS TO SAFE WATER

Country	Percent
Rwanda	41
Oman	39
Angola	38
Mauritania	37
Cambodia	30
Sierra Leone	28
Chad	27
Ethiopia	24

SCALE 1 : 140 000 000

0   2000   4000   6000   8000 km

Eckert IV projection

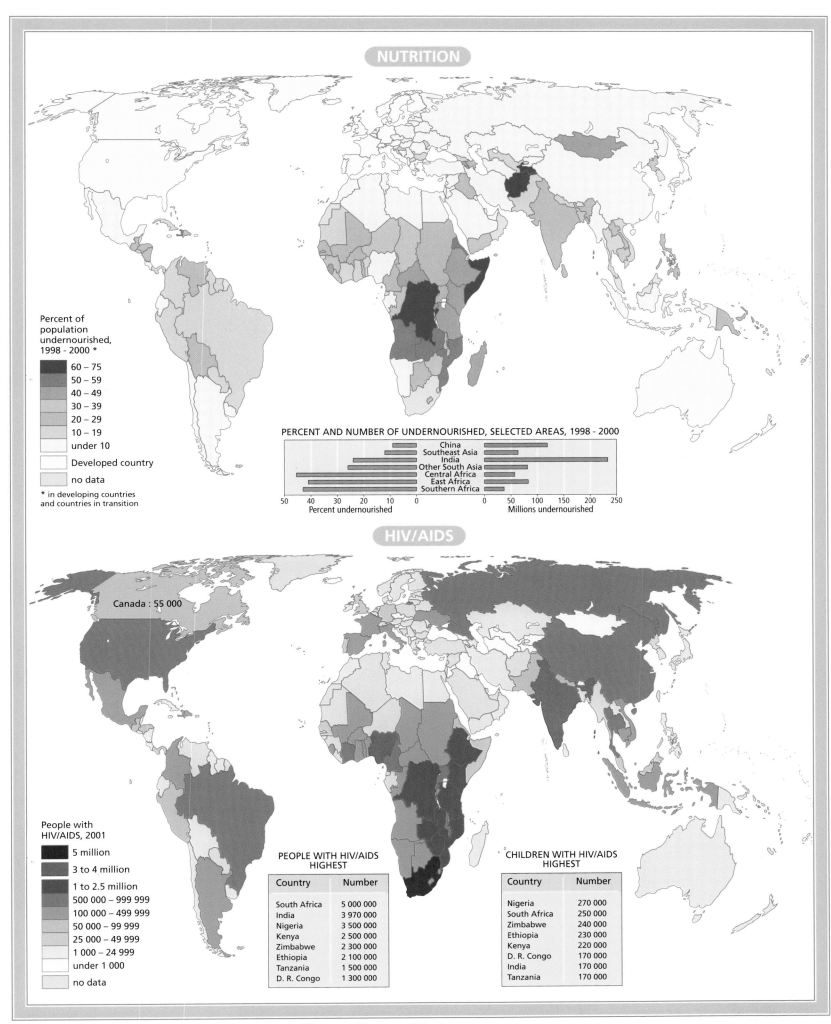

NUTRITION

Percent of population undernourished, 1998 - 2000 *

- 60 – 75
- 50 – 59
- 40 – 49
- 30 – 39
- 20 – 29
- 10 – 19
- under 10
- Developed country
- no data

* in developing countries and countries in transition

PERCENT AND NUMBER OF UNDERNOURISHED, SELECTED AREAS, 1998 - 2000

China
Southeast Asia
India
Other South Asia
Central Africa
East Africa
Southern Africa

Percent undernourished   Millions undernourished

HIV/AIDS

Canada : 55 000

People with HIV/AIDS, 2001

- 5 million
- 3 to 4 million
- 1 to 2.5 million
- 500 000 – 999 999
- 100 000 – 499 999
- 50 000 – 99 999
- 25 000 – 49 999
- 1 000 – 24 999
- under 1 000
- no data

PEOPLE WITH HIV/AIDS HIGHEST

Country	Number
South Africa	5 000 000
India	3 970 000
Nigeria	3 500 000
Kenya	2 500 000
Zimbabwe	2 300 000
Ethiopia	2 100 000
Tanzania	1 500 000
D. R. Congo	1 300 000

CHILDREN WITH HIV/AIDS HIGHEST

Country	Number
Nigeria	270 000
South Africa	250 000
Zimbabwe	240 000
Ethiopia	230 000
Kenya	220 000
D. R. Congo	170 000
India	170 000
Tanzania	170 000

SCALE 1 : 140 000 000

0   2000   4000   6000   8000 km

Eckert IV projection

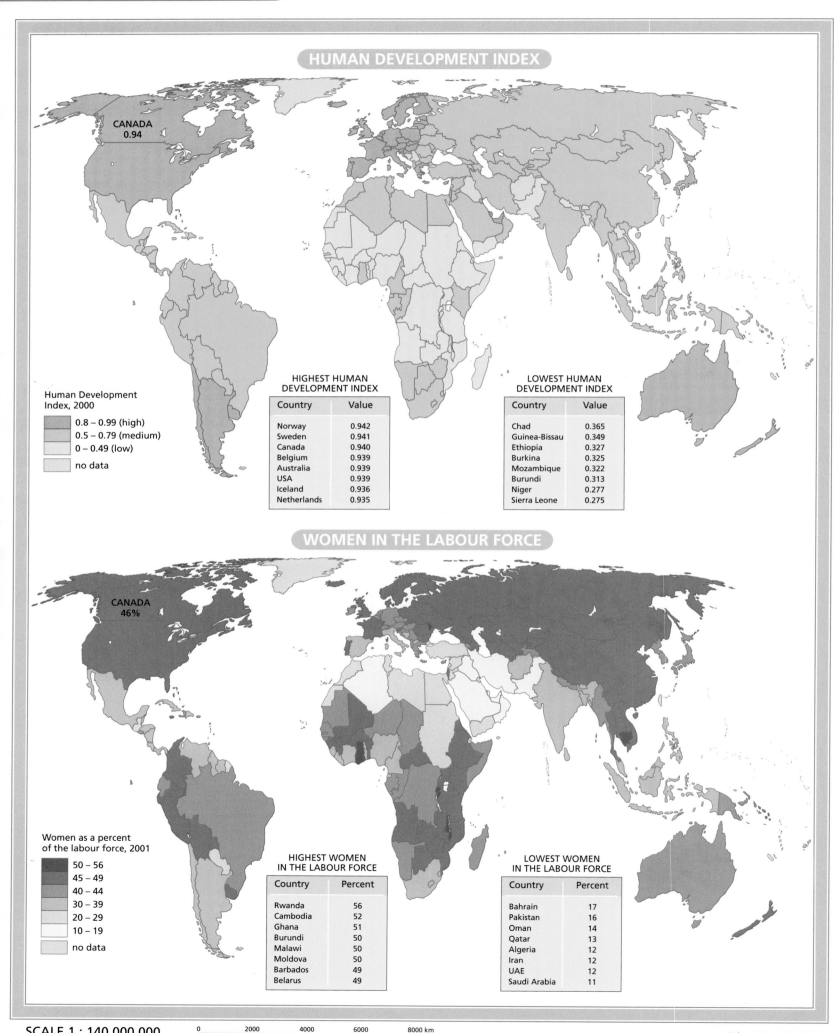

HUMAN DEVELOPMENT INDEX

CANADA
0.94

Human Development
Index, 2000

- 0.8 – 0.99 (high)
- 0.5 – 0.79 (medium)
- 0 – 0.49 (low)
- no data

HIGHEST HUMAN DEVELOPMENT INDEX

Country	Value
Norway	0.942
Sweden	0.941
Canada	0.940
Belgium	0.939
Australia	0.939
USA	0.939
Iceland	0.936
Netherlands	0.935

LOWEST HUMAN DEVELOPMENT INDEX

Country	Value
Chad	0.365
Guinea-Bissau	0.349
Ethiopia	0.327
Burkina	0.325
Mozambique	0.322
Burundi	0.313
Niger	0.277
Sierra Leone	0.275

WOMEN IN THE LABOUR FORCE

CANADA
46%

Women as a percent
of the labour force, 2001

- 50 – 56
- 45 – 49
- 40 – 44
- 30 – 39
- 20 – 29
- 10 – 19
- no data

HIGHEST WOMEN IN THE LABOUR FORCE

Country	Percent
Rwanda	56
Cambodia	52
Ghana	51
Burundi	50
Malawi	50
Moldova	50
Barbados	49
Belarus	49

LOWEST WOMEN IN THE LABOUR FORCE

Country	Percent
Bahrain	17
Pakistan	16
Oman	14
Qatar	13
Algeria	12
Iran	12
UAE	12
Saudi Arabia	11

SCALE 1 : 140 000 000

0   2000   4000   6000   8000 km

Eckert IV projection

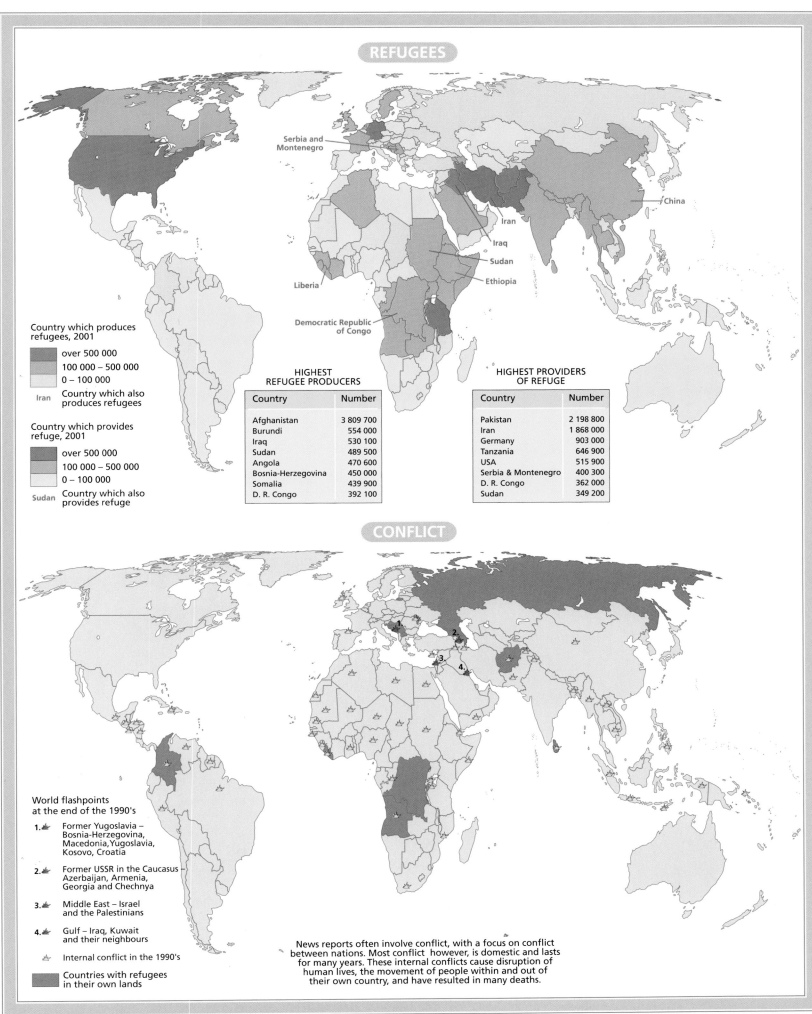

REFUGEES

Country which produces refugees, 2001
- over 500 000
- 100 000 – 500 000
- 0 – 100 000

Iran Country which also produces refugees

Country which provides refuge, 2001
- over 500 000
- 100 000 – 500 000
- 0 – 100 000

Sudan Country which also provides refuge

Serbia and Montenegro

Iran
Iraq
Sudan
Ethiopia
Liberia
China

Democratic Republic of Congo

HIGHEST REFUGEE PRODUCERS

Country	Number
Afghanistan	3 809 700
Burundi	554 000
Iraq	530 100
Sudan	489 500
Angola	470 600
Bosnia-Herzegovina	450 000
Somalia	439 900
D. R. Congo	392 100

HIGHEST PROVIDERS OF REFUGE

Country	Number
Pakistan	2 198 800
Iran	1 868 000
Germany	903 000
Tanzania	646 900
USA	515 900
Serbia & Montenegro	400 300
D. R. Congo	362 000
Sudan	349 200

CONFLICT

World flashpoints at the end of the 1990's

1. Former Yugoslavia – Bosnia-Herzegovina, Macedonia, Yugoslavia, Kosovo, Croatia

2. Former USSR in the Caucasus – Azerbaijan, Armenia, Georgia and Chechnya

3. Middle East – Israel and the Palestinians

4. Gulf – Iraq, Kuwait and their neighbours

- Internal conflict in the 1990's

- Countries with refugees in their own lands

News reports often involve conflict, with a focus on conflict between nations. Most conflict however, is domestic and lasts for many years. These internal conflicts cause disruption of human lives, the movement of people within and out of their own country, and have resulted in many deaths.

SCALE 1 : 140 000 000

0   2000   4000   6000   8000 km

Eckert IV projection

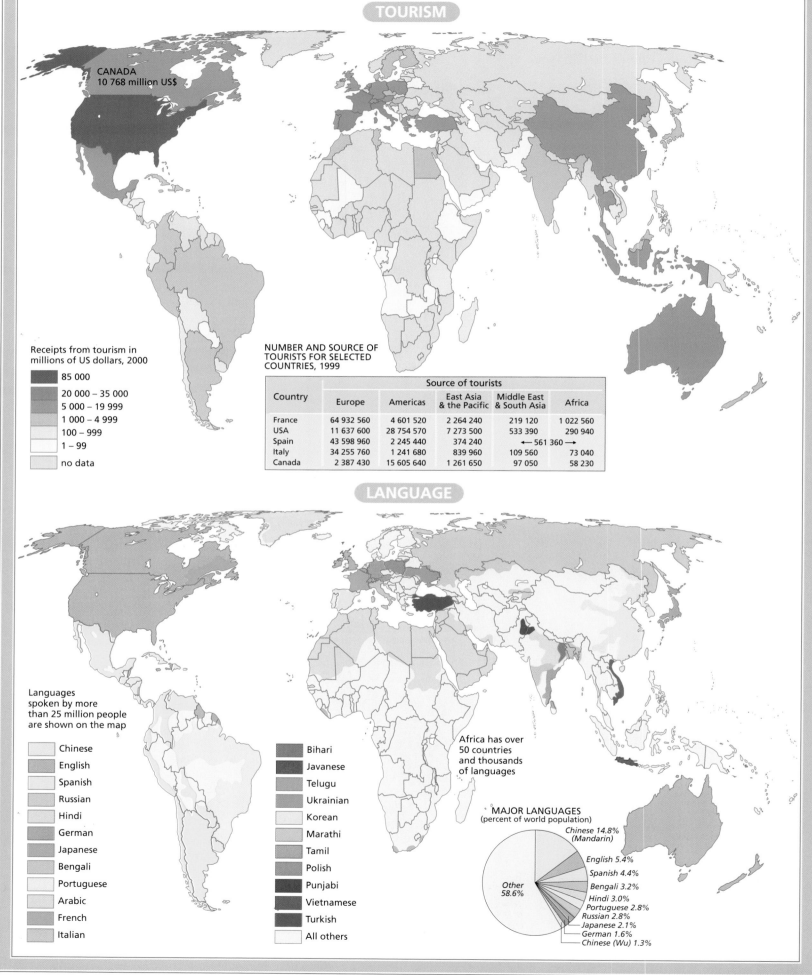

TOURISM

CANADA
10 768 million US$

Receipts from tourism in
millions of US dollars, 2000

- 85 000
- 20 000 – 35 000
- 5 000 – 19 999
- 1 000 – 4 999
- 100 – 999
- 1 – 99
- no data

NUMBER AND SOURCE OF TOURISTS FOR SELECTED COUNTRIES, 1999

Country	Source of tourists				
	Europe	Americas	East Asia & the Pacific	Middle East & South Asia	Africa
France	64 932 560	4 601 520	2 264 240	219 120	1 022 560
USA	11 637 600	28 754 570	7 273 500	533 390	290 940
Spain	43 598 960	2 245 440	374 240	← 561 360 →	
Italy	34 255 760	1 241 680	839 960	109 560	73 040
Canada	2 387 430	15 605 640	1 261 650	97 050	58 230

LANGUAGE

Languages
spoken by more
than 25 million people
are shown on the map

- Chinese
- English
- Spanish
- Russian
- Hindi
- German
- Japanese
- Bengali
- Portuguese
- Arabic
- French
- Italian

- Bihari
- Javanese
- Telugu
- Ukrainian
- Korean
- Marathi
- Tamil
- Polish
- Punjabi
- Vietnamese
- Turkish
- All others

Africa has over
50 countries
and thousands
of languages

MAJOR LANGUAGES
(percent of world population)

- Chinese 14.8% (Mandarin)
- English 5.4%
- Spanish 4.4%
- Bengali 3.2%
- Hindi 3.0%
- Portuguese 2.8%
- Russian 2.8%
- Japanese 2.1%
- German 1.6%
- Chinese (Wu) 1.3%
- Other 58.6%

SCALE 1 : 140 000 000

0   2000   4000   6000   8000 km

Eckert IV projection

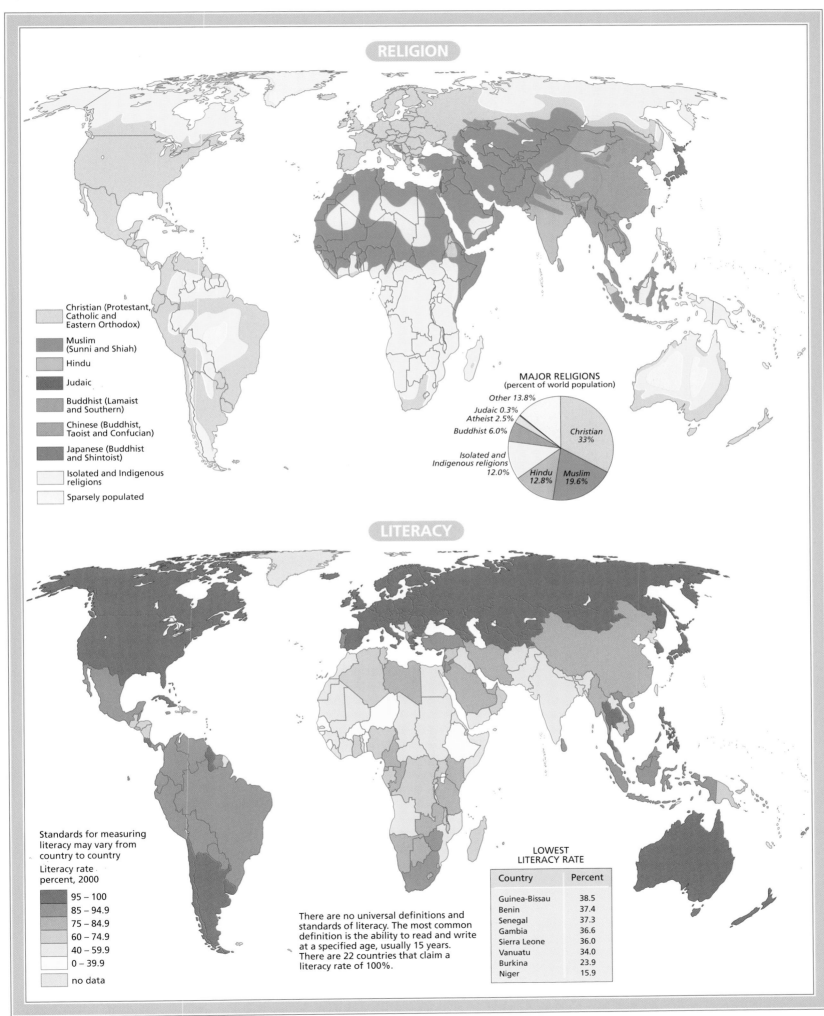

RELIGION

Christian (Protestant, Catholic and Eastern Orthodox)

Muslim (Sunni and Shiah)

Hindu

Judaic

Buddhist (Lamaist and Southern)

Chinese (Buddhist, Taoist and Confucian)

Japanese (Buddhist and Shintoist)

Isolated and Indigenous religions

Sparsely populated

MAJOR RELIGIONS
(percent of world population)

Other 13.8%
Judaic 0.3%
Atheist 2.5%
Buddhist 6.0%
Christian 33%
Isolated and Indigenous religions 12.0%
Hindu 12.8%
Muslim 19.6%

LITERACY

Standards for measuring literacy may vary from country to country

Literacy rate percent, 2000

95 – 100
85 – 94.9
75 – 84.9
60 – 74.9
40 – 59.9
0 – 39.9

no data

There are no universal definitions and standards of literacy. The most common definition is the ability to read and write at a specified age, usually 15 years. There are 22 countries that claim a literacy rate of 100%.

LOWEST LITERACY RATE

Country	Percent
Guinea-Bissau	38.5
Benin	37.4
Senegal	37.3
Gambia	36.6
Sierra Leone	36.0
Vanuatu	34.0
Burkina	23.9
Niger	15.9

SCALE 1 : 140 000 000

0   2000   4000   6000   8000 km

Eckert IV projection

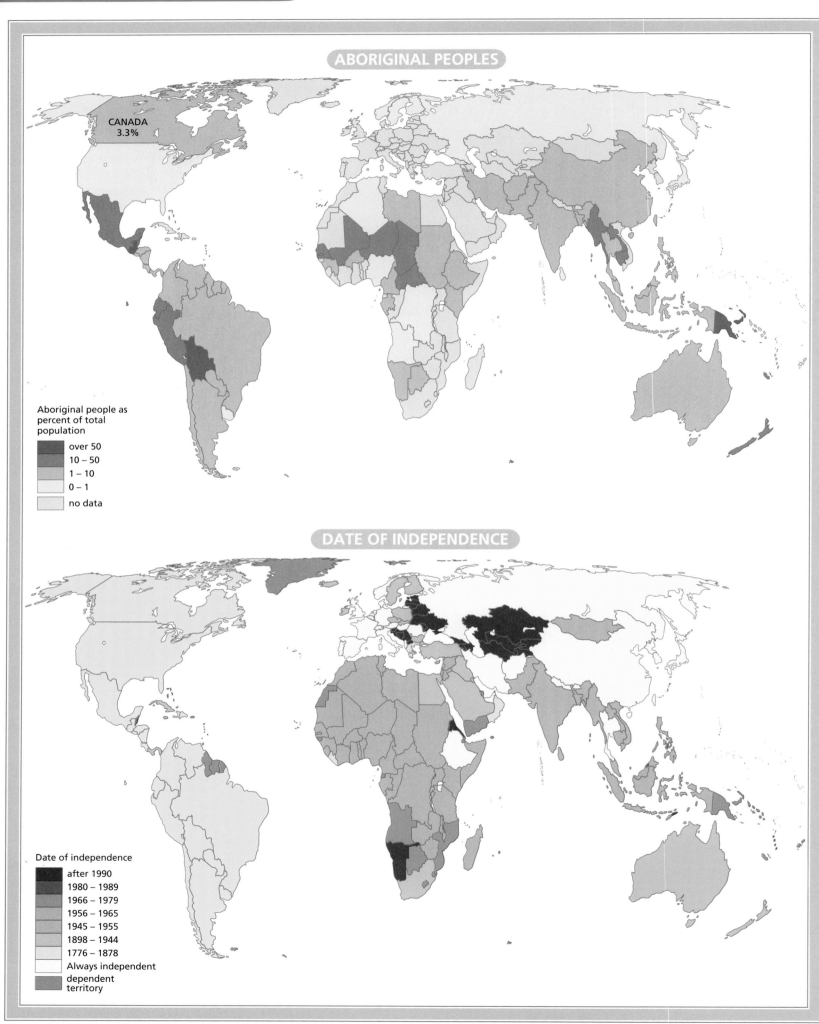

ABORIGINAL PEOPLES

CANADA
3.3%

Aboriginal people as
percent of total
population

- over 50
- 10 – 50
- 1 – 10
- 0 – 1
- no data

DATE OF INDEPENDENCE

Date of independence
- after 1990
- 1980 – 1989
- 1966 – 1979
- 1956 – 1965
- 1945 – 1955
- 1898 – 1944
- 1776 – 1878
- Always independent
- dependent territory

SCALE 1 : 140 000 000

0   2000   4000   6000   8000 km

Eckert IV projection

TYPES OF GOVERNMENT

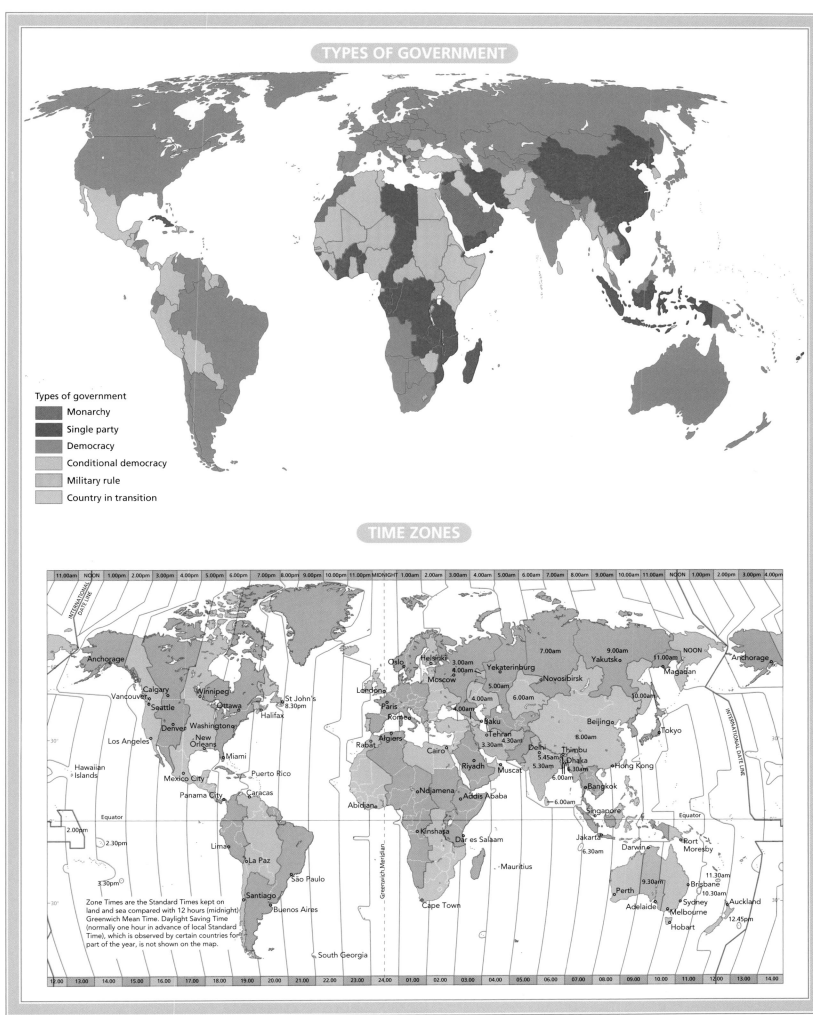

Types of government

- Monarchy
- Single party
- Democracy
- Conditional democracy
- Military rule
- Country in transition

TIME ZONES

| 11.00am | NOON | 1.00pm | 2.00pm | 3.00pm | 4.00pm | 5.00pm | 6.00pm | 7.00pm | 8.00pm | 9.00pm | 10.00pm | 11.00pm | MIDNIGHT | 1.00am | 2.00am | 3.00am | 4.00am | 5.00am | 6.00am | 7.00am | 8.00am | 9.00am | 10.00am | 11.00am | NOON | 1.00pm | 2.00pm | 3.00pm | 4.00pm |

INTERNATIONAL DATE LINE

Anchorage

Vancouver
Calgary
Seattle
Winnipeg
Denver
Ottawa
Washington
Los Angeles
New Orleans
Miami
Hawaiian Islands
Mexico City
Panama City
Caracas

St John's
8.30pm
Halifax

Puerto Rico

Oslo
London
Paris
Rome
Rabat
Algiers

Helsinki
Moscow

3.00am
4.00am

Yekaterinburg
5.00am

4.00am
6.00am

Novosibirsk

7.00am

Yakutsk

9.00am

Magadan

11.00am

NOON

Anchorage

10.00am

Tokyo

INTERNATIONAL DATE LINE

4.00am
Baku
Tehran
3.30am

Cairo

Riyadh
Muscat

4.30am

Delhi
5.45am
5.30am

Beijing
8.00am

Thimbu
Dhaka
6.30am
6.00am

Hong Kong

Bangkok

Equator

2.00pm

2.30pm

3.30pm

Lima
La Paz
São Paulo
Santiago
Buenos Aires

South Georgia

Ndjamena

Abidjan

Kinshasa

Addis Ababa

Dar es Salaam

Greenwich Meridian

Mauritius

Cape Town

6.00am

Singapore

Jakarta
6.30am

Darwin

Perth

9.30am

Adelaide

Port Moresby

11.30am
Brisbane

Sydney
Melbourne

10.30am

Hobart

Auckland

12.45pm

Equator

Zone Times are the Standard Times kept on land and sea compared with 12 hours (midnight) Greenwich Mean Time. Daylight Saving Time (normally one hour in advance of local Standard Time), which is observed by certain countries for part of the year, is not shown on the map.

| 12.00 | 13.00 | 14.00 | 15.00 | 16.00 | 17.00 | 18.00 | 19.00 | 20.00 | 21.00 | 22.00 | 23.00 | 24.00 | 01.00 | 02.00 | 03.00 | 04.00 | 05.00 | 06.00 | 07.00 | 08.00 | 09.00 | 10.00 | 11.00 | 12.00 | 13.00 | 14.00 |

SCALE 1 : 140 000 000

0   2000   4000   6000   8000 km

Eckert IV projection

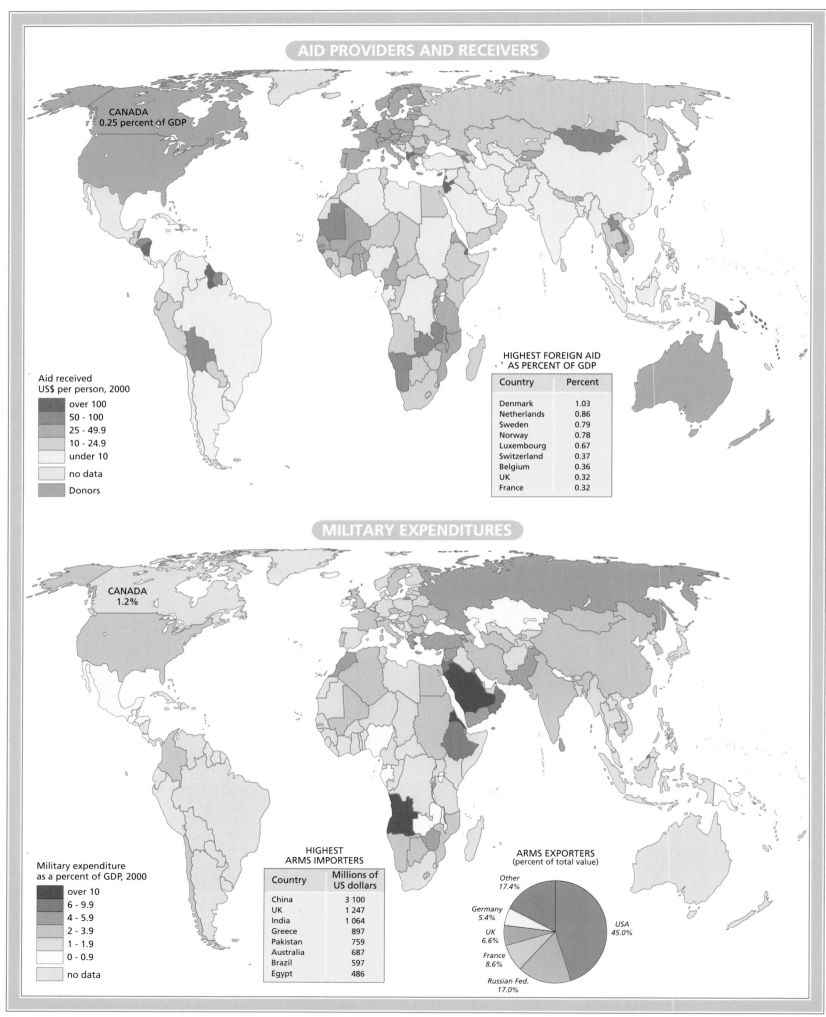

AID PROVIDERS AND RECEIVERS

CANADA
0.25 percent of GDP

Aid received
US$ per person, 2000
- over 100
- 50 - 100
- 25 - 49.9
- 10 - 24.9
- under 10
- no data
- Donors

HIGHEST FOREIGN AID AS PERCENT OF GDP

Country	Percent
Denmark	1.03
Netherlands	0.86
Sweden	0.79
Norway	0.78
Luxembourg	0.67
Switzerland	0.37
Belgium	0.36
UK	0.32
France	0.32

MILITARY EXPENDITURES

CANADA
1.2%

Military expenditure
as a percent of GDP, 2000
- over 10
- 6 - 9.9
- 4 - 5.9
- 2 - 3.9
- 1 - 1.9
- 0 - 0.9
- no data

HIGHEST ARMS IMPORTERS

Country	Millions of US dollars
China	3 100
UK	1 247
India	1 064
Greece	897
Pakistan	759
Australia	687
Brazil	597
Egypt	486

ARMS EXPORTERS
(percent of total value)

- Other 17.4%
- Germany 5.4%
- UK 6.6%
- France 8.6%
- Russian Fed. 17.0%
- USA 45.0%

SCALE 1 : 140 000 000

0   2000   4000   6000   8000 km

Eckert IV projection

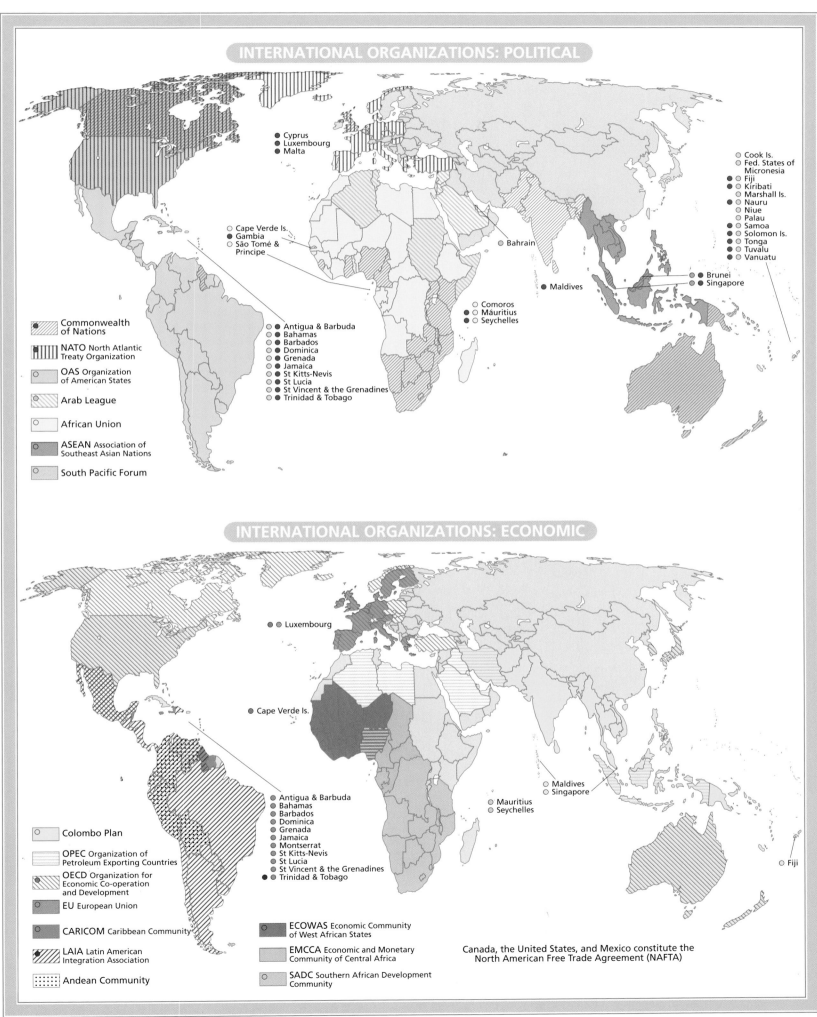

INTERNATIONAL ORGANIZATIONS: POLITICAL

- Cyprus
- Luxembourg
- Malta

- Cape Verde Is.
- Gambia
- São Tomé & Principe

- Bahrain

- Maldives

- Comoros
- Mauritius
- Seychelles

- Cook Is.
- Fed. States of Micronesia
- Fiji
- Kiribati
- Marshall Is.
- Nauru
- Niue
- Palau
- Samoa
- Solomon Is.
- Tonga
- Tuvalu
- Vanuatu

- Brunei
- Singapore

- Antigua & Barbuda
- Bahamas
- Barbados
- Dominica
- Grenada
- Jamaica
- St Kitts-Nevis
- St Lucia
- St Vincent & the Grenadines
- Trinidad & Tobago

Commonwealth of Nations

NATO North Atlantic Treaty Organization

OAS Organization of American States

Arab League

African Union

ASEAN Association of Southeast Asian Nations

South Pacific Forum

INTERNATIONAL ORGANIZATIONS: ECONOMIC

- Luxembourg

- Cape Verde Is.

- Maldives
- Singapore

- Mauritius
- Seychelles

- Fiji

- Antigua & Barbuda
- Bahamas
- Barbados
- Dominica
- Grenada
- Jamaica
- Montserrat
- St Kitts-Nevis
- St Lucia
- St Vincent & the Grenadines
- Trinidad & Tobago

Colombo Plan

OPEC Organization of Petroleum Exporting Countries

OECD Organization for Economic Co-operation and Development

EU European Union

CARICOM Caribbean Community

LAIA Latin American Integration Association

Andean Community

ECOWAS Economic Community of West African States

EMCCA Economic and Monetary Community of Central Africa

SADC Southern African Development Community

Canada, the United States, and Mexico constitute the North American Free Trade Agreement (NAFTA)

SCALE 1 : 140 000 000

0   2000   4000   6000   8000 km

Eckert IV projection

ARCTIC OCEAN

RUSSIAN FEDERATION

Bering Sea

PACIFIC OCEAN

GREENLAND

Arctic Circle

ICELAND

U.S.A.
ALASKA
Fairbanks
Olnuvik
Anchorage
Whitehorse
Yellowknife
NUUK

Yukon
Mackenzie

C A N A D A

Churchill
Hudson Bay

Peace
Churchill
Nelson
Seven

St John's

Edmonton
Saskatoon
Vancouver
Victoria
Seattle
Calgary
Regina
Winnipeg
Portland
Spokane
Thunder Bay
Charlottetown
Saint John
Halifax

Fraser
Columbia

Québec
Sudbury
Montréal
OTTAWA
Toronto
Boston
Providence

Boundaries
— International

Urban population
- ■ ● over 1 000 000
- □ ○ 500 000 - 1 000 000
- □ ○ 100 000 - 500 000
- □ ○ under 100 000

Square symbols denote national capital cities.

D.R. DOMINICAN REPUBLIC
E.S. EL SALVADOR
H. HAITI
P.R. PUERTO RICO

SCALE 1 : 40 000 000
0   400   800   1200 km

Billings
Minneapolis-St Paul
Duluth
Hamilton
Buffalo
Detroit
Cleveland
New York
Philadelphia
Baltimore
Boise
Milwaukee
Chicago
Pittsburgh
WASHINGTON D.C.
San Francisco
Reno
Salt Lake City
Sacramento
Fresno
UNITED
Omaha
STATES
Cincinnati
Norfolk
Denver
Kansas City
Indianapolis
St Louis
Greensboro
Las Vegas
OF
Los Angeles
Colorado
Arkansas
Tulsa
Little Rock
Memphis
Greenville
ATLANTIC OCEAN
BERMUDA (UK)

San Diego
Phoenix
Tucson
Albuquerque
Oklahoma City
AMERICA
Atlanta
Birmingham
Savannah
Tijuana
El Paso
Fort Worth
Dallas
Jackson
Mobile
Jacksonville
Ciudad Juárez
Austin
Houston
New Orleans
Tampa-St Petersburg
San Antonio
Fort Lauderdale
Miami
NASSAU
Monterrey
Gulf of Mexico
THE BAHAMAS

Snake
Yellowstone
Missouri
Ohio
Mississippi
Rio Grande

Tropic of Cancer

Mazatlán
M E X I C O
HAVANA
CUBA
H. D.R. P.R.(USA) SAN JUAN
Guadalajara
León
Cancún
JAMAICA
PORT-AU PRINCE
SANTO DOMINGO
MEXICO CITY
Puebla
KINGSTON
Caribbean Sea
Acapulco
BELMOPAN
BELIZE
HONDURAS
GUATEMALA
TEGUCIGALPA
GUATEMALA CITY
SAN SALVADOR
E.S. NICARAGUA
MANAGUA
VENEZUELA

SAN JOSE
COSTA RICA
PANAMA
PANAMA CITY

PACIFIC OCEAN

COLOMBIA

ECUADOR
Equator

PERU
BRAZIL

POPULATION

Arctic Circle

Persons per km²
- over 100
- 50-100
- 10-50
- 1-10
- 0-1

Toronto
Detroit
Montréal
Boston
Chicago
New York
Philadelphia
Washington D.C.
San Francisco
San Diego
Los Angeles
Phoenix
Dallas
Atlanta
Monterrey
Houston
Miami
Tropic of Cancer
Guadalajara
Mexico City
Santo Domingo
Guatemala City

Urban population
- ■ over 10 000 000
- ■ 5 000 000 - 10 000 000
- ● 2 500 000 - 5 000 000
- • 1 000 000 - 2 500 000

SCALE 1 : 100 000 000

Chamberlin Trimetric projection

Relief

Relief metres
5000
3000
2000
1000
500
200
sea level
below sea level
0
200
4000
6000

Permanent ice

6194 ▲ Mountain height (in metres)

SCALE 1 : 40 000 000

0   400   800   1200 km

PHYSICAL REGIONS

Pacific Ranges
Rocky Mountains
Canadian Shield
Appalachian Highlands
Interior Plains and Lowlands
Western Plateaus, Ranges and Basins
Coastal Lowlands
Tropic of Cancer
Caribbean Islands
Central American Highlands

SCALE 1 : 100 000 000

ARCTIC OCEAN

PACIFIC OCEAN

ATLANTIC OCEAN

Greenland

Iceland
Faeroes

Wrangel I.
Pt Barrow
Brooks Range
Beaufort Sea
Banks Island
Queen Elizabeth Islands
Parry Islands
Ellesmere Island
Baffin Bay
Denmark Strait
Arctic Circle
Cape Farewell
Davis Strait

Bering Strait
Bering Sea
St Lawrence I.
Nunivak I.
Yukon
Alaska Range ▲ Mt McKinley 6194
Aleutian Range
Bristol Bay
Kodiak I.
Gulf of Alaska
Mt Logan ▲ 5959
Mackenzie Mts
Great Bear Lake
Victoria Island
Southampton I.
Foxe Basin
Baffin Island
Labrador Sea

Alexander Archipelago
Queen Charlotte Islands
Coast Mountains
Mt Waddington ▲ 4042
Vancouver Island
Mt Rainier ▲ 4392
Fraser
Peace
Great Slave Lake
Lake Athabasca
Churchill
Nelson
Saskatchewan
Lake Winnipeg
Albany
Severn
CANADIAN SHIELD
Hudson Bay
Belcher Is
Péninsule d'Ungava
Hudson Strait
Churchill
St Lawrence
Newfoundland
Gulf of St Lawrence
Cape Breton I.
C. Sable

ROCKY MOUNTAINS
GREAT PLAINS
Cascade Range
Columbia
Snake
Yellowstone
Gannett Pk 4202 ▲
Great Salt L.
Sierra Nevada
Great Basin
Mt Whitney ▲ 4418
Grand Canyon
Colorado
Colorado Plateau
Missouri
Platte
Arkansas
Red
Lake Superior
Lake Michigan
Lake Huron
Lake Erie
Lake Ontario
Ohio
Tennessee
Mississippi
Ozark Plateau
Alabama
Appalachian Mts
Chesapeake B.
C. Cod
Long I.
Bermuda
ATLANTIC OCEAN
C. Hatteras
C. Fear
C. Sable

Guadalupe
Lower California
Gulf of California
Sierra Madre Occidental
C. San Lucas
Sierra Madre Oriental
Altiplano Mexicano
Popocatépetl ▲ 5452
Edwards Plateau
Brazos
Rio Grande
C. Canaveral
Tropic of Cancer
Bahamas
Gulf of Mexico
Campeche Bay
Yucatán
Str. of Florida
Yucatán Channel
Cuba
Jamaica
Greater Antilles
Hispaniola
Puerto Rico
Lesser Antilles
Curaçao
Caribbean Sea

Sierra Madre del Sur
Sierra Madre
G. of Honduras
G. of Panama
L. Nicaragua
Isthmus of Panama
G. of Darién
Cordillera Occidental
Cordillera Central
Orinoco

PACIFIC OCEAN
I. de Coco
I. de Malpelo
Galapagos Islands
G. of Guayaquil
Equator
Cotopaxi ▲ 5896
Chimborazo ▲ 6310

Chamberlin Trimetric projection

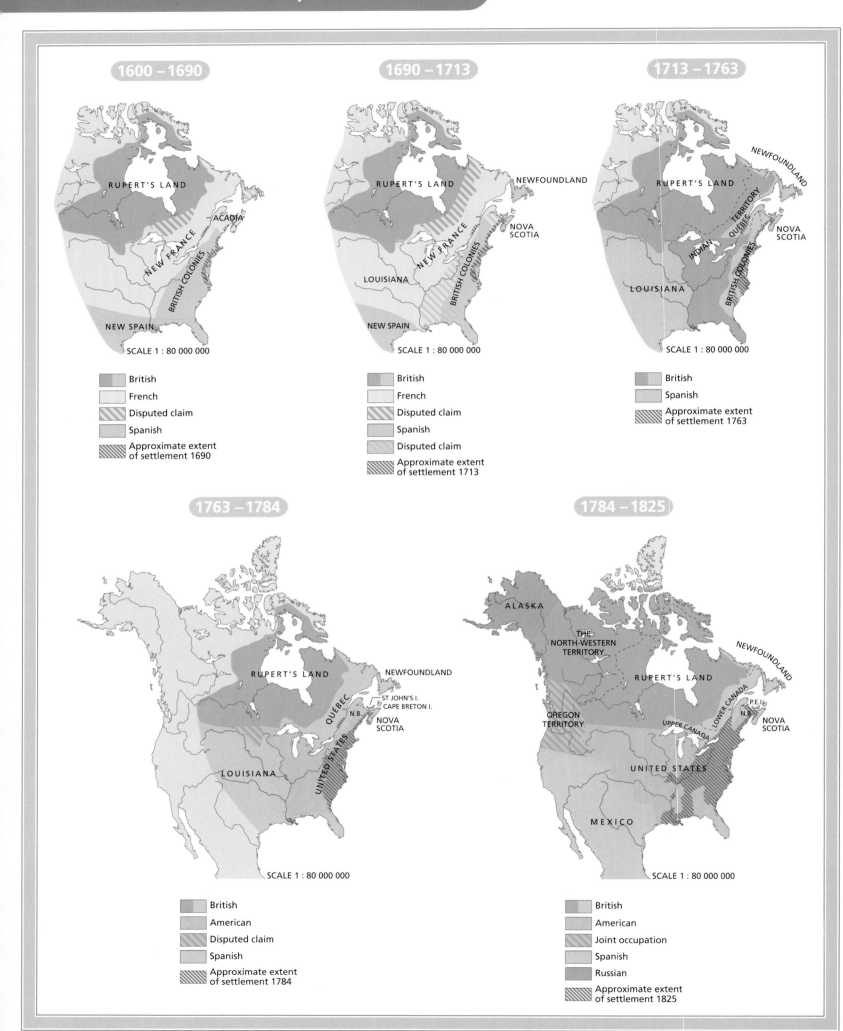

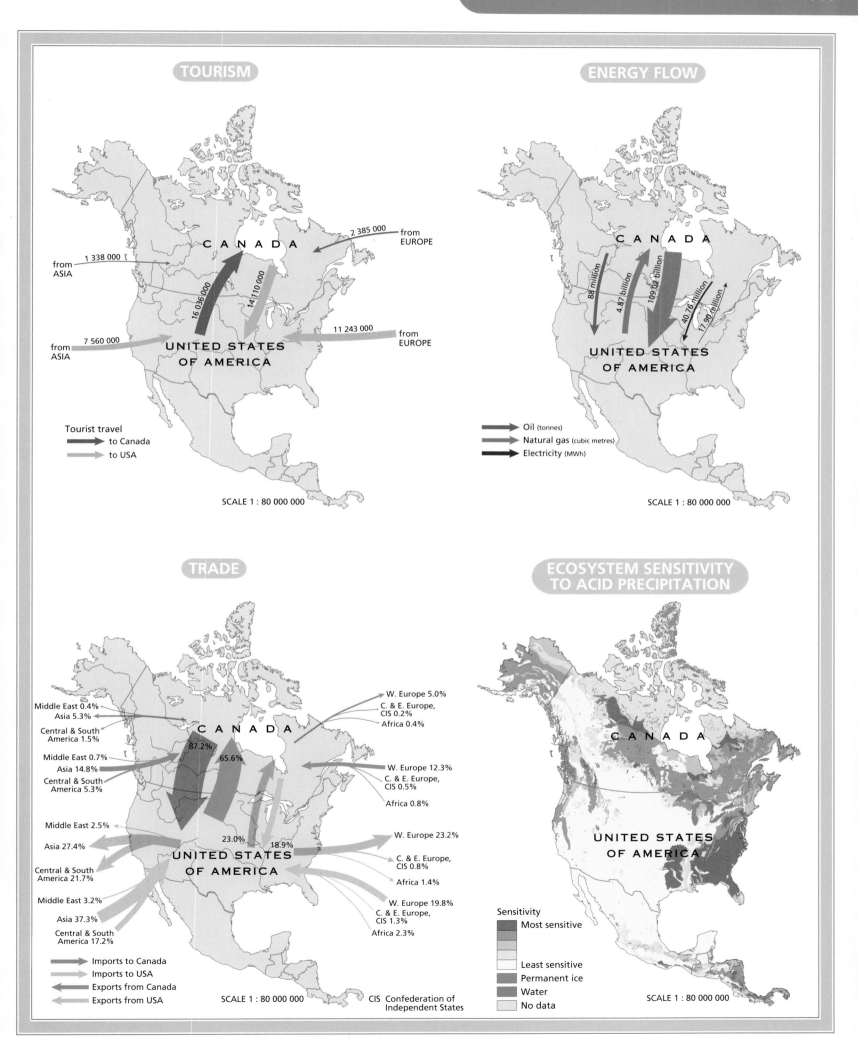

TOURISM

CANADA

2 385 000 from EUROPE

from ASIA 1 338 000

16 036 000

14 110 000

from ASIA 7 560 000

11 243 000 from EUROPE

UNITED STATES OF AMERICA

Tourist travel
→ to Canada
→ to USA

SCALE 1 : 80 000 000

ENERGY FLOW

CANADA

88 million

4.87 billion

109.02 billion

40.76 million

17.90 million

UNITED STATES OF AMERICA

→ Oil (tonnes)
→ Natural gas (cubic metres)
→ Electricity (MWh)

SCALE 1 : 80 000 000

TRADE

W. Europe 5.0%
C. & E. Europe, CIS 0.2%
Africa 0.4%

Middle East 0.4%
Asia 5.3%
Central & South America 1.5%

Middle East 0.7%
Asia 14.8%
Central & South America 5.3%

CANADA

87.2%

65.6%

W. Europe 12.3%
C. & E. Europe, CIS 0.5%

Africa 0.8%

Middle East 2.5%

Asia 27.4%

23.0%   18.9%

W. Europe 23.2%

Central & South America 21.7%

UNITED STATES OF AMERICA

C. & E. Europe, CIS 0.8%

Africa 1.4%

Middle East 3.2%

Asia 37.3%

W. Europe 19.8%
C. & E. Europe, CIS 1.3%

Central & South America 17.2%

Africa 2.3%

→ Imports to Canada
→ Imports to USA
← Exports from Canada
← Exports from USA

SCALE 1 : 80 000 000

CIS Confederation of Independent States

ECOSYSTEM SENSITIVITY TO ACID PRECIPITATION

CANADA

UNITED STATES OF AMERICA

Sensitivity
- Most sensitive
- Least sensitive
- Permanent ice
- Water
- No data

SCALE 1 : 80 000 000

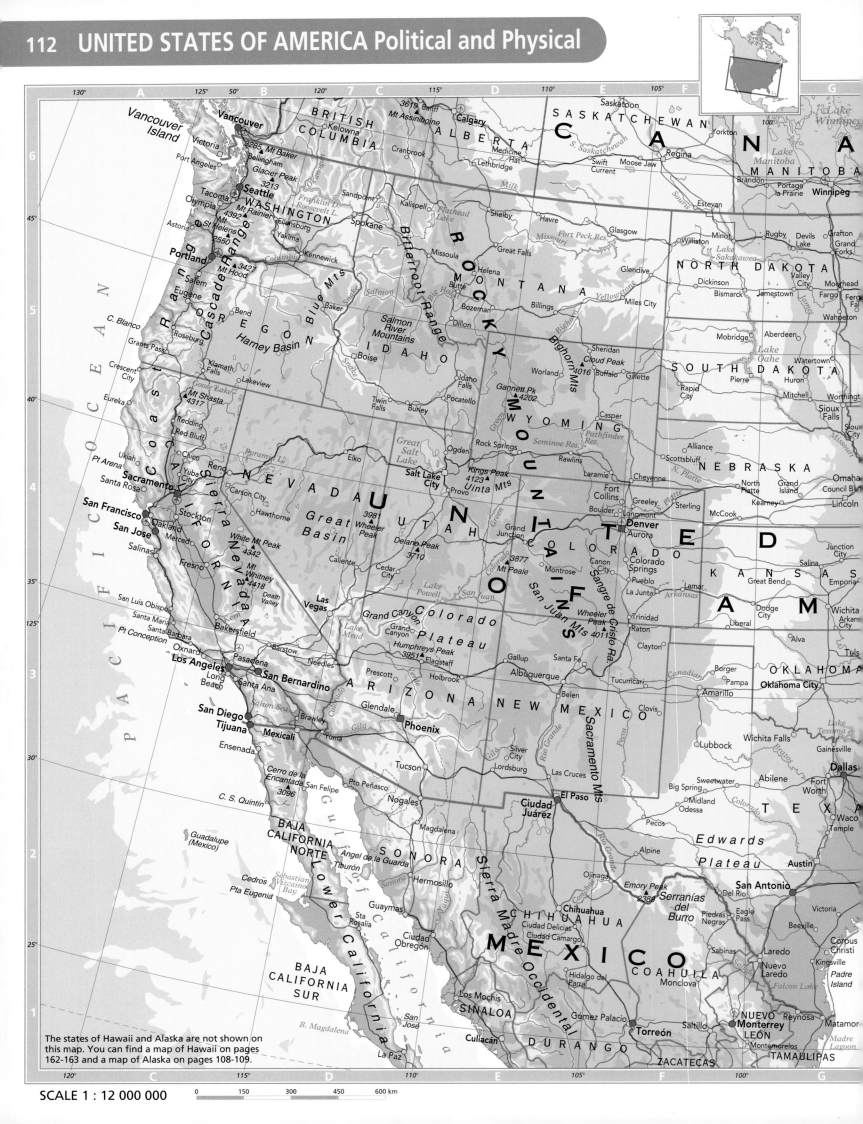

The states of Hawaii and Alaska are not shown on this map. You can find a map of Hawaii on pages 162-163 and a map of Alaska on pages 108-109.

SCALE 1 : 12 000 000

0   150   300   450   600 km

Relief and physical features

Relief metres

5000
3000
2000
1000
500
200
sea level
below sea level
0
200
4000
6000

▲ 4418 Mountain height
(in metres)

Water features

～～ River

～～ Intermittent river

Lake / Reservoir

Intermittent lake

Marsh

Communications

—— Railway

—— Road

⊕ Main airport

Administration

Boundaries

—— International

—— Internal

Urban population

■ ● over 1 000 000

□ ○ 500 000 - 1 000 000

□ ○ 100 000 - 500 000

▫ ○ under 100 000

Square symbols denote national,
provincial, territorial or state capital cities.

Lambert Conformal Conic projection

LAND USE

ALASKA

SCALE 1 : 40 000 000

Legend:
- Urban
- Cropland
- Cropland and woodland
- Grassland and grazing
- Temperate forest
- Coniferous forest
- Tropical forest
- Scrubland or desert
- Swamp and marsh
- Tundra
- • Climograph station

The United States is the third largest country in the world, both in area and population. Blessed with abundant resources, it has developed into an economic and political leader. Over 40 percent of the land is used for agriculture, a sector that is largely mechanized and scientifically controlled. The United States is the world's largest exporter of grain. The country also produces almost 14 percent of the world's oil, and 25 percent of the world's natural gas and coal. It is the leading producer of nuclear power and the second largest producer of hydroelectric power. However, the United States consumes even more natural resources than it produces.

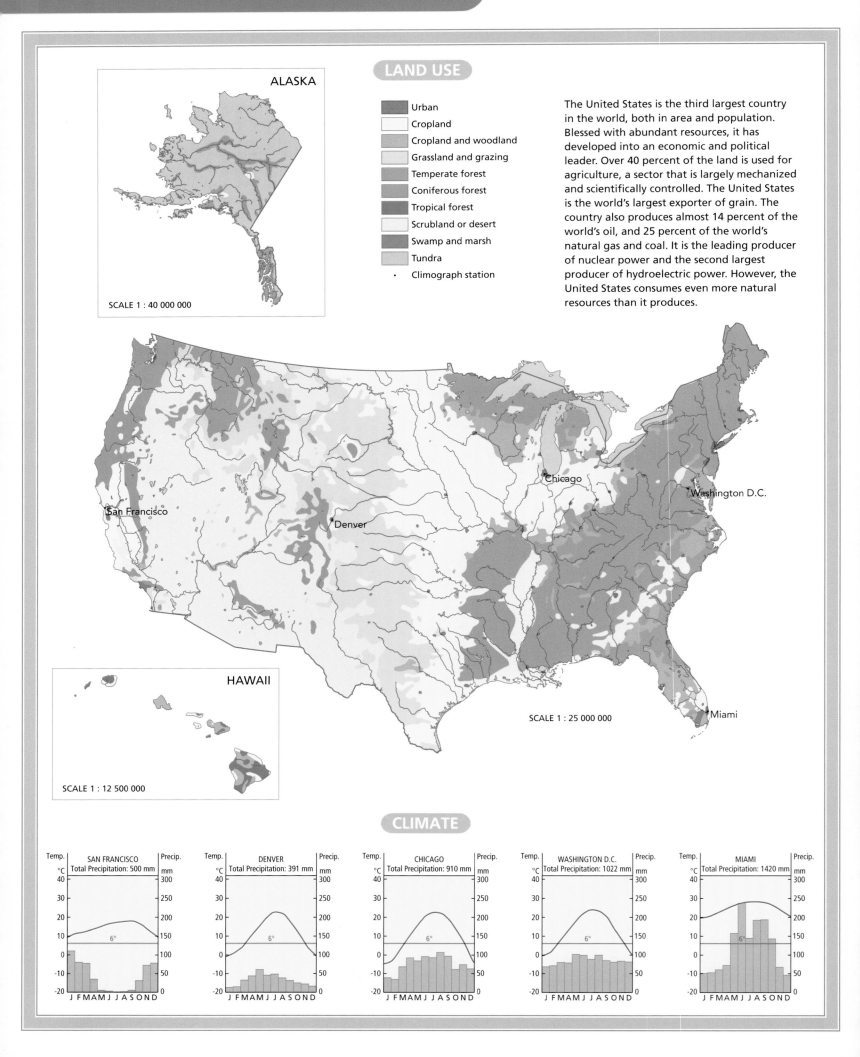

Chicago

Washington D.C.

San Francisco

Denver

Miami

SCALE 1 : 25 000 000

HAWAII

SCALE 1 : 12 500 000

CLIMATE

SAN FRANCISCO — Total Precipitation: 500 mm

DENVER — Total Precipitation: 391 mm

CHICAGO — Total Precipitation: 910 mm

WASHINGTON D.C. — Total Precipitation: 1022 mm

MIAMI — Total Precipitation: 1420 mm

POPULATION CHANGE

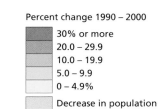

Percent change 1990 – 2000

- 30% or more
- 20.0 – 29.9
- 10.0 – 19.9
- 5.0 – 9.9
- 0 – 4.9%
- Decrease in population

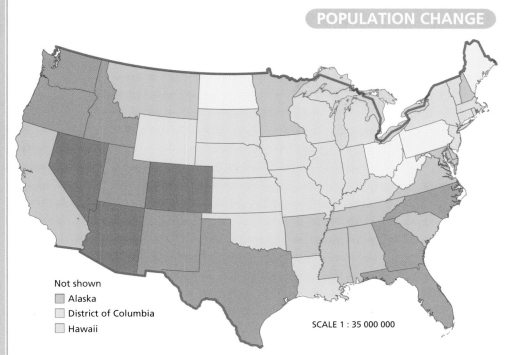

Not shown
- Alaska
- District of Columbia
- Hawaii

SCALE 1 : 35 000 000

Population change is often linked to economic change. People pursuing jobs move to areas where the economy is strong. However, retirees can also stimulate an area's economy, as they have in Florida and the Southwest. Generally, the American population continues to move west and southwest. California and Texas are becoming the centers for the fast-growing high-tech industry. The Northeast still features heavy industry.

TOURISM

Top Destinations, 1999

State	Income from tourism	
	Millions, US$	Percent of GDP
Hawaii	7 092	17.5
Florida	16 648	3.8
Nevada	2 661	3.8
D.C.	1 613	2.9
New York	9 448	1.3
Arizona	1 620	1.1
California	13 828	1.1
Alaska	215	0.8
Vermont	130	0.8
Maine	246	0.7
Massachusetts	1 939	0.7
Utah	359	0.6
Colorado	731	0.5
Texas	3 242	0.5
Illinois	1 647	0.4
Louisiana	459	0.4
Montana	91	0.4
Oregon	389	0.4
Rhode Island	113	0.4
South Carolina	448	0.4
Washington	931	0.4

ECONOMY

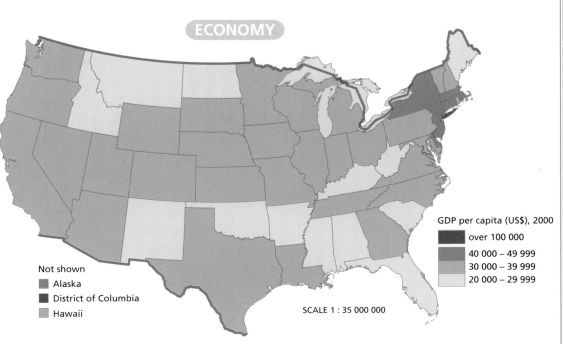

Not shown
- Alaska
- District of Columbia
- Hawaii

SCALE 1 : 35 000 000

GDP per capita (US$), 2000
- over 100 000
- 40 000 – 49 999
- 30 000 – 39 999
- 20 000 – 29 999

Imports, 2001 / Exports, 2001

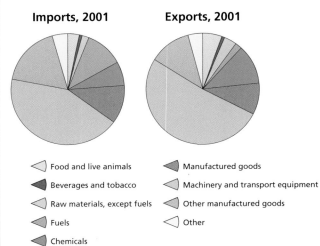

- Food and live animals
- Beverages and tobacco
- Raw materials, except fuels
- Fuels
- Chemicals
- Manufactured goods
- Machinery and transport equipment
- Other manufactured goods
- Other

GDP by sector, 2000

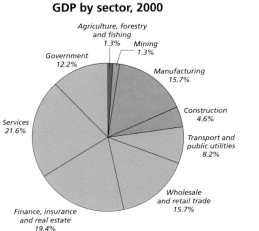

Agriculture, forestry and fishing 1.3%
Mining 1.3%
Government 12.2%
Manufacturing 15.7%
Construction 4.6%
Transport and public utilities 8.2%
Services 21.6%
Wholesale and retail trade 15.7%
Finance, insurance and real estate 19.4%

Trade, 2001

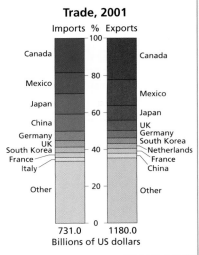

Imports % Exports

Imports: Canada, Mexico, Japan, China, Germany, UK, South Korea, France, Italy, Other
Exports: Canada, Mexico, Japan, UK, Germany, South Korea, Netherlands, France, China, Other

731.0 / 1180.0
Billions of US dollars

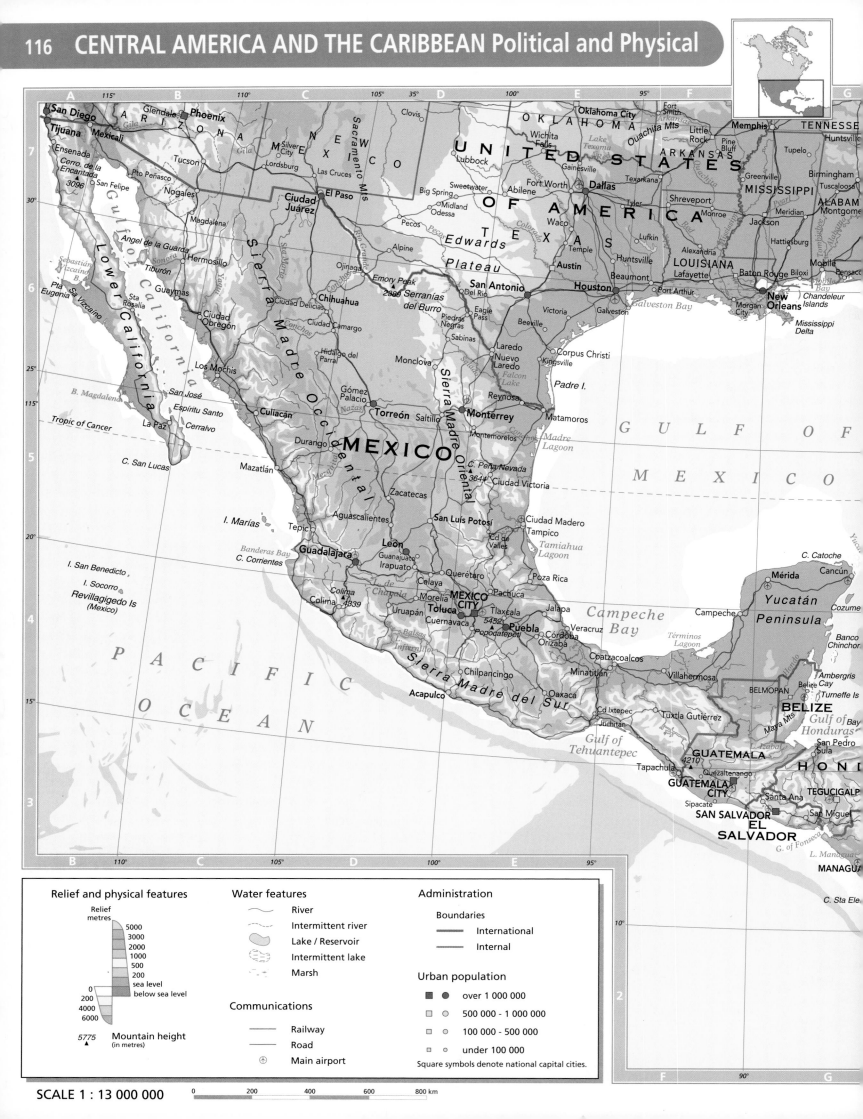

This false-colour view of central Mexico illustrates the area of wintering of the Monarch butterfly. The butterflies winter in the "red" fir forests at high altitudes. Over the past 30 years, almost half of these forests have been subjected to intense logging, reducing the available winter habitat and putting the Monarch cycle of life in danger.

Lambert Azimuthal Equal Area projection

LAND USE

Although small in size and population, this region is physically and culturally diverse. Dominated by fold and volcanic mountains, there are more than 30 active volcanoes in the region. Land use reflects the variety of climate, which ranges from the deserts of the Baja peninsula to the tropical forests of Nicaragua, Costa Rica, and Honduras. Culturally, the region reflects the influence of the Mayans and Toltecs, who developed highly advanced agriculture and urban development long before the incursion of the Spanish into the region.

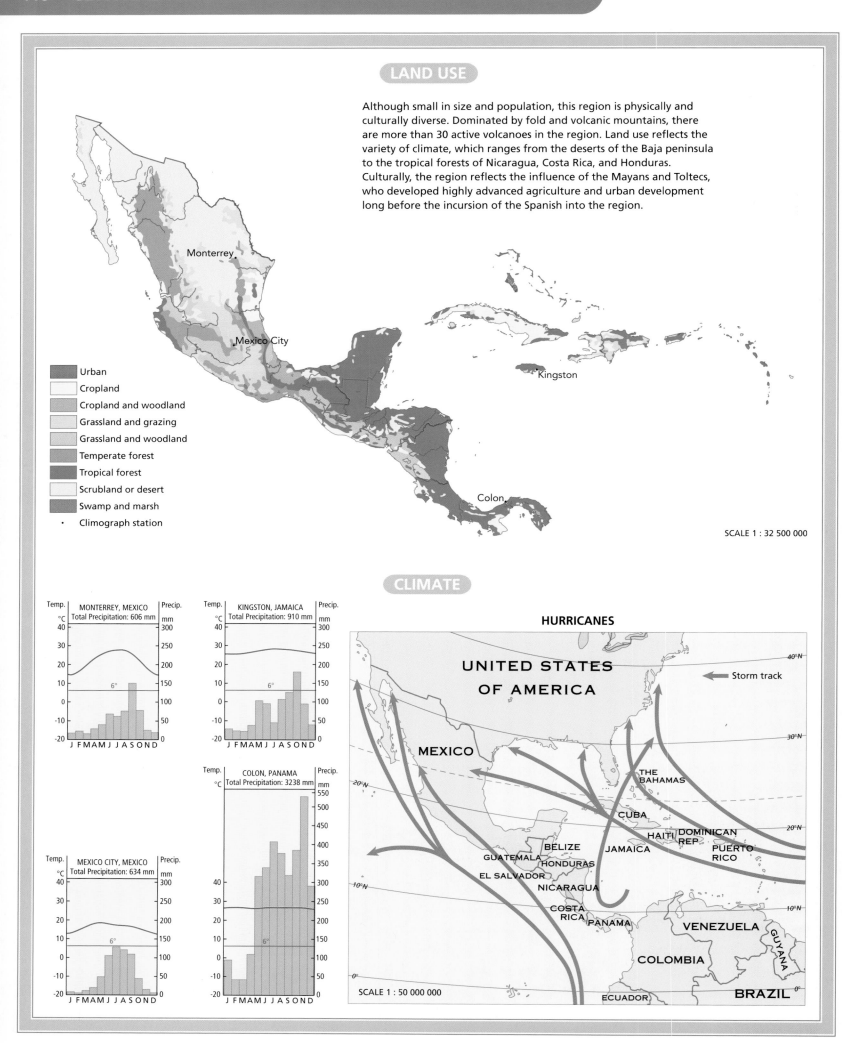

Monterrey

Mexico City

Kingston

Colon

Legend:
- Urban
- Cropland
- Cropland and woodland
- Grassland and grazing
- Grassland and woodland
- Temperate forest
- Tropical forest
- Scrubland or desert
- Swamp and marsh
- Climograph station

SCALE 1 : 32 500 000

CLIMATE

MONTERREY, MEXICO
Total Precipitation: 606 mm
Temp. °C / Precip. mm
6°

KINGSTON, JAMAICA
Total Precipitation: 910 mm
Temp. °C / Precip. mm
6°

MEXICO CITY, MEXICO
Total Precipitation: 634 mm
Temp. °C / Precip. mm
6°

COLON, PANAMA
Total Precipitation: 3238 mm
Temp. °C / Precip. mm
6°

HURRICANES

Storm track

UNITED STATES OF AMERICA

MEXICO

THE BAHAMAS

CUBA

HAITI — DOMINICAN REP.

BELIZE — JAMAICA — PUERTO RICO

GUATEMALA

HONDURAS

EL SALVADOR

NICARAGUA

COSTA RICA — PANAMA

VENEZUELA

COLOMBIA

GUYANA

ECUADOR

BRAZIL

40°N, 30°N, 20°N, 10°N, 0°

SCALE 1 : 50 000 000

PANAMA CANAL

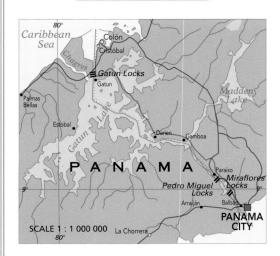

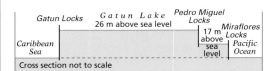

PANAMA CANAL
Opened *1914*
Length *64 km*
Minimum depth *12 m*
Minimum width *152 m*

POLITICAL CONFLICT

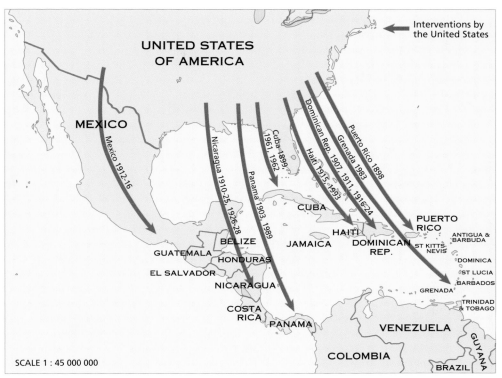

Interventions by the United States

SCALE 1 : 45 000 000

TOURISM

Top Destinations, 2000

Country	Income from tourism Millions, US$	Percent of GDP
Virgin Islands (USA)	965	53.6
St Lucia	311	46.7
Antigua and Barbuda	291	44.5
Cayman Islands	439	37.2
The Bahamas	1 503	33.2
Barbados	745	28.7
St Vincent and the Grenadines	77	23.4
St Kitts and Nevis	70	23.3
Bermuda	431	19.5
Dominica	49	18.5
Jamaica	1 333	18.0
Grenada	63	16.7

Country	Income from tourism Millions, US$	Percent of GDP
Belize	112	15.4
Dominican Republic	2 918	14.8
Costa Rica	1 102	7.0
Cuba	1 756	6.9
Panama	576	5.8
Puerto Rico	2 541	5.8
Nicaragua	116	4.8
Honduras	240	4.0
Trinidad and Tobago	210	3.1
Guatemala	518	2.7
El Salvador	254	1.9
Mexico	8 295	1.4
Haiti	55	1.3

ECONOMY

CUBA

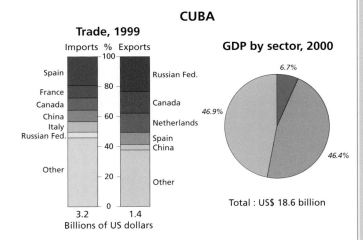

MEXICO / COSTA RICA

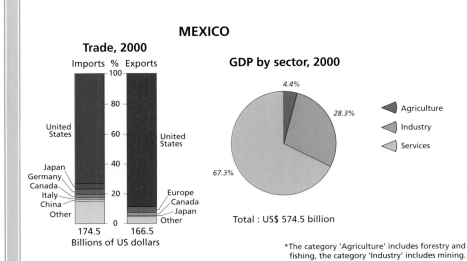

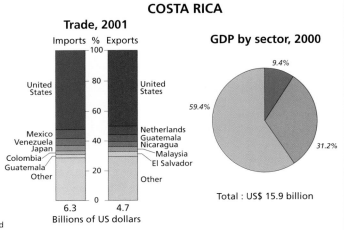

*The category 'Agriculture' includes forestry and fishing, the category 'Industry' includes mining.

MEXICO
BELIZE
GUATEMALA
HONDURAS
EL SALVADOR
NICARAGUA
COSTA RICA
PANAMA
G. of Honduras

CUBA
THE BAHAMAS
JAMAICA
HAITI
DOMINICAN REP.
PUERTO RICO (USA)

CARIBBEAN SEA

ATLANTIC OCEAN

Barranquilla
Cartagena
Maracaibo
Valencia
Cabimas
CARACAS
Maracay
TRINIDAD AND TOBAGO

Cúcuta
San Cristóbal
Ciudad Bolívar
Ciudad Guayana
Orinoco
GEORGETOWN
PARAMARIBO
CAYENNE

Medellín
Bucaramanga
VENEZUELA
GUYANA
SURINAME
FRENCH GUIANA

Manizales
Meta
Buenaventura
BOGOTÁ
COLOMBIA
Cali

I. de Coco (Costa Rica)
I. de Malpelo (Colombia)

QUITO
ECUADOR
Guayaquil
G. of Guayaquil

Galapagos Islands (Ecuador)

Japurá
Negro
Amazon
Manaus
Belém
São Luis
Equator
Fernando de Noronha (Brazil)

Iquitos
Marañón
Juruá
Purús
Madeira
Tapajós
Xingu
Amazon
Fortaleza
Teresina
Natal
Campina Grande
João Pessoa
Recife

Chiclayo
Trujillo
PERU
Rio Branco
BRAZIL
Araguaia
Tocantins
Parnaíba
Maceió
Aracaju

LIMA
Callao
Huancayo
Cuzco

Salvador

Arequipa
L. Titicaca
BOLIVIA
LA PAZ
Santa Cruz
Cuiabá
BRASÍLIA
Goiânia
São Francisco

Arica
L. Poopó
SUCRE
Cochabamba
Corumbá
Belo Horizonte

Iquique
Vitória
Campos
Ribeirão Prêto
Nova Iguaçu
Trindade (Brazil)
Martin Vaz Is

Antofagasta
PARAGUAY
Campinas
São Paulo
Santos
Rio de Janeiro
Tropic of Capricorn

Salta
ASUNCIÓN
Paraná
Curitiba

San Miguel de Tucumán
Corrientes
Florianopolis

CHILE
Córdoba
Santa Fé
Paraná
Uruguay
Porto Alegre

Valparaíso
Rosario
Parana
Pelotas
URUGUAY
ATLANTIC OCEAN

SANTIAGO
Mendoza
BUENOS AIRES
MONTEVIDEO
La Plata
Río de la Plata

Talcahuano
Concepción
ARGENTINA
Mar del Plata

Puerto Montt
Bahía Blanca

PACIFIC OCEAN

Golfo San Matías

Comodoro Rivadavia

Bahía Grande
Str. of Magellan
Stanley
Falkland Islands (UK)

Punta Arenas

South Georgia (UK)

South Sandwich Is (UK)

Lambert Azimuthal Equal Area projection

POPULATION

Persons per km²
over 100
50-100
10-50
1-10
0-1

Caracas
Medellín
Bogotá
Equator
Fortaleza
Recife
Lima
Salvador
Belo Horizonte
Tropic of Capricorn
Río de Janeiro
São Paulo
Curitiba
Porto Alegre
Santiago
Buenos Aires

Urban population
■ over 10 000 000
■ 5 000 000 - 10 000 000
● 2 500 000 - 5 000 000
· 1 000 000 - 2 500 000

SCALE 1 : 80 000 000

Boundaries
International

Urban population
■ ● over 1 000 000
□ ○ 500 000 - 1 000 000
□ ○ 100 000 - 500 000
□ ○ under 100 000

Square symbols denote national capital cities.

SCALE 1 : 35 000 000
0   400   800   1200 km

A 90° B 80° C 70° D 60° E 50° F 40° G 30° H

Bahamas
Cuba
Greater Antilles
Yucatan Channel
Yucatán
Hispaniola
Puerto Rico
Jamaica
Leeward Is
Sierra Madre
G. of Honduras
C A R I B B E A N   S E A
Lesser Antilles
Windward Is
A T L A N T I C
L. Nicaragua
G. of Darien
Gallinas Pt
Curaçao
O C E A N
Trinidad
Orinoco Delta
I. de Coco
Cordillera Central
Llanos
L. Maracaibo
Orinoco
2810 Mt Roraima ▲
Essequibo
Guiana Highlands
Amazon Delta
Equator
I. de Malpelo
5897 ▲ Cotopaxi
6310 ▲ Chimborazo
Meta
Japurá
Amazon
Negro
Amazon
Fernando de Noronha
Galapagos Islands
G. of Guayaquil
Marañón
Juruá
Purús
Madeira
Tapajós
Xingu
C. de São Roque
Pta Negra
S e l v a s
A N D E S
6768 ▲ Huascarán
Mato Grosso Plateau
Tocantins
Parnaíba
Brazilian
Araguaia
São Francisco
Highlands
P A C I F I C
Atacama Desert
Altiplano
L. Titicaca
L. Poopó
Paraná
O C E A N
Gran Chaco
Paraguay
2797 ▲ Agulhas Negras
Trindade Martin Vaz Is
Tropic of Capricorn
6908 ▲ Ojos del Salado
Paraná
Uruguay
A T L A N T I C
6960 ▲ Aconcagua
P a m p a s
Rio de la Plata
O C E A N
Patagonia
Golfo San Matías
Isla de Chiloé
Bahía Grande
Falkland Islands
Str. of Magellan
Tierra del Fuego
South Georgia
Cape Horn
South Sandwich Is

PHYSICAL REGIONS

A 90° B 80° C

Guiana Highlands
Equator
Central Plains and Lowlands
Brazilian Plateau
Andes Mountains
Tropic of Capricorn

SCALE 1 : 80 000 000

Relief

Relief metres	
	5000
	3000
	2000
	1000
	500
	200
0	sea level
	below sea level
200	
3000	
5000	

6960 ▲ **Mountain height** (in metres)

SCALE 1 : 35 000 000

0   400   800   1200 km

Lambert Azimuthal Equal Area projection

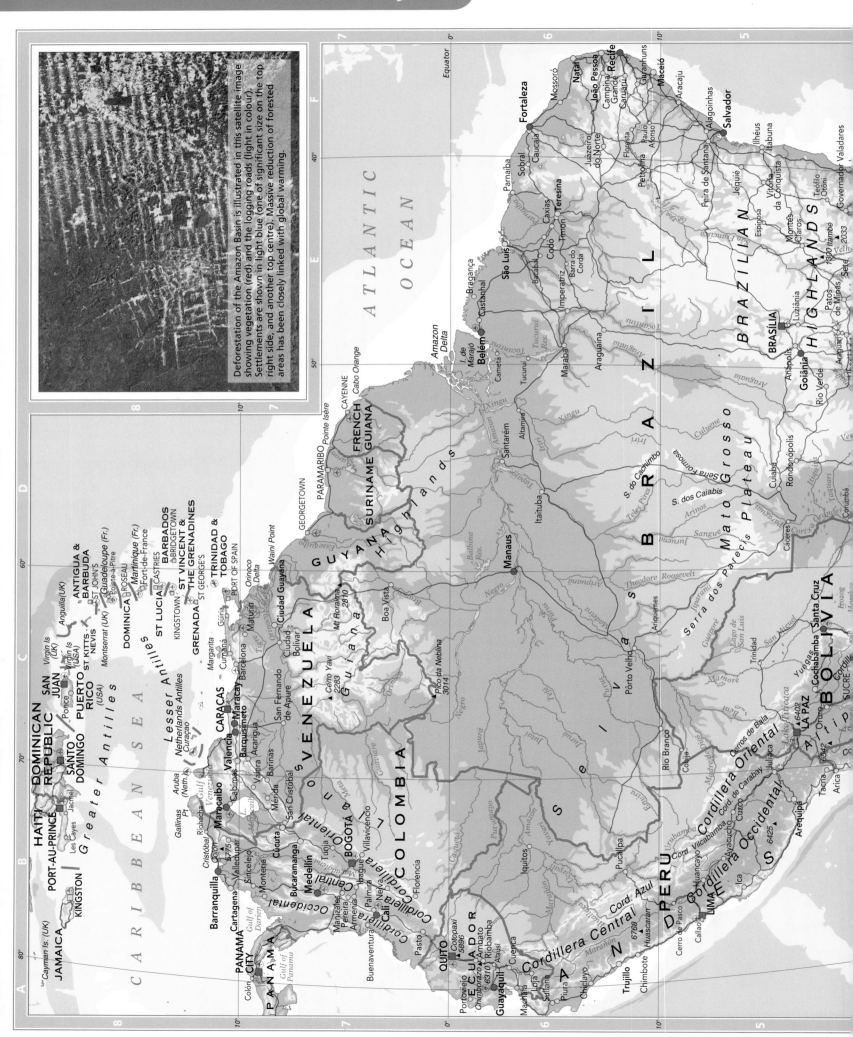

Deforestation of the Amazon Basin is illustrated in this satellite image showing vegetation (red) and the logging roads (light in blue). Settlements are shown in light blue (one of significant size on the top right side, and another top centre). Massive reduction of forested areas has been closely linked with global warming.

ATLANTIC OCEAN

CARIBBEAN SEA

JAMAICA
KINGSTON
HAITI
PORT-AU-PRINCE
DOMINICAN REPUBLIC
SANTO DOMINGO
SAN JUAN
PUERTO RICO (USA)
ANTIGUA & BARBUDA
ST KITTS-NEVIS
DOMINICA
MARTINIQUE (Fr.)
ST LUCIA
BARBADOS
ST VINCENT & THE GRENADINES
GRENADA
TRINIDAD & TOBAGO
PORT OF SPAIN

Greater Antilles
Lesser Antilles
Netherlands Antilles

PANAMA
PANAMA CITY

VENEZUELA
CARACAS
Maracay
Valencia
Barquisimeto
Maracaibo

COLOMBIA
BOGOTÁ
Medellín
Cali
Bucaramanga

ECUADOR
QUITO
Guayaquil

PERU
LIMA

GUYANA
GEORGETOWN
SURINAME
PARAMARIBO
FRENCH GUIANA
CAYENNE

GUYANA HIGHLANDS
Guiana Highlands

BRAZIL
BRAZILIAN HIGHLANDS
BRASÍLIA
Goiânia
Fortaleza
Recife
Salvador
Natal
João Pessoa
Maceió
Belém
São Luís
Manaus
Teresina

Mato Grosso Plateau

BOLIVIA
LA PAZ
SUCRE
Santa Cruz
Cochabamba

ANDES
Cordillera Oriental
Cordillera Occidental
Cordillera Central

Amazon Delta

A N D E S

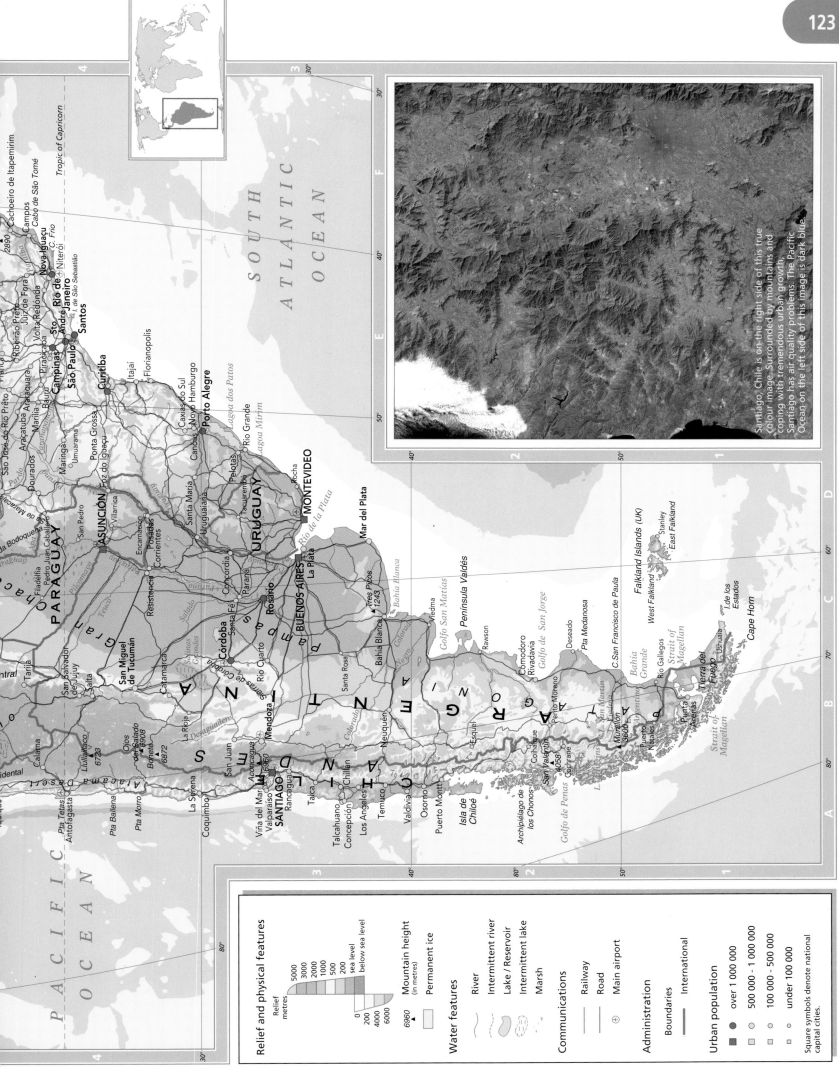

LAND USE

Legend:
- Urban
- Cropland
- Cropland and woodland
- Grassland and grazing
- Grassland and woodland
- Temperate forest
- Tropical forest
- Scrubland or desert
- Swamp and marsh
- Tundra
- • Climograph station

Bogota

Manaus

Recife

Antofagasta

Buenos Aires

Punta Arenas

SCALE 1 : 35 000 000

A continent as vast as South America differs greatly in land use, resources, economic development and culture. The vast tropical rain forests of Amazonia are in sharp contrast to the Atacama Desert, which is one of the driest areas in the world. Although dominated by tropical conditions, the extreme south and the high altitude areas along the plateaus and mountains of the Andes are very cold. Land use in southern Chile is similar to that in Mediterranean areas. Extremes of wealth and poverty have led to political and economic instability in many South American countries. However, most countries are currently moving towards increased democracy and greater social justice.

CLIMATE

BOGOTA, COLOMBIA
Total Precipitation: 944 mm
Temp. °C / Precip. mm
6°
J F M A M J J A S O N D

MANAUS, BRAZIL
Total Precipitation: 2088 mm
Temp. °C / Precip. mm
6°
J F M A M J J A S O N D

RECIFE, BRAZIL
Total Precipitation: 1813 mm
Temp. °C / Precip. mm
6°
J F M A M J J A S O N D

ANTOFAGASTA, CHILE
Total Precipitation: 3.5 mm
Temp. °C / Precip. mm
6°
J F M A M J J A S O N D

PUNTA ARENAS, CHILE
Total Precipitation: 397 mm
Temp. °C / Precip. mm
6°
J F M A M J J A S O N D

BUENOS AIRES, ARGENTINA
Total Precipitation: 1005 mm
Temp. °C / Precip. mm
6°
J F M A M J J A S O N D

TOURISM

Top Destinations, 2000

Country	Income from tourism	
	Millions, US$	Percent of GDP
Guyana	59	8.7
Suriname	53	6.1
Uruguay	652	3.3
Trinidad and Tobago	210	3.1
Ecuador	402	3.0
Bolivia	160	1.9
Peru	1 001	1.9
Colombia	1 028	1.3
Chile	827	1.2
Argentina	2 903	1.0
Paraguay	66	0.9
Brazil	4 228	0.7
Venezuela	656	0.6

COLONIZATION

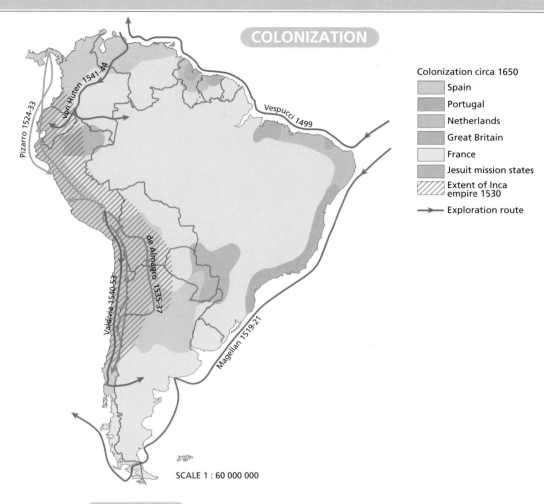

Colonization circa 1650
- Spain
- Portugal
- Netherlands
- Great Britain
- France
- Jesuit mission states
- Extent of Inca empire 1530
- Exploration route

SCALE 1 : 60 000 000

ECONOMY

VENEZUELA

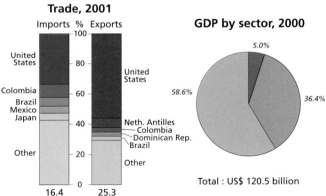

Trade, 2001

Imports % Exports

United States

Colombia
Brazil
Mexico
Japan

United States

Neth. Antilles
Colombia
Dominican Rep.
Brazil

Other

Other

16.4   25.3
Billions of US dollars

GDP by sector, 2000

5.0%
58.6%
36.4%

Total : US$ 120.5 billion

BRAZIL

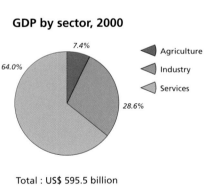

Trade, 2001

Imports % Exports

United States

Argentina
Germany
Japan
Italy
France
South Korea
China
Nigeria
UK
Other

United States

Argentina
Netherlands
Germany
Japan
China
Mexico
Italy
Belgium
UK
Other

58.5   58.2
Billions of US dollars

GDP by sector, 2000

7.4%
64.0%
28.6%

- Agriculture
- Industry
- Services

Total : US$ 595.5 billion

CHILE

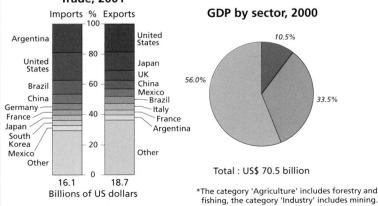

Trade, 2001

Imports % Exports

Argentina

United States

Brazil
China
Germany
France
Japan
South Korea
Mexico
Other

United States

Japan
UK
China
Mexico
Brazil
Italy
France
Argentina

Other

16.1   18.7
Billions of US dollars

GDP by sector, 2000

10.5%
56.0%
33.5%

Total : US$ 70.5 billion

*The category 'Agriculture' includes forestry and fishing, the category 'Industry' includes mining.

EXTERNAL DEBT, 2000

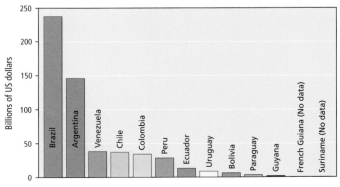

Billions of US dollars

Brazil
Argentina
Venezuela
Chile
Colombia
Peru
Ecuador
Uruguay
Bolivia
Paraguay
Guyana
French Guiana (No data)
Suriname (No data)

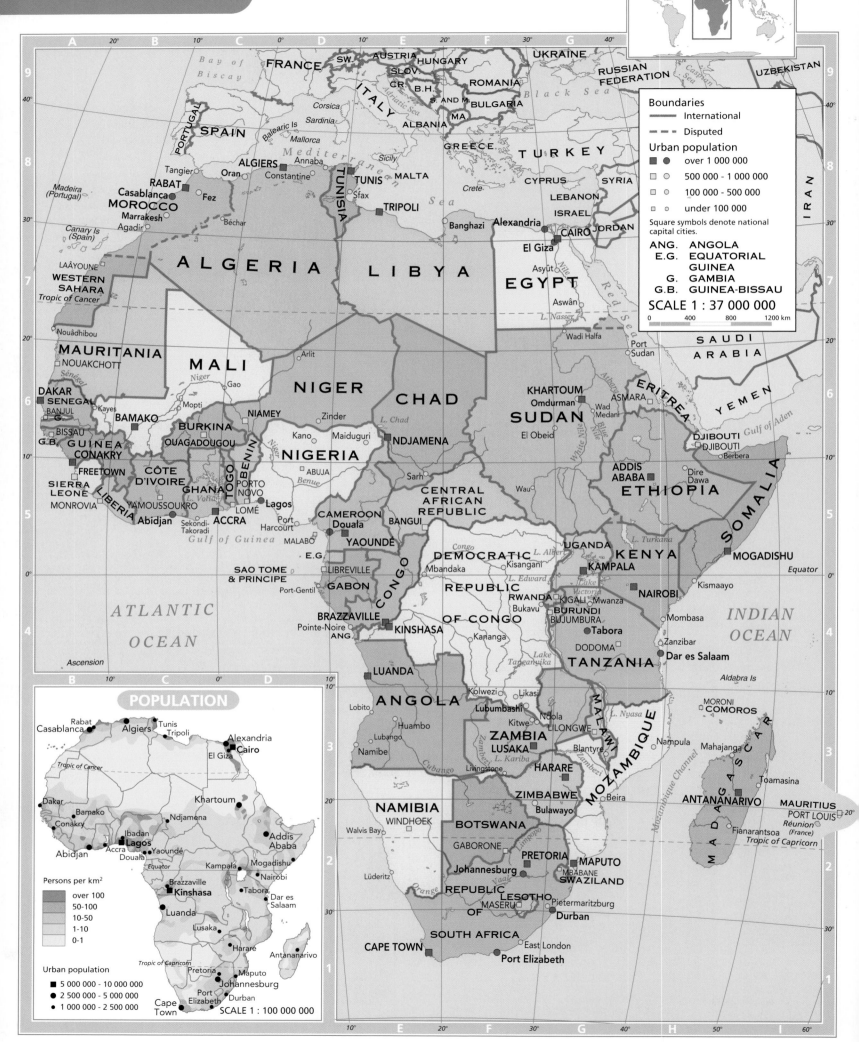

Lambert Azimuthal Equal Area projection

Relief

Relief metres

5000
3000
2000
1000
500
200
0 sea level
200 below sea level
3000
5000

5895 ▲ Mountain height (in metres)

SCALE 1 : 37 000 000

0 400 800 1200 km

Bay of Biscay
C. Finisterre
Pyrenees
Corsica
Sardinia
Balearic Is
Mallorca
Sierra Nevada
C. St Vincent
Madeira
Canary Is
Tenerife
Alps
Apennines
Adriatic Sea
Danube
Black Sea
Caspian Sea
Mediterranean Sea
Sicily
Crete
Taurus Mts
Cyprus
G. of Gabès
Gulf of Sirte
4167 ▲ Jbel Toubkal
Atlas Mountains

S A H A R A   D E S E R T

El Djouf
2918 ▲ Mt Tahat
Hoggar
Djado Plateau
Tibesti
3415 ▲ Emi Koussi
1800 ▲ Mt Gréboun
Aïr
Libyan Desert
Qattara Depression
Suez Canal
Sinai
Nile
L. Nasser
Red Sea
Hijaz
Nubian Desert
'Asir
Rub 'al Khali
Tropic of Cancer

Sénégal
Gambia
Fouta Djallon
C. Palmas
Niger
Bani
Black Volta
White Volta
Lake Volta
L. Chad
Chari
Logone
Benue
Jos Plateau
Darfur
3070 ▲ J. Gimbala
Blue Nile
White Nile
Gezira
Athara
Akobo
4620 ▲ Ras Dashen
Denakil
L. Tana
Ethiopian Highlands
Gulf of Aden
Shabeelle

Bight of Benin
Gulf of Guinea
Adamawa Highlands
4100 ▲ Mt Cameroun
Bioco
Príncipe
São Tomé
Sanaga
Ubangi
Uele
Aruwimi
Congo
Congo Basin
Kasai
Kwilu
Cuanza
Cuango
L. Albert
L. Edward
5110 ▲ Mt Stanley
Lake Victoria
5199 ▲ Mt Kenya
L. Turkana
Juba
Sudd
Masai Steppe
5895 ▲ Kilimanjaro
Pemba I.
Zanzibar I.
Mafia I.
Rufiji
Equator

ATLANTIC OCEAN
Ascension

INDIAN OCEAN
Aldabra Is

Congo
Lake Tanganyika
Chaîne des Mitumba
Great Rift Valley
L. Mweru
Luapula
Muchinga Mts
Luangwa
L. Nyasa
Comoro Islands

Bié Plateau
Okavango
Cubango
Cunene
Etosha Pan
Makgadikgadi
Namib Desert
K a l a h a r i   D e s e r t
Zambezi
L. Kariba
Victoria Falls
Matabèle Upland
Save
Limpopo
Mozambique Channel
Madagascar
Mauritius
Réunion
Tropic of Capricorn

Orange
Vaal
3482 ▲ Thabana Ntlenyana
Drakensberg
Great Karoo
Cape of Good Hope
C. Agulhas

Lambert Azimuthal Equal Area projection

PHYSICAL REGIONS

Northern Highlands
Tropic of Cancer
Western Plateau
Nile Basin
Coastal Lowlands
Equator
Congo Basin
Eastern Highlands
Great Rift Valley
Great Rift Valley
Coastal Lowlands
Southern Plateau
Tropic of Capricorn
Central Highlands

SCALE 1 : 100 000 000

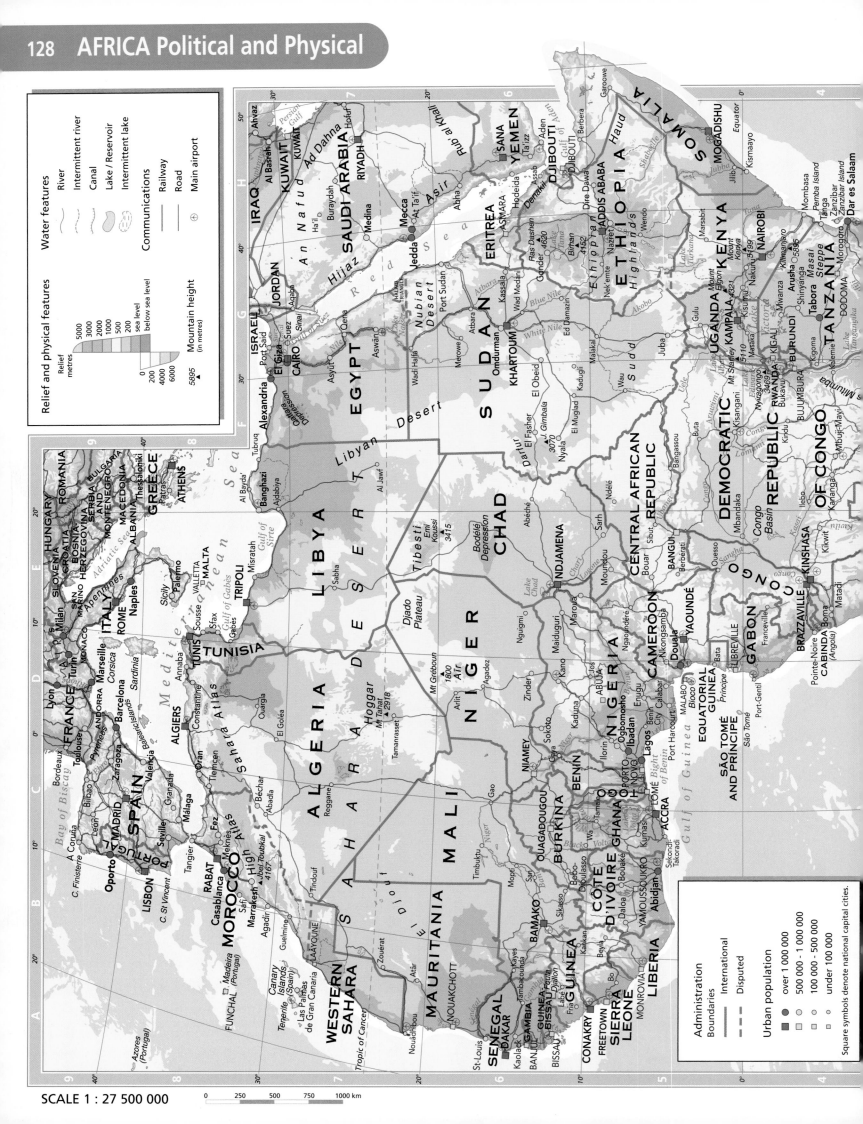

Relief and physical features

Water features

- River
- Intermittent river
- Canal
- Lake / Reservoir
- Intermittent lake

Communications

- Railway
- Road
- ⊕ Main airport

Relief
metres
5000
3000
2000
1000
500
200
sea level
below sea level

0
200
4000
6000

5895 ▲ Mountain height
(in metres)

Administration

Boundaries
— International
--- Disputed

Urban population
- ● over 1 000 000
- ○ 500 000 - 1 000 000
- ○ 100 000 - 500 000
- ○ under 100 000

Square symbols denote national capital cities.

SCALE 1 : 27 500 000

0   250   500   750   1000 km

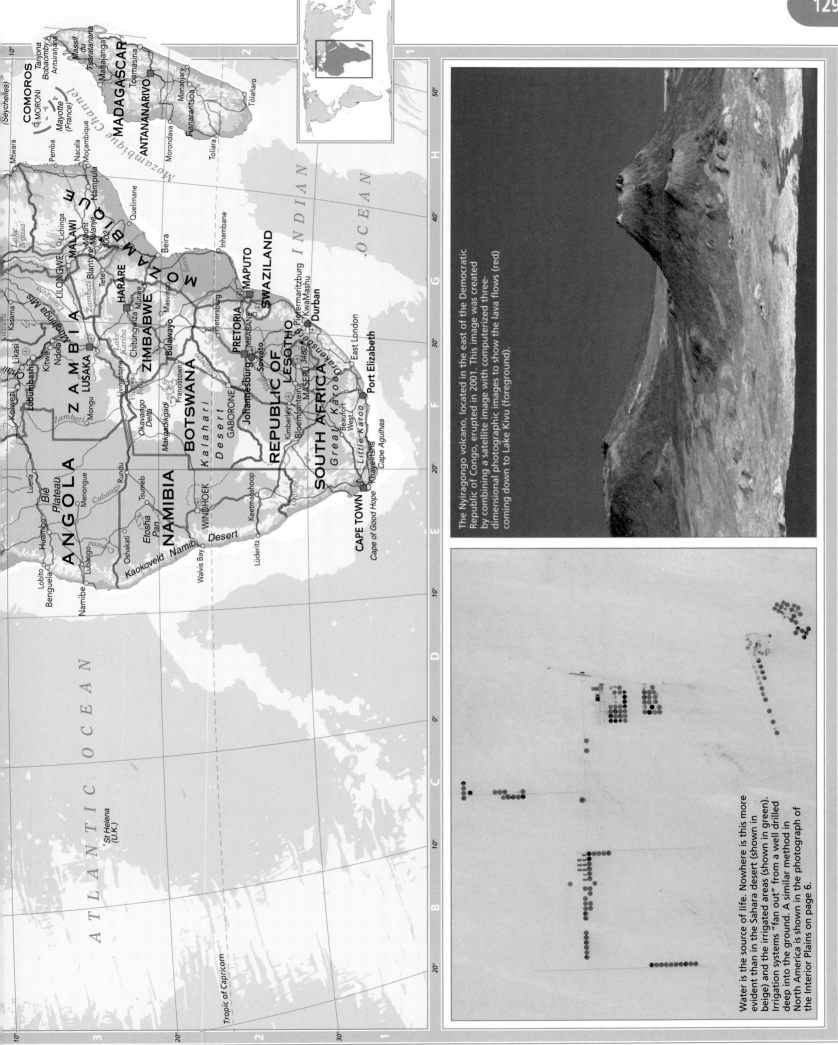

(Seychelles)

COMOROS
MORONI
Mayotte (France)

MADAGASCAR
ANTANANARIVO

Tanjona Bobaomby
Massif du Tsaratanana
Antsiranana
Mahajanga
Toamasina
Mananjary
Fianarantsoa
Morondava
Toliara
Tôlañaro

Mozambique Channel

Mtwara
Pemba
Nacala
Moçambique
Nampula

Lake Nyasa
Lichinga
Quelimane

MALAWI
MOZAMBIQUE

LILONGWE
Blantyre
Mount Mlanje 3002

Luangwa Mts

Kasama

Tete
Zambezi
HARARE
Mutare
Beira
Inhambane

ZAMBIA
LUSAKA

ZIMBABWE
Masvingo

Chitungwiza
Bulawayo

MAPUTO
SWAZILAND
MBABANE

Kariba
Lake Kariba
Livingstone

Victoria Falls

Kabwe
Ndola
Kitwe
Kwekwe

Pietersburg
PRETORIA
Johannesburg
Soweto

Pietermaritzburg
KwaMashu
Durban

LESOTHO
MASERU 3482

Kolwezi
Likasi
Lubumbashi

Mongu

Okavango Delta
Francistown
GABORONE

Bloemfontein
Kimberley

BOTSWANA
Makgadikgadi
Kalahari Desert

SOUTH AFRICA
Beaufort West
Great Karoo
Little Karoo

East London
Port Elizabeth

ANGOLA

Luena
Bié Plateau
Menongue
Cubango

Rundu
Tsumeb

Drakensberg

Huambo
Benguela
Lobito

Cunene

NAMIBIA
Etosha Pan
Oshakati

WINDHOEK

Keetmanshoop
Upington

Knysna
Khayelitsha
Cape Agulhas

CAPE TOWN
Cape of Good Hope

Namibe
Namib Desert
Walvis Bay
Lüderitz

Kaokoveld

Orange

ATLANTIC OCEAN

St Helena (U.K.)

Tropic of Capricorn

INDIAN OCEAN

The Nyiragongo volcano, located in the east of the Democratic Republic of Congo, erupted in 2001. This image was created by combining a satellite image with computerized three-dimensional photographic images to show the lava flows (red) coming down to Lake Kivu (foreground).

Water is the source of life. Nowhere is this more evident than in the Sahara desert (shown in beige) and the irrigated areas (shown in green). Irrigation systems "fan out" from a well drilled deep into the ground. A similar method in North America is shown in the photograph of the Interior Plains on page 6.

Lambert Azimuthal Equal Area projection

LAND USE

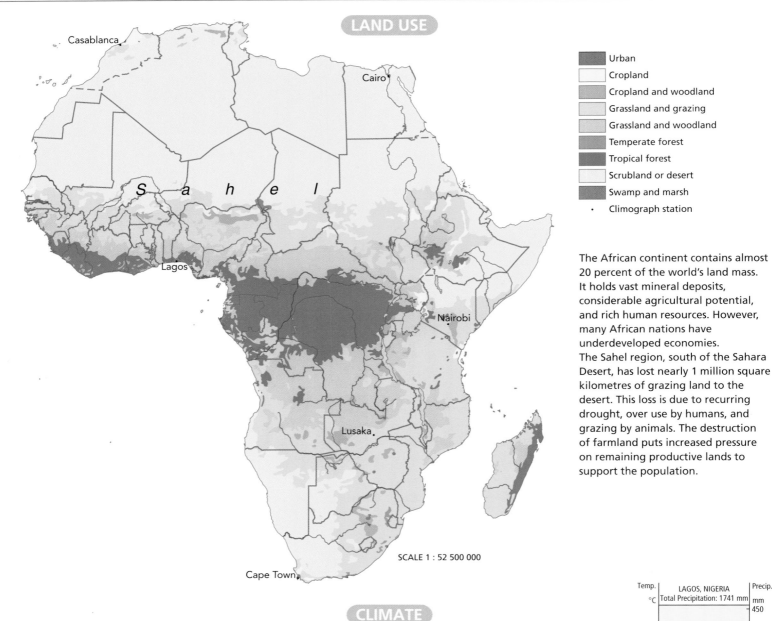

Legend:
- Urban
- Cropland
- Cropland and woodland
- Grassland and grazing
- Grassland and woodland
- Temperate forest
- Tropical forest
- Scrubland or desert
- Swamp and marsh
- Climograph station

SCALE 1 : 52 500 000

The African continent contains almost 20 percent of the world's land mass. It holds vast mineral deposits, considerable agricultural potential, and rich human resources. However, many African nations have underdeveloped economies.
The Sahel region, south of the Sahara Desert, has lost nearly 1 million square kilometres of grazing land to the desert. This loss is due to recurring drought, over use by humans, and grazing by animals. The destruction of farmland puts increased pressure on remaining productive lands to support the population.

CLIMATE

RAINFALL VARIABILITY IN THE SAHEL

All areas of the world experience variations in precipitation. In the Sahel, variability is high – very different from one year to the next. The black line in the graph below indicates average rainfall, while the red bars indicate years of lower-than-average rainfall. Even in the years of above-average rainfall (green bars), precipitation has not been enough to replenish the soil moisture and meet the needs of plants.

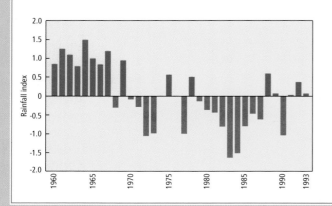

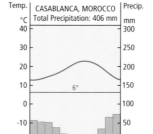

CASABLANCA, MOROCCO — Total Precipitation: 406 mm

CAIRO, EGYPT — Total Precipitation: 25 mm

LAGOS, NIGERIA — Total Precipitation: 1741 mm

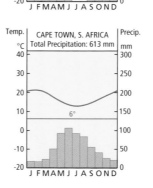

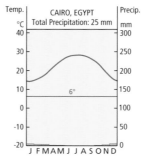

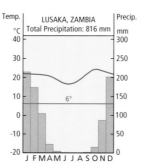

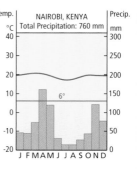

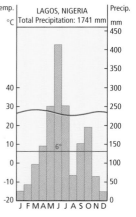

CAPE TOWN, S. AFRICA — Total Precipitation: 613 mm

LUSAKA, ZAMBIA — Total Precipitation: 816 mm

NAIROBI, KENYA — Total Precipitation: 760 mm

TOURISM

Top Destinations, 2000

Country	Income from tourism	
	Millions, US$	Percent of GDP
Seychelles	110	17.9
Mauritius	585	13.4
Comoros	19	8.5
Tanzania	739	8.2
Tunisia	1 496	7.7
Morocco	2 040	6.1
Eritrea	36	5.9
Botswana	234	4.6
Egypt	4 345	4.4
Cape Verde	23	3.9
Ghana	304	3.9
Zimbabwe	202	3.7
Senegal	166	3.5
Zambia	91	3.1
Madagascar	116	3.0
Kenya	304	2.9
Mauritania	28	2.9
Swaziland	35	2.6
Uganda	149	2.3
Mali	50	2.2
Lesotho	19	2.1
Sierra Leone	12	1.9
South Africa	2 526	1.9
Malawi	27	1.6
Niger	24	1.2
Rwanda	17	0.9
Libya	28	0.7
Ethiopia	24	0.4
Guinea	12	0.4
Togo	6	0.4

COLONIZATION AND INDEPENDENCE

Colonial powers in 1914

- Belgium
- France
- Germany
- United Kingdom
- Italy
- Portugal
- Spain
- Independent

1960 Year of independence

BU.: BURUNDI
G.: GAMBIA
G.B.: GUINEA BISSAU
R.: RWANDA
T.: TOGO

SCALE 1 : 70 000 000

ECONOMY

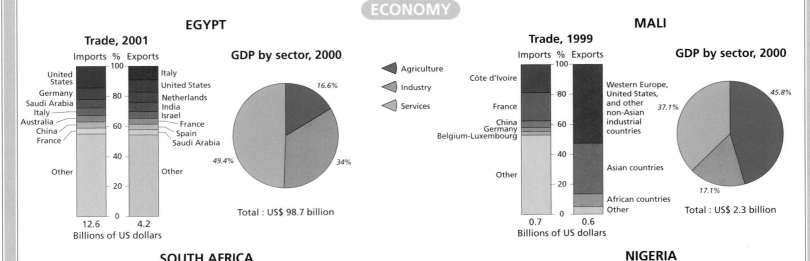

EGYPT

Trade, 2001

Imports % Exports

Imports: United States, Germany, Saudi Arabia, Italy, Australia, China, France, Other
Exports: Italy, United States, Netherlands, India, Israel, France, Spain, Saudi Arabia, Other

12.6   4.2
Billions of US dollars

GDP by sector, 2000

16.6%
49.4%   34%

Total : US$ 98.7 billion

Agriculture
Industry
Services

MALI

Trade, 1999

Imports % Exports

Imports: Côte d'Ivoire, France, China, Germany, Belgium-Luxembourg, Other
Exports: Western Europe, United States, and other non-Asian industrial countries, Asian countries, African countries, Other

0.7   0.6
Billions of US dollars

GDP by sector, 2000

45.8%
37.1%
17.1%

Total : US$ 2.3 billion

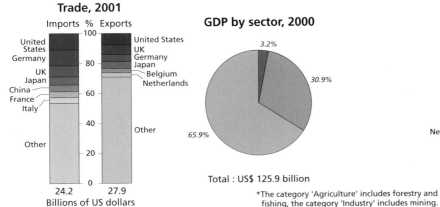

SOUTH AFRICA

Trade, 2001

Imports % Exports

Imports: United States, Germany, UK, Japan, China, France, Italy, Other
Exports: United States, UK, Germany, Japan, Belgium, Netherlands, Other

24.2   27.9
Billions of US dollars

GDP by sector, 2000

3.2%
30.9%
65.9%

Total : US$ 125.9 billion

*The category 'Agriculture' includes forestry and fishing, the category 'Industry' includes mining.

NIGERIA

Trade, 2000

Imports % Exports

Imports: UK, United States, Germany, France, Belgium, Japan, Italy, China, Netherlands, Other
Exports: United States, India, Spain, France, Italy, Côte d'Ivoire, Other

5.8   27.0
Billions of US dollars

GDP by sector, 2000

24.5%   29.5%
46%

Total : US$ 41.1 billion

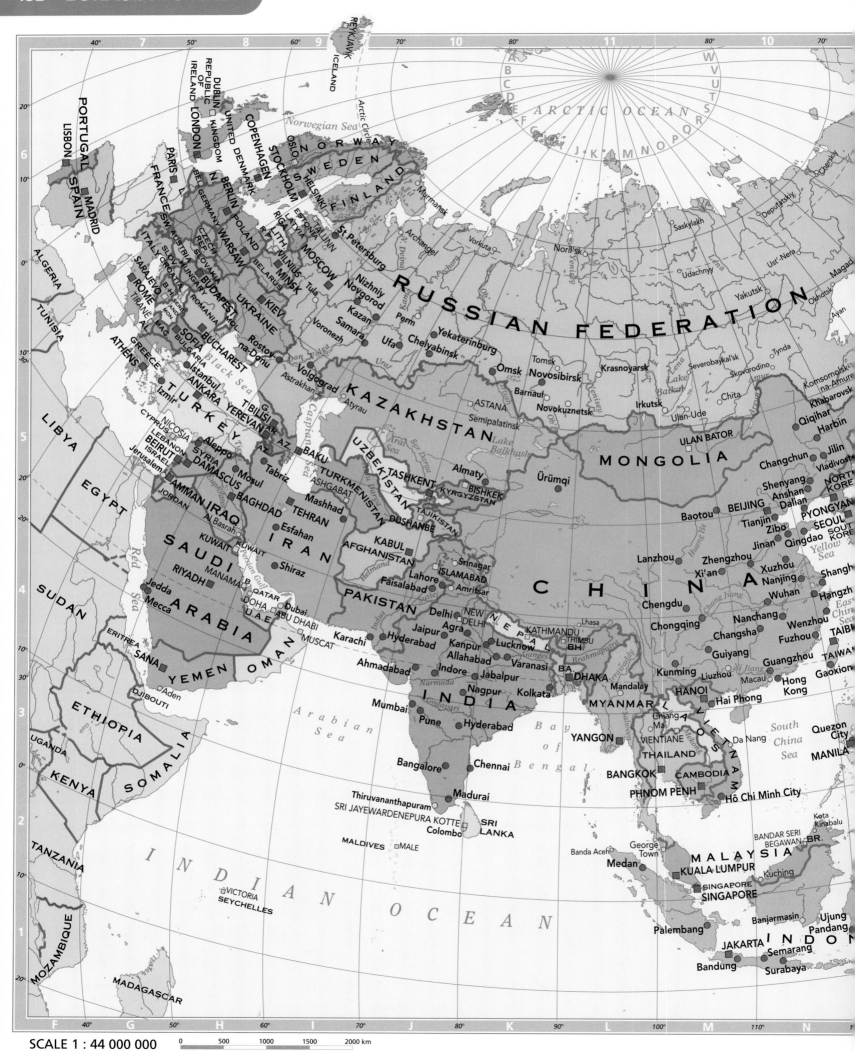

SCALE 1 : 44 000 000

0   500   1000   1500   2000 km

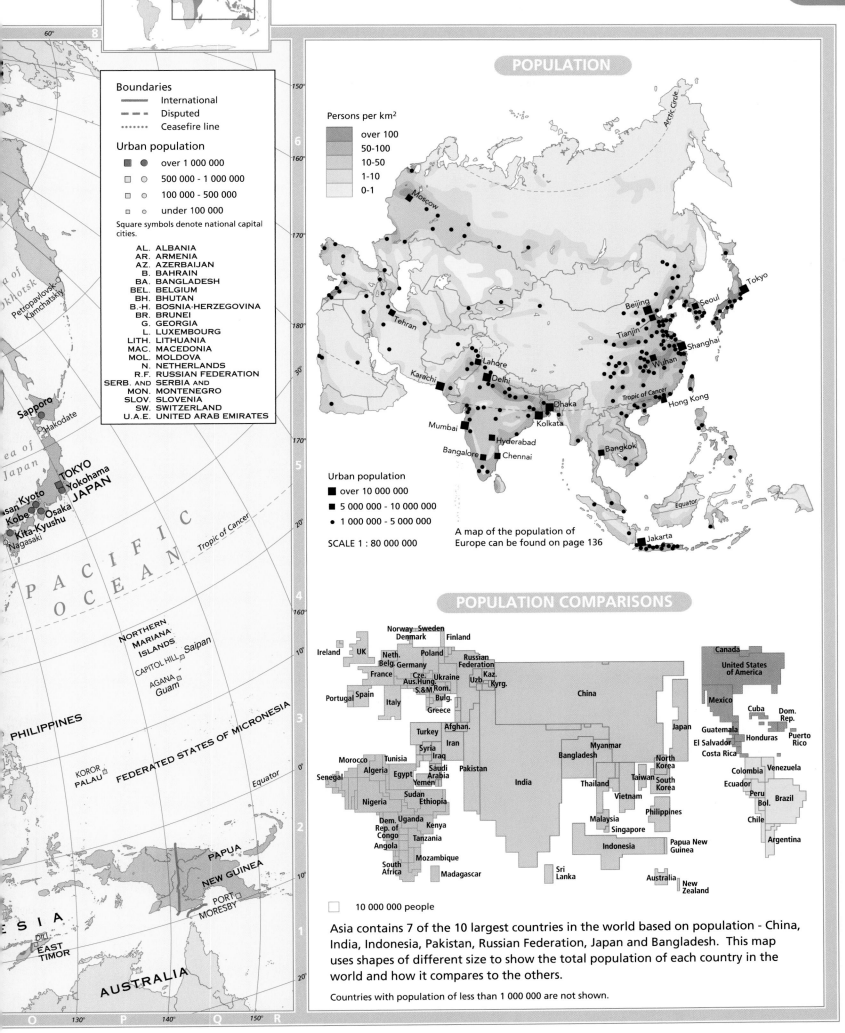

POPULATION

Persons per km²
- over 100
- 50-100
- 10-50
- 1-10
- 0-1

Urban population
- ■ over 10 000 000
- ■ 5 000 000 - 10 000 000
- • 1 000 000 - 5 000 000

SCALE 1 : 80 000 000

A map of the population of Europe can be found on page 136

Boundaries
- International
- Disputed
- Ceasefire line

Urban population
- over 1 000 000
- 500 000 - 1 000 000
- 100 000 - 500 000
- under 100 000

Square symbols denote national capital cities.

AL. ALBANIA
AR. ARMENIA
AZ. AZERBAIJAN
B. BAHRAIN
BA. BANGLADESH
BEL. BELGIUM
BH. BHUTAN
B.-H. BOSNIA-HERZEGOVINA
BR. BRUNEI
G. GEORGIA
L. LUXEMBOURG
LITH. LITHUANIA
MAC. MACEDONIA
MOL. MOLDOVA
N. NETHERLANDS
R.F. RUSSIAN FEDERATION
SERB. AND SERBIA AND
MON. MONTENEGRO
SLOV. SLOVENIA
SW. SWITZERLAND
U.A.E. UNITED ARAB EMIRATES

POPULATION COMPARISONS

☐ 10 000 000 people

Asia contains 7 of the 10 largest countries in the world based on population - China, India, Indonesia, Pakistan, Russian Federation, Japan and Bangladesh. This map uses shapes of different size to show the total population of each country in the world and how it compares to the others.

Countries with population of less than 1 000 000 are not shown.

Lambert Azimuthal Equal Area projection

SCALE 1 : 44 000 000

0   500   1000   1500   2000 km

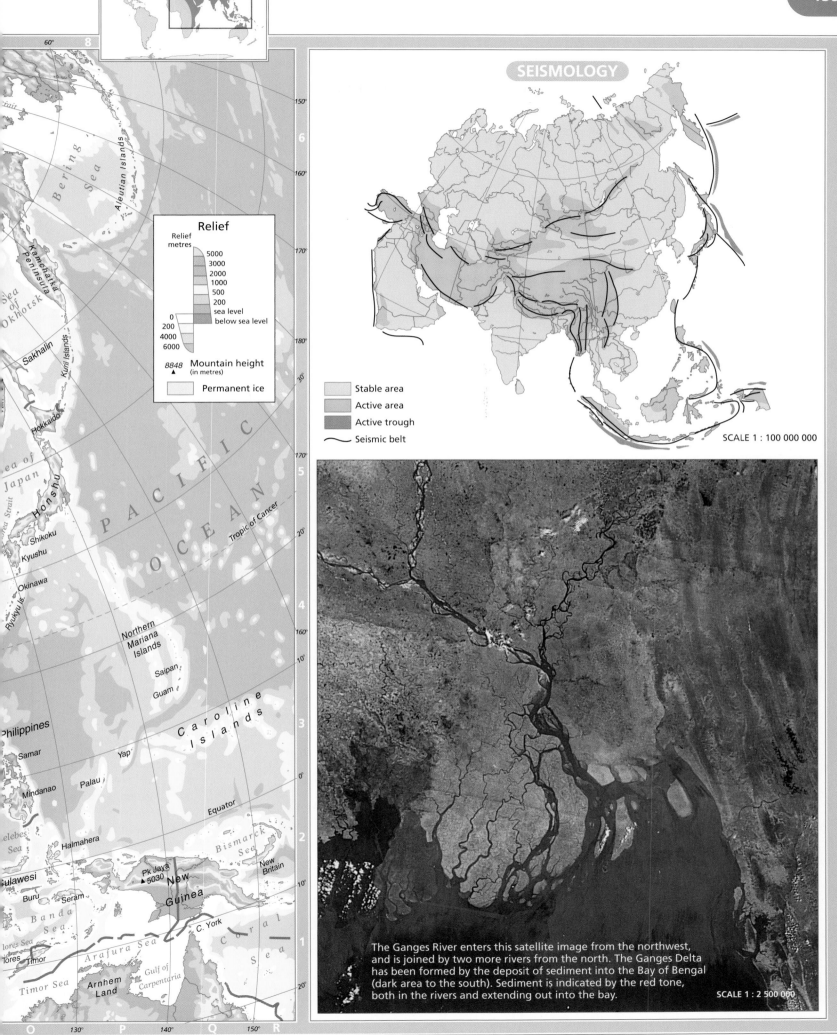

Relief

Relief
metres

5000
3000
2000
1000
500
200
0 sea level
below sea level
200
4000
6000

8848 ▲ Mountain height
(in metres)

Permanent ice

SEISMOLOGY

Stable area

Active area

Active trough

Seismic belt

SCALE 1 : 100 000 000

The Ganges River enters this satellite image from the northwest, and is joined by two more rivers from the north. The Ganges Delta has been formed by the deposit of sediment into the Bay of Bengal (dark area to the south). Sediment is indicated by the red tone, both in the rivers and extending out into the bay.

SCALE 1 : 2 500 000

Lambert Azimuthal Equal Area projection

Boundaries

——————	International
– – – – –	Disputed
··········	Ceasefire line

Urban population

■	●	over 1 000 000
□	○	500 000 - 1 000 000
□	○	100 000 - 500 000
□	○	under 100 000

Square symbols denote national capital cities.

Country abbreviations

A.	ANDORRA
AZ.	AZERBAIJAN
B.H.	BOSNIA-HERZEGOVINA
BEL.	BELGIUM
L.	LIECHTENSTEIN
LUX.	LUXEMBOURG
MAC.	MACEDONIA
NETH.	NETHERLANDS
SL.	SLOVENIA
SW.	SWITZERLAND

SCALE 1 : 25 000 000

0   300   600   900 km

POPULATION

Urban population
- ■ 5 000 000 - 10 000 000
- ● 2 500 000 - 5 000 000
- • 1 000 000 - 2 500 000

Persons per km²

	over 100
	50-100
	10-50
	1-10
	0-1

SCALE 1 : 45 000 000

Lambert Azimuthal Equal Area projection

EUROPE'S CHANGING BOUNDARIES

1914, The Eve of the First World War

SCALE 1 : 42 500 000

1925, The Aftermath of the First World War

SCALE 1 : 42 500 000

1949, Cold War Europe

SCALE 1 : 42 500 000

2003, The European Union

Member of the E.U.

Countries expected to join the E.U.

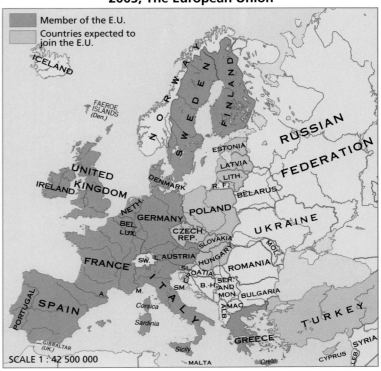

SCALE 1 : 42 500 000

Abbreviations

ALB.	ALBANIA
A.	ANDORRA
B.-H.	BOSNIA-HERZEGOVINA
BEL.	BELGIUM
CZECH REP.	CZECH REPUBLIC
FED. REP. OF GER.	FEDERAL REPUBLIC OF GERMANY
F. S. OF TR.	FREE STATE OF TRIESTE
GER.	GERMANY
GER. DEM. REP.	GERMAN DEMOCRATIC REPUBLIC
L.	LIECHTENSTEIN
LEB.	LEBANON
LITH.	LITHUANIA
LUX.	LUXEMBOURG
M.	MONACO
MAC.	MACEDONIA
MOL.	MOLDOVA
MONT.	MONTENEGRO
NETH.	NETHERLANDS
R. F.	RUSSIAN FEDERATION
SER. AND MON.	SERBIA AND MONTENEGRO
SL.	SLOVENIA
SM.	SAN MARINO
SW.	SWITZERLAND

0   200   400   600   800 km

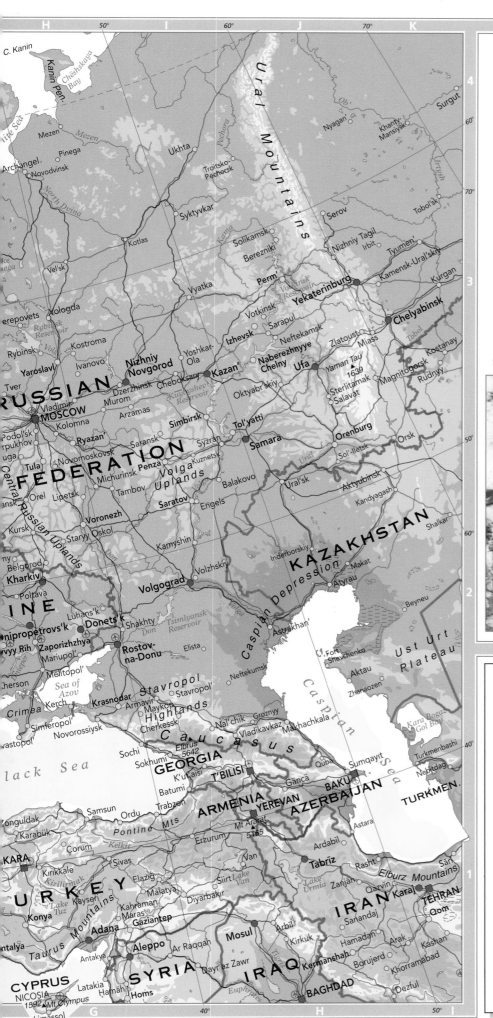

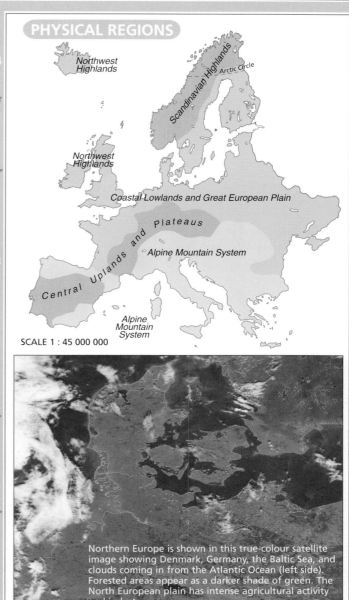

PHYSICAL REGIONS

Northwest Highlands

Scandinavian Highlands

Arctic Circle

Northwest Highlands

Coastal Lowlands and Great European Plain

Central Uplands and Plateaus

Alpine Mountain System

Alpine Mountain System

SCALE 1 : 45 000 000

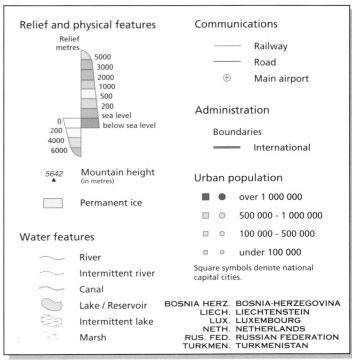

Northern Europe is shown in this true-colour satellite image showing Denmark, Germany, the Baltic Sea, and clouds coming in from the Atlantic Ocean (left side). Forested areas appear as a darker shade of green. The North European plain has intense agricultural activity and industry.

Relief and physical features

Relief metres

5000
3000
2000
1000
500
200
0 sea level
   below sea level
200
4000
6000

5642 ▲ Mountain height (in metres)

Permanent ice

Water features

~~~ River

~~~ Intermittent river

~~~ Canal

Lake / Reservoir

Intermittent lake

Marsh

Communications

——— Railway

——— Road

⊕ Main airport

Administration

Boundaries

━━━ International

Urban population

■ ● over 1 000 000

□ ○ 500 000 - 1 000 000

□ ○ 100 000 - 500 000

□ ○ under 100 000

Square symbols denote national capital cities.

BOSNIA HERZ. BOSNIA-HERZEGOVINA
LIECH. LIECHTENSTEIN
LUX. LUXEMBOURG
NETH. NETHERLANDS
RUS. FED. RUSSIAN FEDERATION
TURKMEN. TURKMENISTAN

Lambert Azimuthal Equal Area projection

LAND USE

Urban
Cropland
Cropland, grassland and woodland
Grassland and grazing
Grassland and woodland
Temperate forest
Coniferous forest
Scrubland or desert
Tundra
• Climograph station

Helsinki

Aberdeen

Warsaw

Paris

Vienna

SCALE 1 : 27 000 000

Athens

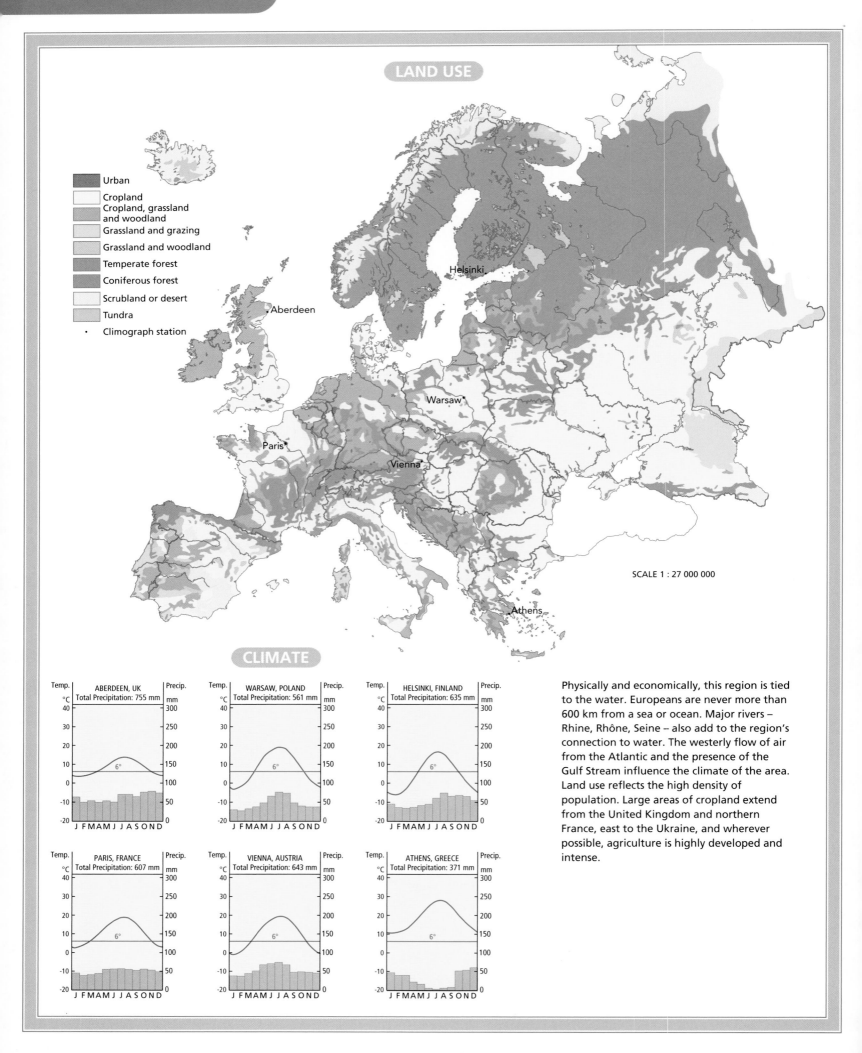

CLIMATE

Physically and economically, this region is tied to the water. Europeans are never more than 600 km from a sea or ocean. Major rivers – Rhine, Rhône, Seine – also add to the region's connection to water. The westerly flow of air from the Atlantic and the presence of the Gulf Stream influence the climate of the area. Land use reflects the high density of population. Large areas of cropland extend from the United Kingdom and northern France, east to the Ukraine, and wherever possible, agriculture is highly developed and intense.

ABERDEEN, UK
Total Precipitation: 755 mm
Temp. °C / Precip. mm
6°

WARSAW, POLAND
Total Precipitation: 561 mm
Temp. °C / Precip. mm
6°

HELSINKI, FINLAND
Total Precipitation: 635 mm
Temp. °C / Precip. mm
6°

PARIS, FRANCE
Total Precipitation: 607 mm
Temp. °C / Precip. mm
6°

VIENNA, AUSTRIA
Total Precipitation: 643 mm
Temp. °C / Precip. mm
6°

ATHENS, GREECE
Total Precipitation: 371 mm
Temp. °C / Precip. mm
6°

TOURISM

Top Destinations by Expenditure, 2000

Country	Income from tourism		Country	Income from tourism	
	Millions, US$	Percent of GDP		Millions, US$	Percent of GDP
Spain	31 000	5.5	Denmark	4 025	2.5
France	29 900	2.3	Ireland	3 571	3.8
Italy	27 439	2.5	Hungary	3 424	7.5
United Kingdom	19 544	1.4	Czech. Republic	2 869	5.6
Germany	17 812	0.9	Croatia	2 758	14.5
Austria	11 440	6.0	Norway	* 2 229	1.4
Greece	9 221	8.2	Ukraine	* 2 124	6.7
Russian Fed.	* 7 510	3.9	Finland	1 401	1.1
Switzerland	7 303	3.0	Bulgaria	1 074	8.9
Belgium	* 7 039	2.8	Slovenia	957	5.3
Netherlands	6 951	1.9	Malta	650	18.2
Poland	6 100	3.9	Estonia	505	10.2
Portugal	5 206	4.9	Slovakia	432	2.2
Sweden	4 107	1.8	Georgia	* 400	14.2

* 1999 figures

Top Destinations by Visitors, 2000

Country	Visitors (thousands)	Country	Visitors (thousands)
France	75 500	Croatia	5 831
Spain	48 201	Czech. Republic	5 700
Italy	41 182	Norway	* 4 481
United Kingdom	25 191	Ukraine	* 4 232
Russian Fed.	21 169	Romania	3 274
Germany	18 983	Andorra	2 949
Austria	17 982	Bulgaria	2 785
Poland	17 400	Sweden	2 746
Greece	12 500	Finland	2 700
Portugal	12 037	Cyprus	2 686
Switzerland	11 400	Denmark	2 088
Netherlands	10 200	Lithuania	1 226
Ireland	6 728	Malta	1 216
Belgium	6 457	Estonia	1 100

* 1999 figures

ECONOMY

WORLD GDP, 2000

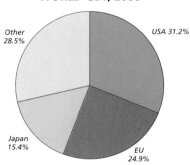

Other 28.5%

USA 31.2%

Japan 15.4%

EU 24.9%

Total World GDP : US$ 31.5 trillion

Europe was the first major world region to construct a modern economy, consisting of a strong base in commercial agriculture and advanced industrial development. During the latter half of the twentieth century, two organizations – the European Economic Community (EEC) and the European Free Trade Association (EFTA) – started the process of economic integration that allowed the region to develop into an economic powerhouse. Average per capita incomes are among the world's highest. The European Union (EU) allows the free flow of people, goods, and services across its members' borders, and continues to incorporate more partner countries. The Council of Ministers, which meets in Brussels, is the EU's decision-making body. The European Court of Justice, located in Luxembourg, rules on disputes among member nations. A common currency, the Euro, has been adopted to replace the local currency in most of the Union nations.

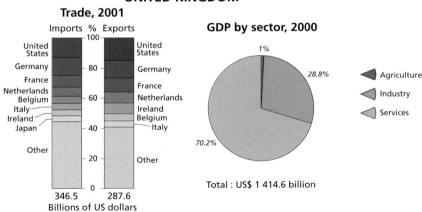

UNITED KINGDOM

Trade, 2001

Imports % Exports

United States, Germany, France, Netherlands, Belgium, Italy, Ireland, Japan, Other

United States, Germany, France, Netherlands, Ireland, Belgium, Italy, Other

346.5   287.6
Billions of US dollars

GDP by sector, 2000

1%
28.8%
70.2%

Total : US$ 1 414.6 billion

- Agriculture
- Industry
- Services

POLAND

Trade, 2001

Imports % Exports

Germany, Russian Fed., Italy, France, UK, Netherlands, Czech Rep., United States, Other

Germany, Italy, France, UK, Netherlands, Czech Rep., Belgium, Russian Fed., Other

50.2   36.1
Billions of US dollars

GDP by sector, 2000

3.8%
36.2%
60%

Total : US$ 157.7 billion

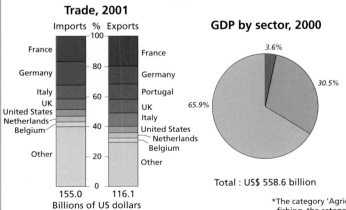

SPAIN

Trade, 2001

Imports % Exports

France, Germany, Italy, UK, United States, Netherlands, Belgium, Other

France, Germany, Portugal, UK, Italy, United States, Netherlands, Belgium, Other

155.0   116.1
Billions of US dollars

GDP by sector, 2000

3.6%
30.5%
65.9%

Total : US$ 558.6 billion

*The category 'Agriculture' includes forestry and fishing, the category 'Industry' includes mining.

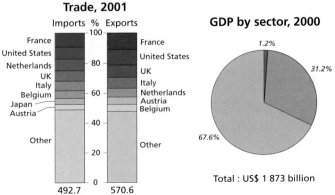

GERMANY

Trade, 2001

Imports % Exports

France, United States, Netherlands, UK, Italy, Belgium, Japan, Austria, Other

France, United States, UK, Italy, Netherlands, Austria, Belgium, Other

492.7   570.6
Billions of US dollars

GDP by sector, 2000

1.2%
31.2%
67.6%

Total : US$ 1 873 billion

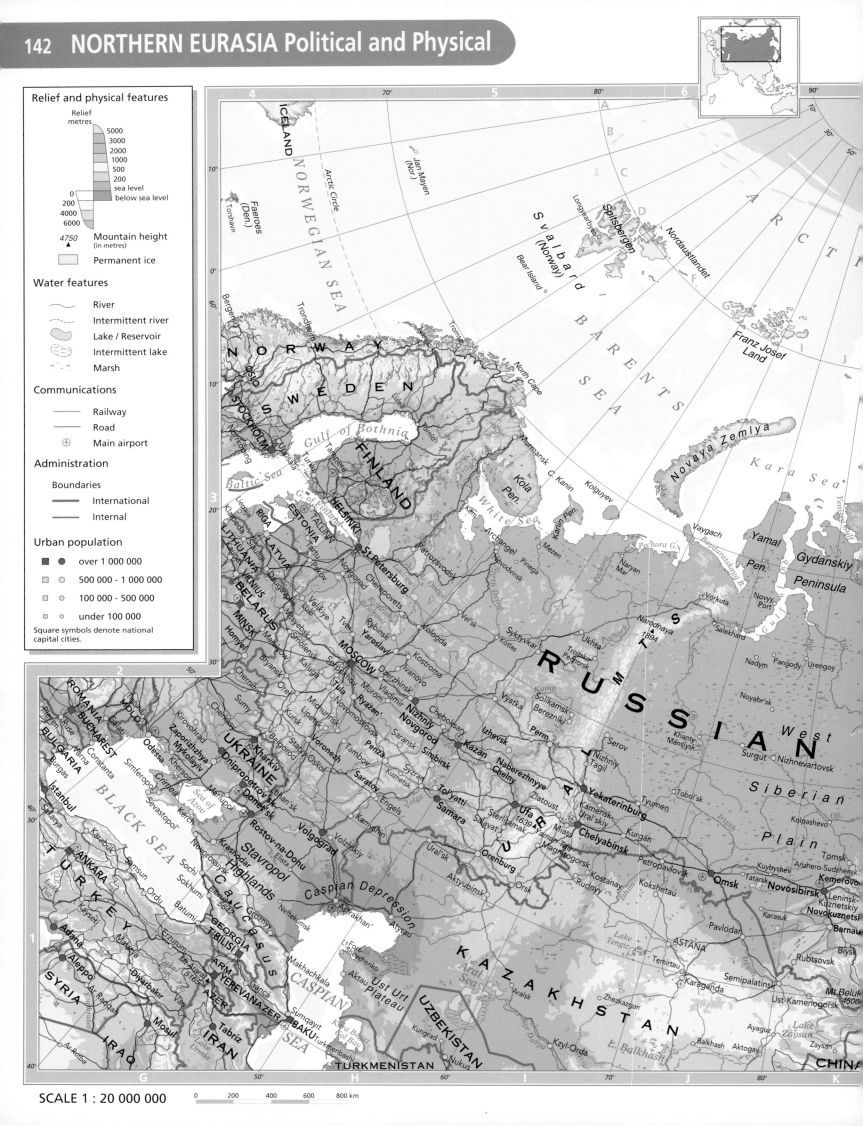

Relief and physical features

Relief
metres

5000
3000
2000
1000
500
200
sea level
0
200
4000
6000
below sea level

4750 ▲ Mountain height (in metres)

Permanent ice

Water features

~ River

Intermittent river

Lake / Reservoir

Intermittent lake

Marsh

Communications

Railway

Road

⊕ Main airport

Administration

Boundaries

International

Internal

Urban population

■ ● over 1 000 000

□ ○ 500 000 - 1 000 000

□ ○ 100 000 - 500 000

□ ○ under 100 000

Square symbols denote national capital cities.

SCALE 1 : 20 000 000

0 200 400 600 800 km

Conic Equidistant projection

LAND USE

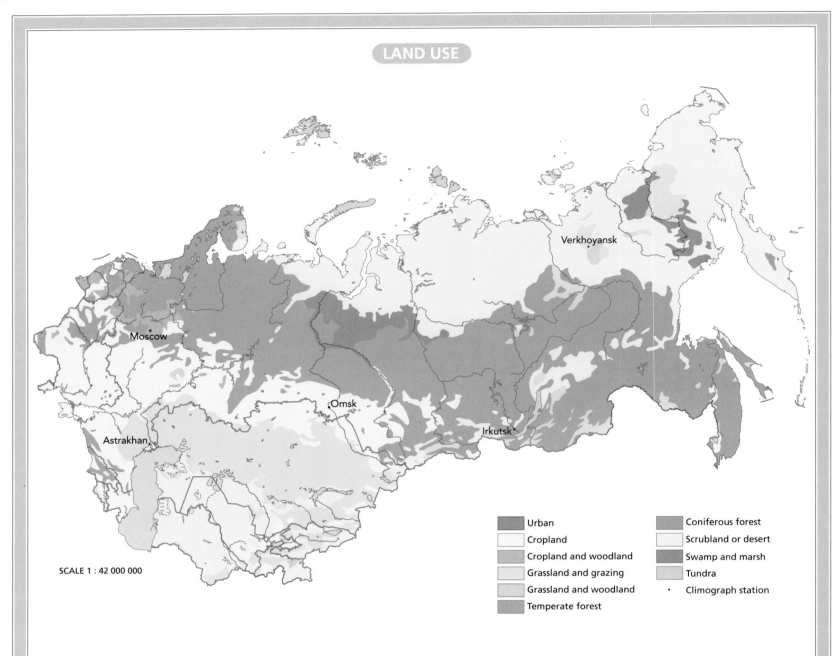

Verkhoyansk

Moscow

Omsk

Irkutsk

Astrakhan

SCALE 1 : 42 000 000

	Urban		Coniferous forest
	Cropland		Scrubland or desert
	Cropland and woodland		Swamp and marsh
	Grassland and grazing		Tundra
	Grassland and woodland	•	Climograph station
	Temperate forest		

Because of its size, no region can match the range of land uses and climatic conditions found in Northern Eurasia, from the polar ice and cold deserts of Siberia to the hot deserts of Turkmenistan. The vast nature of the region is also emphasized in its longitudinal extent: from 20°E to 170°W – almost half the circumference of the earth.

The Russian Federation continues to dominate the region, although the former Soviet Union collapsed in the late 1980s. In recent years, the former Soviet states have had difficulty reaching an appropriate balance in achieving economic development, political stability, human rights and environmental goals.

CLIMATE

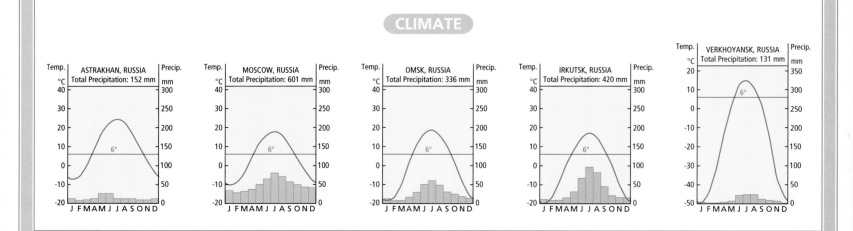

LANGUAGE

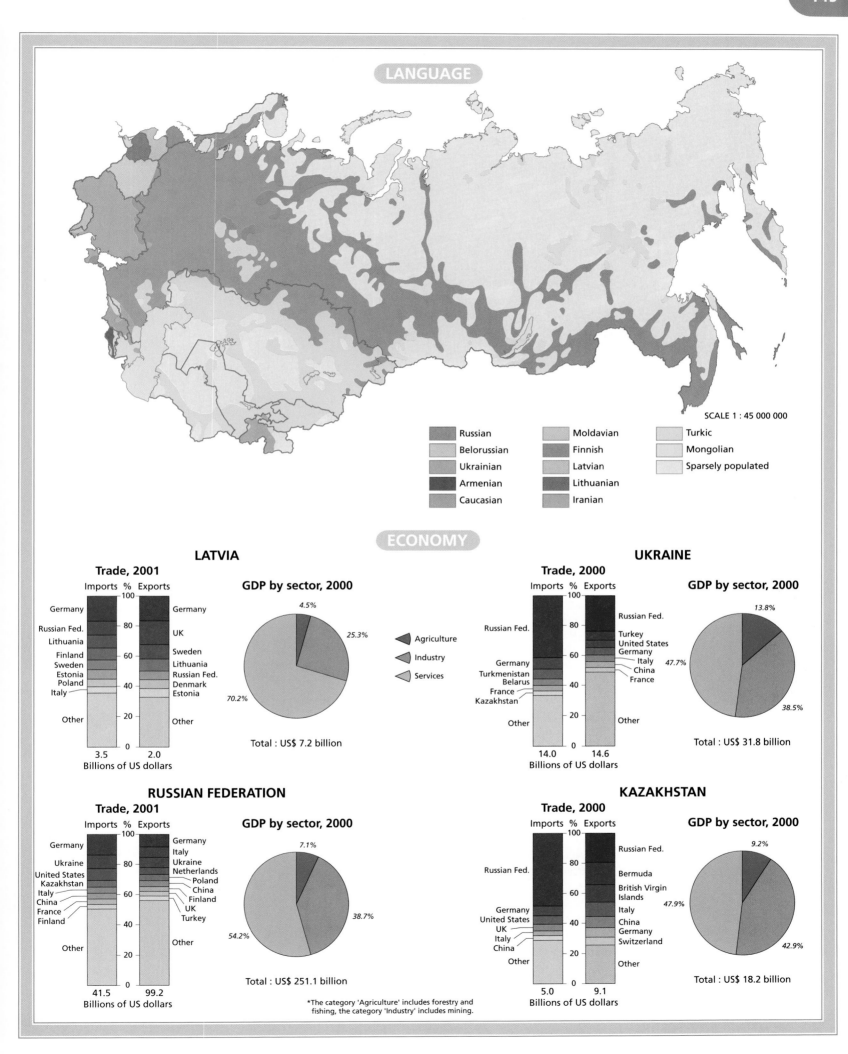

SCALE 1 : 45 000 000

Legend:
- Russian
- Belorussian
- Ukrainian
- Armenian
- Caucasian
- Moldavian
- Finnish
- Latvian
- Lithuanian
- Iranian
- Turkic
- Mongolian
- Sparsely populated

ECONOMY

LATVIA

Trade, 2001

Imports % Exports

Imports (top to bottom): Germany, Russian Fed., Lithuania, Finland, Sweden, Estonia, Poland, Italy, Other

Exports (top to bottom): Germany, UK, Sweden, Lithuania, Russian Fed., Denmark, Estonia, Other

3.5   2.0
Billions of US dollars

GDP by sector, 2000

- 4.5%
- 25.3%
- 70.2%

Agriculture
Industry
Services

Total : US$ 7.2 billion

UKRAINE

Trade, 2000

Imports % Exports

Imports (top to bottom): Russian Fed., Germany, Turkmenistan, Belarus, France, Kazakhstan, Other

Exports (top to bottom): Russian Fed., Turkey, United States, Germany, Italy, China, France, Other

14.0   14.6
Billions of US dollars

GDP by sector, 2000

- 13.8%
- 47.7%
- 38.5%

Total : US$ 31.8 billion

RUSSIAN FEDERATION

Trade, 2001

Imports % Exports

Imports (top to bottom): Germany, Ukraine, United States, Kazakhstan, Italy, China, France, Finland, Other

Exports (top to bottom): Germany, Italy, Ukraine, Netherlands, Poland, China, Finland, UK, Turkey, Other

41.5   99.2
Billions of US dollars

GDP by sector, 2000

- 7.1%
- 38.7%
- 54.2%

Total : US$ 251.1 billion

KAZAKHSTAN

Trade, 2000

Imports % Exports

Imports (top to bottom): Russian Fed., Germany, United States, UK, Italy, China, Other

Exports (top to bottom): Russian Fed., Bermuda, British Virgin Islands, Italy, China, Germany, Switzerland, Other

5.0   9.1
Billions of US dollars

GDP by sector, 2000

- 9.2%
- 47.9%
- 42.9%

Total : US$ 18.2 billion

*The category 'Agriculture' includes forestry and fishing, the category 'Industry' includes mining.

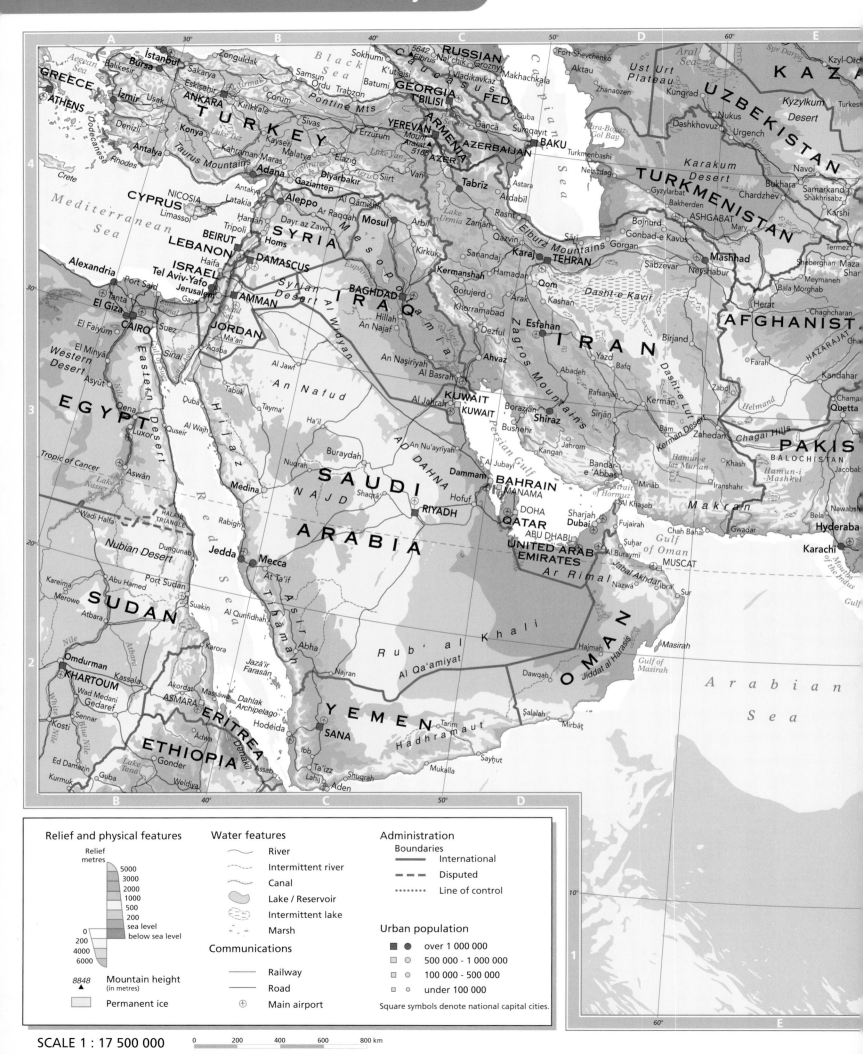

Relief and physical features

Relief metres
5000
3000
2000
1000
500
200
sea level
below sea level
200
4000
6000

▲ 8848 Mountain height (in metres)

Permanent ice

Water features

River
Intermittent river
Canal
Lake / Reservoir
Intermittent lake
Marsh

Communications

Railway
Road
⊕ Main airport

Administration

Boundaries
International
Disputed
Line of control

Urban population

■ ● over 1 000 000
□ ○ 500 000 – 1 000 000
□ ○ 100 000 – 500 000
□ ○ under 100 000

Square symbols denote national capital cities.

SCALE 1 : 17 500 000

0   200   400   600   800 km

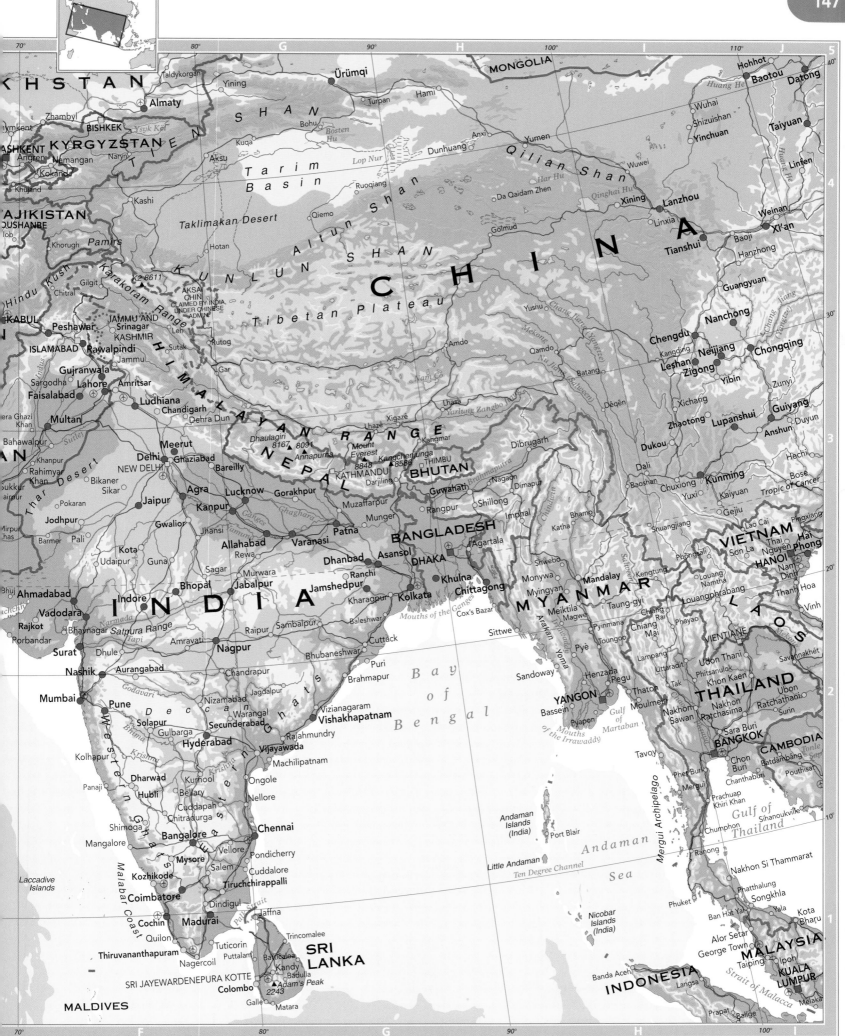

Lambert Azimuthal Equal Area projection

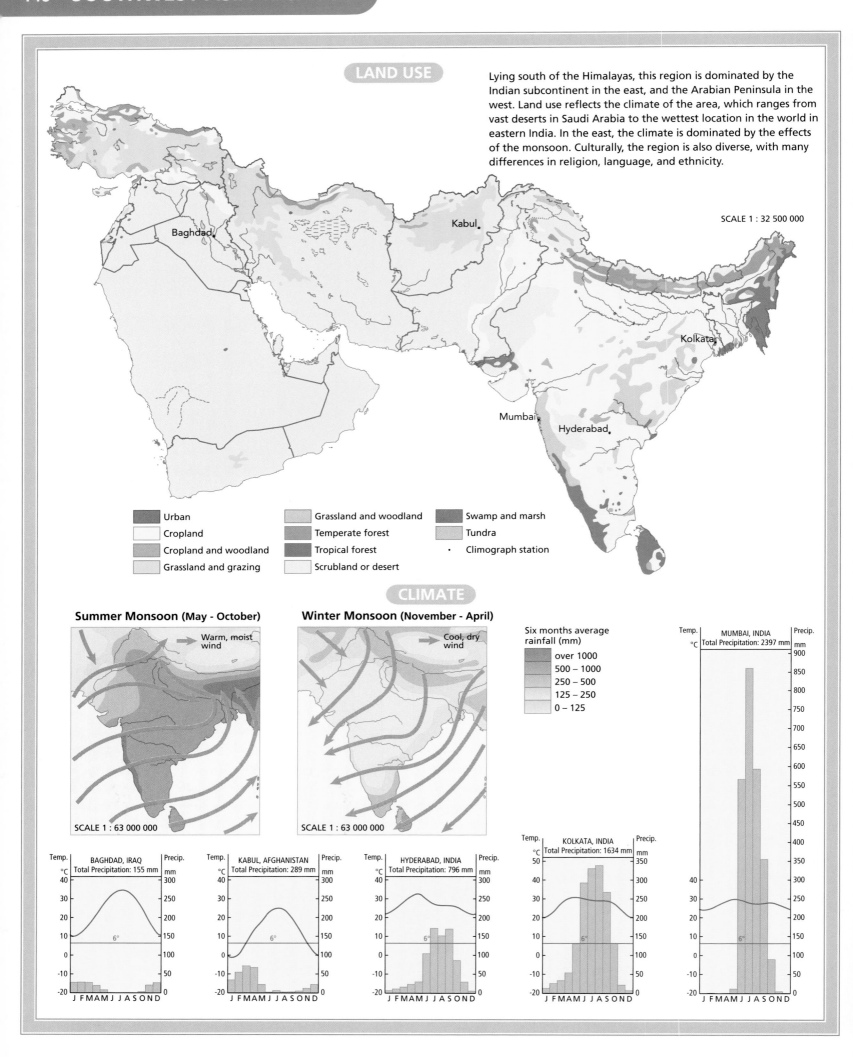

LAND USE

Lying south of the Himalayas, this region is dominated by the Indian subcontinent in the east, and the Arabian Peninsula in the west. Land use reflects the climate of the area, which ranges from vast deserts in Saudi Arabia to the wettest location in the world in eastern India. In the east, the climate is dominated by the effects of the monsoon. Culturally, the region is also diverse, with many differences in religion, language, and ethnicity.

SCALE 1 : 32 500 000

Baghdad
Kabul
Kolkata
Mumbai
Hyderabad

Urban
Cropland
Cropland and woodland
Grassland and grazing
Grassland and woodland
Temperate forest
Tropical forest
Scrubland or desert
Swamp and marsh
Tundra
· Climograph station

CLIMATE

Summer Monsoon (May - October)

Warm, moist wind

SCALE 1 : 63 000 000

Winter Monsoon (November - April)

Cool, dry wind

SCALE 1 : 63 000 000

Six months average rainfall (mm)

over 1000
500 – 1000
250 – 500
125 – 250
0 – 125

MUMBAI, INDIA
Total Precipitation: 2397 mm

BAGHDAD, IRAQ
Total Precipitation: 155 mm

KABUL, AFGHANISTAN
Total Precipitation: 289 mm

HYDERABAD, INDIA
Total Precipitation: 796 mm

KOLKATA, INDIA
Total Precipitation: 1634 mm

TOURISM

Top Destinations, 2000

Country	Income from tourism	
	Millions, US$	Percent of GDP
Maldives	344	61.8
Cyprus	1 894	21.8
Jordan	722	8.7
Bahrain	408	6.2
Lebanon	742	4.5
Turkey	7 636	3.8
Nepal	168	3.3
Israel	3 100	2.8
Syria	474	2.8
Sri Lanka	253	1.6
UAE	607	1.2
Yemen	76	0.9
Iran	850	0.8
Kuwait	243	0.8
India	3 296	0.7
Oman	104	0.5
Bangladesh	59	0.1
Pakistan	86	0.1

RELIGION

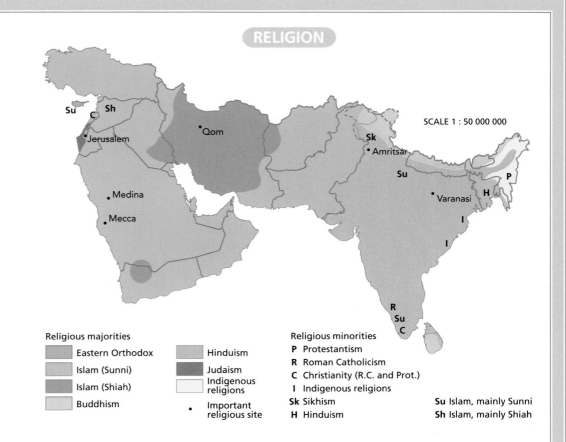

SCALE 1 : 50 000 000

Religious majorities

- Eastern Orthodox
- Islam (Sunni)
- Islam (Shiah)
- Buddhism
- Hinduism
- Judaism
- Indigenous religions
- ● Important religious site

Religious minorities

- **P** Protestantism
- **R** Roman Catholicism
- **C** Christianity (R.C. and Prot.)
- **I** Indigenous religions
- **Sk** Sikhism
- **H** Hinduism
- **Su** Islam, mainly Sunni
- **Sh** Islam, mainly Shiah

REFUGEES

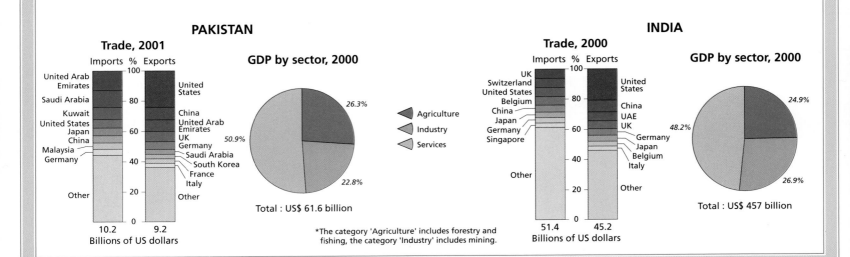

Number of refugees (thousands), 2001

Arrivals ■ Departures

ECONOMY

IRAN

Trade, 2000

Imports % Exports

Imports: Germany, Italy, Japan, Belgium, UAE, Argentina, Other

Exports: UK, Japan, Italy, UAE, South Korea, Greece, Turkey, Other

15.2   30.0
Billions of US dollars

GDP by sector, 2000

18.9%
22.3%
58.8%

Total : US$ 104.9 billion

PAKISTAN

Trade, 2001

Imports % Exports

Imports: United Arab Emirates, Saudi Arabia, Kuwait, United States, Japan, China, Malaysia, Germany, Other

Exports: United States, China, United Arab Emirates, UK, Germany, Saudi Arabia, South Korea, France, Italy, Other

10.2   9.2
Billions of US dollars

GDP by sector, 2000

26.3%
50.9%
22.8%

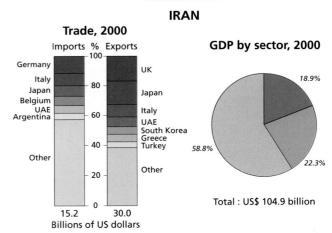

- Agriculture
- Industry
- Services

Total : US$ 61.6 billion

*The category 'Agriculture' includes forestry and fishing, the category 'Industry' includes mining.

INDIA

Trade, 2000

Imports % Exports

Imports: UK, Switzerland, United States, Belgium, China, Japan, Germany, Singapore, Other

Exports: United States, China, UAE, UK, Germany, Japan, Belgium, Italy, Other

51.4   45.2
Billions of US dollars

GDP by sector, 2000

24.9%
48.2%
26.9%

Total : US$ 457 billion

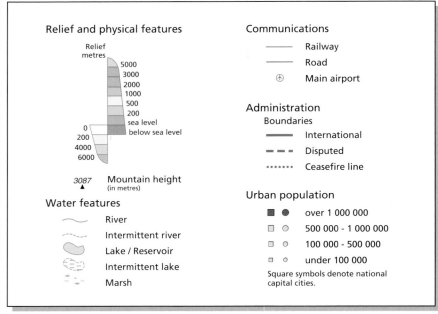

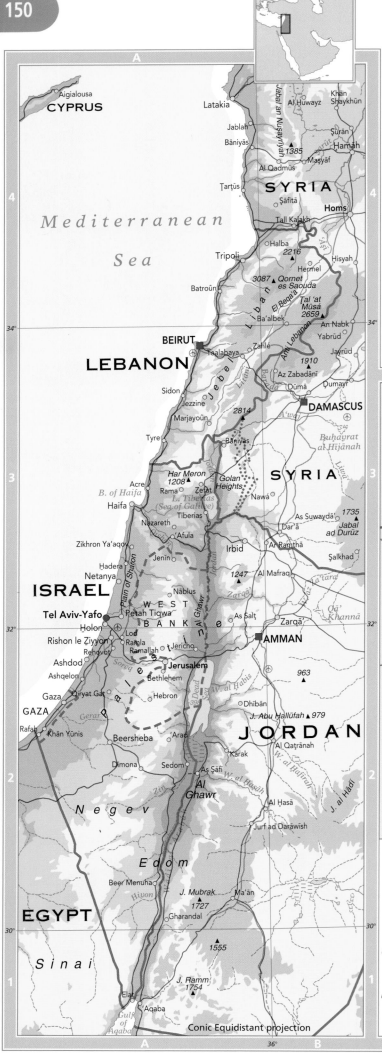

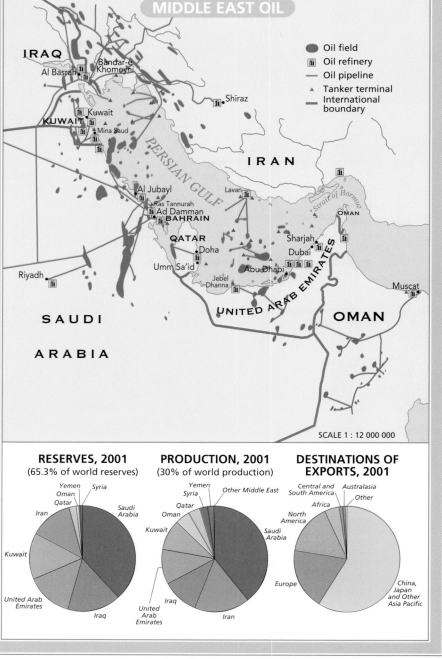

CHANGING BORDERS

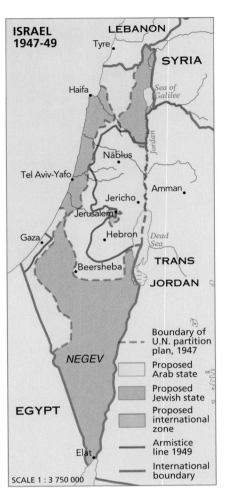

ISRAEL 1947-49

LEBANON
Tyre
SYRIA
Haifa
Sea of Galilee
Nablus
Tel Aviv-Yafo
Jericho
Amman
Jerusalem
Gaza
Hebron
Dead Sea
Beersheba
TRANS JORDAN
NEGEV
EGYPT
Elat

Boundary of U.N. partition plan, 1947
Proposed Arab state
Proposed Jewish state
Proposed international zone
Armistice line 1949
International boundary

SCALE 1 : 3 750 000

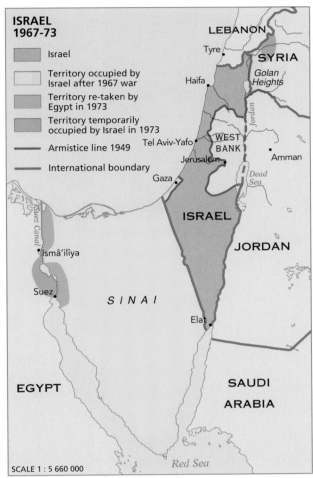

ISRAEL 1967-73

Israel
Territory occupied by Israel after 1967 war
Territory re-taken by Egypt in 1973
Territory temporarily occupied by Israel in 1973
Armistice line 1949
International boundary

LEBANON
Tyre
SYRIA
Golan Heights
Haifa
Jordan
WEST BANK
Tel Aviv-Yafo
Jerusalem
Amman
Gaza
Dead Sea
ISRAEL
JORDAN
Suez Canal
Ismâ'iliya
Suez
SINAI
Elat
EGYPT
SAUDI ARABIA
Red Sea

SCALE 1 : 5 660 000

ISRAEL 2003

LEBANON
Tyre
SYRIA
Golan Heights
Haifa
Nazareth
Nablus
Tel Aviv-Yafo
WEST BANK
Jericho
Amman
Jerusalem
GAZA Gaza
Dead Sea
Beersheba
ISRAEL
JORDAN
NEGEV
EGYPT
Elat

Israel
Occupied territories
Buffer zone
International boundary
Disputed International boundary

SCALE 1 : 3 750 000

ARAB POPULATION

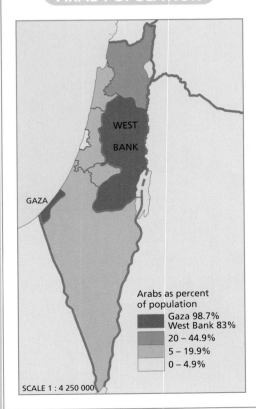

WEST BANK
GAZA

Arabs as percent of population
Gaza 98.7%
West Bank 83%
20 – 44.9%
5 – 19.9%
0 – 4.9%

SCALE 1 : 4 250 000

Jerusalem is the holy city for Judaism, Christianity, and Islam. All three faiths have historic interest in this area. From the late 1850s Jewish nationalists advocated a homeland for their people who had been scattered since the time of the Romans. During the 1920s and 1930s, Jews fleeing persecution in Europe came to Palestine. Following World War II, and the genocide of millions of Jews by Nazi Germany, migration to Palestine increased. The Arab majority who lived there did not welcome the Jews' arrival, and there was frequent fighting. In 1948, the United Nations took up the cause of a Jewish homeland and Israel was created out of Palestine. Warfare erupted. Hundreds of thousands of Palestinian Arabs were displaced from their homes and became refugees. Since then, the area has endured almost constant strife between Israel and its Arab neighbours. Wars in 1967 and 1973 resulted in changing borders. Attempts at creating a lasting peace among the peoples of the region have not been successful.

Israel's own population of about 6 million is more than 80% Jewish. The West Bank and Gaza, areas that were occupied by Israel in 1967, are inhabited predominantly by Arabs.

COMPARISON OF SELECTED DATA

	Israel	Gaza	West Bank
Area	20 770 km²	363 km²	5800 km²
Compares in size to...	Half of Nova Scotia	Washington, DC	Prince Edward Island
Resources	Copper, phosphates, potash, manganese, natural gas	Natural gas	Negligible
Arable land	17%	26%	na
Population	6.2 million	1.2 million	2.2 million
Ethnicity	81.4% Jewish 18.6% Arab and Druze	98.7% Palestinian Arab	83% Palestinian Arab
Religion	80.1% Jewish	98.7% Sunni Muslim	75% Sunni Muslim
GDP per capita (US$)	20 000	625	1000

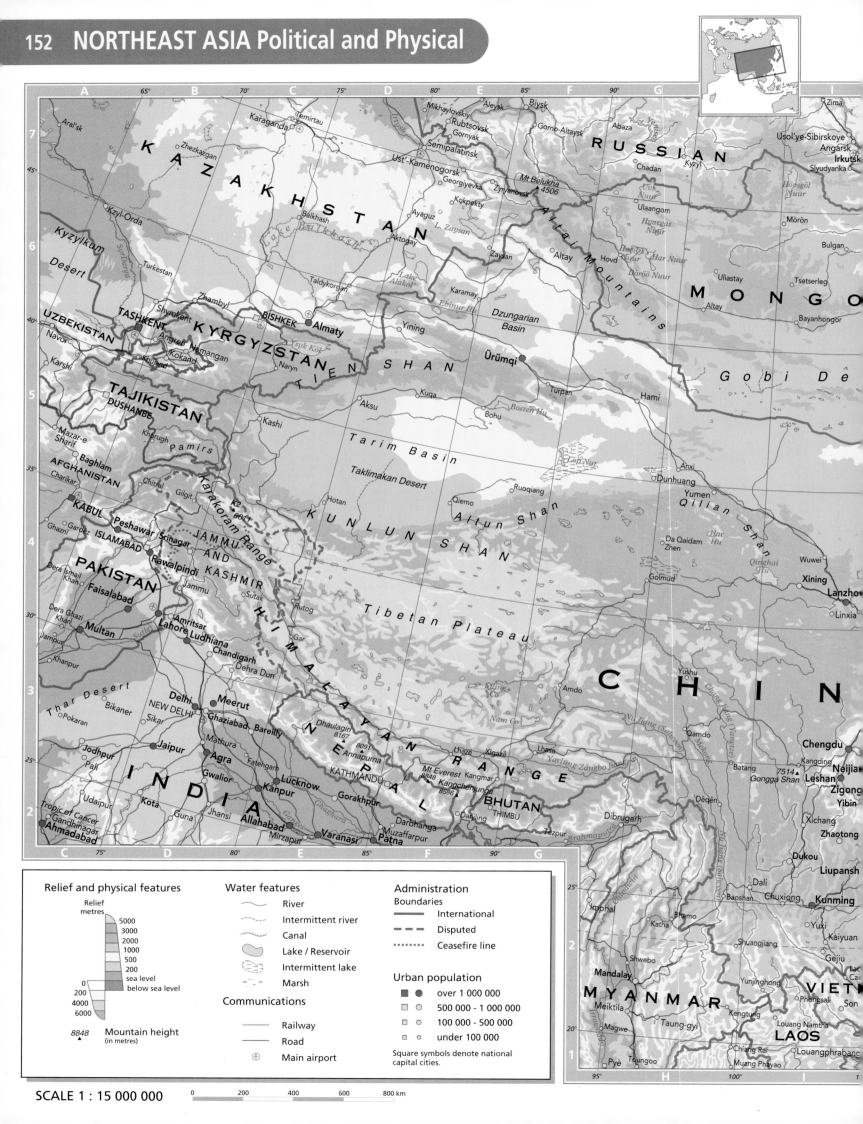

Relief and physical features

Relief metres
5000
3000
2000
1000
500
200
sea level
below sea level
200
4000
6000

8848 Mountain height (in metres)

Water features

River
Intermittent river
Canal
Lake / Reservoir
Intermittent lake
Marsh

Communications

Railway
Road
Main airport

Administration

Boundaries
International
Disputed
Ceasefire line

Urban population
over 1 000 000
500 000 - 1 000 000
100 000 - 500 000
under 100 000

Square symbols denote national capital cities.

SCALE 1 : 15 000 000

0   200   400   600   800 km

Conic projection

INDIA
Chittagong
BANGLA-DESH
Mt Pakokku
Victoria ▲ 3053
Sittwe
Monywa
Shwebo
Monywa
Mandalay
Myingyan
Meiktila
Magwe
Pyinmana
Sandoway
Henzada
Pye
Pegu
Shwegyin
Bassein
YANGON
Pyapon
Thaton
Martaban
Moulmein
Gulf of Martaban
Mouths of the Irrawaddy

MYANMAR

Arakan Yoma

Bay of Bengal

Preparis I.

Andaman Islands (India)

Port Blair
Little Andaman

Ten Degree Channel
Car Nicobar

Nicobar Islands (India)

Great Nicobar

Andaman Sea

CHINA
Shwebo
Yunjinghong
Phongsali
Kengtung
Louang Namtha
Chiang Rai
Chiang Mai
Phayao
Nan
Phrae
Lampang
Uttaradit
Phitsanulok
Tak
Sara Buri
Nakhon Sawan
Ayutthaya
Nonthaburi
BANGKOK
Chon Buri
Phet Buri
Rat Buri
Chanthaburi
Prachuap Khiri Khan
Chumphon
Ranong
Phuket
Krabi
Nakhon Si Thammarat
Phatthalung
Songkhla
Ban Hat Yai
Yala

THAILAND

Tavoy
Mergui
Tenasserim
Mergui Archipelago

Gulf of Thailand

Lao Cai
Cao Bang
Pingxiang
Thai Nguyen
HANOI
Nam Dinh
Thai Binh
Hai Phong
Son La
Louangphrabang
Xiangkhoang
VIENTIANE
Udon Thani
Khon Kaen
Savannakhet
Pakxé
Ubon Ratchathani
Surin
Nakhon Ratchasima
Sisophon
Batdâmbâng
Pouthisat
Tônlé Sap
CAMBODIA
PHNOM PENH
Sihanoukville
Kâmpôt
Long Xuyên
Rach Gia
Can Tho
Bac Liêu
Mui Ca Mau
Con Son
Mouths of the Mekong

LAOS

Thanh Hoa
Vinh
Ha Tinh
Dong Hoi
Quang Tri
Huê
Da Nang
Quang Ngai
Qui Nhon
Buôn Ma Thuôt
Nha Trang
Cam Ranh
Da Lat
Phan Thiêt
Tây Ninh
Kâmpóng Cham
Krâchéh
My Tho
Hô Chi Minh City
Vung Tau

VIETNAM

CHINA
Nanning
Yulin
Qinzhou
Beihai
Zhanjiang
Macau
Hong Kong
Gaoxion
TAIWAN
Leizhou Pen.
Haikou
Qionghai
Dongfang
Hainan

Gulf of Tongking

Paracel Is

SOUTH CHINA SEA

Spratly Is

Laoag
San Fernando
Baguio
Dagupan
Cabanatuan
Mt Pinatubo 1600
Olongapo
Quezo City
MANILA
Pasig
Batangas
Calapa
Mindoro

Calamian Group

Palawan
Puerto Princesa
Brooke's Point
Taytay

MALAYSIA
BRUNEI
BANDAR SERI BEGAWAN
Miri
Seria
Kota Kinabalu
G. Kinabalu ▲ 4094
Sandakan
Lahad Datu
SABAH
Tawau
Tarakan
Tanjungredeb
Igan
Bintulu
Sibu
Debak
SARAWAK
Iran Ha. ▲ 2988
Kuching
Simanggang
Singkawang
Sambas
Pontianak
Sukadana
BORNEO
Schwaner Mts
KALIMANTAN
Samarinda
Balikpapan
Kendawangan
Ketapang
Palangkaraya
Amuntai
Sampit
Pangkalanbuun
Banjarmasin
Tg Puting
Tg Selatan
Laut

Balabac Strait
Jolo
Tawitaw
Su Sea
Ce

MALAYA
Alor Setar
George Town
Pinang
Butterworth
Taiping
Ipoh
KUALA LUMPUR
Putrajaya
Seremban
Melaka
Keluang
Muar
Johor Bahru
SINGAPORE
SINGAPORE
Kota Bharu
Kuala Terengganu
Dungun
Kuantan
Natuna Besar
Anambas Is
Natuna Is
Tambelan Is
Riau Is

Strait of Malacca

Banda Aceh
Lhokseumawe
Langsa
Medan
G. Leuser ▲ 3145
Tebingtinggi
Prapat
Lake Toba
Balige
Sibolga
Rantauprapat
Pakanbaru
SUMATRA
Nias
Batu Is
Bukittinggi
Padangpanjang
Padang
Siberut
Sipura
Utara I.
Muarabungo
Jambi
G. Kerinci 3805
Sungaipenuh
Lubuklinggau
Prabumulih
Palembang
Bangka
Mentok
Pangkalpinang
Tanjungpandan
Toboali
Belitung
Karimata Strait

Barisan Range

Mentawai Is

INDIAN OCEAN

Selatan I.
Bengkulu
Dempo ▲ 3159
Lahat
Martapura
Kotabumi
Tanjungkarang Telukbetung
Enggano

Sunda Str.
Serang
JAKARTA
Bogor
Sukabumi
Bandung
Cirebon
Pekalongan
Tasikmalaya
Cilacap
Slamet ▲ 3428
Semarang
Surakarta
Yogyakarta
Malang ▲ 3676
JAVA
Tuban
Madura
Surabaya
Probolinggo
Singaraja
Bali ▲ 3726
Denpasar
Mataram
Lombok

Java Sea

Bawean
Kangean Is

Bali Sea
Flores

INDONES

Ujung Pandang
Bontosunggu
Bulukum
Salayar
Sulawes
Mamuju
Bt Gandadiwata ▲ 3074
Majene
Parepare
Watampone
Makassar Strait
Makassar Gulf of Bone
Palu
Poso
Sidoa
Toli
Tomi Gulf

Christmas I. (Aust.)

Sumbawa
Sumba
Waingapu
Raba
Ruteng
Ende

SCALE 1 : 15 000 000

0   200   400   600   800 km

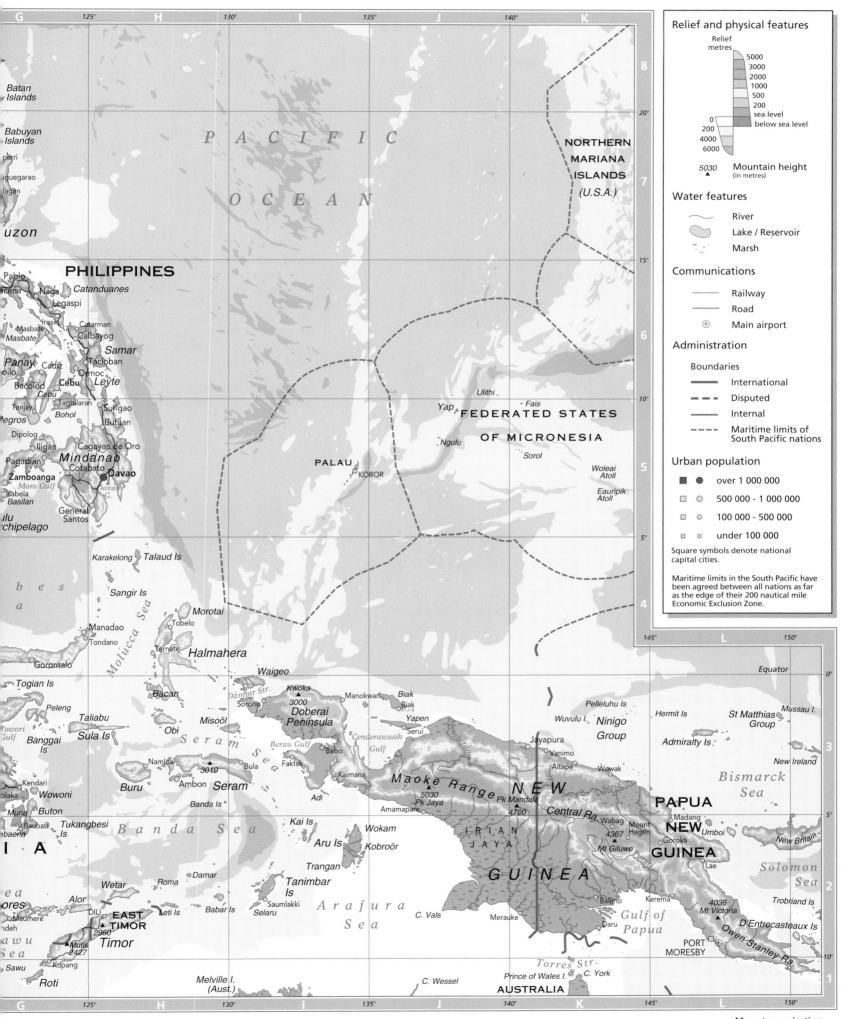

Relief and physical features

Relief
metres
5000
3000
2000
1000
500
200
sea level
below sea level

▲ 5030 Mountain height (in metres)

Water features

River
Lake / Reservoir
Marsh

Communications

Railway
Road
⊕ Main airport

Administration

Boundaries

International
Disputed
Internal
Maritime limits of South Pacific nations

Urban population

■ ● over 1 000 000
□ ○ 500 000 - 1 000 000
□ ○ 100 000 - 500 000
□ ○ under 100 000

Square symbols denote national capital cities.

Maritime limits in the South Pacific have been agreed between all nations as far as the edge of their 200 nautical mile Economic Exclusion Zone.

PACIFIC OCEAN

Batan Islands
Babuyan Islands
parri
guegarao
lagan
uzon

PHILIPPINES

Pablo
cena
Naga
Legaspi
Irosin
Catarman
Catanduanes
Masbate
Calbayog
Masbate
Samar
Panay
Cadiz
Tacloban
oilo
Ormoc
Leyte
Bacolod
Cebu
Cebu
Tagbilaran
Tanjay
Bohol
Surigao
egros
Butuan
Dipolog
Iligan
Cagayan de Oro
Pagadian
Mindanao
Cotabato
Davao
Zamboanga
Moro Gulf
Dava
G.
Isabela
Basilan
General Santos
lu
chipelago

NORTHERN MARIANA ISLANDS (U.S.A.)

Ulithi
Yap
Fais
FEDERATED STATES
Ngulu
OF MICRONESIA
Sorol
PALAU
KOROR
Woleai Atoll
Eauripik Atoll

Karakelong Talaud Is
bes
a
Sangir Is
Manadao
Tobelo
Molucca Sea
Morotai
Tondano
Ternate
Halmahera
Gorontalo
Waigeo
Togian Is
Bacan
Danpir Str.
Kwoka
Manokwari
Biak
Peleng
Taliabu
Sorong
3000
Biak
Obi
Misoöl
Doberai
Peninsula
Yapen
Pelelehu Is
Wuvulu I.
Ninigo
Group
Hermit Is
St Matthias Group
Mussau I.
owori
Gulf
Banggai
Is
Sula Is
Seram Sea
Cenderawasih
Gulf
Serui
Wuwulu I.
Jayapura
Admiralty Is
New Ireland
Namlea
3019
Bula
Berau Gulf
Babo
Vanimo
Kendari
Ambon
Seram
Fakfak
Kaimana
Aitape
Wewak
Bismarck Sea
Wowoni
Buru
Banda Is
Adi
Maoke Range
Sepik
PAPUA
Muna
Buton
5030
Pk Mandala
N E W
Wabag
Madang
Baubau
Tukangbesi
Is
Kai Is
Wokam
Amamapare
Pk Jaya
Central Ra.
4700
Mount Hagen
4367
NEW
Umboi
baena
Is
Aru Is
Kobroör
I R I A N
Goroka
New Britain
J A Y A
Mt Giluwe
Purari
GUINEA
I A
Trangan
G U I N E A
Lae
Banda Sea
Damar
Tanimbar
Is
Arafura
Sea
Balimo
Kerema
4036
Mt Victoria
Solomon Sea
Wetar
Alor
Roma
Saumlakki
Selaru
C. Vals
Gulf of Papua
Trobriand Is
ores
DILI
EAST
TIMOR
Leti Is
Babar Is
Merauke
Daru
D'Entrecasteaux Is
Maumere
ndeh
2960
Mutis
2427
Timor
Sawu
Roti
Kupang
Melville I.
(Aust.)
C. Wessel
Torres Str.
Prince of Wales I.
C. York
PORT MORESBY
Owen-Stanley Ra.
AUSTRALIA

Equator

Mercator projection

LAND USE

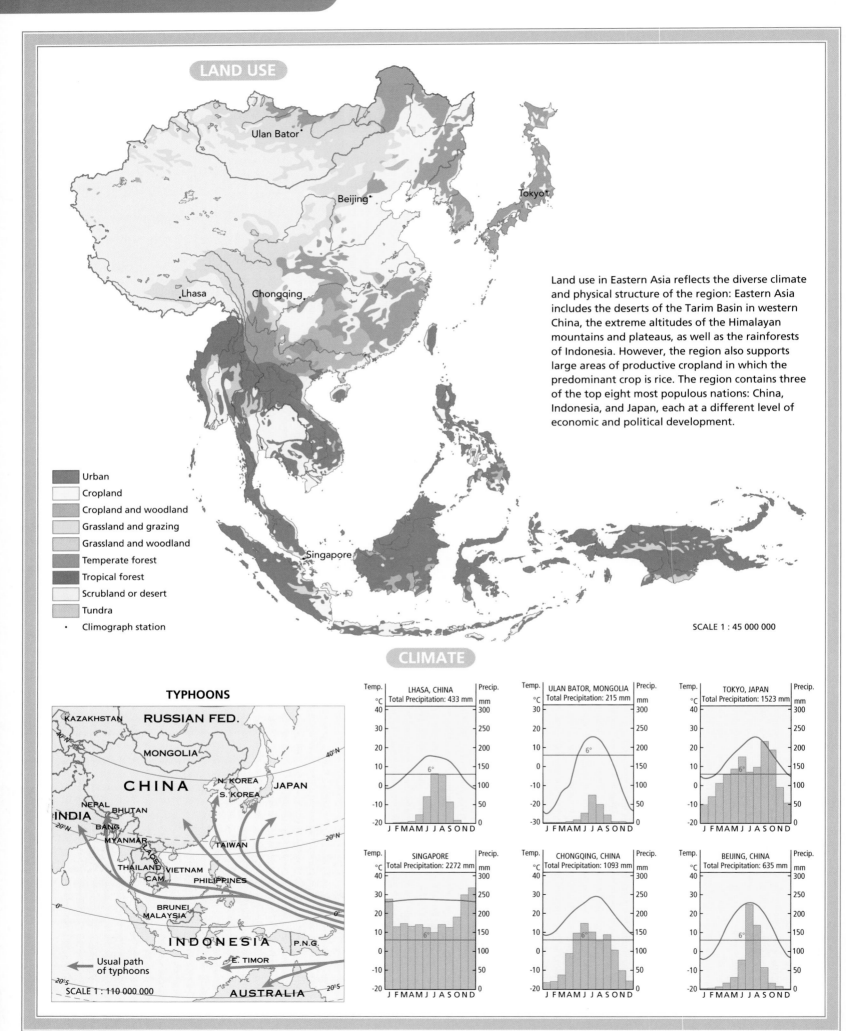

Ulan Bator

Beijing

Tokyo

Lhasa

Chongqing

Singapore

Land use in Eastern Asia reflects the diverse climate and physical structure of the region: Eastern Asia includes the deserts of the Tarim Basin in western China, the extreme altitudes of the Himalayan mountains and plateaus, as well as the rainforests of Indonesia. However, the region also supports large areas of productive cropland in which the predominant crop is rice. The region contains three of the top eight most populous nations: China, Indonesia, and Japan, each at a different level of economic and political development.

Urban
Cropland
Cropland and woodland
Grassland and grazing
Grassland and woodland
Temperate forest
Tropical forest
Scrubland or desert
Tundra
• Climograph station

SCALE 1 : 45 000 000

CLIMATE

TYPHOONS

KAZAKHSTAN RUSSIAN FED.

MONGOLIA

CHINA N. KOREA JAPAN

S. KOREA

NEPAL BHUTAN

INDIA

BANG.

MYANMAR

TAIWAN

THAILAND VIETNAM

CAM. PHILIPPINES

BRUNEI
MALAYSIA

INDONESIA P.N.G.

E. TIMOR

← Usual path of typhoons

SCALE 1 : 110 000 000

AUSTRALIA

LHASA, CHINA
Total Precipitation: 433 mm

ULAN BATOR, MONGOLIA
Total Precipitation: 215 mm

TOKYO, JAPAN
Total Precipitation: 1523 mm

SINGAPORE
Total Precipitation: 2272 mm

CHONGQING, CHINA
Total Precipitation: 1093 mm

BEIJING, CHINA
Total Precipitation: 635 mm

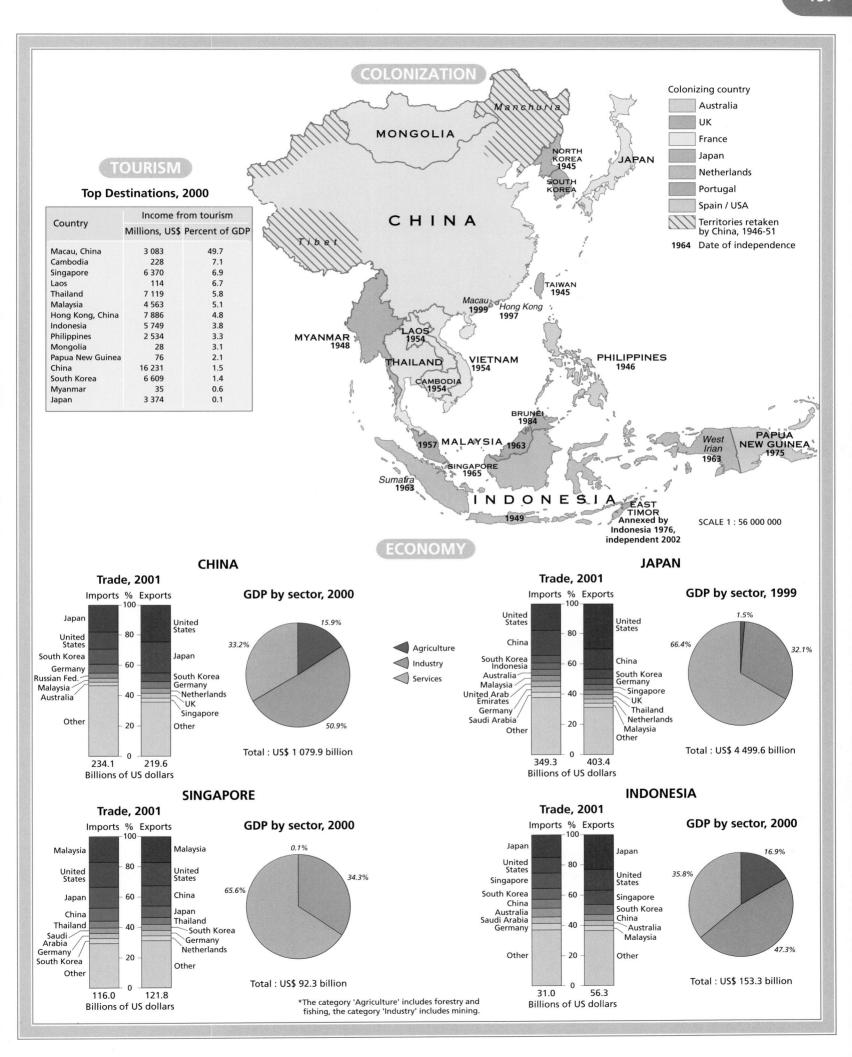

SCALE 1 : 16 500 000

0   200   400   600   800 km

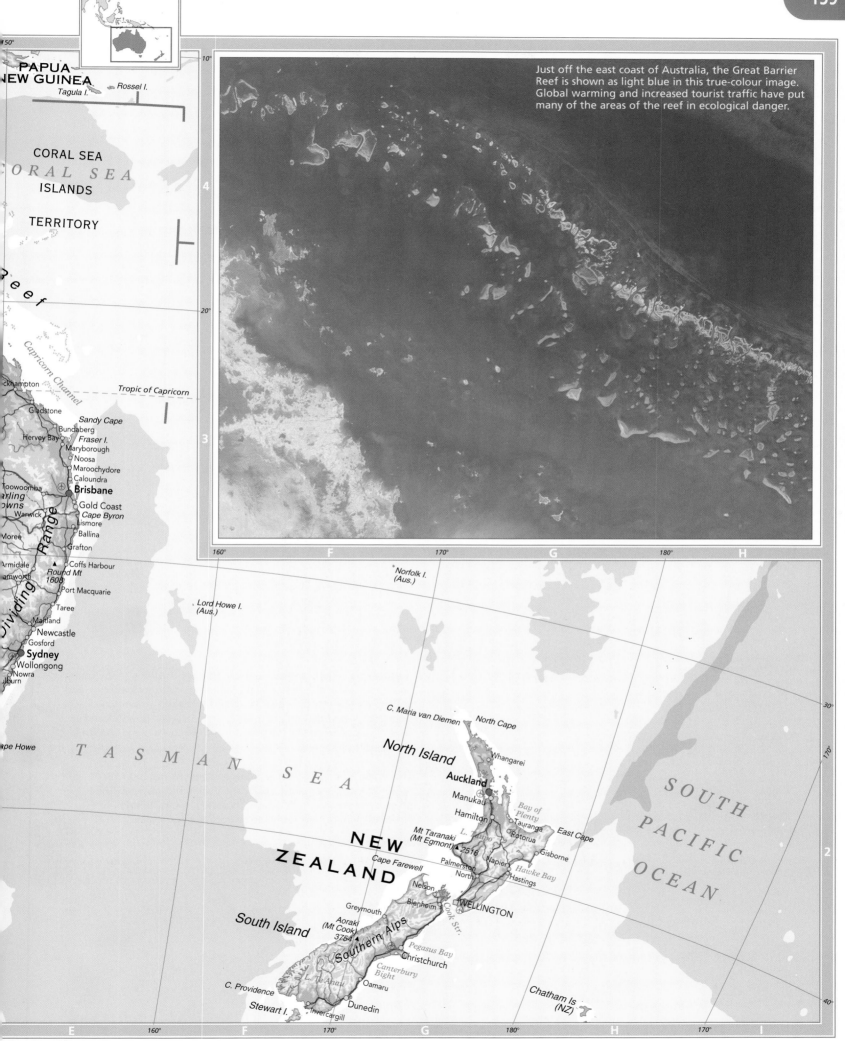

PAPUA NEW GUINEA

Tagula I.   Rossel I.

CORAL SEA

CORAL SEA ISLANDS

TERRITORY

Reef

Capricorn Channel

ckhampton

Tropic of Capricorn

Gladstone

Bundaberg   Sandy Cape
Hervey Bay   Fraser I.
Maryborough
Noosa
Maroochydore
Caloundra
Toowoomba   **Brisbane**
arling   Gold Coast
owns   Cape Byron
Warwick   Lismore
Ballina
Moree   Grafton
Armidale   Coffs Harbour
amworth   Round Mt
1608

Port Macquarie

Taree

Maitland
Newcastle
Gosford
Sydney
Wollongong
Nowra
lburn

Just off the east coast of Australia, the Great Barrier Reef is shown as light blue in this true-colour image. Global warming and increased tourist traffic have put many of the areas of the reef in ecological danger.

TASMAN SEA

ape Howe

Norfolk I. (Aus.)

Lord Howe I. (Aus.)

C. Maria van Diemen   North Cape

North Island   Whangarei

Auckland

Manukau
Bay of
Plenty   East Cape
Hamilton   Tauranga
Rotorua
NEW   L. Taupo   Gisborne
Mt Taranaki
(Mt Egmont)   2516
ZEALAND   Napier
Cape Farewell   Palmerston   Hawke Bay
North   Hastings

Nelson
Greymouth   Blenheim   **WELLINGTON**
South Island   Cook Str.
Aoraki
(Mt Cook)   Southern Alps   Pegasus Bay
3754   Christchurch
Canterbury
Bight
C. Providence   L. Te Anau   Oamaru
Stewart I.   Dunedin
Invercargill

SOUTH

PACIFIC

OCEAN

Chatham Is (NZ)

Lambert Azimuthal Equal Area projection

LAND USE

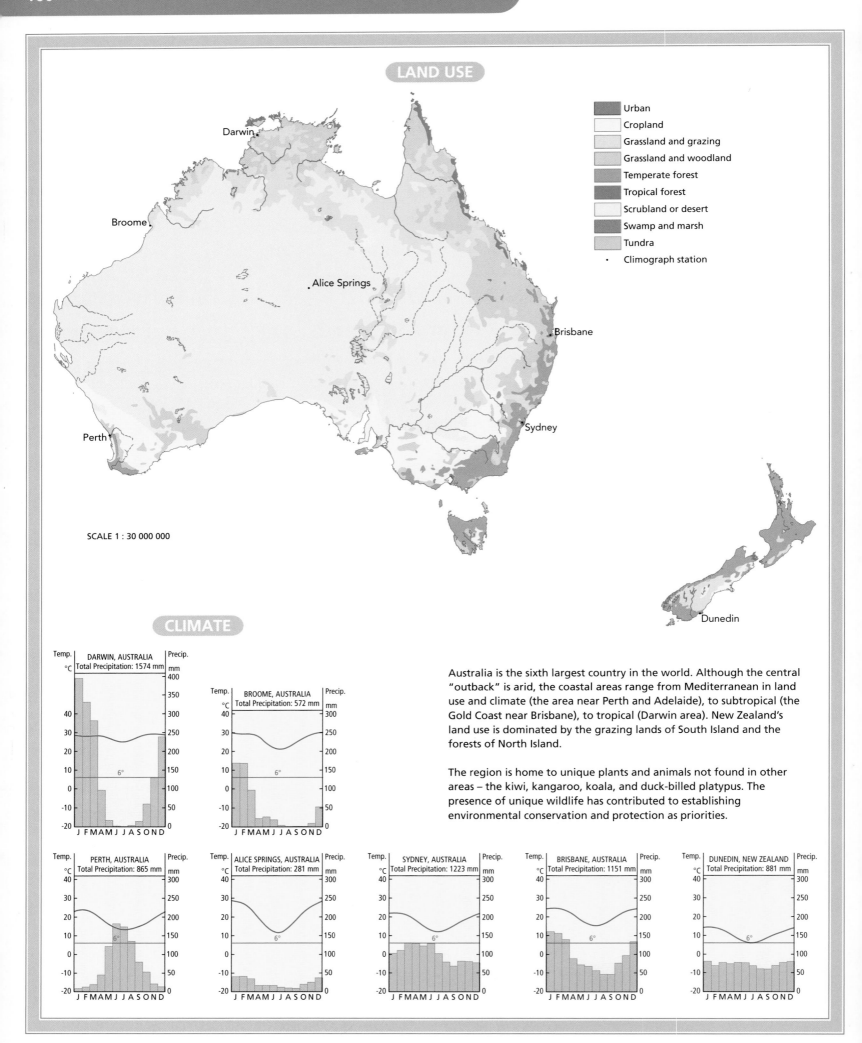

Legend:
- Urban
- Cropland
- Grassland and grazing
- Grassland and woodland
- Temperate forest
- Tropical forest
- Scrubland or desert
- Swamp and marsh
- Tundra
- • Climograph station

Darwin

Broome

Alice Springs

Brisbane

Perth

Sydney

Dunedin

SCALE 1 : 30 000 000

CLIMATE

DARWIN, AUSTRALIA
Total Precipitation: 1574 mm

BROOME, AUSTRALIA
Total Precipitation: 572 mm

Australia is the sixth largest country in the world. Although the central "outback" is arid, the coastal areas range from Mediterranean in land use and climate (the area near Perth and Adelaide), to subtropical (the Gold Coast near Brisbane), to tropical (Darwin area). New Zealand's land use is dominated by the grazing lands of South Island and the forests of North Island.

The region is home to unique plants and animals not found in other areas – the kiwi, kangaroo, koala, and duck-billed platypus. The presence of unique wildlife has contributed to establishing environmental conservation and protection as priorities.

PERTH, AUSTRALIA
Total Precipitation: 865 mm

ALICE SPRINGS, AUSTRALIA
Total Precipitation: 281 mm

SYDNEY, AUSTRALIA
Total Precipitation: 1223 mm

BRISBANE, AUSTRALIA
Total Precipitation: 1151 mm

DUNEDIN, NEW ZEALAND
Total Precipitation: 881 mm

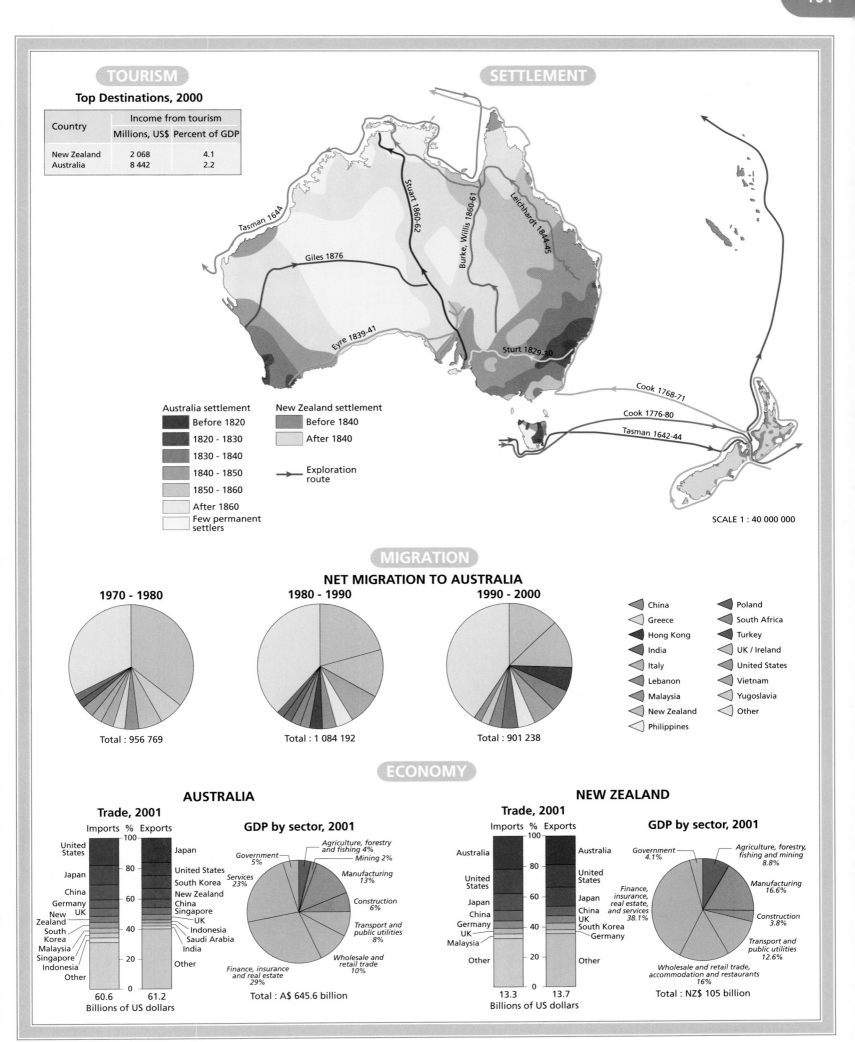

TOURISM

Top Destinations, 2000

Country	Income from tourism	
	Millions, US$	Percent of GDP
New Zealand	2 068	4.1
Australia	8 442	2.2

SETTLEMENT

Tasman 1644

Stuart 1860-62

Burke, Willis 1860-61

Leichhardt 1844-45

Giles 1876

Eyre 1839-41

Sturt 1829-30

Cook 1768-71

Cook 1776-80

Tasman 1642-44

Australia settlement
- Before 1820
- 1820 - 1830
- 1830 - 1840
- 1840 - 1850
- 1850 - 1860
- After 1860
- Few permanent settlers

New Zealand settlement
- Before 1840
- After 1840

→ Exploration route

SCALE 1 : 40 000 000

MIGRATION

NET MIGRATION TO AUSTRALIA

1970 - 1980

Total : 956 769

1980 - 1990

Total : 1 084 192

1990 - 2000

Total : 901 238

- China
- Greece
- Hong Kong
- India
- Italy
- Lebanon
- Malaysia
- New Zealand
- Philippines
- Poland
- South Africa
- Turkey
- UK / Ireland
- United States
- Vietnam
- Yugoslavia
- Other

ECONOMY

AUSTRALIA

Trade, 2001

Imports % Exports

Imports: United States, Japan, China, Germany, New Zealand, UK, South Korea, Malaysia, Singapore, Indonesia, Other

Exports: Japan, United States, South Korea, New Zealand, China, Singapore, UK, Indonesia, Saudi Arabia, India, Other

60.6   61.2
Billions of US dollars

GDP by sector, 2001

- Government 5%
- Agriculture, forestry and fishing 4%
- Mining 2%
- Manufacturing 13%
- Services 23%
- Construction 6%
- Transport and public utilities 8%
- Wholesale and retail trade 10%
- Finance, insurance and real estate 29%

Total : A$ 645.6 billion

NEW ZEALAND

Trade, 2001

Imports % Exports

Imports: Australia, United States, Japan, China, Germany, UK, Malaysia, Other

Exports: Australia, United States, Japan, China, UK, South Korea, Germany, Other

13.3   13.7
Billions of US dollars

GDP by sector, 2001

- Government 4.1%
- Agriculture, forestry, fishing and mining 8.8%
- Manufacturing 16.6%
- Finance, insurance, real estate, and services 38.1%
- Construction 3.8%
- Transport and public utilities 12.6%
- Wholesale and retail trade, accommodation and restaurants 16%

Total : NZ$ 105 billion

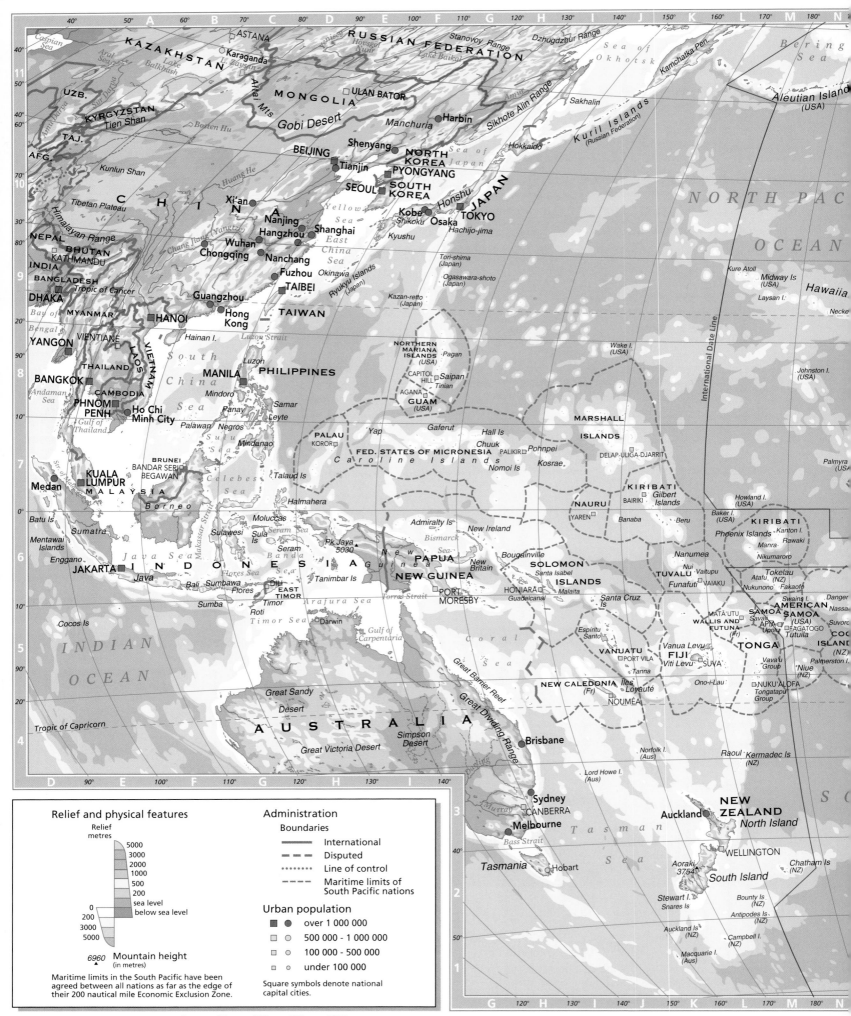

Relief and physical features

Relief
metres
5000
3000
2000
1000
500
200
0 sea level
200
below sea level
3000
5000

6960 Mountain height
(in metres)

Maritime limits in the South Pacific have been
agreed between all nations as far as the edge of
their 200 nautical mile Economic Exclusion Zone.

Administration
Boundaries
International
Disputed
Line of control
Maritime limits of
South Pacific nations

Urban population
over 1 000 000
500 000 - 1 000 000
100 000 - 500 000
under 100 000

Square symbols denote national
capital cities.

SCALE 1 : 50 000 000

0   500   1000   1500   2000 km

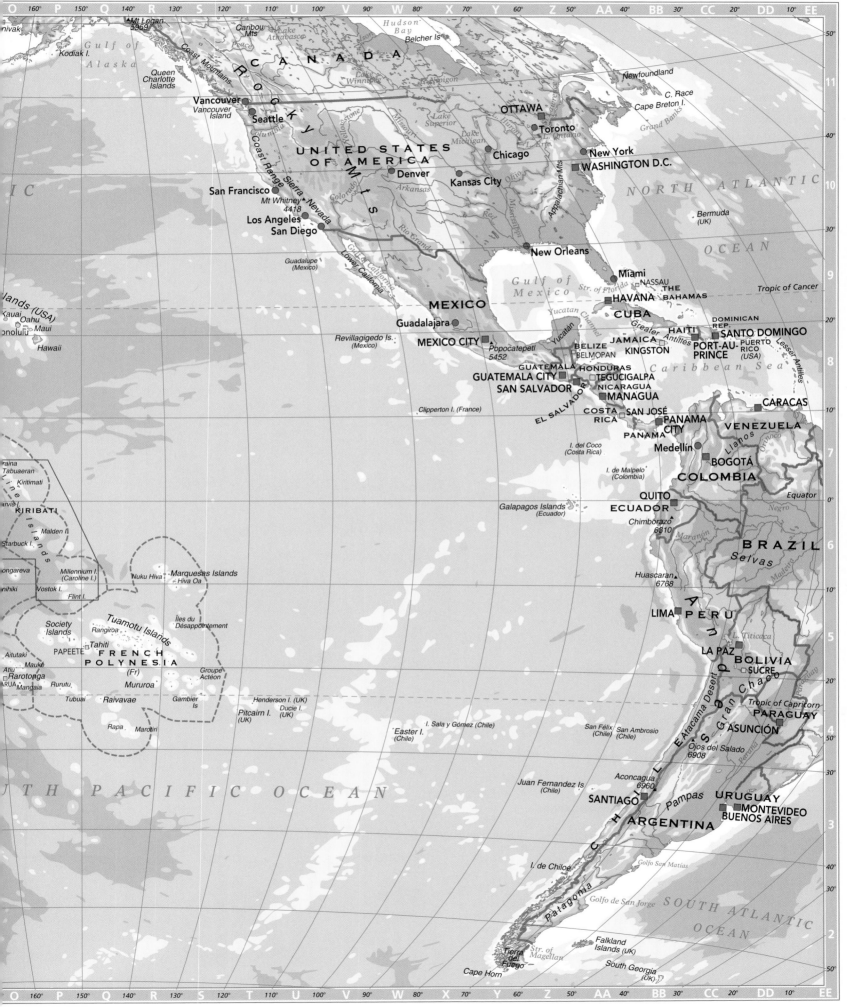

Hammer - Aitoff projection

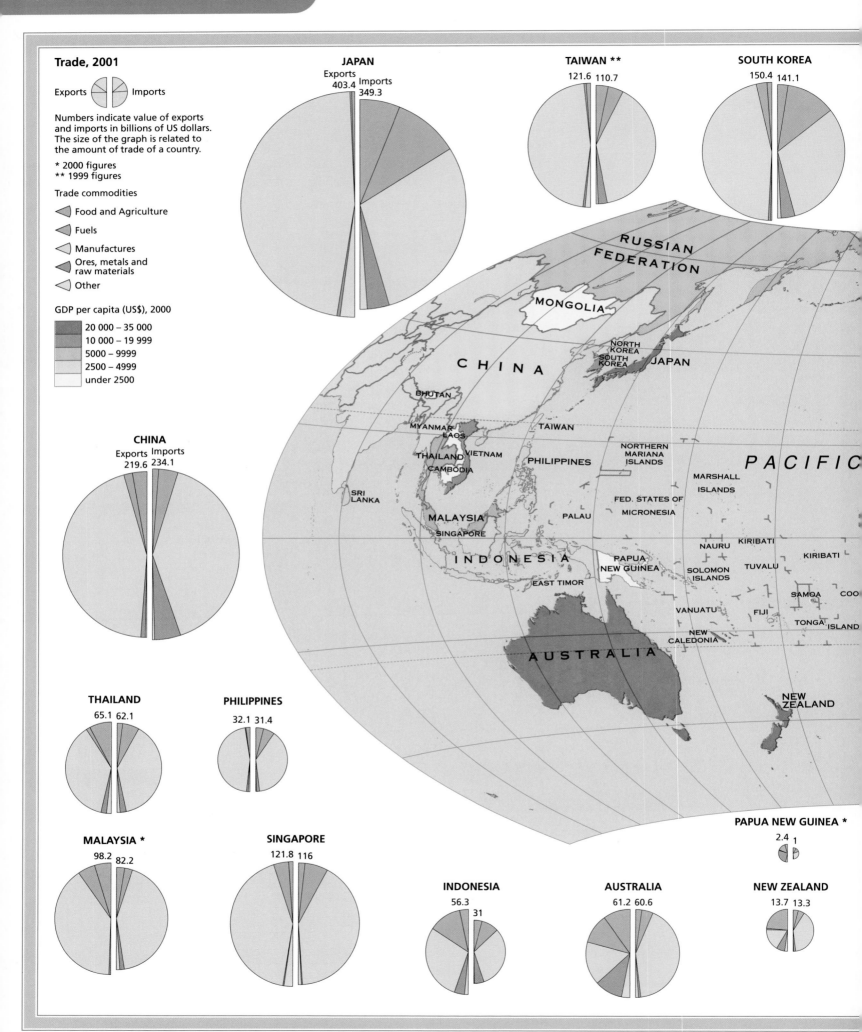

Trade, 2001

Exports | Imports

Numbers indicate value of exports and imports in billions of US dollars. The size of the graph is related to the amount of trade of a country.

* 2000 figures
** 1999 figures

Trade commodities

Food and Agriculture

Fuels

Manufactures

Ores, metals and raw materials

Other

GDP per capita (US$), 2000

20 000 – 35 000
10 000 – 19 999
5000 – 9999
2500 – 4999
under 2500

JAPAN
Exports 403.4 | Imports 349.3

TAIWAN **
121.6 | 110.7

SOUTH KOREA
150.4 | 141.1

CHINA
Exports 219.6 | Imports 234.1

THAILAND
65.1 | 62.1

PHILIPPINES
32.1 | 31.4

MALAYSIA *
98.2 | 82.2

SINGAPORE
121.8 | 116

INDONESIA
56.3 | 31

AUSTRALIA
61.2 | 60.6

PAPUA NEW GUINEA *
2.4 | 1

NEW ZEALAND
13.7 | 13.3

RUSSIAN FEDERATION

MONGOLIA

NORTH KOREA

SOUTH KOREA

JAPAN

CHINA

BHUTAN

MYANMAR

LAOS

TAIWAN

THAILAND

VIETNAM

PHILIPPINES

CAMBODIA

NORTHERN MARIANA ISLANDS

PACIFIC

SRI LANKA

MARSHALL ISLANDS

MALAYSIA

SINGAPORE

PALAU

FED. STATES OF MICRONESIA

INDONESIA

PAPUA NEW GUINEA

NAURU

KIRIBATI

KIRIBATI

EAST TIMOR

SOLOMON ISLANDS

TUVALU

SAMOA

COO

VANUATU

FIJI

TONGA ISLAND

NEW CALEDONIA

AUSTRALIA

NEW ZEALAND

0   1000   2000   3000   4000 km

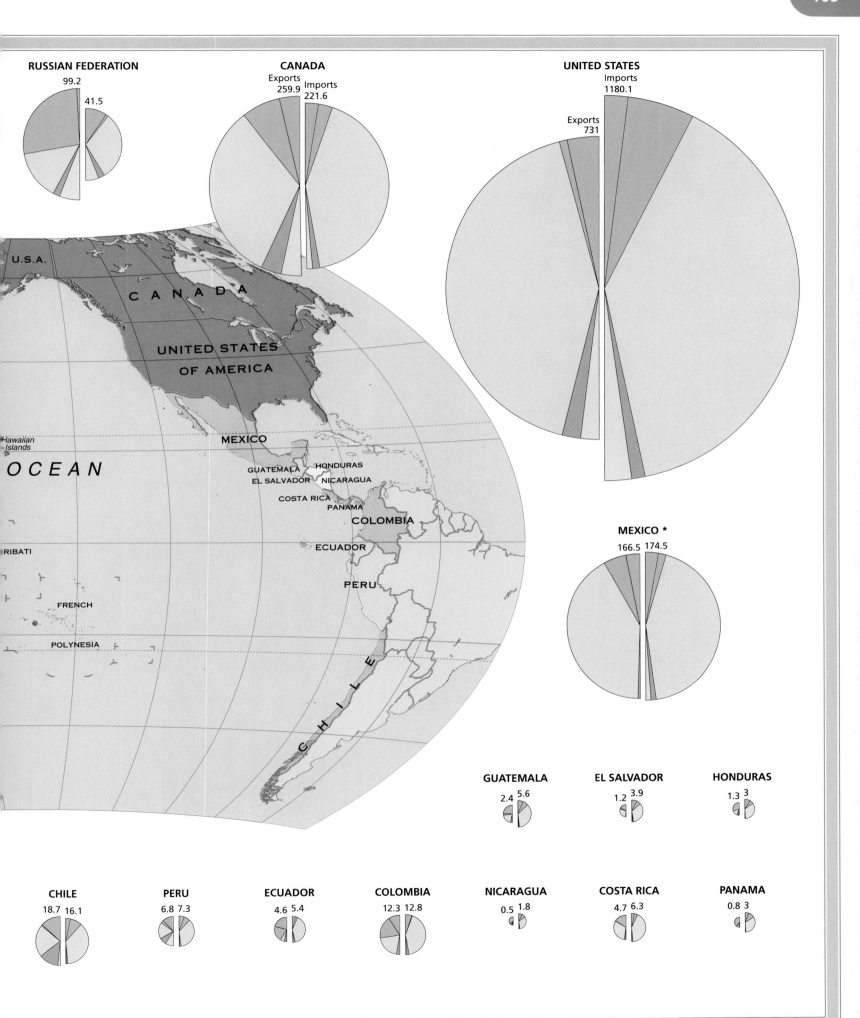

RUSSIAN FEDERATION
99.2
41.5

CANADA
Exports
259.9   Imports
221.6

UNITED STATES
Imports
1180.1
Exports
731

U.S.A.

C A N A D A

UNITED STATES
OF AMERICA

Hawaiian
Islands

O C E A N

MEXICO

GUATEMALA   HONDURAS
EL SALVADOR   NICARAGUA
COSTA RICA
PANAMA
COLOMBIA

ECUADOR

PERU

RIBATI

FRENCH

POLYNESIA

C H I L E

MEXICO *
166.5 174.5

GUATEMALA
2.4 5.6

EL SALVADOR
1.2 3.9

HONDURAS
1.3 3

CHILE
18.7 16.1

PERU
6.8 7.3

ECUADOR
4.6 5.4

COLOMBIA
12.3 12.8

NICARAGUA
0.5 1.8

COSTA RICA
4.7 6.3

PANAMA
0.8 3

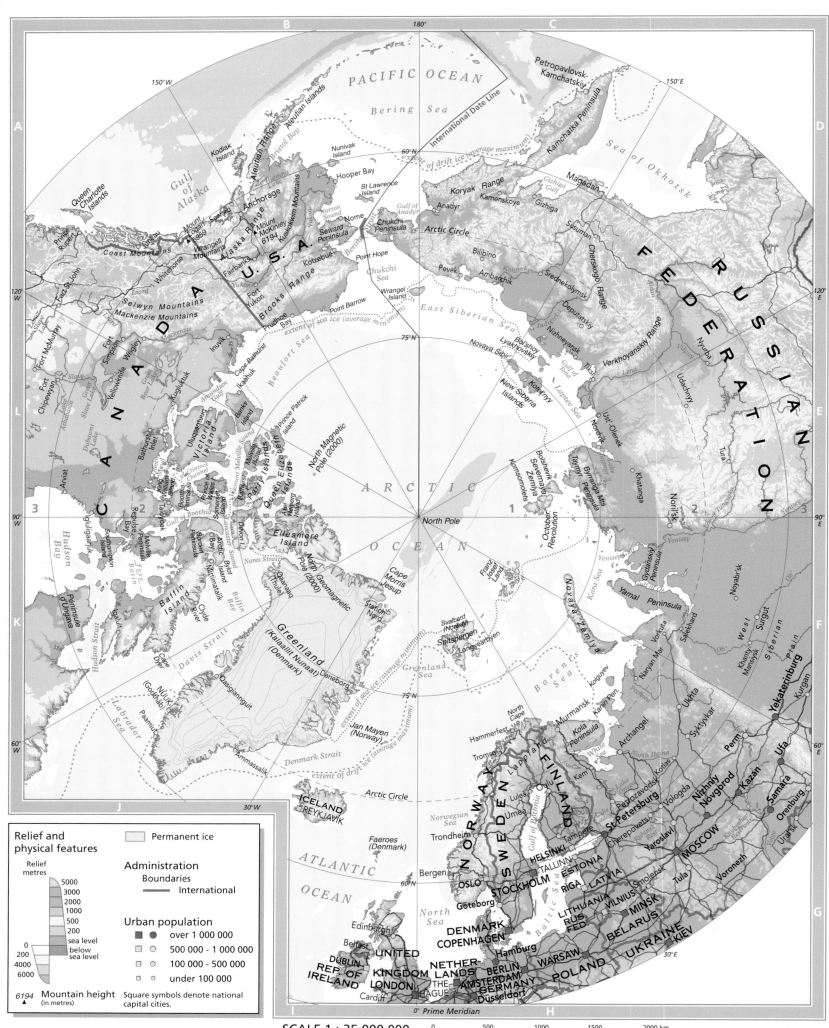

Relief and physical features

Relief metres
5000
3000
2000
1000
500
200
0 sea level
200 below
4000 sea level
6000

6194 ▲ Mountain height (in metres)

Permanent ice

Administration
Boundaries
International

Urban population
over 1 000 000
500 000 - 1 000 000
100 000 - 500 000
under 100 000

Square symbols denote national capital cities.

SCALE 1 : 35 000 000

0   500   1000   1500   2000 km

Polar Stereographic projection

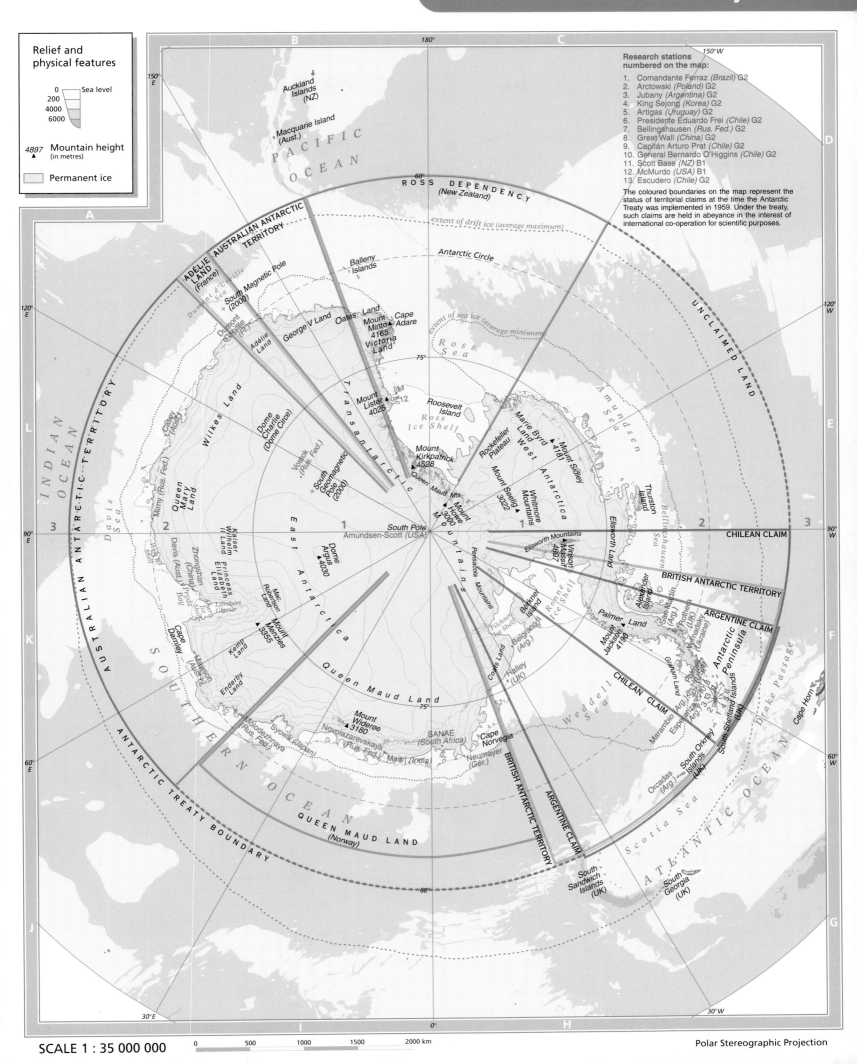

Relief and physical features

0	Sea level
200	
4000	
6000	

4897 ▲ Mountain height (in metres)

Permanent ice

Research stations numbered on the map:

1. Comandante Ferraz *(Brazil)* G2
2. Arctowski *(Poland)* G2
3. Jubany *(Argentina)* G2
4. King Sejong *(Korea)* G2
5. Artigas *(Uruguay)* G2
6. Presidente Eduardo Frei *(Chile)* G2
7. Bellingshausen *(Rus. Fed.)* G2
8. Great Wall *(China)* G2
9. Capitán Arturo Prat *(Chile)* G2
10. General Bernardo O'Higgins *(Chile)* G2
11. Scott Base *(NZ)* B1
12. McMurdo *(USA)* B1
13. Escudero *(Chile)* G2

The coloured boundaries on the map represent the status of territorial claims at the time the Antarctic Treaty was implemented in 1959. Under the treaty, such claims are held in abeyance in the interest of international co-operation for scientific purposes.

SCALE 1 : 35 000 000

0 500 1000 1500 2000 km

Polar Stereographic Projection

1 MAP SYMBOLS

Symbols are used on a map to show the location of features such as roads, rivers and towns. The meaning of each symbol used on a map is explained in the legend.

Map symbols often look like the features they represent. The colour of the symbol also provides a clue to its meaning (e.g. water is usually blue). The importance of a feature might be shown by the size of the symbol (e.g. larger cities are usually represented by larger circles).

Some examples of the symbols used in this atlas are shown below :

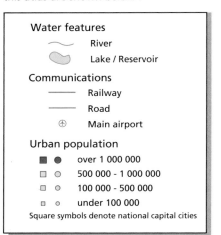

2 DIRECTION

Determining direction on a map is important because it indicates where one place is in relation to other places. The points of the compass are used to show the difference in direction between one place and another.

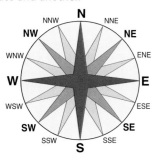

North, south, east and west are called the cardinal points of the compass. The other points are called intermediate points. Many maps have an arrow to indicate the direction toward north. If a map does not have a north arrow, north is assumed to be at the top of the map. Accurate direction can also be determined using the degrees of a circle. Zero degrees and 360 degrees are north (like 12 o'clock on a clock), and the numbers proceed clockwise. East is 90°, south is 180° and west is 270°.

3 MAP TYPES

Part of Central America

Political maps provide an overview of the size and location of countries in a specific area, such as a continent. Coloured squares indicate capital cities. Coloured circles represent other cities, with the size of the circle indicating the approximate size of the city.
See pages 108 and 126 for examples of this type of map.

Part of East Africa

Physical maps use colour to show oceans, seas, rivers, lakes, and height of the land. The names and heights of major landforms are also indicated. More information about land height, relief, and colour layers can be found on pages 172 and 175.
See pages 109 and 127 for examples of this type of map.

Part of the eastern seaboard of the United States

Physical/political maps bring together the information provided in the two types of map described above. They show relief and physical features as well as country borders, major cities and towns, roads, railways, and airports.
See pages 112–113 and 122–123 for examples of this type of map.

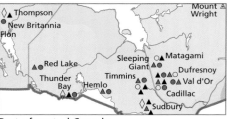

Part of central Canada

Distribution maps use different colours, symbols, or shading to show the location and distribution of natural or human-made features. In this map, different symbols have been used to show the location of iron ore, zinc, copper, nickel, silver and gold.
See pages 20 and 86 for examples of this type of map.

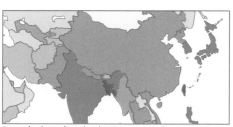

Population density in Eastern Asia

Graduated colour maps use dots, colours, or shading to show a feature's location and intensity. Generally, the highest numbers are shaded with the darkest colours. In this map, colours are used to show population density.
See pages 88 and 92 for examples of this type of map.

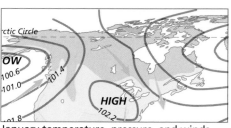

January temperature, pressure, and winds over Canada

Isoline maps use thin lines to show the distribution of a feature. An isoline passes through places that have the same value or quantity. Isolines may show features such as temperature (isotherm), air pressure (isobar), or height of land (contour). The value of the line is usually written on it; on either side, the value will be higher or lower.
See pages 10–11 and 82 for examples of this type of map.

1 SCALE

To draw a map of any part of the world, the area must be reduced, or "scaled down," to the size of a page in this atlas, a foldable road map, or a topographic map. The scale of the map indicates the amount by which an area has been reduced.

The scale of a map can also be used to determine the actual distance between two or more places or the actual size of an area on a map. The scale indicates the relationship between distances on the map and distances on the ground.

Scale can be shown

- **using words:** for example, "one centimetre to one kilometre" (one centimetre on the map represents one kilometre on the ground), or "one centimetre to 100 kilometres" (one centimetre on the map represents 100 kilometres on the ground).
- **using numbers:** for example, "1: 100 000 or 1/100 000" (one centimetre on the map represents 100 000 centimetres on the ground), or "1: 40 000 000 or 1/40 000 000" (one centimetre on the map represents 40 million centimetres on the ground). Normally, the large numbers with centimetres would be converted to metres or kilometres.
- **as a line scale:** for example,

```
0      200     400     600     800 km
```

2 USING MAPS OF DIFFERENT SCALE

The scale of the map will determine how much and what type of information can be shown. As the area shown on the map becomes larger and larger, the amount of detail and accuracy of the map becomes less and less.

Excerpt from the topographic map of Montréal at a scale of 1: 250 000. At this scale, the islands and bridges across the St Lawrence River are visible and urban areas (pink) can be seen.

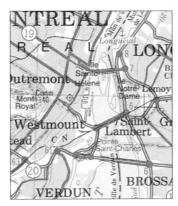

Excerpt from the map of Québec at a scale of 1: 7 500 000. At this scale, the general location of Montréal is indicated at the junction of the Ottawa and St Lawrence rivers, along with many of the surrounding towns and cities.

3 USING THE SCALE TO MEASURE DISTANCE

The instructions below show you how to determine how far apart places are on the map, then using the line scale, to determine the actual distance on the ground.

To use the line scale to measure the straight-line distance between two places on a map:
1. place the edge of a sheet of paper on the two places on a map,
2. on the paper, place a mark at each of the two places,
3. place the paper on the line scale,
4. measure the distance on the ground using the scale.

To find the distance between Calgary and Regina, line up the edge of a piece of paper between the two places and mark off the distance.

Compare this distance with the marks on the line scale. The straight-line distance between Calgary and Regina is about 650 kilometres.

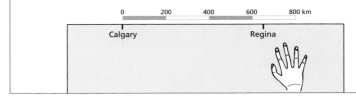

Often, the road or rail distance between two places is greater than the straight-line distance. To measure this distance:
1. place the edge of a sheet of paper on the map and mark off the start point on the paper,
2. move the paper so that its edge follows the bends and curves on the map (Hint: use the tip of your pencil to pin the edge of the paper to the curve as you pivot the paper around each curve),
3. mark off the end point on the sheet of paper,
4. place the paper on the line scale and read the actual distance following a road or railroad.

To find the distance by road between Calgary and Regina, mark off the start point, then twist the paper to follow the curve of the road through Medicine Hat, Swift Current, Moose Jaw, and then into Regina. The actual distance is about 750 kilometres.

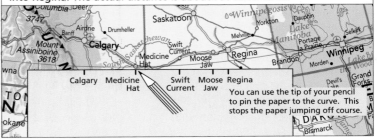

There are several ways of finding places on a map. This atlas uses three different methods:
- letters and numbers around the edge of the map
- lines of latitude and longitude drawn on the map
- the military grid system (see page 175) for Canadian topographic maps

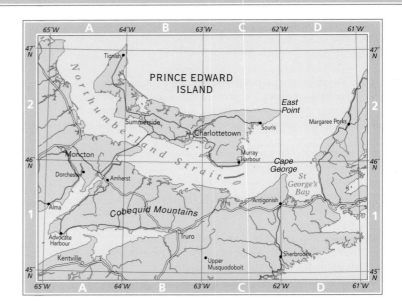

1 LETTERS AND NUMBERS

1. Find the name of the place in the gazetteer.
2. Find the page number and area reference (e.g., page 2, F2).
3. Go to the correct page in the atlas.
4. Find F in the border below the map, and find 2 on the side of the map.
5. Follow the letter up and follow the number across to find the correct square (F2).
6. Locate the place by searching the square.

Look at the map of Atlantic Canada. Charlottetown is located at B2, Truro is located at B1, and Moncton is located at A2.

2 LATITUDE

Latitude is distance, measured in degrees, north and south of the equator. Lines of latitude circle the globe in an east-west direction. The distance between lines of latitude is always the same; therefore, they are also known as parallels of latitude. Because the circumference of Earth gets smaller toward the poles, the lines of latitude are shorter nearer the poles.

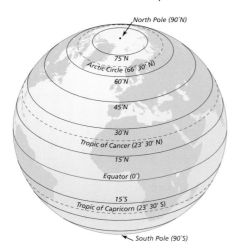

All lines of latitude have numbers between 0° and 90° and a direction, either north or south of the equator. The equator is at 0° latitude. It divides Earth into two halves: the Northern and Southern Hemispheres. The North Pole is at 90° north and the South Pole is at 90° south. The "tilt" of Earth has given particular importance to some lines of latitude . They include:
- the Arctic Circle at 66° 30' north
- the Antarctic Circle at 66° 30' south
- the Tropic of Cancer at 23° 30' north
- the Tropic of Capricorn at 23° 30' south

3 LONGITUDE

Longitude is distance, measured in degrees, east and west of the prime meridian. Lines of longitude join the poles in a north-south direction. Because the lines join the poles, they are always the same length, but are farthest apart at the equator and closest together at the poles. These lines are also called meridians of longitude.

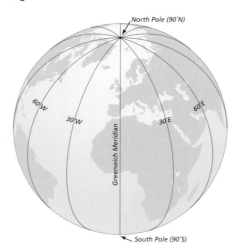

Longitude begins along the Prime Meridian, or Greenwich Meridian, at 0°, in London, England. On the opposite side of Earth is the 180° meridian, which is the International Date Line. These two lines can be used to divide Earth into two halves: the Western Hemisphere and the Eastern Hemisphere. To the west of the Prime Meridian are Canada, the United States, and Brazil; to the east of the Prime Meridian are Germany, India, and China. All lines of longitude have numbers between 0° and 180° and a direction, either east or west of the prime meridian.

4 FINDING PLACES

When lines of latitude and longitude are drawn on a map, they form a grid, which looks like a pattern of squares. This pattern is used to find places on a map. Latitude is always stated before longitude (e.g., 42°N, 78°W).

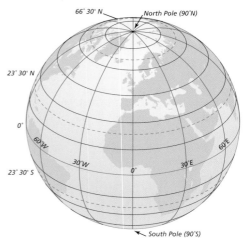

On the map of Atlantic Canada (above), Murray Harbour is directly on a line of **latitude** – representing 46°N. Similarly, Antigonish is directly on a line of **longitude** – representing 62°W. Other places, not exactly on lines, use subdivisions of degrees called minutes. There are 60 minutes in a degree. Truro is located almost halfway between 45°N and 46°N and about one quarter of the distance between the lines 63°W and 64°W longitude. Its latitude and longitude would be 45° 25'N, and 63° 15'W.

Since Earth is a sphere and maps are flat, map makers (cartographers) have invented different ways of drawing the round surface of Earth on a flat piece of paper. These methods are called map projections.

There are many different types of map projections, but none of them can perfectly match the sphere of Earth. Every map projection must "stretch" or "squash" the round surface to make it fit onto a flat piece of paper. As a result, no map projection can correctly show all four aspects of a map – shape, area, direction, and distance – at the same time. In drawing any ONE of these four aspects accurately, the other three become distorted or inaccurate. Each map projection has advantages and disadvantages.

1 CYLINDRICAL PROJECTIONS

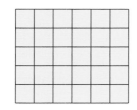

Cylindrical projections are constructed by projecting the surface of the globe or sphere (Earth) onto a cylinder that just touches the outside edges of that globe. Two examples of cylindrical projections are Mercator and Times.

Mercator (see pages 154-155 for an example of this projection)

The Mercator cylindrical projection is a useful projection for areas near the equator and to about 15 degrees north or south of the equator, where distortion of shape is minimal. The projection is useful for navigation, since directions are plotted as straight lines.

Times (see pages 80-81 for an example of this projection)

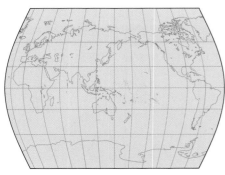

The Times projection is similar to the Mercator projection, but the meridians of longitude are slightly curved. The Times projection is most accurate halfway between the poles at 45°N and 45°S.

2 CONIC PROJECTIONS

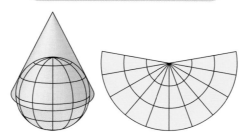

Conic projections are constructed by projecting the surface of a globe or sphere (Earth) onto a cone that just touches the outside edges of that globe. Examples of conic projections are Albers Equal Area Conic and Chamberlin Trimetric.

Conic Equidistant (see pages 142-143 for an example of this projection)

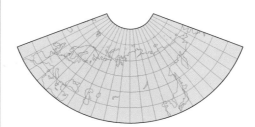

Conic projections are best suited for areas between 30° and 60° north and south of the equator when the east-west distance is greater than the north-south distance (such as Northern Eurasia). The meridians are straight and spaced at equal intervals.

Chamberlin Trimetric (see page 108 for an example of this projection)

Chamberlin Trimetric is an equidistant projection. It is used to show areas with greater north-south extent than east-west extent (such as North America).

3 AZIMUTHAL PROJECTIONS

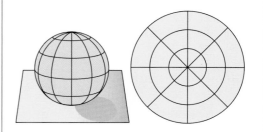

Azimuthal projections are constructed by projecting the surface of the globe or sphere (Earth) onto a flat surface that touches the globe at one point only. Some examples of azimuthal projections are Lambert Azimuthal Equal Area and Polar Stereographic.

Lambert Azimuthal Equal Area (see pages 158-159 for an example of this projection)

Lambert's projection is useful for areas that have similar east-west and north-south dimensions such as Australia.

Polar Stereographic (see page 167 for an example of this projection)

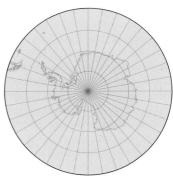

This projection is a good choice for showing travel routes from a central point because points on the map are in constant relative position and distance from the centre.

1 CLIMATE STATISTICS AND TABLES

Climate statistics (temperatures and precipitation) can be found in a number of locations, including textbooks, reference texts in the library, and Web sites dealing with weather and climate. In this atlas, the climate statistics have been transformed into climate graphs (see below). The statistics are usually shown in three rows: the station name (and altitude) and months of the year in the first row; the average temperature for each month in the second row; and the average precipitation for each month in the third row. This information can be used to develop a climate graph similar to the one below.

Saskatoon (515 metres)	Jan	Feb	Mar	Apr	May	Jun	Jul	Aug	Sep	Oct	Nov	Dec
Temperature - (°C)	-17.0	-13.0	-5.8	4.4	11.5	16.0	18.2	17.3	11.2	4.5	-6.2	-14.3
Precipitation - (mm)	15.2	10.3	14.7	23.9	49.4	61.1	60.1	38.8	30.7	16.7	13.3	15.9

2 CLIMATE GRAPHS

A climate graph is a combination of a line graph and a bar graph. The line is used to indicate temperature and is related to the scale at the left side of the graph. The precipitation is shown as a series of 12 bars, each one representing a month, and is related to the scale on the right side. The total annual precipitation is shown at the top of the graph.

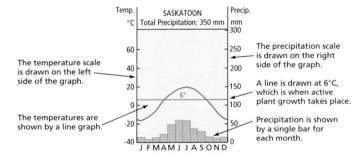

The temperature scale is drawn on the left side of the graph.

The temperatures are shown by a line graph.

The precipitation scale is drawn on the right side of the graph.

A line is drawn at 6°C, which is when active plant growth takes place.

Precipitation is shown by a single bar for each month.

3 UNDERSTANDING CLIMATE GRAPHS

- A temperature line that is almost flat indicates a location close to the equator that has even temperatures all year round.
- A temperature line that has a large bump (∩) or dip (∪) indicates a location that has a definite winter and summer season. If the period from May to September is shown by a bump (∩), indicating higher temperatures in that period, then the location is in the northern hemisphere. If the same time period shows a dip (∪), indicating lower temperatures, then the location is in the southern hemisphere.
- When a number of high precipitation bars are grouped together, this is an indication of a distinctive wet season. If there are few or no bars for a series of months, then this indicates a distinctive dry season. If all the precipitation bars are high throughout the year, the location is wet all year round. If the precipitation bars are quite low or non-existent for most of the year, the location is very dry.

The climate graph for Saskatoon indicates a location that has low winter temperatures, high summer temperatures, and a concentration of precipitation during the summer months.

4 UNDERSTANDING RELIEF

Relief refers to differences in the height of land. In this atlas, the height of land is shown in three ways: colour layers, spot heights, and contours. Contours are dealt with on pages 174 and 175.
- Colour layers: different colours are used to show different heights.
- Spot heights: dots or triangles (with an associated number) show the location and height of significant places on the map.

5 COLOUR LAYERS

A relief scale is placed in the legend or at the side of the page to show the colour layers that have been used to illustrate ranges of elevation. To make comparisons easy, this atlas uses the same colours to represent the same range of elevations on all maps of this type.

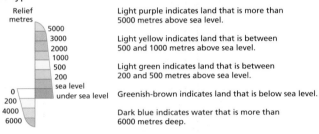

Light purple indicates land that is more than 5000 metres above sea level.

Light yellow indicates land that is between 500 and 1000 metres above sea level.

Light green indicates land that is between 200 and 500 metres above sea level.

Greenish-brown indicates land that is below sea level.

Dark blue indicates water that is more than 6000 metres deep.

6 SPOT HEIGHTS

Physical maps often use spot heights to show the highest mountain in an area. The map of the island of New Guinea illustrates both the coloured layers of relief and spot heights. From this map, the following information can be determined:

Doberai Peninsula, New Guinea

3000 ▲ Mountain height (in metres)

- The area in the north-eastern portion of the Doberai Peninsula is high.
- The mountainous area covers nearly half of the peninsula.
- Mount Kwoka is 3000 metres in elevation and is located at the northern end of the mountain range.

7 BUT, WHAT DOES IT LOOK LIKE?

The next step is to imagine what the area would look like if we could fly over the area at the bottom edge of the map and look north toward the Doberai Peninsula on a very clear day.

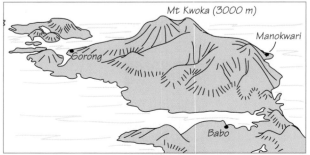

Field sketch of Doberai Peninsula

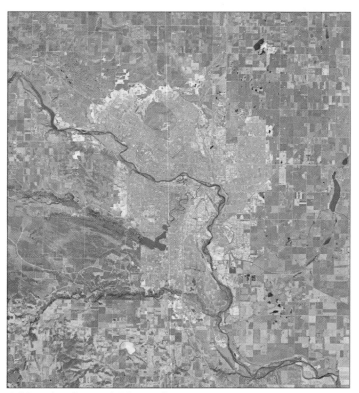

A false-colour image of Calgary, Alberta.

A true-colour image of Calgary, Alberta.

1 REMOTE SENSING

Maps, aerial photographs, and satellite images provide unique views of the Earth – views from above Earth. Geographers use photographs and electronic images taken from aircraft and satellites to determine patterns, trends, and basic characteristics of Earth. Aerial photographs can be used to produce three-dimensional images, which can then be converted into maps.

Since the 1960s, satellites fitted with cameras, scanners, and sensors have been programmed to collect useful information about Earth's lands and waters. The information is gathered using types of electromagnetic radiation – X - ray, ultraviolet, visible, and microwave. It is recorded in digital form, sent back to Earth, and processed into images. Satellites collect information on soil moisture conditions, vegetation coverage, land use, marine resources, ozone levels, geology, air and water pollution, and weather patterns.

2 LANDSAT AND RADARSAT

The United States has a series of satellites, including Landsat, that use different wavelengths to record characteristics of Earth's surface. When the data is sent back to Earth, colours are artificially added to make it easier to interpret the images. In recent years, Landsat imagery has changed from the "false-colour" images to more natural colours. This trend is reflected in the images shown to the left.

Canada has had extensive involvement with remote sensing and has been effective in gathering information from areas that may not be easily accessible. Radarsat is an orbiting satellite that uses radar signals to provide complete coverage of Canada's land area every three days. Since these images are not light sensitive, Radarsat can provide 24-hour coverage in all weather conditions. Radarsat was launched with the assistance of United States facilities in exchange for the sharing of data. The main purposes for Radarsat include monitoring environmental changes and providing resource development data.

3 SATELLITE IMAGES IN THIS ATLAS

The Pearson School Atlas includes a variety of images and maps derived from satellite data. Three of the numerous examples included are:
• a false-colour image of the Amazon Basin (page 122)
• a satellite image of the Great Barrier Reef (page 159)
• a computer-generated, three-dimensional image of Nyirangongo volcano in the Democratic Republic of Congo, which combines both Landsat imagery and radar-topography techniques (page 129)

In a false-colour satellite image, colours are used to signify the following characteristics:

White	bare ground, sand, salt, clouds, ice and snow
Yellow	little vegetation cover, heavily grazed areas
Pink/red	early growth in crops and grasslands
Red	healthy green vegetation, rainforest (deep red), mangroves (red-brown)
Brown	woodland, bare rock
Light green	moist ploughed fields, poor grazing lands
Dark green	forests or scrub, clear shallow water
Blue/light blue	arid scrubland, very shallow water
Blue/grey	urban areas, concrete, houses
Dark blue/black	ocean, deep water, cloud shadows

Topographic maps illustrate the characteristics of an area in great detail. Both natural features (e.g. rivers, wooded areas) and human-made features (e.g. roads, buildings, cemeteries) are identified. This is possible because the scale is usually large.

Most countries have topographic maps in a range of scales from 1: 50 000 to 1: 250 000. Topographic maps are used for a variety of purposes including camping, hiking, biking, urban planning and surveying.

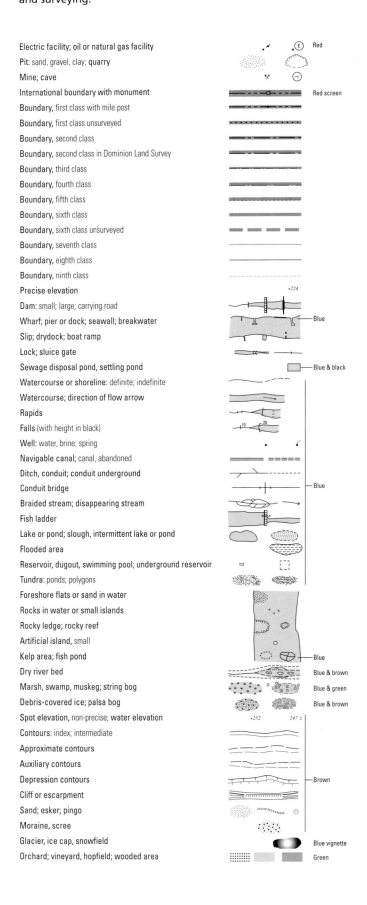

Dual highway, hard surface

Road, hard surface, more than 2 lanes

Road, hard surface, 2 lanes — Red

Road, hard surface, less than 2 lanes

Street

Road, loose or stabilized surface, all season, 2 lanes or more

Road, loose or stabilized surface, all season, less than 2 lanes — Orange

Road, loose surface, dry weather

Unclassified road, street

Vehicle track or winter road; gate

Trail, cut line or portage; portage, short or position uncertain

Road, under construction — Orange or red

Highway interchange with number; traffic circle — Red

Highway route number — Orange or red

Built-up area; street; park/sports field — Red screen; black screen

Indian reserve; small

Railway, single track; railway station; turntable

Railway, multiple tracks

Railway, under construction

Railway, abandoned

Railway on road; special track railway

Rapid transit route: rail; road

Bridge; footbridge; snowshed

Bridge: swing, draw, lift; tunnel

Cut; embankment, causeway

Dyke or levee; with road

Ferry

Ford

Submarine cable

Navigation light; navigation beacon

Coast Guard station; exposed shipwreck

Seaplane base; seaplane anchorage

Crib or abandoned bridge pier

Airfield, position approximate; heliport

Building(s)

Church; non-Christian place of worship; shrine

School; elevator; fire station

Sports track; stadium

Silo; kiln; dome

Cemetery; historic site or point of interest

Landmark object (with height): tower, chimney, etc.

Campground; picnic site; service centre

Golf course; golf driving range; drive-in theatre

Wind-operated device; ruins; greenhouse

Aerial cableway, ski lift, conveyor

Ski area, ski jump

Wall; fence

Tank(s): vertical; horizontal

Warden, ranger station; Customs

Well: oil, gas

Crane: vertical; horizontal

Rifle range with butts

Power transmission line; multiple lines

Telephone line; firebreak

Pipeline with control valve

Pipeline underground; multiple pipelines underground

Electric facility; oil or natural gas facility — Red

Pit: sand, gravel, clay; quarry

Mine; cave

International boundary with monument — Red screen

Boundary, first class with mile post

Boundary, first class unsurveyed

Boundary, second class

Boundary, second class in Dominion Land Survey

Boundary, third class

Boundary, fourth class

Boundary, fifth class

Boundary, sixth class

Boundary, sixth class unsurveyed

Boundary, seventh class

Boundary, eighth class

Boundary, ninth class

Precise elevation

Dam: small; large; carrying road

Wharf; pier or dock; seawall; breakwater — Blue

Slip; drydock; boat ramp

Lock; sluice gate

Sewage disposal pond, settling pond — Blue & black

Watercourse or shoreline: definite; indefinite

Watercourse; direction of flow arrow

Rapids

Falls (with height in black)

Well: water, brine; spring

Navigable canal; canal, abandoned

Ditch, conduit; conduit underground

Conduit bridge — Blue

Braided stream; disappearing stream

Fish ladder

Lake or pond; slough, intermittent lake or pond

Flooded area

Reservoir, dugout, swimming pool; underground reservoir

Tundra: ponds; polygons

Foreshore flats or sand in water

Rocks in water or small islands

Rocky ledge; rocky reef

Artificial island, small

Kelp area; fish pond — Blue

Dry river bed — Blue & brown

Marsh, swamp, muskeg; string bog — Blue & green

Debris-covered ice; palsa bog — Blue & brown

Spot elevation, non-precise; water elevation

Contours: index; intermediate

Approximate contours

Auxiliary contours

Depression contours — Brown

Cliff or escarpment

Sand; esker; pingo

Moraine, scree

Glacier, ice cap, snowfield — Blue vignette

Orchard; vineyard, hopfield; wooded area — Green

1 SYMBOLS

There are four different kinds of symbols on topographic maps. These are illustrated on page 174. *Point* symbols show locations of features such as schools, cemeteries, or historic sites. *Line* symbols are used for such things as roads, power lines, rivers and political boundaries. *Contours* are special line symbols representing places at the same elevation. *Area* symbols cover a specific area on a map, such as marshes, forests, sand pits and urban areas.

2 ELEVATION AND RELIEF

Contours indicate the height of land above sea level or the depth of water. When contours are close together, they indicate a steep slope (a large change in elevation over a short distance). When contours are far apart, the landscape varies little over large areas. The distance between contours may change from one map to another and may be expressed in metres or in feet. Eventually, all Canadian topographic maps will be in metric figures. Contours can be helpful in determining the direction of water flow, since they form a V-pattern pointing upstream.
On topographic maps, individual elevations – for example, the top of a mountain – are shown by a spot height or a benchmark to indicate a permanent marker set in concrete or in the bedrock.

The example above shows part of the Wolfville, Nova Scotia topographic sheet. The contours are 10 metres apart. There are relatively flat areas on the left and right sides and steep slopes along the stream. The contours point in a V upstream indicating that the three streams all flow from south to north.

3 GRIDS AND CO-ORDINATES

Topographic maps use grid lines that are numbered from the bottom to the top of the map and from the left to the right side (or, from south to north and from west to east). In this atlas, the grid lines are numbered around the edges of the map, similar to topographic maps.

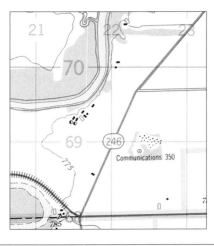

In the sample (at the bottom of the previous column) from the Morris, Manitoba topographic sheet, the communications tower is at grid point 224689. This means that it is 4/10ths of the way between lines 22 and 23 (224), and 9/10ths of the way between lines 68 and 69 (689). Similarly the house at the very top of the example is located at 2/10ths to the east of line 22 (222) and 6/10ths north of line 70 (706). Putting these three digit numbers together provides the co-ordinates 222706 for the location of the house.

4 CROSS-SECTIONAL DIAGRAMS

Cross-sectional diagrams (or profiles) help you to visualize the landscape. However, the vertical scale is different from the horizontal scale and therefore the slope becomes exaggerated.

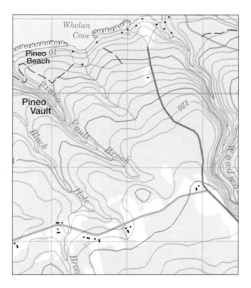

To draw a profile from Whelan Cove to the road junction in the bottom right-hand corner, follow these instructions.
• Determine the contour interval, for example, 10 metres.
• Draw a line on the map joining the two locations.
• Lay a piece of paper along the line, and indicate the elevation at each end of the line.
• Put a mark on the piece of paper where each contour crosses the line.
• Label each mark with the elevation (e.g. edge of the water, 10 m, 20 m, etc.)
• On a second piece of paper, draw a graph scale using the contour interval as the vertical scale, for example 10 metres.
• Place the first piece of paper along the horizontal part of the graph and transfer each mark up to the corresponding value on the vertical scale.
• Join the dots with a smoothly flowing line to create a profile of the landscape.

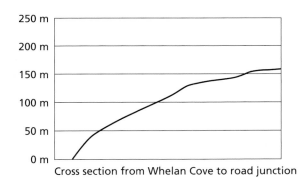

Cross section from Whelan Cove to road junction

1 Land and Fresh Water Areas

	NL	PE	NS	NB	QC	ON	MB	SK	AB	BC	YT	NWT	NU	CANADA
Total Land and Fresh Water Area	405 212	5 660	55 284	72 908	1 542 056	1 076 395	647 797	651 036	661 848	944 735	482 443	1 346 106	2 093 190	9 984 670
Percent of Canada's Total Area (land and fresh water)	4.1	0.1	0.6	0.7	15.4	10.8	6.5	6.5	6.6	9.5	4.8	13.5	21.0	100
Percent of Canada's Fresh Water Area	3.5	0	0.2	0.2	19.8	17.8	10.6	6.7	2.2	2.2	0.9	18.3	17.6	100

SOURCE: Natural Resources Canada

2 Land Cover

Type	Description	Area (000 km²)	Percentage of Total Land and Fresh Water Area
Forest and Taiga	Forests, some wetlands, barren lands	4 456	45
Tundra	Barrens in arctic or high altitude environments	2 302	23
Wetlands	Swamps, bogs, marshes (including coastal marshes), some with trees	1 244	12
Fresh Water	Lakes, rivers, streams, reservoirs	755	8
Cropland	Farms (including orchards and vineyards), fenced pasture land	658	6
Rangeland	Grazing land (non-fenced)	203	2
Ice and Snow	Permanent glaciers, snow, ice caps	272	3
Human Use	Urban, transportatation, industrial uses	79	1
TOTAL		9 970	100

Based on a variety of sources; some data has been recently adjusted to reflect the results of new satellite imaging techniques

POPULATION

3 Population Growth in Canada, 1851 to 2001

	Population (000)	Change From Last Major Census Year (000)	Change From Last Major Census Year Percent	Annual Rate of Growth (percent)
1851	2 436.3	na	na	na
1861	3 229.6	793.3	32.6	2.9
1871	3 689.3	459.6	14.2	1.3
1881	4 324.8	635.6	17.2	1.6
1891	4 833.2	508.4	11.8	1.1
1901	5 371.3	538.1	11.1	1.1
1911	7 206.6	1 835.3	34.2	3.0
1921	8 787.9	1 581.3	21.9	2.0
1931	10 376.8	1 588.8	18.1	1.7
1941	11 506.7	1 129.9	10.9	1.0
1951[a]	14 009.4	2 502.8	21.8	1.7
1961	18 238.2	2 157.5	13.4	2.5
1971	21 568.3	3 330.1	18.3	1.8
1981	24 343.2	2 774.9	12.9	1.3
1991	27 297.0	2 953.8	12.1	1.2
2001	30 007.1	2 710.1	9.9	1.0

[a]Newfoundland included for the first time. Excluding Newfoundland, the increase would have been 2 141 358 or 18.6%.
SOURCE: Census of Canada

4 Population Growth by Province and Territory, 1867 to 2001

	NL (000)	PE (000)	NS (000)	NB (000)	QC (000)	ON (000)	MB (000)	SK (000)	AB (000)	BC (000)	YT (000)	NWT (000)	NU[a] (000)	CANADA (000)
1867	na	88	364	271	1 123	1 525	15	na	na	32	na	45	na	3 463
1871	na	94	388	286	1 191	1 621	25	na	na	36	na	48	na	3 689
1881	na	109	441	321	1 360	1 927	62	na	na	49	na	56	na	4 325
1891	na	109	450	321	1 489	2 114	153	na	na	98	na	99	na	4 833
1901	na	103	460	331	1 649	2 183	255	91	73	179	27	20	na	5 371
1911	na	94	492	352	2 006	2 527	461	492	374	393	9	7	na	7 207
1921	na	88.6	523.8	387.9	2 360.5	2 933.7	610.1	757.5	588.5	524.6	4.1	8.1	na	8 787.4
1931	na	88.0	512.8	408.2	2 874.7	3 431.7	700.1	921.8	731.6	694.3	4.2	9.3	na	10 376.7
1941	na	95.0	578.0	457.4	3 331.9	3 787.7	729.7	896.0	796.2	817.8	5.0	12.0	na	11 506.7
1951	361.4	98.4	642.6	515.7	4 055.7	4 597.6	776.5	831.7	939.5	1 165.2	9.1	16.0	na	14 009.4
1961	457.9	104.6	737.0	597.9	5 259.2	6 236.1	921.7	925.2	1 332.0	1 629.1	14.6	23.0	na	18 238.3
1971	522.1	111.6	789.0	634.6	6 027.8	7 703.1	988.2	926.2	1 627.9	2 184.6	18.4	34.8	na	21 568.3
1981	567.7	122.5	847.4	696.4	6 438.4	8 625.1	1 026.2	968.3	2 237.7	2 744.5	23.2	45.7	na	24 343.2
1991	568.0	130.0	900.0	724.0	6 896.0	10 085.0	1 092.0	989.0	2 546.0	3 282.0	26.9	54.8	na	27 297.0
2001	512.9	135.3	908.0	729.5	7 237.5	11 410.0	1 119.6	978.9	2 974.8	3 907.7	28.7	37.4	26.7	30 007.1

[a]Part of Northwest Territories until 1999
SOURCE: Census of Canada

5 Demographics of Canada, 1851 to 2001

	Total Population Growth[a] (000)	Births (000)	Deaths (000)	Natural Increase (000)	Immigration (000)	Emigration (000)	Net Migration (000)	Population at End of Period (000)
1851–1861	793	1 281	670	611	352	170	182	3 230
1861–1871	460	1 370	760	610	260	410	-150	3 689
1871-1881	636	1 480	790	690	350	404	-54	4 325
1881–1891	508	1 524	870	654	680	826	-146	4 833
1891–1901	538	1 548	880	668	250	380	-130	5 371
1901–1911	1 835	1 925	900	1 025	1 550	740	810	7 207
1911–1921	1 581	2 340	1 070	1 270	1 400	1 089	311	8 788
1921–1931	1 589	2 420	1 060	1 360	1 200	970	230	10 377
1931–1941	1 130	2 294	1 072	1 222	149	241	-92	11 507
1941–1951	2 503	3 212	1 220	1 992	548	382	166	14 009
1951–1961	4 229	4 468	1 320	3 148	1 543	563	980	18 238
1961–1971	3 330	4 105	1 497	2 608	1 429	707	722	21 568
1971–1981	2 775	3 575	1 667	1 908	1 824	636	1 188	24 343
1981–1991	2 954	3 805	1 831	1 974	1 876	491	1 385	27 297
1991–2001	2 710	3 640	2 119	1 521	2 229	410	1 819	30 007

[a] Total population growth is the difference in the census population count at the end of the period
SOURCE: Statistics Canada

6 Demographics by Province and Territory, 2002

		NL	PE	NS	NB	QC	ON	MB	SK	AB	BC	YT	NWT	NU	CANADA
Birth Rate/1000		8.8	10.2	9.4	9.5	9.7	10.6	12.1	11.8	12.0	9.7	11.7	15.6	26.5	10.4
Death Rate/1000		8.3	8.5	8.6	8.5	7.3	7.4	9.0	9.3	6.1	6.9	4.9	4.2	4.9	7.4
Natural Increase Rate/1000		0.5	1.7	0.8	1.0	2.4	3.2	3.1	2.5	5.9	2.8	6.8	11.4	21.6	3.0
International Migration															
Immigration Rate/1000		0.8	1.0	1.7	1.0	5.2	12.7	4.2	1.8	5.3	9.1	2.3	2.2	0.6	8.1
Emigration Rate/1000		0.8	0.3	0.8	0.5	1.7	2.9	1.7	1.2	2.7	2.3	3.6	2.4	2.3	2.3
Net Migration Rate/1000		0.0	0.7	0.9	0.5	3.5	9.8	2.5	0.6	2.6	6.8	-1.3	-0.2	-1.7	5.8
Interprovincial Migration															
Net Migration Rate/1000		-4.7	4.9	-1.3	-1.1	-1.1	0.6	-4.6	-8.5	8.6	-1.7	-13.2	-7.5	0.8	–
Total Net Migration Rate/1000		-4.7	5.6	-0.4	-0.6	2.4	10.4	-2.1	-7.9	11.2	5.1	-14.5	-7.7	-0.9	–
Total Growth Rate/1000		-4.2	7.3	0.4	0.4	4.8	13.6	1.0	-5.4	17.1	7.9	-7.7	3.7	20.7	8.8
Infant Mortality Rate/1000[a]		5.2	4.4	4.4	5.7	5.6	5.5	7.5	8.9	4.8	4.7	8.4	10.9	na	5.5
Life Expectancy at Birth (years)[b]	M	75.0	73.9	74.9	75.2	75.2	76.1	75.5	75.5	76.0	76.1	72.3	69.9	na	75.7
	F	80.5	80.7	80.7	81.2	81.5	81.4	80.8	81.4	81.3	81.9	84.7	75.8	na	81.4

[a] 1997 figures
[b] 1996 figures
SOURCE: Statistics Canada

7 Population of Census Metropolitan Areas, 1951 to 2001

Census Metropolitan Area	1951 (000)	1961 (000)	1971 (000)	1981 (000)	1991 (000)	2001 (000)	Percent Change 1991–2001	Rank 2001 (1951)
Toronto	1 261.9	1 919.4	2 628.0	2 998.9	3 893.0	4 682.9	20.3	1 (2)
Montréal	1 539.3	2 215.6	2 743.2	2 828.4	3 127.2	3 426.4	9.6	2 (1)
Vancouver	586.2	826.8	1 082.4	1 268.2	1 602.5	1 987.0	24.0	3 (3)
Ottawa-Hull	311.6	457.0	602.5	718.0	920.9	1 063.7	15.5	4 (5)
Calgary	142.3	279.1	403.3	592.7	754.0	951.4	26.2	5 (12)
Edmonton	193.6	359.8	495.7	657.1	839.9	937.8	11.7	6 (8)
Québec	289.3	379.1	480.5	576.1	645.6	682.8	5.8	7 (6)
Winnipeg	357.2	476.5	540.3	548.8	652.4	671.3	2.9	8 (4)
Hamilton	281.9	401.1	498.5	542.1	599.8	662.4	10.4	9 (7)
London	167.7	226.7	286.0	283.7	381.5	432.5	13.4	10 (11)
Kitchener	107.5	154.9	226.8	287.8	356.4	414.3	16.2	11 (15)
St Catharines-Niagara	189.0	257.8	303.4	304.4	364.6	377.0	3.4	12 (9)
Halifax	138.4	193.4	222.6	277.7	320.5	359.2	12.1	13 (13)
Victoria	114.9	155.8	195.8	233.5	288.0	311.9	8.3	14 (14)
Windsor	182.6	217.2	258.6	246.1	262.1	307.9	17.5	15 (10)
Oshawa[a]			120.3	154.2	240.1	296.3	23.4	16 (-)
Saskatoon	55.7	95.6	126.4	154.2	210.0	225.9	7.6	17 (22)
Regina	72.7	113.7	140.7	164.3	191.7	192.8	0.6	18 (21)
St John's, Nfld.	80.9	106.7	131.8	154.8	171.9	172.9	0.6	19 (17)
Greater Sudbury	80.5	127.4	155.4	149.9	157.6	155.6	-1.3	20 (19)
Chicoutimi-Jonquière	91.2	127.6	133.7	135.2	160.9	154.9	-3.7	21 (16)
Sherbrooke[a]				74.1	139.2	153.8	10.5	22 (-)
Abbotsford[a]						147.4		23 (-)
Kingston[a]						146.8		24 (-)
Trois-Rivières	46.1	53.5	55.9	111.5	136.3	137.5	0.9	25 (23)
Saint John, N.B.	80.7	98.1	106.7	114.0	125.0	122.7	-1.8	26 (18)
Thunder Bay	73.7	102.1	112.1	121.4	124.4	122.0	-1.9	27 (20)

[a] Although there may have been an urban centre here, it was not a Census Metropolitan Area until the date indicated
SOURCE: Statistics Canada

8 Population by Age Group, 1911 to 2001

	0–4 years (000)	5–9 years (000)	10–14 years (000)	15–24 years (000)	25–34 years (000)	35–44 years (000)	45–54 years (000)	55–64 years (000)	65 years and over (000)	Total Population (000)
1911	890	785	702	1 398	1 219	863	620	393	336	7 207
1921	1 059	1 050	914	1 518	1 343	1 163	799	521	420	8 787
1931	1 074	1 133	1 074	1 952	1 495	1 334	1 075	662	576	10 377
1941	1 052	1 046	1 101	2 152	1 811	1 436	1 227	914	768	11 507
1951	1 722	1 398	1 131	2 147	2 174	1 869	1 407	1 077	1 086	14 009
1961	2 256	2 080	1 856	2 616	2 481	2 390	1 879	1 289	1 391	18 238
1971	1 817	2 254	2 310	4 004	2 890	2 527	2 292	1 731	1 745	21 568
1981	1 783	1 777	1 921	4 659	4 216	2 968	2 499	2 159	2 361	24 343
1991	1 907	1 908	1 878	3 831	4 866	4 372	2 966	2 400	3 170	27 297
2001	1 696	1 976	2 053	4 009	3 995	5 102	4 419	2 868	3 889	30 007

SOURCE: Census of Canada 2001

9 Population by Age and Sex, 2001

Sex and Age	NL (000)	PE (000)	NS (000)	NB (000)	QC (000)	ON (000)	MB (000)	SK (000)	AB (000)	BC (000)	YT (000)	NWT (000)	NU (000)	CANADA (000)
Male														
0–4 years	12.7	3.9	24.3	19.4	192.3	343.3	36.4	31.0	95.3	105.4	0.9	1.5	1.7	868.1
5–9	15.0	4.7	28.4	22.6	232.7	396.4	41.0	35.4	106.9	123.8	1.0	1.8	1.7	1 011.5
10–14	17.9	5.0	31.5	24.8	234.1	405.0	42.3	39.4	114.1	132.7	1.2	1.8	1.7	1 051.5
15–24	36.8	9.5	58.9	49.3	482.0	754.6	77.7	73.5	223.8	261.1	2.0	2.9	2.4	2 034.4
25–34	31.8	8.0	55.3	46.4	460.0	760.7	71.4	56.8	216.4	253.0	1.8	3.0	2.3	1 966.8
35–44	41.2	10.3	74.1	60.1	617.5	963.8	88.2	73.7	259.5	320.4	2.7	3.5	1.8	2 516.7
45–54	41.1	9.9	67.8	56.0	548.1	801.5	77.3	66.0	213.3	297.0	2.6	2.6	1.2	2 184.5
55–64	26.5	6.6	45.5	36.4	371.0	520.6	49.4	41.8	120.8	188.9	1.4	1.2	0.6	1 410.8
65–74	17.1	4.6	31.2	24.1	248.7	383.6	36.8	34.7	83.9	139.5	0.6	0.6	0.3	1 005.6
75–84	8.9	2.5	17.5	14.1	121.0	202.3	22.7	22.4	42.3	77.3	0.2	0.2	0.09	531.5
85 years and over	2.0	0.7	4.6	3.6	25.6	45.3	6.5	7.0	10.4	19.8	0.06	0.05	0.02	125.6
Female														
0–4 years	12.1	3.7	23.1	18.3	183.5	327.9	34.3	29.9	91.2	100.3	0.8	1.5	1.6	828.2
5–9	14.1	4.4	27.5	21.5	224.6	376.3	39.3	33.9	101.6	117.2	1.0	1.8	1.6	964.7
10–14	17.0	5.0	30.3	23.5	224.4	383.9	40.4	37.6	108.6	126.6	1.1	1.7	1.5	1 001.7
15–24	36.5	9.5	59.0	48.1	467.5	733.3	75.6	70.7	214.3	253.2	1.9	2.7	2.3	1 974.7
25–34	34.8	8.5	60.0	48.4	461.8	797.8	71.8	58.3	213.8	265.6	2.1	3.1	2.3	2 028.2
35–44	44.0	11.0	78.3	62.1	626.5	995.7	88.9	75.6	259.0	335.8	3.0	3.3	1.7	2 584.9
45–54	41.8	10.2	70.4	57.1	561.9	833.7	78.5	64.9	207.6	302.7	2.5	2.3	1.1	2 234.8
55–64	26.5	6.6	47.0	36.5	389.9	543.4	50.7	42.8	120.3	190.8	1.1	1.0	0.6	1 457.2
65–74	18.4	5.1	35.5	28.0	298.5	434.5	41.8	37.9	89.3	147.2	0.5	0.5	0.2	1 137.2
75–84	12.4	3.9	26.9	21.0	197.2	301.7	34.2	31.5	60.1	109.0	0.2	0.2	0.06	798.3
85 years and over	4.3	1.7	10.9	8.3	68.9	104.8	14.5	14.1	22.5	40.2	0.08	0.09	0.01	290.3

SOURCE: Statistics Canada

10 Immigrants by Class and Category, 2001

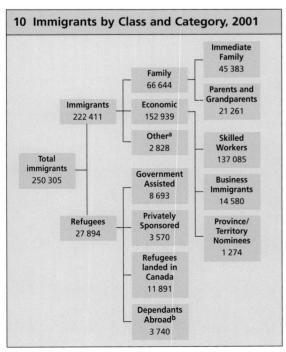

Total immigrants 250 305
- Immigrants 222 411
  - Family 66 644
    - Immediate Family 45 383
    - Parents and Grandparents 21 261
  - Economic 152 939
    - Skilled Workers 137 085
    - Business Immigrants 14 580
    - Province/Territory Nominees 1 274
  - Other[a] 2 828
- Refugees 27 894
  - Government Assisted 8 693
  - Privately Sponsored 3 570
  - Refugees landed in Canada 11 891
  - Dependants Abroad[b] 3 740

[a] Includes live-in care-givers, post determination refugee claimants, deferred removal orders, retirees
[b] Dependants (of a refugee landed in Canada) who live abroad
SOURCE: Statistics Canada

11 Aboriginal Population, 2001

	First Nations (000)	Métis (000)	Inuit (000)	Total[a] (000)
NL	7.0	5.5	4.6	18.8
PE	1.0	0.2	0.02	1.3
NS	12.9	3.1	0.4	17.0
NB	11.5	4.3	0.2	17.0
QC	51.1	15.9	9.5	79.4
ON	131.6	48.3	1.4	188.3
MB	90.3	56.8	0.3	150.0
SK	83.7	43.7	0.2	130.2
AB	85.0	66.1	1.1	156.2
BC	118.3	44.3	0.8	170.0
YT	5.6	0.5	0.1	6.5
NWT	10.6	3.6	3.9	18.7
NU	0.1	0.06	22.6	22.7
CANADA	608.9	292.3	45.1	976.3

[a] Totals include categories not shown
SOURCE: Statistics Canada

12 Status Indian[a] Population, 2001

	Total Indian[a] Population	On Reserve	Off Reserve
NL	7 040	755	6 285
PE	1 035	370	665
NS	12 920	7 285	5 630
NB	11 490	5 955	5 530
QC	51 125	32 200	18 925
ON	131 560	40 120	91 440
MB	90 345	50 970	39 370
SK	83 745	43 695	40 045
AB	84 990	36 245	48 750
BC	118 295	44 085	74 205
YT	5 600	1 815	3 790
NWT	10 615	8 915	1 700
NU	95	0	95
CANADA	608 850	272 410	336 435

[a] Terms used by Statistics Canada, as defined by the *Indian Act*.
SOURCE: Statistics Canada

13 Population by Ethnic Origin, 2001

	NL	PE	NS	NB	QC	ON	MB	SK	AB	BC	YT	NWT	NU	CANADA
Canadian	208 285	31 985	251 350	242 220	3 414 220	1 598 050	113 060	111 745	387 445	382 135	3 485	3 540	605	6 748 135
British	147 045	26 140	152 820	89 780	125 615	1 259 615	86 350	71 505	267 665	437 535	2 520	2 600	1 190	2 670 360
French	5 005	6 460	27 160	55 985	678 370	190 170	22 710	15 055	42 945	37 670	465	440	260	1 082 700
Chinese	710	150	2 580	1 310	51 640	443 695	10 245	7 015	88 500	329 945	215	185	30	936 210
Italian	215	140	2 150	1 090	161 825	481 735	7 665	1 690	23 105	46 470	60	95	20	726 275
German	845	435	16 350	3 410	20 765	226 220	75 115	84 280	153 185	123 475	925	510	85	705 600
East Indian	670	40	1 920	850	26 680	329 455	9 575	2 365	50 740	159 075	165	120	20	581 665
Aboriginal	11 110	600	9 675	9 140	63 890	89 920	89 045	83 010	82 855	87 355	4 085	14 070	20 290	565 040
Ukrainian	85	50	1 220	300	9 170	90 065	54 925	40 710	88 355	40 785	255	235	50	326 195
Caribbean	60	40	655	320	85 145	219 235	4 175	660	7 875	5 300	40	55	20	323 580
Multiple responses	129 335	64 990	401 495	304 660	1 876 360	4 401 645	500 790	481 920	1 420 680	1 717 615	14 680	13 520	3 795	11 331 490

SOURCE: Statistics Canada

14 Population by First Language, 1991 to 2001

	1991	2001	Percent Change 1991–2001
English[a]	16 169 875	17 352 315	7.3
French[a]	6 502 860	6 703 325	3.1
Chinese	498 845	853 745	71.1
Indo-Iranian	301 335	627 860	108.4
Italian	510 990	469 485	-8.1
German	466 245	438 080	-6.0
Spanish	177 425	245 500	38.4
Portuguese	212 090	213 815	0.8
Polish	189 815	208 375	9.8
Arabic	107 750	199 940	85.6
Aboriginal	172 610	187 675	8.7
Tagalog (Filipino)	99 715	174 060	74.6
Ukrainian	187 010	148 090	-20.8
Dutch	149 870	128 670	-14.1
Vietnamese	78 570	122 055	55.3
Greek	126 205	120 365	-4.6
Russian	35 300	94 555	167.9
Tamil	30 535	92 010	201.3
Korean (Filipino)	36 185	85 070	135.1
Hungarian	79 770	75 555	-5.3
Croatian	39 660	54 880	38.4
Finnish	27 705	22 405	-19.1
Total Single Responses	26 686 850	29 257 885	
Total Multiple Responses	307 190	381 145	
Canada	26 994 045	29 639 035	

[a]Official language
SOURCE: Statistics Canada

15 Refugees to Canada by Country, 1990 to 2001

1990 Country	Total	Rank	1995 Country	Total	Rank	2001 Country	Total	Rank
Poland	11 902	1	Bosnia-Herzegovina	5 964	1	Afghanistan	2 916	1
Vietnam	5 279	2	Sri Lanka	4 792	2	Sri Lanka	2 504	2
El Salvador	3 750	3	Iraq	1 276	3	Pakistan	2 111	3
Ethiopia	2 174	4	Iran	1 263	4	Yugoslavia	1 745	4
Iran	2 019	5	Afghanistan	1 094	5	Iran	1 474	5
Sri Lanka	1 234	6	Somalia	1 083	6	Colombia	1 281	6
USSR	1 153	7	China	684	7	India	1 153	7
Czechoslovakia	1 151	8	Yugoslavia	579	8	Iraq	1 076	8
Somalia	1 072	9	Ethiopia	415	9	Sudan	1038	9
Romania	1 016	10	Croatia	405	10	Dem. Rep. of Congo	928	10
Others	8 939		Others	7 409		Others	11 673	

SOURCE: Citizenship and Immigration Canada

ECONOMICS

16 Employment by Industry, 1970 to 2001

	1970	1975	1980	1986	1991	1996	2001
Agricultural (000)	–	–	–	513	521	486	
Forestry (000)	–	–	–	113	106	103	568
Fishing (000)	–	–	–	46	48	46	
Mining (000)	–	–	–	193	192	168	170
Manufacturing (000)	1 768	1 871	2 111	2 197	2 084	2 040	2 174
Construction (000)	467	603	624	759	933	822	879
Trans., Comm., Utilities (000)	698	812	906	977	1 061	1 046	893
Trade (000)	1 328	1 637	1 837	2 191	2 446	2 493	2 441
Finance, Insurance, and Real Estate (000)	379	474	611	691	811	788	895
Services (000)	2 040	2 520	3 096	4 090	4 906	5 439	6 651
Public Administration (000)	510	665	744	969	1 111	887	904
Total (000)	–	–	–	12 740	14 220	14 318	15 576

SOURCE: Statistics Canada

181

17 Employment by Industry by Province and Territory, 2001

	NL (000)	PE (000)	NS (000)	NB (000)	QC (000)	ON (000)	MB (000)	SK (000)	AB (000)	BC (000)	YT (000)	NWT (000)	NU (000)
Agricultural, Forestry and Fishing	15.5	9.5	22.9	20.4	101.6	123.7	37.4	72.7	84.6	78.6	0.3	0.3	0.1
Mining	4.9	0.2	3.4	3.2	16.3	21.1	4.2	14.5	86.0	14.0	0.4	1.4	0.2
Manufacturing	24.0	7.8	44.2	45.9	640.7	984.3	68.0	29.4	134.9	194.4	0.4	0.3	0.2
Construction	15.0	5.3	26.8	23.3	168.4	332.3	28.7	27.2	130.0	118.7	1.4	1.5	0.7
Transportation, Communication, and Other Utilities	13.7	2.6	22.8	23.8	198.3	326.4	41.1	29.0	106.0	125.8	0.9	1.8	0.9
Trade	36.6	10.0	71.1	53.6	581.8	950.7	84.2	73.4	258.7	315.4	2.3	2.2	1.4
Finance, Insurance, and Real Estate	7.1	2.0	20.6	14.8	186.8	401.4	28.8	25.3	84.3	122.2	0.6	0.7	0.4
Services	95.1	28.4	192.9	151.5	1 521.1	2 543.9	244.8	201.3	720.0	932.6	7.7	7.9	4.0
Public Administration	20.4	7.1	37.8	28.5	229.4	309.0	40.2	31.3	77.5	112.8	3.7	4.3	2.6
Total	232.3	72.9	442.4	365.0	3 644.4	5 992.8	577.3	504.0	1 682.0	2 014.5	17.7	20.4	10.7

SOURCE: Statistics Canada

PRIMARY INDUSTRY

18 Agricultural Land Use, 2001

	NL	PE	NS	NB	QC	ON	MB	SK	AB	BC	CANADA
Farmland Area (000 ha)	40.6	261.5	407.0	388.1	3 417.0	5 466.2	7 601.8	26 265.6	21 067.5	2 587.1	67 502.4
Percent Change 1991–2001	-14.3	+1.0	+2.5	+3.3	-0.4	+0.3	-1.6	-2.2	+1.2	+8.1	-0.4
Number of Farms	643	1 845	3 923	3 034	32 139	59 728	21 071	50 598	53 652	20 290	246 923
Average Farm Size (ha)	63.0	142.0	104.0	128.0	106.0	92.0	361.0	519.0	393.0	128.0	273.0
Average Farm Size Percent Change 1991–2001	-3.1	+29.1	+4.0	+10.3	+17.8	+16.5	+19.9	+17.4	+8.0	+3.2	+12.8
Cropland Area (000 ha)	8.4	175.5	119.2	148.9	1 850.0	3 656.7	4 714.8	15 375.9	9 728.2	617.5	36 395.2
Summer Fallow Area (000 ha)	0.1	0.2	0.6	0.6	4.9	14.2	255.7	3 131.6	1 235.6	36.8	4 680.4
Tame or Seeded Pasture (000 ha)	2.5	11.8	22.9	18.2	182.8	313.1	383.5	1 405.7	2 230.9	233.0	4 804.5

SOURCE: Statistics Canada

19 Census Farms by Product, 2001

	NL	PE	NS	NB	QC	ON	MB	SK	AB	BC	CANADA
Total Farms	519	1 739	3 318	2 563	30 539	55 092	19 818	48 990	50 580	17 382	230 540
Cattle Ranching and Farming	119	734	1 123	975	13 390	19 152	7 544	12 294	23 301	5 295	83 927
Hog and Pig Farming	9	95	68	83	2 224	2 491	980	298	868	153	7 269
Poultry and Egg Production	33	22	111	47	759	1 614	286	113	450	977	4 412
Sheep and Goat Farming	27	9	69	28	640	1 017	172	219	626	461	3 268
Other Animal Production	38	124	307	176	1 426	5 428	1 298	2 009	5 387	3 305	19 498
Oilseed and Grain Farming	0	57	17	30	3 210	13 371	7 358	30 842	13 133	250	68 268
Vegetable and Melon Farming	90	398	119	304	1 092	1 416	193	119	241	538	4 510
Fruit and Tree Nut Farming	23	91	653	304	1 044	1 739	74	49	75	2 528	6 580
Greenhouse, Nursery and Floriculture Production	102	33	456	251	1 386	2 430	237	242	688	1 678	7 503
Other Crop Farming	78	176	395	365	5 368	6 434	1 676	2 805	5 811	2 197	25 305

SOURCE: Statistics Canada

20 Farm Cash Receipts, 1998 to 2002

	1998 ($000 000)	1999 ($000 000)	2000 ($000 000)	2001 ($000 000)	2002 ($000 000)
Total	29 796	30 481	33 027	36 323	35 775
Canadian Wheat Board Payments	949	948	814	1 032	975
Wheat	2 413	2 337	2 352	2 544	2 315
Oats	193	175	196	276	305
Barley	510	421	477	622	500
Deferred Grain Receipts	84	357	45	-248	203
Canola	2 663	1 771	1 560	1 723	1 635
Other Cereals and Oilseeds	1 841	1 639	1 615	1 433	1 760
Other Crops	5 260	5 674	6 114	6 339	6 666
Cattle and Calves	5 720	6 204	6 826	7 824	7 547
Hogs	2 229	2 434	3 388	3 853	3 315
Hens and Chickens	1 352	1 320	1 362	1 519	1 453
Dairy Products	3 846	3 921	4 030	4 142	4 135
Other Livestock Products	1 312	1 314	1 421	1 534	1 556
Payments	1 423	1 965	2 827	3 750	3 409

SOURCE: Statistics Canada

21 Forest Land and Harvest, 2000

	Total Area (000 ha)	Area of Forest (000 ha)	Area of Productive Forest (000 ha)	Total Area Harvested (000 ha) and (Percent Clear-cut)	Total Volume of Wood Cut (000 000m³)
NL	40 600	22 500	11 270	23 (100)	2.7[a]
PE	570	290	280	6 (99.6)	0.7[a]
NS	5 600	3 900	3 770	54 (97.1)	6.2[a]
NB	7 300	6 100	5 950	112 (71.5)	11.3[a]
QC	154 100	83 900	53 990	349 (83.6)	43.3
ON	106 900	58 000	42 200	202 (94.5)	28.1
MB	65 000	26 300	15 240	16 (100)	2.2[a]
SK	65 200	28 800	12 630	21 (100)	4.5
AB	66 100	38 200	25 710	65 (99.5)	21.9
BC	94 800	60 600	51 740	204 (94.5)	75.0
YT	48 300	27 500	7 470	0.01 (100)	0.3[a]
NWT	342 600	61 400	14 320	0.05 (100)	0.1[a]

[a] 1999 figures
SOURCES: The State of Canada's Forests
       Statistics Canada

22 Fishing, 2001[a]

	Atlantic Coast			Pacific Coast		
	Quantity (000 metric tonnes)	Percent Change 1991–2001	Value ($000 000)	Quantity (000 metric tonnes)	Percent Change 1991–2001	Value ($000 000)
Total Groundfish	157.6	-74.9	178.7	114.2	-31.1	104.8
Cod	40.3	-87.0	58.4	0.5	-95.8	0.6
Haddock	15.6	-29.0	27.9	0	0	0
Redfish	19.7	-78.7	12.6	21.6	-7.7	29.7
Halibut	1.6	-19.2	12.1	4.5	+4.6	20.6
Flatfish	25.1	-61.0	21.8	5.5	-30.4	6.5
Greenland Turbot	13.8	-31.7	14.8	8.3	+260.9	2.4
Pollock	7.2	-82.4	5.6	1.7	-32.3	0.8
Hake	23.0	-64.1	17.6	61.0	-38.4	12.3
Cusk	1.5	-65.9	1.4	0	0	0
Catfish	0.6	-58.4	0.3	0	0	0
Skate	2.6	+131.3	0.8	1.5	+523.0	0.4
Dogfish	3.8	+1 128.8	1.9	4.3	+38.7	2.7
Other	2.8	-24.3	3.5	5.3	-52.3	28.8
Total Pelagic	250.3	-17.7	81.1	50.4	-60.0	59.8
Herring	199.3	-7.5	42.0	24.2	-39.1	16.8
Mackerel	24.5	-5.4	10.5	0.02	+100.0	0.01
Swordfish	1.1	–	8.5	0	0	0
Tuna	0.9	+73.6	13.4	3.1	+2 040.6	12.0
Alewife	2.8	+63.1	0.7	0	0	0
Eel	0.2	-77.6	0.9	0	0	0
Salmon	0	-100.0	0	22.9	-73.3	30.9
Smelt	0.3	-75.2	0.4	0	0	0
Capelin	19.7	-60.5	3.1	0	0	0
Other	1.5	-33.0	1.6	0.2	+468.3	0.08
Total Shellfish	423.1	+86.3	1 490.2	17.6	-27.7	117.8
Clam/quahaugs	26.9	+111.8	28.5	2.5	-48.8	37.7
Oyster	3.0	+57.9	7.8	0	-100.0	0
Scallop	90.5	+13.8	122.0	0.04	-52.4	0.3
Squid	0.1	-97.5	0.02	0	-100.0	0
Mussel	11.8	+227.8	15.4	0	0	0
Lobster	51.4	+6.0	638.7	0	0	0
Shrimp	125.6	+210.1	261.3	4.2	-0.3	33.8
Crab, Queen	95.3	+171.0	396.3	0	0	0
Crab, Other	12.3	+1 018.2	11.6	5.7	+200.0	36.8
Sea Urchin	2.8	–	6.4	4.3	-	7.8
Other	3.4	+161.5	2.2	0.9	-89.9	1.4
Total All Fisheries	831.0	-28.2	1 750.0	182.2	-42.3	282.4

[a] Statistics do not include Aquaculture production
SOURCE: Fisheries and Oceans Canada

23 Mineral Production, 2001

							$000 000							
	NL	PE	NS	NB	QC	ON	MB	SK	AB	BC	YT	NWT	NU	CANADA
Metals														
Cobalt	0	0	0	0	12.3	53.7	14.9	0	0	0	0	0	0	80.9
Copper	0	0	0	22.6	245.0	455.7	97.1	27.0	0	687.8	0	0	0	1 535.2
Gold	20.2	0	0.6	3.5	456.9	1 073.3	86.3	25.5	0.5	317.4	37.3	54.3	59.4	2 135.2
Iron Ore	7 98.2	0	0	0	na	0	0	0	0	na	0	0	0	1 188.9
Lead	0	0	0	60.0	0	0	0	0	0	25.7	0	0	23.8	109.5
Molybdenum	0	0	0	0	0	0	0	0	0	73.8	0	0	0	73.8
Nickel	0	0	0	0	235.5	1 129.7	412.2	0	0	0	0	0	0	1 777.4
Platinum Group	0	0	0	0	na	na	na	0	0	0	0	0	0	651.9
Silver	0.07	0	0	49.4	52.5	32.1	6.9	0.4	0	132.8	0.2	0.2	3.3	277.9
Zinc	0	0	0	441.1	355.3	109.6	129.3	2.9	0	153.4	0	0	234.4	1 426.0
Uranium	0	0	0	0	0	0	0	605.4	0	0	0	0	0	605.4
Total Metals	818.5	0	0.6	580.2	2 238.8	3 460.5	791.5	661.3	0.5	1 394.5	37.5	54.5	320.9	10 359.3
Non-metals														
Asbestos	0	0	0	0	118.7	0	0	0	0	0	0	0	0	118.7
Peat	0.2	3.2	na	53.8	55.4	0	na	na	24.5	na	0	0	0	186.4
Potash	0	0	0	na	0	0	0	na	0	0	0	0	0	1 617.4
Salt	0	0	na	na	na	270.7	0	35.8	19.2	0	0	0	0	426.1
Sulphur	na	0	na	0	0	na	0	0.2	0.6	na	0	0	0	1.3
Total Structural Minerals (e.g. sand, gravel, cement, stone)	41.8	0.8	73.1	29.8	638.8	1 480.7	50.8	48.1	260.9	448.8	3.6	6.2	0	3367.5
Total Non-Metals	44.7	4.0	241.3	207.1	1 365.1	2 170.8	93.6	1 649.9	600.1	513.0	3.6	724.0	0	7 617.2
Fuels														
Coal	0	0	na	19.9	0	0	0	na	389.4	959.3	0	0	0	1 557.1
Natural Gas	0	0	na	0	0	na	0	1 224.4	26 321.5	4 810.3	98.1	207.3	0	33 677.5
Crude Oil	2 038.2	0	na	0	0	na	138.2	4 040.7	17 721.4	na	0	337.6	0	25 181.4
Total Fuels	2 038.2	0	1 168.7	19.9	0	137.6	138.2	5 422.3	48 707.6	6 715.8	98.1	544.8	0	64 991.3
Total All Minerals	2 901.4	4.0	1 410.6	807.2	3 603.9	5 768.9	1 023.3	7 733.5	49 308.2	8 623.3	139.2	1 323.4	320.9	82 967.8

SOURCE: Natural Resources Canada

MANUFACTURING

24 Manufacturers, 1965 to 1999

	Number of Establishments	Number of Production Employees	Salaries ($000 000)	Cost of Fuel and Electricity ($000 000)	Cost of Materials and Supplies ($000 000)	Value of Shipments of Goods ($000 000)	Value Added ($000 000)
1965	33 310	1 115 892	5 012	676	18 622	33 889	14 927
1970	31 928	1 167 063	7 232	903	25 700	46 380	20 047
1975	30 100	1 271 786	12 699	1 805	51 178	88 427	36 105
1980	35 495	1 346 187	22 162	4 449	99 898	168 058	65 851
1984	36 464	1 240 816	28 294	7 306	136 134	230 070	88 667
1990	39 864	1 393 324	40 406	7 936	168 664	298 918	122 972
1995	31 445	1 276 941	43 400	9 300	226 000	389 800	157 100
1999	29 822	1 494 809	53 300	11 100	277 800	488 600	202 800

SOURCE: Industry Canada

25 Manufacturers by Province and Territory, 1997

	NL	PE	NS	NB	QC	ON	MB	SK	AB	BC	YT/NWT/NU
Number of Establishments	314.0	154.0	727.0	696.0	10 176.0	13 906.0	1 098.0	787.0	2 804.0	4 228.0	45.0
Number of Production Employees	9 071.0	3 823.0	28 330.0	26 637.0	362 788.0	694 624.0	48 114.0	20 376.0	91 878.0	123 722.0	489.0
Salaries ($000 000)	266.1	82.2	845.7	779.9	11 272.3	25 642.1	1 324.5	629.2	3 112.8	4 880.4	12.4
Cost of Fuel and Electricity ($000 000)	82.0	19.7	208.2	374.5	3 265.4	3 968.0	226.8	165.4	813.2	1 050.6	1.1
Cost of Materials and Supplies ($000 000)	780.8	530.9	3 867.1	5 336.8	54 583.9	136 050.5	5 459.8	3 636.7	20 810.0	19 955.0	26.6
Value of Shipments of Goods ($000 000)	1 658.2	802.3	6 464.6	8 434.6	102 825.6	228 505.2	9 969.3	6 114.5	34 675.7	34 582.7	50.4

SOURCE: Statistics Canada

TOURISM

26 Where Canadians Visit, 2000

	Overnight Visits		
Country Visited	Visits (000)	Nights Spent (000)	Spending in Country ($000 000)
USA	14 648	103 024	8 975
United Kingdom	803	9 617	974
Mexico	731	7 451	716
France	442	4 455	561
Germany	277	2 332	234
Cuba	273	2 366	210
Italy	211	2 578	332
Dominican Republic	195	1 737	152
Netherlands	154	1 341	115
Spain	132	1 946	172
Japan	124	1 636	191
Switzerland	124	916	97
Republic of Ireland	97	1 025	115
Belgium	93	549	52
Austria	88	515	65

SOURCE: Statistics Canada

27 Who Visits Canada, 2000

	Overnight Visits		
Country of Origin	Visits (000)	Nights Spent (000)	Spending in Canada ($000 000)
USA	15 225	58 649	7 448
United Kingdom	866	9 324	1 004
Japan	500	3 299	573
France	404	5 198	425
Germany	385	4 732	413
Australia	160	2 055	224
Taiwan	173	2 275	246
Mexico	143	1 372	180
Hong Kong	137	1 327	135
South Korea	134	1 104	175
Netherlands	128	1 658	146
Italy	108	1 048	105
Switzerland	104	1 266	146
Israel	75	707	73
China	74	978	110

SOURCE: Statistics Canada

TRADE

28 Exports from Canada, 1993 to 2002

	1993 ($000 000)	1996 ($000 000)	1999 ($000 000)	2002 ($000 000)
USA	150 657	223 177	308 076	345 427
Japan	8 496	11 210	8 573	8 398
United Kingdom	2 975	4 040	4 828	4 427
China	1 681	3 015	2 664	4 093
Germany	2 568	3 338	2 415	2 950
Mexico	826	1 259	1 613	2 412
South Korea	1 721	2 817	1 989	1 998
France	1 316	1 752	1 890	1 994
Belgium	1 038	1 539	1 881	1 907
Netherlands	1 383	1 668	1 558	1 768
Others	14 855	22 005	19 933	20 747
Total (all countries)	187 515	275 819	355 420	396 121

SOURCE: Statistics Canada

29 Imports to Canada, 1993 to 2002

	1993 ($000 000)	1996 ($000 000)	1999 ($000 000)	2002 ($000 000)
USA	113 846	156 953	215 575	218 308
China	3 098	4 931	8 951	15 978
Japan	10 718	10 439	15 039	15 412
Mexico	3 710	6 035	9 536	12 708
United Kingdom	4 473	5 908	8 107	9 728
Germany	3 522	4 824	6 949	8 290
France	2 275	3 402	5 316	5 843
Re-Imports (Canada)	3 114	4 195	5 538	5 423
South Korea	2 199	2 729	3 572	4 860
Italy	1 936	2 719	3 621	4 438
Others	21 064	30 431	38 204	47 655
Total (all countries)	169 953	232 566	320 409	348 644

SOURCE: Statistics Canada

30 Commodities, 2002

		Imports ($000 000)	Exports ($000 000)			Imports ($000 000)	Exports ($000 000)
1	Transport Equipment	93 381	101583	9	Food	12 627	17 097
2	Mining and Oil and Gas	16 126	47 435	10	Plastics and Rubber Products	10 990	12 643
3	Paper	6 571	23 767	11	Petroleum and Coal Products	2 874	9 971
4	Machinery	32 988	22 328	12	Furniture	3 722	7 487
5	Chemicals	32 837	20 209	13	Electrical Equipment, Appliances and Components	12 550	6 685
6	Primary Metal Products	12 898	19 804		Other	66 440	69 229
7	Computer and Electronic Products	41 855	19 448		**Total**	**348 644**	**396 121**
8	Wood Products	2 785	18 435				

SOURCE: Industry Canada

GOVERNMENT

31 National Political Party Representation, 1953 to 2000

	Election Year														
Region	1953	1958	1962	1963	1965	1968	1972	1974	1979	1980	1984	1988	1993	1997	2000
Atlantic Canada – Total Seats	33	33	33	33	32	32	32	31	32	32	32	32	32	32	32
Liberal	27	8	14	20	15	7	10	13	12	19	7	20	31	11	19
Progressive Conservative	5	25	18	13	18	25	22	17	17	13	25	12	1	13	9
New Democratic Party	1	–	1	–	–	–	–	1	2	–	–	–	–	8	4
Québec– Total Seats	70	75	75	75	73	74	73	74	75	75	75	75	75	75	75
Liberal	66	25	35	47	56	56	56	60	67	74	17	12	19	26	36
Progressive Conservative	4	50	14	8	8	4	2	3	2	1	58	63	1	5	1
Bloc Québécois	–	–	–	–	–	–	–	–	–	–	–	–	54	44	38
Others	–	–	–	–	–	–	–	–	–	–	–	–	1	–	–
Ontario – Total Seats	85	85	85	85	85	88	87	88	95	95	95	99	99	103	103
Liberal	51	15	44	52	51	64	36	55	32	52	15	42	98	101	100
Progressive Conservative	33	67	35	27	25	17	40	25	57	38	66	47	–	1	–
New Democratic Party	1	3	6	6	9	6	11	8	6	5	13	10	–	–	1
Reform Party	–	–	–	–	–	–	–	–	–	–	–	–	1	–	2
Others	–	–	–	–	–	–	–	–	–	–	–	–	–	1	–
Western – Total Seats	72	72	72	72	72	70	68	68	80	80	80	89	89	91	91
Liberal	27	1	7	10	9	28	7	13	3	2	2	8	29	17	17
Progressive Conservative	9	66	49	47	46	26	42	49	60	51	61	48	–	1	2
New Democratic Party	21	5	12	11	12	16	19	6	18	27	17	33	9	13	8
Social Credit	15	–	4	4	5	–	–	–	–	–	–	–	–	–	–
Reform Party	–	–	–	–	–	–	–	–	–	–	–	–	51	60	64
Canada – Total Seats in House of Commons	265	265	265	265	265	265	265	282	282	282	282	295	295	301	301
Liberal	171	49	100	129	131	155	109	141	114	147	40	82	177	155	172
Progressive Conservative	51	208	116	95	97	72	107	95	136	103	211	170	2	20	12
New Democratic Party	23	8	19	17	21	22	31	16	26	32	30	43	9	21	13
Social Credit	15	–	30	24	14	14	15	11	6	–	–	–	–	–	–
Bloc Québécois	–	–	–	–	–	–	–	–	–	–	–	–	54	44	38
Reform Party	–	–	–	–	–	–	–	–	–	–	–	–	52	60	66
Others	5	–	–	–	2	2	2	1	–	–	–	1	–	1	1

SOURCE: Elections Canada

FLAG	COUNTRY	CAPITAL CITY	AREA	LAND USE				POPULATION			
			km²	CROP km²	PASTURE km²	FOREST km²	OTHER km²	TOTAL 2002	BIRTH RATE / DEATH RATE per 1000 people 2000	DOUBLING TIME (years) 2000	TOTAL FERTILITY RATE 1995–2000
	AFGHANISTAN	Kabul	652 225	1 440	300 000	17 000	333 785	23 294 000	48/22	28	-
	ALBANIA	Tiranë	28 748	1 210	4 450	10 480	12 608	3 164 000	17/6	55	2.6
	ALGERIA	Algiers	2 381 741	5 200	315 000	39 500	2 022 041	31 403 000	25/5	29	3.2
	ANGOLA	Luanda	1 246 700	3 000	540 000	230 000	473 700	13 936 000	48/19	23	7.2
	ARGENTINA	Buenos Aires	2 766 889	22 000	1 420 000	509 000	815 889	37 944 000	19/8	62	2.6
	ARMENIA	Yerevan	29 800	650	8 340	4 200	16 610	3 790 000	11/6	161	1.4
	AUSTRALIA	Canberra	7 682 300	2 960	4 049 000	1 450 000	2 180 340	19 536 000	13/7	110	1.8
	AUSTRIA	Vienna	83 855	710	19 200	32 400	31 545	8 069 000	10/10	2 310	1.4
	AZERBAIJAN	Baku	86 600	2 630	25 620	9 500	48 850	8 147 000	15/6	77	1.9
	BAHAMAS, THE	Nassau	13 939	40	20	3 240	10 639	312 000	19/6	45	2.4
	BAHRAIN	Manama	691	40	40	-	-	663 000	20/3	37	2.6
	BANGLADESH	Dhaka	143 998	3 450	6 000	18 920	115 628	143 364 000	28/9	38	3.8
	BARBADOS	Bridgetown	430	10	20	50	350	269 000	14/9	130	1.5
	BELARUS	Minsk	207 600	1 240	29 950	72 000	104 410	10 106 000	9/14	-	1.3
	BELGIUM	Brussels	30 520	220	6 850	7 090	16 360	10 276 000	11/10	770	1.5
	BELIZE	Belmopan	22 965	250	500	21 000	1 215	236 000	27/4	26	3.4
	BENIN	Porto Novo	112 620	2 650	5 500	34 000	70 470	6 629 000	39/13	24	6.1
	BERMUDA	Hamilton	54	-	-	10	-	64 000	-	-	-
	BHUTAN	Thimbu	46 620	200	3 000	31 000	12 420	2 198 000	38/9	22	5.5
	BOLIVIA	La Paz	1 098 581	2 620	338 310	580 000	177 651	8 705 000	31/9	34	4.4
	BOSNIA-HERZEGOVINA	Sarajevo	51 130	1 500	12 000	27 100	10 530	4 126 000	12/8	141	-
	BOTSWANA	Gaborone	581 370	30	256 000	265 000	60 340	1 564 000	32/20	45	4.4
	BRAZIL	Brasília	8 511 965	120 000	1 850 000	5 550 000	991 965	174 706 000	20/7	45	2.3
	BRUNEI	Bandar Seri Begawan	5 765	40	60	4 500	1 165	341 000	21/3	32	2.8
	BULGARIA	Sofia	110 994	2 120	16 150	33 480	59 244	7 790 000	9/14	-	1.1
	BURKINA	Ouagadougou	274 200	500	60 000	138 000	75 700	12 207 000	44/19	24	6.9
	BURUNDI	Bujumbura	27 835	3 600	9 350	3 250	11 635	6 688 000	40/20	28	6.8
	CAMBODIA	Phnom Penh	181 000	1 070	15 000	122 000	42 930	13 776 000	30/12	27	5.2
	CAMEROON	Yaoundé	475 442	12 000	20 000	359 000	84 442	15 535 000	37/14	27	5.1
	CANADA	Ottawa	9 984 670	658 000	203 000	4 176 000	4 947 670	30 007 094	11/8	178	1.6
	CENTRAL AFRICAN REPUBLIC	Bangui	622 436	900	31 250	467 000	123 286	3 844 000	36/20	34	5.3
	CHAD	Ndjamena	1 284 000	300	450 000	324 000	509 700	8 390 000	45/16	21	6.6
	CHILE	Santiago	756 945	3 180	129 350	165 000	459 415	15 589 000	17/6	54	2.4
	CHINA	Beijing	9 562 000	114 210	4 000 010	1 305 180	4 142 600	1 279 557 000	15/7	79	1.8
	COLOMBIA	Bogotá	1 141 748	17 270	409 200	530 000	185 278	43 495 000	23/6	34	2.8
	COMOROS	Moroni	1 862	500	150	400	812	749 000	33/8	25	5.4
	CONGO	Brazzaville	342 000	450	100 000	199 000	42 550	3 206 000	43/14	29	6.3
	CONGO, DEM. REP. OF	Kinshasa	2 345 410	11 800	150 000	1 660 000	523 610	54 275 000	46/17	22	6.7
	COSTA RICA	San José	51 100	2 800	23 400	15 700	9 200	4 200 000	20/4	39	2.8
	CÔTE D'IVOIRE	Yamoussoukro	322 463	44 000	130 000	96 000	52 463	16 691 000	37/17	32	5.1
	CROATIA	Zagreb	56 538	1 280	15 700	20 760	18 798	4 657 000	10/12	-	1.7
	CUBA	Havana	110 860	8 350	22 000	26 080	54 430	11 273 000	13/7	103	1.6
	CYPRUS	Nicosia	9 251	420	40	1 230	7 561	797 000	13/8	124	2.0
	CZECH REPUBLIC	Prague	78 864	2 360	9 610	26 290	40 604	10 250 000	9/11	-	1.2
	DENMARK	Copenhagen	43 075	80	3 580	4 170	35 245	5 343 000	12/11	472	1.7
	DJIBOUTI	Djibouti	23 200	-	13 000	220	-	652 000	37/18	30	6.1

LABOUR FORCE			GDP, 2000				COMMUNICATIONS, 2000			
AGRI-CULTURE percent employed	MANU-FACTURING percent employed	SERVICE INDUSTRIES percent employed	PER CAPITA PPP US$	EXTERNAL DEPT repayments percent of GDP	EDUCATION spending percent of GDP	MILITARY spending percent of GDP	INTERNET USERS (000)	TELEPHONES main lines in use (000)	TELEVISIONS per 1000 people	PASSENGER CARS per 1000 people
70	11	19	-	-	-	-	-	29	14	-
24	45	31	3 506	0.7	-	1.2	12	120	123	29
26	31	43	5 308	8.4	6	3.5	180	2 300	110	-
75	8	17	2 187	13.6	3	21.2	60	72	19	-
1	25	74	12 377	9.6	-	1.3	3 880	7 500	-	140
-	-	-	2 559	2.2	2	4.4	30	600	244	-
5	21	74	25 693	-	5	1.7	10 630	10 050	738	-
6	30	63	26 765	-	6	0.8	3 700	4 000	536	495
42	12	46	2 936	3.4	3	2.7	25	865	259	38
4	15	81	17 012	-	3	-	17	96	247	-
1	55	43	15 084	-	4	4.0	140	152	402	250
63	10	25	1 602	1.7	-	1.3	150	500	7	0
4	22	74	15 494	-	5	-	6	108	310	229
21	35	40	7 544	0.8	6	1.3	422	2 313	342	135
2	27	71	27 178	-	-	1.4	3 760	4 769	541	448
28	17	55	5 606	8.1	-	-	18	31	183	44
64	8	28	990	3.5	3	-	25	51	45	-
1	10	82	-	-	-	-	25	52	1 086	-
94	1	5	1 412	1.4	-	-	3	6	20	-
2	29	69	2 424	8.0	-	1.5	78	328	119	-
11	48	41	-	-	-	-	45	303	111	-
3	31	67	7 184	1.3	9	3.7	33	131	25	30
23	20	57	7 625	10.5	5	1.3	13 980	17 039	343	-
2	64	34	16 779	-	4	7.6	35	79	640	293
27	29	44	5 710	9.9	3	3.0	585	3 187	449	233
92	2	6	976	2.5	3	1.6	25	53	12	-
15	22	59	591	3.1	4	5.4	6	20	30	-
75	5	21	1 446	1.0	6	2.4	10	22	8	-
70	9	22	1 703	6.3	3	1.3	45	95	34	-
4	22	74	27 840	-	6	1.2	16 840	20 803	-	459
80	4	16	1 172	1.5	2	-	2	10	6	-
83	4	13	871	1.9	2	1.0	4	10	1	-
14	26	60	9 417	8.7	4	3.3	3 100	2 603	242	88
48	22	13	3 976	2.0	-	2.1	45 800	135 000	293	-
1	24	75	6 248	6.4	-	2.3	1 150	5 434	282	43
77	9	13	1 588	1.3	-	-	3	7	-	-
49	15	37	825	1.3	5	-	0.5	22	-	-
68	13	19	765	0.3	-	-	6	20	-	-
20	23	56	8 650	4.1	6	0.0	384	450	231	88
60	10	31	1 630	10.9	4	-	70	264	60	-
17	31	53	8 091	12.8	-	3.0	480	1 721	293	-
18	30	52	-	-	-	-	120	473	250	-
11	25	63	20 824	-	6	3.2	150	488	179	341
5	40	55	13 991	9.4	4	2.0	2 690	3 869	508	335
4	27	70	27 627	-	8	1.5	3 370	4 785	807	353
-	-	-	PER CAPITA PPP US$	2.4	spending	4.4	3	10	71	-

FLAG	COUNTRY	CAPITAL CITY	AREA	LAND USE				POPULATION			
			km²	CROP km²	PASTURE km²	FOREST km²	OTHER km²	TOTAL 2002	BIRTH RATE / DEATH RATE per 1000 people 2000	DOUBLING TIME (years) 2000	TOTAL FERTILITY RATE 1995–2000
	DOMINICA	Roseau	750	120	20	500	110	70 000	-	83	-
	DOMINICAN REPUBLIC	Santo Domingo	48 442	5 000	21 000	6 000	16 442	8 639 000	23/6	32	2.9
	EAST TIMOR	Dili	14 874	100	1 500	11 000	2 274	779 000	-	39	-
	ECUADOR	Quito	272 045	14 270	51 070	156 000	50 705	13 112 000	24/6	33	3.1
	EGYPT	Cairo	1 000 250	4 660	-	340	995 250	70 278 000	25/6	35	3.4
	EL SALVADOR	San Salvador	21 041	2 500	7 940	1 050	9 551	6 520 000	26/6	29	3.2
	EQUATORIAL GUINEA	Malabo	28 051	1 000	1 040	18 300	7 711	483 000	41/16	28	5.9
	ERITREA	Asmara	117 400	30	69 670	7 360	40 340	3 993 000	39/13	23	5.7
	ESTONIA	Tallinn	45 200	140	2 990	20 170	21 900	1 361 000	9/13	-	1.2
	ETHIOPIA	Addis Ababa	1 133 880	7 280	200 000	133 000	793 600	66 040 000	44/20	29	6.8
	FIJI	Suva	18 330	850	1 750	11 850	3 880	832 000	22/6	46	3.2
	FINLAND	Helsinki	338 145	40	210	231 860	106 035	5 183 000	11/10	433	1.7
	FRANCE	Paris	543 965	11 420	101 240	150 120	281 185	59 670 000	13/9	204	1.7
	FRENCH GUIANA	Cayenne	90 000	40	100	79 900	9 960	176 000	-	29	-
	GABON	Libreville	267 667	1 700	46 650	199 000	20 317	1 293 000	36/16	32	5.4
	GAMBIA, THE	Banjul	11 295	50	4 590	930	5 725	1 371 000	39/13	29	5.2
	GEORGIA	T'bilisi	69 700	2 690	19 380	29 880	17 750	5 213 000	9/9	462	1.6
	GERMANY	Berlin	357 868	2 160	50 480	107 000	198 228	81 990 000	9/11	-	1.3
	GHANA	Accra	238 537	22 000	83 500	92 000	41 037	20 176 000	30/11	29	4.6
	GREECE	Athens	131 957	11 130	46 750	26 200	47 877	10 631 000	12/11	-	1.3
	GRENADA	St George's	378	100	10	30	238	94 000	25/7	30	-
	GUATEMALA	Guatemala City	108 890	5 450	26 020	52 120	25 300	11 995 000	33/7	24	4.9
	GUINEA	Conakry	245 857	6 000	107 000	67 000	65 857	8 381 000	39/17	29	6.3
	GUINEA-BISSAU	Bissau	36 125	500	10 800	10 700	14 125	1 257 000	42/20	31	6.0
	GUYANA	Georgetown	214 969	160	12 300	165 000	37 509	765 000	23/9	40	2.4
	HAITI	Port-au-Prince	27 750	3 500	4 900	1 400	17 950	8 400 000	32/13	40	4.4
	HONDURAS	Tegucigalpa	112 088	3 590	15 080	60 000	33 418	6 732 000	31/6	25	4.3
	HUNGARY	Budapest	93 030	2 010	10 510	17 190	63 320	9 867 000	10/14	-	1.4
	ICELAND	Reykjavík	102 820	-	22 740	1 200	-	283 000	14/7	81	2.0
	INDIA	New Delhi	3 287 263	79 000	109 100	685 000	2 414 163	1 041 144 000	25/9	39	3.3
	INDONESIA	Jakarta	1 919 445	130 460	111 770	1 117 740	559 475	217 534 000	22/7	44	2.6
	IRAN	Tehran	1 648 000	20 020	440 000	114 000	1 073 980	72 376 000	22/6	48	3.2
	IRAQ	Baghdad	438 317	3 400	40 000	1 920	392 997	24 246 000	31/9	25	-
	IRELAND, REPUBLIC OF	Dublin	70 282	30	33 500	5 700	31 052	3 878 000	14/8	116	1.9
	ISRAEL	Jerusalem	20 770	850	1 400	1 260	17 260	6 303 000	21/6	45	2.9
	ITALY	Rome	301 245	28 410	44 460	68 090	160 285	57 449 000	9/10	-	1.2
	JAMAICA	Kingston	10 991	1 000	2 290	1 850	5 851	2 621 000	21/6	45	2.5
	JAPAN	Tokyo	377 727	3 560	4 050	246 210	123 907	127 538 000	9/8	462	1.4
	JORDAN	Amman	89 206	1 570	7 910	700	79 026	5 196 000	29/4	24	4.7
	KAZAKHSTAN	Astana	2 717 300	1 360	1 850 980	96 000	768 960	16 027 000	15/10	161	2.1
	KENYA	Nairobi	582 646	5 200	213 000	168 000	196 446	31 904 000	35/14	33	4.6
	KIRIBATI	Tarawa	717	370	-	20	-	85 000	29/7	28	-
	KUWAIT	Kuwait	17 818	20	1 360	20	16 418	2 023 000	20/2	32	2.9
	KYRGYZSTAN	Bishkek	198 500	670	92 910	7 300	97 620	5 047 000	21/7	47	2.9
	LAOS	Vientiane	236 800	810	8 780	125 500	101 710	5 530 000	37/13	26	5.3
	LATVIA	Riga	63 700	290	6 110	28 700	28 600	2 392 000	9/14	-	1.1

LABOUR FORCE			GDP, 2000				COMMUNICATIONS, 2000			
AGRI-CULTURE percent employed	MANU-FACTURING percent employed	SERVICE INDUSTRIES percent employed	PER CAPITA PPP US$	EXTERNAL DEPT repayments percent of GDP	EDUCATION spending percent of GDP	MILITARY spending percent of GDP	INTERNET USERS (000)	TELEPHONES main lines in use (000)	TELEVISIONS per 1000 people	PASSENGER CARS per 1000 people
24	18	54	5 880	3.8	5	-	2	19	220	-
20	25	55	6 033	2.6	-	-	186	709	-	-
-	-	-	-	-	-	-	-	-	-	-
7	21	71	3 203	9.4	-	-	328	1 115	218	41
30	22	48	3 635	1.8	-	2.3	600	3 972	189	-
25	25	50	4 497	2.8	-	0.7	40	380	201	-
75	5	20	15 073	0.4	2	-	1	6	-	-
81	5	15	837	0.5	5	22.9	10	30	26	-
9	32	59	10 066	8.6	7	1.6	430	502	591	331
98	2	10	668	2.2	4	9.4	20	232	6	1
2	34	64	4 668	2.0	-	1.5	15	81	113	-
6	28	66	24 996	-	-	1.3	2 690	2 848	692	403
1	25	74	24 223	-	6	2.6	16 970	34 860	628	469
-	-	-	-	-	-	-	2	47	-	-
52	16	33	6 237	9.5	3	0.3	18	39	326	-
82	8	11	1 649	4.4	5	1.1	5	32	3	-
49	9	40	2 664	3.9	-	0.9	25	620	474	49
3	35	63	25 103	-	5	1.5	32 100	50 900	586	508
62	10	28	1 964	9.1	4	1.0	200	240	118	-
18	23	59	16 501	-	-	4.9	1 400	5 431	488	254
14	24	59	7 580	2.9	-	-	5	27	-	-
26	22	52	3 821	2.3	2	0.8	200	665	61	52
87	2	11	1 982	4.4	2	1.5	15	37	44	-
85	2	13	755	2.9	0	1.3	4	10	-	-
29	20	48	3 963	16.2	-	-	95	70	81	-
-	-	-	1 467	1.0	-	-	30	60	5	-
35	22	43	2 453	9.7	4	0.6	40	234	96	52
7	35	58	12 416	17.4	5	1.5	1 200	3 095	437	238
9	25	66	29 581	-	7	0.0	220	197	509	546
67	13	-	2 358	2.2	-	2.4	7 000	27 700	78	-
45	16	39	3 043	12.2	1	1.1	4 400	5 588	149	14
23	31	45	5 884	3.3	5	3.8	420	6 313	163	-
16	18	66	-	-	-	-	13	675	83	-
9	29	62	29 866	-	4	0.7	1 310	1 600	399	-
2	25	72	20 131	-	8	8.0	1 940	2 800	335	220
6	33	62	23 626	-	5	2.1	19 250	25 000	494	-
21	19	60	3 639	8.7	6	-	100	353	194	-
5	32	63	26 755	-	3	1.0	56 000	60 381	725	395
6	25	69	3 966	8.0	-	9.5	212	403	84	-
22	18	60	5 871	10.1	-	0.7	100	1 920	241	66
19	20	62	1 022	4.6	7	1.8	500	310	25	-
6	6	87	-	-	-	-	1	4	36	-
-	-	-	15 799	-	6	8.2	200	412	486	-
52	12	36	2 711	13.3	5	1.9	52	351	49	39
78	6	16	1 575	2.5	2	-	10	25	10	-
15	26	59	7 045	7.9	7	1.0	312	735	789	218

FLAG	COUNTRY	CAPITAL CITY	AREA km²	LAND USE				POPULATION			
				CROP km²	PASTURE km²	FOREST km²	OTHER km²	TOTAL 2002	BIRTH RATE / DEATH RATE per 1000 people 2000	DOUBLING TIME (years) 2000	TOTAL FERTILITY RATE 1995–2000
	LEBANON	Beirut	10 452	1 420	160	800	8 072	3 614 000	20/6	43	2.3
	LESOTHO	Maseru	30 355	-	20 000	-	-	2 076 000	33/17	33	4.8
	LIBERIA	Monrovia	111 369	2 150	20 000	46 000	43 219	3 298 000	44/17	21	-
	LIBYA	Tripoli	1 759 540	3 350	133 000	8 400	1 614 790	5 529 000	27/5	28	3.8
	LITHUANIA	Vilnius	65 200	590	4 970	19 830	39 810	3 682 000	9/11	-	1.4
	LUXEMBOURG	Luxembourg	2 586	-	-	-	-	448 000	13/9	198	1.7
	MACEDONIA	Skopje	25 713	440	6 360	10 200	8 713	2 051 000	13/8	112	1.9
	MADAGASCAR	Antananarivo	587 041	6 000	240 000	232 000	109 041	16 913 000	40/12	24	6.1
	MALAWI	Lilongwe	118 484	1 400	18 500	37 000	61 584	11 828 000	46/24	36	6.8
	MALAYSIA	Kuala Lumpur	332 965	57 850	2 850	222 480	49 785	23 036 000	25/4	34	3.3
	MALDIVES	Male	298	20	10	10	258	309 000	29/5	23	5.8
	MALI	Bamako	1 240 140	440	300 000	116 500	823 200	12 019 000	46/20	22	7.0
	MALTA	Valletta	316	10	-	-	-	393 000	11/8	182	1.9
	MAURITANIA	Nouakchott	1 030 700	120	392 500	44 100	593 980	2 830 000	42/15	25	6.0
	MAURITIUS	Port Louis	2 040	60	70	440	1 470	1 180 000	17/7	66	2.0
	MEXICO	Mexico City	1 972 545	25 000	800 000	487 000	660 545	101 842 000	25/5	36	2.8
	MICRONESIA, FEDERATED STATES OF	Pohnpei	701	320	100	-	-	129 000	26/6	27	-
	MOLDOVA	Chişinău	33 700	3 700	3 780	3 580	22 640	4 273 000	10/11	1 733	1.6
	MONGOLIA	Ulan Bator	1 565 000	10	1 292 940	137 500	134 559	2 587 000	22/6	50	2.7
	MOROCCO	Rabat	446 550	9 670	210 000	89 700	137 180	30 988 000	24/6	41	3.4
	MOZAMBIQUE	Maputo	799 380	2 350	440 000	173 000	184 030	18 986 000	40/20	32	6.3
	MYANMAR	Yangon	676 577	5 950	3 160	324 000	343 467	48 956 000	25/12	35	3.3
	NAMIBIA	Windhoek	824 292	40	380 000	125 000	319 252	1 819 000	36/17	42	5.3
	NEPAL	Kathmandu	147 181	700	17 570	57 500	71 411	24 153 000	33/10	28	4.8
	NETHERLANDS	Amsterdam/The Hague	41 526	350	10 120	3 340	27 716	15 990 000	13/9	193	1.5
	NEW ZEALAND	Wellington	270 534	17 250	133 000	76 670	43 614	3 837 000	15/7	89	2.0
	NICARAGUA	Managua	130 000	2 890	48 150	32 000	46 960	5 347 000	30/5	23	4.3
	NIGER	Niamey	1 267 000	100	120 000	25 000	1 121 900	11 641 000	51/19	23	8.0
	NIGERIA	Abuja	923 768	26 500	392 000	143 000	362 268	120 047 000	40/16	24	5.9
	NORTH KOREA	Pyonyang	120 538	3 000	500	73 700	43 338	22 586 000	18/11	48	-
	NORWAY	Oslo	323 878	-	1 570	83 300	-	4 505 000	13/10	217	1.8
	OMAN	Muscat	309 500	610	10 000	-	-	2 709 000	28/3	18	5.8
	PAKISTAN	Islamabad	803 940	6 580	50 000	34 800	712 560	148 721 000	34/8	25	5.5
	PANAMA	Panama City	77 082	1 550	14 770	32 600	28 162	2 942 000	21/5	41	2.6
	PAPUA NEW GUINEA	Port Moresby	462 840	6 500	1 750	420 000	34 590	5 032 000	32/9	29	4.6
	PARAGUAY	Asunción	406 752	880	217 000	128 500	60 372	5 778 000	30/5	26	4.2
	PERU	Lima	1 285 216	5 100	271 000	848 000	161 116	26 523 000	23/7	32	3.0
	PHILIPPINES	Manila	300 000	45 000	12 800	136 000	106 200	78 611 000	27/5	31	3.6
	POLAND	Warsaw	312 683	3 370	40 830	87 320	181 163	38 542 000	10/10	-	1.5
	PORTUGAL	Lisbon	88 940	7 150	14 370	31 020	36 400	10 049 000	12/11	990	1.5
	PUERTO RICO	San Juan	9 104	460	2 100	1 460	5 084	3 988 000	15/8	75	-
	QATAR	Doha	11 437	30	500	-	-	584 000	14/3	38	3.7
	ROMANIA	Bucharest	237 500	5 000	49 440	66 800	116 260	22 332 000	10/11	-	1.3
	RUSSIAN FEDERATION	Moscow	17 075 400	18 450	899 700	7 659 120	8 498 130	143 752 000	9/15	-	1.2
	RWANDA	Kigali	26 338	2 500	5 450	2 500	15 888	8 148 000	44/22	30	6.2
	ST LUCIA	Castries	616	140	20	80	376	151 000	18/6	56	2.7

AGRI-CULTURE percent employed	MANU-FACTURING percent employed	SERVICE INDUSTRIES percent employed	PER CAPITA PPP US$	EXTERNAL DEPT repayments percent of GDP	EDUCATION spending percent of GDP	MILITARY spending percent of GDP	INTERNET USERS (000)	TELEPHONES main lines in use (000)	TELEVISIONS per 1000 people	PASSENGER CARS per 1000 people
7	31	62	4 308	11.0	2	3.6	300	700	335	-
40	28	32	2 031	7.3	13	3.1	5	22	16	-
72	6	22	-	-	-	-	0.5	7	25	-
11	23	66	-	-	-	-	20	500	137	-
20	27	53	7 106	8.0	6	1.8	341	1 142	422	294
2	25	73	50 061	-	-	0.7	100	315	589	587
9	49	39	5 086	4.5	-	2.1	100	408	282	-
78	7	15	840	2.4	2	1.2	35	55	24	-
54	22	24	615	3.5	5	0.8	35	38	3	-
18	32	50	9 068	6.7	-	1.9	5 700	4 600	168	170
22	24	50	4 485	3.6	4	-	6	21	40	-
86	2	12	797	4.2	3	2.5	30	45	14	-
3	34	64	17 273	-	5	0.8	59	187	556	455
55	10	34	1 677	10.7	4	-	8	27	-	-
15	40	46	10 017	12.6	4	0.2	158	281	268	73
21	25	53	9 023	10.1	-	0.5	3 500	12 332	283	102
-	-	-	-	-	-	-	2	11	20	-
49	14	38	2 109	10.5	-	0.4	15	627	297	54
49	15	14	1 783	3.0	-	2.5	40	104	65	17
6	33	61	3 546	10.0	-	4.2	400	1 391	166	41
83	8	9	854	2.3	3	2.5	23	90	5	-
63	12	25	-	-	-	1.7	10	250	7	-
53	18	29	6 431	-	8	3.3	45	110	38	-
79	6	21	1 327	1.8	3	0.9	60	237	7	-
3	22	73	25 657	-	5	1.6	9 730	9 132	538	383
10	23	67	20 070	-	7	1.0	2 060	1 920	522	481
42	15	38	2 366	12.5	4	1.1	20	140	69	3
8	48	44	746	1.6	3	1.4	12	20	37	-
3	22	75	896	2.5	-	0.9	100	500	68	-
38	32	30	-	-	-	-	-	1 100	54	-
5	22	73	29 918	-	8	1.8	2 680	2 735	669	407
45	24	32	-	7.7	4	9.7	120	201	563	-
47	17	36	1 928	4.6	-	4.5	1 200	2 861	131	5
17	18	64	6 000	9.4	-	1.2	45	396	194	83
79	7	14	2 280	8.0	-	0.8	135	61	17	-
5	22	73	4 426	4.4	5	1.0	20	290	218	-
6	19	76	4 799	8.1	3	-	3 000	1 800	148	27
39	16	45	3 971	9.0	3	1.2	4 500	3 100	144	10
19	32	49	9 051	6.5	5	1.9	6 400	8 070	400	240
13	35	52	17 290	-	6	2.1	4 400	5 300	630	-
2	22	76	-	-	-	-	600	1 322	330	-
3	32	65	-	-	-	-	75	142	869	-
42	28	31	6 423	6.4	4	2.1	1 000	3 777	381	133
12	29	59	8 377	4.6	-	4.0	18 000	30 000	-	-
92	3	5	943	2.0	-	3.0	20	11	-	-
22	19	59	5 703	5.7	9	-	3	37	365	-

FLAG	COUNTRY	CAPITAL CITY	AREA km²	LAND USE CROP km²	PASTURE km²	FOREST km²	OTHER km²	POPULATION TOTAL 2002	BIRTH RATE / DEATH RATE per 1000 people 2000	DOUBLING TIME (years) 2000	TOTAL FERTILITY RATE 1995–2000
	SAMOA	Apia	2 831	670	10	1 340	811	159 000	30/6	28	4.5
	SÃO TOMÉ AND PRÍNCIPE	São Tomé	964	430	10	-	-	143 000	31/9	20	-
	SAUDI ARABIA	Riyadh	2 200 000	1 910	1 700 000	18 000	480 090	21 701 000	33/4	23	6.2
	SENEGAL	Dakar	196 720	380	56 500	74 500	65 340	9 908 000	37/13	25	5.6
	SERBIA AND MONTENEGRO	Belgrade	102 173	3 300	18 510	17 690	62 673	10 522 000	12/11	866	-
	SEYCHELLES	Victoria	455	60	-	50	-	83 000	19/7	65	-
	SIERRA LEONE	Freetown	71 740	600	22 000	20 400	28 740	4 814 000	44/23	26	6.5
	SINGAPORE	Singapore	639	-	-	30	-	4 188 000	12/4	84	1.6
	SLOVAKIA	Bratislava	49 035	1 260	8 650	19 890	19 235	5 408 000	10/10	866	1.4
	SLOVENIA	Ljubljana	20 251	310	3 140	10 770	6 031	1 983 000	9/10	-	1.2
	SOLOMON ISLANDS	Honiara	28 370	180	400	24 500	3 290	479 000	39/5	23	5.6
	SOMALIA	Mogadishu	637 657	240	430 000	160 000	47 417	9 557 000	51/17	24	-
	SOUTH AFRICA, REPUBLIC OF	Pretoria/Cape Town	1 219 080	9 590	839 280	82 000	288 210	44 203 000	26/16	55	3.1
	SOUTH KOREA	Seoul	99 274	2 000	540	64 560	32 174	47 389 000	13/6	82	1.5
	SPAIN	Madrid	504 782	49 000	114 500	161 370	179 912	39 924 000	10/9	6 931	1.2
	SRI LANKA	Colombo	65 610	10 200	4 400	21 000	30 010	19 287 000	18/6	60	2.1
	SUDAN	Khartoum	2 505 813	2 000	1 171 800	420 000	912 013	32 559 000	34/11	32	4.9
	SURINAME	Paramaribo	163 820	100	210	150 000	13 510	421 000	23/7	37	2.2
	SWAZILAND	Mbabane	17 364	120	12 000	1 000	4 244	948 000	36/15	37	4.8
	SWEDEN	Stockholm	449 964	-	4 470	280 250	-	8 823 000	10/11	-	1.5
	SWITZERLAND	Bern	41 293	240	11 440	11 860	17 753	7 167 000	10/9	315	1.5
	SYRIA	Damascus	185 180	8 100	83 590	4 840	88 650	17 040 000	29/5	25	4.0
	TAIWAN	Taibei	36 179	-	-	-	-	22 548 000	-/-	97	-
	TAJIKISTAN	Dushanbe	143 100	1 300	35 000	5 370	101 430	6 177 000	19/5	43	3.7
	TANZANIA	Dodoma	945 087	9 500	350 000	327 000	258 587	36 820 000	39/17	24	5.5
	THAILAND	Bangkok	513 115	33 000	8 000	145 000	327 115	64 344 000	17/7	70	2.1
	TOGO	Lomé	56 785	1 200	10 000	9 000	36 585	4 779 000	37/15	23	5.8
	TONGA	Nuku'alofa	748	310	40	80	318	100 000	25/7	33	-
	TRINIDAD AND TOBAGO	Port of Spain	5 130	470	110	2 350	2 200	1 306 000	15/7	103	1.6
	TUNISIA	Tunis	164 150	21 050	40 620	6 760	95 720	9 670 000	17/6	44	2.3
	TURKEY	Ankara	779 452	25 340	123 780	201 990	428 342	68 569 000	20/6	46	2.7
	TURKMENISTAN	Ashgabat	488 100	650	307 000	40 000	140 450	4 930 000	21/7	48	3.6
	UGANDA	Kampala	241 038	19 000	18 000	63 000	141 038	24 780 000	45/19	24	7.1
	UKRAINE	Kiev	603 700	9 320	79 100	92 390	422 890	48 652 000	9/15	-	1.3
	UNITED ARAB EMIRATES	Abu Dhabi	83 600	1 870	3 050	30	78 650	2 701 000	17/3	32	3.2
	UNITED KINGDOM	London	244 082	520	110 330	23 900	109 332	59 657 000	11/11	546	1.7
	UNITED STATES OF AMERICA	Washington D.C.	9 809 386	20 500	2 392 500	2 959 900	4 436 486	288 530 000	15/9	120	2.0
	URUGUAY	Montevideo	176 215	400	135 430	9 300	31 085	3 385 000	16/10	107	2.4
	UZBEKISTAN	Tashkent	447 400	3 750	228 000	13 000	202 650	25 618 000	22/6	40	2.8
	VANUATU	Port Vila	12 190	900	420	9 140	1 730	207 000	32/7	25	4.6
	VENEZUELA	Caracas	912 050	9 600	182 400	445 000	275 050	25 093 000	22/4	34	3.0
	VIETNAM	Hanoi	329 565	16 000	6 420	96 500	210 645	80 226 000	19/6	48	2.5
	VIRGIN ISLANDS (USA)	Charlotte Amalie	352	10	50	20	272	124 000	16/5	-	-
	YEMEN	Sana	527 968	1 240	160 650	20 000	346 078	19 912 000	40/11	25	7.6
	ZAMBIA	Lusaka	752 614	190	300 000	320 000	132 424	10 872 000	40/21	35	6.0
	ZIMBABWE	Harare	390 759	1 300	172 000	87 500	129 959	13 076 000	30/18	69	5.0

LABOUR FORCE			GDP, 2000				COMMUNICATIONS, 2000			
AGRI-CULTURE percent employed	MANU-FACTURING percent employed	SERVICE INDUSTRIES percent employed	PER CAPITA PPP US$	EXTERNAL DEPT repayments percent of GDP	EDUCATION spending percent of GDP	MILITARY spending percent of GDP	INTERNET USERS (000)	TELEPHONES main lines in use (000)	TELEVISIONS per 1000 people	PASSENGER CARS per 1000 people
-	-	-	5 041	3.6	-	-	3	8	61	-
-	-	-	-	9.5	4	-	9	5	228	-
19	20	61	11 367	-	-	11.6	570	3 100	264	-
77	8	16	1 510	5.2	3	1.4	100	235	40	-
-	-	-	-	-	4	-	400	2 017	282	176
-	-	-	-	2.8	6	1.8	9	20	203	-
67	15	17	490	6.7	1	1.4	20	25	13	-
0	29	71	23 356	-	-	4.8	2 310	1 950	304	97
7	39	54	11 243	13.5	4	1.8	700	1 935	407	229
11	38	51	17 367	-	6	1.2	600	722	368	418
27	12	38	1 648	3.3	-	-	8	8	23	-
75	8	16	-	-	-	-	0.2	15	14	-
-	-	-	9 401	3.1	6	1.5	3 068	5 000	127	94
12	27	61	17 380	5.1	4	2.8	25 600	24 000	364	167
7	31	62	19 472	-	5	1.3	7 890	17 336	591	-
42	23	33	3 530	4.5	-	4.5	122	495	111	15
70	9	22	1 797	0.5	4	3.0	56	400	273	-
6	25	66	3 799	-	-	-	15	64	253	-
26	27	48	4 492	1.6	6	1.6	14	39	119	34
3	25	72	24 277	-	8	2.1	6 020	6 017	574	437
5	26	69	28 769	-	5	1.1	3 850	4 820	548	486
28	25	47	3 556	2.0	-	5.5	60	1 313	67	9
-	-	-	-	-	-	-	11 600	12 490	-	-
46	17	29	1 152	8.8	-	1.2	5	363	326	-
84	4	12	523	2.4	2	1.3	300	127	20	-
49	18	33	6 402	11.5	5	1.6	1 200	5 600	284	-
66	10	24	1 442	2.4	4	-	50	25	32	-
34	24	43	-	-	-	-	1	8	66	-
8	28	64	8 964	6.8	-	-	120	252	340	-
22	34	43	6 363	9.8	8	1.7	400	654	198	-
47	21	32	6 974	10.6	-	4.9	2 500	19 500	449	63
43	20	11	3 956	10.9	-	3.8	2	363	196	-
90	6	4	1 208	2.6	2	1.8	60	50	27	2
26	26	17	3 816	11.5	4	3.6	750	9 450	456	104
8	27	65	17 935	-	2	-	900	915	292	-
2	26	72	23 509	-	5	2.5	34 300	34 878	653	373
3	23	74	34 142	-	5	3.1	165 700	194 000	854	-
4	25	71	9 035	6.7	3	1.1	400	929	530	-
44	14	10	2 441	11.7	-	1.7	100	1 980	276	-
-	-	-	2 802	1.0	9	-	3	6	12	-
13	25	61	5 794	4.9	-	1.2	1 300	2 600	185	-
69	13	17	1 996	4.2	-	-	400	2 600	185	-
0	14	54	-	-	-	-	12	62	594	-
61	17	22	893	2.6	7	5.2	17	291	283	-
75	8	17	780	6.4	2	0.6	25	130	134	-
26	28	47	2 635	6.4	11	4.8	100	212	30	-

Aboriginal peoples The descendants of the original inhabitants of North America. The Canadian Constitution recognizes three groups of Aboriginal peoples: First Nations (Indians), Métis, and Inuit. These are three separate peoples with unique heritages, languages, cultural practices, and spiritual beliefs.

Aboriginal rights Rights that some Aboriginal peoples of Canada hold as a result of their ancestors' longstanding use and occupancy of the land. The rights of certain Aboriginal peoples to hunt, trap, and fish on ancestral lands are examples of Aboriginal rights. Aboriginal rights will vary from group to group, depending on the customs, practices, and traditions that have formed part of their distinctive cultures.

Acid precipitation Also called acid deposition or acid rain. It is produced by sulphur and nitrogen emissions from the burning of fossil fuels. Coal and oil used in energy production, industrial boilers, and automobile engines all promote acid precipitation. When washed from the atmosphere, the precipitation increases the level of acidity in lakes, streams, and soil, and severely damages vegetation, fish, and wildlife.

Agriculture Farming; this involves the work of cultivating soil, producing field or tree crops and raising animals.

AIDS Acquired immune deficiency syndrome. Caused by HIV (human immunodeficiency virus), transmitted by some body fluids. It breaks down the body's ability to fight off infection. In 2002, 14 000 people were newly infected with AIDS every day, many of them children and heterosexual adults.

Air mass A large body of air with generally the same temperature and moisture conditions throughout. Warm and moist or cool and moist air masses usually develop over large bodies of water. Hot and dry or cold and dry air masses develop over large land areas (continents).

Alluvial soil An azonal soil developed from materials (mud, silt, and sand) deposited by moving water. Alluvial soil is often found in the deltas of rivers. It is usually young, rich in minerals, and valuable for agricultural production.

Alpine Occurring at high altitudes – for example, an alpine climate or alpine vegetation.

Aquaculture Using "farming" methods to cultivate and harvest fish, shellfish, and aquatic plants. This is an increasingly important component of the seafood production sector of both the Canadian and world economies.

Aquifer An underground reservoir in a layer of permeable rock, such as sandstone or limestone that contains water. The water accumulates because its movement is blocked by non-porous rock.

Arable land Land suitable for ploughing and cultivation. Arable land does not include pastureland or forested areas not capable of growing crops.

Arctic The high latitudes in the northern or southern hemispheres with low precipitation, very cold winters, and cold summers.

Assembly of First Nations The Assembly of First Nations (AFN) is the national representative organization of the First Nations in Canada. There are over 630 First Nations communities in Canada. It presents views on areas such as: Aboriginal and treaty rights, economic development, education, languages and literacy, health, housing, social development, justice, taxation, land claims, environment, and other issues as they arise.

Asthenosphere A layer of Earth's interior extending from 80 to 250 kilometres beneath the surface where convection currents exist in its partially molten state.

Atmosphere The vast gaseous envelope of air that surrounds Earth. Its boundaries are not easily defined. The atmosphere contains a complex system of gases and suspended particles. The main components are nitrogen, oxygen and carbon dioxide along with some other gases and water vapour.

Azonal soil One of the three major soil groups, known as orders; these soils are young and have indistinct horizons (layers). Alluvial soil is an example.

Barometric pressure A measurement of the air pressure in the atmosphere, measured in kilopascals.

Barrel A unit of measurement in the imperial system equal to approximately 160 litres.

Bedrock The solid rock that usually lies beneath the soil.

Billion In North America, this number represents one thousand million; elsewhere, the term means one million million.

Biosphere That part of Earth which supports life; it consists of two layers, the atmosphere (above Earth) and the lithosphere (or crust).

Birth rate The number of live births per thousand people in one year.

Boreal The coniferous forest area of Canada, Russia and northern Europe; the term means "of the north". It is also applied to the climate region in the same locations.

Broadleaf trees Trees with wide, flat leaves rather than needle-like leaves. In Canada, broadleaf trees lose their leaves in winter. Examples include oak, maple, birch, and poplar.

Cambrian period The first geological period of the Palaeozoic Era, extending from about 600 000 000 to 500 000 000 years ago. Much of the world was covered by water. Small water animals (invertebrates) flourished.

Canadian Shield An area of Precambrian rock, mostly igneous, that covers almost half of Canada.

Capital Money, property, or goods than can be used to generate income for a person, company, or country.

Census metropolitan area (CMA) In Canada, a city and its nearby area with a population over 100 000.

CFCs Chlorofluorocarbons. Synthetic gases containing chlorine, fluorine, and carbon. When released, they reduce the amount of ozone in the atmosphere. Sources of chlorofluorocarbons include some foam materials (e.g., Styrofoam cups), some refrigerants, aerosol sprays, and cleaning solvents.

Chernozem Fertile black or dark brown soil, rich in humus. Cherozems are found in the grassland environments in the Canadian prairies, Ukraine, Eastern Europe, the United States, South America, and Australia.

Clear-cutting The harvesting of all trees that are large enough for commercial use.

Climatic region An area in which the general conditions of temperature and precipitation are reasonably similar. For example, a "desert climate" describes an area of dry conditions.

Climograph Also called a climate graph. A combination line and bar graph used to illustrate long term average monthly temperature and precipitation for a climatic station. Temperature is shown as a line and precipitation as a series of bars.

Confederation The union of independent political units to form one nation. Canada's confederation took place on July 1, 1867. The British North America Act established the Dominion of Canada by joining Nova Scotia, New Brunswick, Québec, and Ontario. In 1991, the now defunct Confederation of Independent States (CIS), joined many of the former Soviet republics.

Coniferous A type of tree with needle-like leaves, cones and softwood trunks. Examples include Douglas fir, cedar, spruce, and hemlock.

Conservation tillage A method of land conservation whereby residues from a harvesting operation including straw and chaff on sloping land is evenly distributed over the acreage being treated. The land is not "turned over" before the next crop is planted.

Constitution The system of fundamental laws and principles of government, in written form. Canada repatriated its constitution in April, 1982.

Continental climate A type of climate where no large body of water moderates the temperature resulting in cold winters and hot summers; precipitation is generally low and occurs in the summer (e.g., Winnipeg).

Continental crust The solid layer above the lithosphere underlying major continents and thicker than under the oceans.

Continental drift Theory that suggests that Earth's crust is composed of plates that move. First proposed in 1858 and developed by Taylor and Wegener in the early 20th century, it was not until the work of Canadian scientist J. Tuzo Wilson in the 1960s that the theory was widely accepted.

Convection The movement of materials in liquids and gases caused by differences in heat. Warmer and less dense materials tend to rise and cooler, more dense materials fall. In the tropics, convection currents refer to the heating, rising, cooling and condensing of air to produce precipitation.

Core The centre of Earth. The temperature of the innermost part, the solid core, exceeds 4000°C. It contains high concentrations of nickel and iron. The liquid core that surrounds the solid core is not actually liquid, but is more fluid than the solid core.

Cropland Land used to raise crops such as wheat, rice, corn, and sugar cane.

Cross section A side view of a landscape between two specific points to illustrate slope and altitude, and important natural features.

Crude oil Oil in its natural, unrefined form, as it comes from Earth.

Crust The relatively thin outer layer of Earth containing both the ocean basins and the continents. It differs from the mantle beneath in both physical and chemical properties.

Crustacean A class of invertebrates with a hard outer shell and joined appendages (e.g., shrimp, crab, lobster).

Cyclonic storm A low pressure area, often accompanied by warm and cold fronts, bringing precipitation to the middle latitudes.

Death rate The number of deaths per 1000 people in one year.

Deciduous tree A tree that regularly sheds its leaves, usually in the autumn. These trees are dormant in winter (e.g., maple, oak, birch)

Delta A river deposit formed where the river enters a large body of water. Water slows down and fine materials (silt, mud) are deposited. This produces a land feature that is triangular in shape, like the Greek letter "delta."

Deposition The laying down of materials carried by water, wind, or ice. (verb: deposit)

Desertification The process by which deserts extend into surrounding areas. It can be caused by climatic changes or human activities. The process has been significant in the Sahel region of Africa.

Developed country One of two basic classifications of countries (see developing country) determined by examining factors such as economic development, gross domestic product per capita, income per capita, potential for development, energy use, literacy, and quantity and quality of food. Based on their available resources, a developed country is thought to be able to provide a reasonable quality of life for inhabitants.

Developing country One of two basic classifications of countries (see developed country) determined by comparison with developed countries. A developing country is becoming more economically advanced and industrialized, but faces many challenges, particularly in providing a reasonable quality of life for inhabitants.

Devonian period The fourth geological period of the Palaeozoic Era, extending from 400 000 000 to 345 000 000 years ago. This was the period in which fish developed.

Differential erosion The wearing away of different types of rock in the same location. For example, softer sedimentary rocks erode more quickly than harder rock, sometimes forming escarpments (e.g., the Niagara Escarpment).

Domestic trade The movement of goods and services within a country (e.g., the movement of goods among provinces of Canada).

Drainage basin An area drained by a river or series of rivers into a common body of water (e.g., Hudson Bay drainage basin in Canada with an area of nearly 3.8 million square kilometres).

Drumlin A hill, usually oval or tear-shaped, formed by glaciers. Drumlins vary in size, are often found in groups (fields), and are common around Guelph and Peterborough, Ontario.

Ecosystem A living community in the water or on land emphasizing the interactions among the host environment and the plants and animals it contains. Ecosystems can be as small as a pond or as large as a tropical rainforest.

El Niño The occasional development of warm ocean surface waters along the coast of Ecuador and Peru. When this warming occurs the tropical Pacific trade winds weaken and the usual up welling of cold, deep ocean water is reduced. El Niño normally occurs late in the calendar year and lasts for a few weeks to a few months. Sometimes an extremely warm event can develop that lasts for much longer time periods.

Emigration The movement of people (or an organism) out of an area or country.

Endangered species An animal or plant threatened with imminent extinction in all or most of its natural area.

Equator An imaginary circle, indicated by a line, which divides Earth into northern and southern hemispheres. It is equally distant from the north and south poles. The equator is used as the base line for latitude.

Equinox Generally, March 21 and September 21. The approximate dates that the sun is directly overhead at noon at the equator. (plural: equinoxes)

Erosion The wearing down and carrying away of material from Earth's surface by water, wind, and ice. (verb: erode)

Escarpment A steep slope or cliff formed by faulting or differential erosion. For example, the Great Rift Valley in Africa was formed by faulting and the Niagara Escarpment in Ontario was formed by differential erosion.

Esker A long narrow ridge of rounded and sorted materials, usually quite coarse (e.g., sand, gravel). Eskers are formed in or under glaciers, as meltwaters deposit materials.

European Union An alliance of member nations to integrate the economy of countries in Europe and to have a common currency (the Euro). Co-ordinated social development and possible political unity are objectives of the organization. Members are increasing on a regular basis as countries apply and are accepted for membership.

Exports Goods or services sold in other countries.

External aid Assistance provided by one nation for another, usually involving goods, money, or technical expertise.

External debt See foreign debt.

External trade Trade with other countries (as compared to domestic trade that takes place within the country). Trade between Canada and the United States is external trade; trade between Alberta and Ontario is domestic trade.

Extinct species A plant or animal that no longer exists (e.g., the passenger pigeon).

Extirpated species A plant or animal that no longer exists in one location, but is found elsewhere. This official designation has been assigned by COSEWIC (Committee on the Status of Endangered Wildlife in Canada) to a species or sub-species of plant or animal formerly native to Canada and no longer known in Canada but may be found elsewhere in the world.

False colour A method of adding colour to digital satellite images to enhance specific features.

Fault A fracture in Earth's crust along which rock strata have moved vertically or horizontally. Faults may trap oil or natural gas.

First Nations A term, describing one of the groups of Aboriginal people, to replace the word "Indian", which many people found offensive. Although the term First Nation is widely used, no legal definition of it exists.

Flora The plant life of a region.

Folding The bending of rock layers, often resulting in the formation of "fold" mountains.

Foreign debt One nation's debt to another. Also called external debt. Developing nations often owe large amounts of money to other countries, especially developed countries.

Fossil The imprint or preserved remains of a prehistoric plant or animal, usually found in sedimentary rock.

Fossil fuel An energy source originating from prehistoric plants and animals, and associated with sedimentary rock (e.g., coal, peat, natural gas, petroleum). The burning of fossil fuels has been associated with global warming, air pollution, and acid precipitation.

Front The surface or line between masses of air that have different characteristics. A warm front marks the advance of warm air into cooler air. A cold front marks the advance of cold air into warmer areas. An occluded front occurs when a cold front runs underneath a warm front.

Frost-free period The total number of days between the average dates of the last frost in the spring and the first frost in the autumn.

Gauging station A point on a river where information on water flow is gathered. Data is interpreted to predict the implications of variations in stream flow.

Generating station A plant where electricity is produced from falling water (hydro), coal, petroleum, natural gas, nuclear fission, or other source.

Geologic time The division of Earth's history of approximately 4.5 billion years into eras and periods.

Geological province A large area whose rock structure, type and age show common characteristics.

Glacier A slow-moving mass of ice. Glaciers are currently found at high latitudes or high altitudes.

Grassland A region where vegetation consists mainly of grasses; moisture is insufficient to support trees. Grassland areas often have regional names (e.g., Pampas: Argentina; Steppe: Ukraine; Prairie: North America).

Greenhouse effect A warming of the atmosphere created by the retention of energy from Earth's ecosystem. Without the greenhouse effect, Earth's atmosphere would be 30 to 35 Celsius degrees colder than the current world-wide average of 15°C. Human activity has affected the gases that make up the atmosphere and may be causing an acceleration of this natural process.

Greenhouse gases The main greenhouse gases are water vapour (H_2O), carbon dioxide (CO_2), methane (CH_4), nitrous oxide (N_2O), ozone (O_3), and halocarbons (CFCs, HFCs, etc.). Fossil fuels for heating and electrical production, gasoline for cars, and manufacturing have added greenhouse gases to the atmosphere. These gases trap the heat and warm the atmosphere.

Gross domestic product The total dollar value of all goods and services produced in a country in a given year. A high gross domestic product (GDP) indicates a high level of development.

Ground water The water in the soil and in the bedrock underlying the soil.

Growing degree days The sum of the number of degrees by which the average temperature of each day in a year exceeds 6°C.

Growing season The season in which the average daily temperature is above 6°C, allowing crops to grow.

Gulf Stream Warm ocean current that originates in and around the Caribbean and flows across the North Atlantic to northwest Europe moderating the climate in that area.

Habitat An environment that supports plant, animal, or human life.

Hardwood Wood produced by most deciduous trees such as oak and maple.

Hazardous waste Discarded materials that pose a risk to humans or the environment.

Hemisphere Any half of a globe or sphere. The Earth has traditionally been divided into hemispheres by the equator (northern and southern hemispheres) and by the prime meridian and international date line (eastern and western hemispheres).

HIV Human immunodeficiency virus (HIV) has been decisively established as the cause of AIDS.

Horizon A distinct layer in a soil profile. Mature soils have three horizons, designated by the letters A, B, and C. There may also be subdivisions of these horizons.

Human development index A measurement of a country's achievements in three areas: longevity, knowledge, and standard of living. Longevity is measured by life expectancy at birth; knowledge is measured by a combination of the adult literacy rate and the combined gross primary, secondary, and tertiary enrolment ratio; and standard of living is measured by GDP per capita (purchasing power).

Humidity The amount of moisture in the air, expressed as a percentage of the total amount of moisture the air could hold. For example, 95% humidity indicates that precipitation will occur shortly since the amount of moisture has almost reached the air's capacity.

Humus The upper layer of the soil consisting of decaying and decayed organic materials.

Hurricane An intense cyclonic storm, which often migrates from its source area in the tropics to temperate areas (e.g., Hurricane Andrew, Hugo, Hazel).

Hydro-electric power Electricity produced by the natural movement of falling water, such as at Niagara Falls in Ontario.

Hydrocarbon A substance containing only compounds of carbon and hydrogen. There are thousands of these compounds (e.g., methane, crude oil).

Ice cap A mass of ice, smaller than an ice sheet, that permanently covers an area of land.

Ice sheet A glacier (thick layer of ice) covering an area greater than 50 000 square kilometres. Greenland and Antarctica are considered ice sheets.

Igneous rock Rock formed by the cooling of molten materials from the interior of Earth.

Immigration The movement of people (or any organism) into an area or country.

Impermeable rock See non-porous rock.

Imports Goods and services purchased from another area, usually another country. Canada's main imports include automobiles, petroleum, and electrical goods.

Improved land Areas of Earth's surface that have been cleared of trees or have been ploughed for the growing of crops.

Indian Act Canadian federal legislation, first passed in 1876, that sets out certain federal government obligations regarding Indian people and regulates the management of Indian reserve lands. The act has been amended several times, most recently in 1985.

Industrial mineral A mineral such as stone, sand, or gravel used in construction.

Industry Extractive processes (mining, forestry, fishing), manufacturing and services such as commerce and insurance. The term does not include agriculture.

Infant mortality rate The number of deaths of children under one year of age, per 1000 live births in a given year. In developed nations, this figure is low (less than 10), but may be as high as 200 in nations where health services are poorly developed.

Inflation A general increase in the price of goods and services over time. In periods of high inflation, the purchasing power of money decreases. High rates of inflation can erode gains made by weak or struggling economies.

Inorganic materials In soil, materials such as rock fragments, liquid, and gases that combine with organic materials to form the soil.

Internal drainage A drainage system with no outlet to the ocean. This occurs when land in the interior is below sea level (e.g., the Dead Sea in Israel, the Caspian Sea in Russia).

International date line An imaginary line that approximately follows 180° longitude. The area of the world just east of the line is one day ahead of the area just west of the line. The line varies slightly from the 180° line to avoid splitting island or countries into separate days.

Intrazonal soil One of the three major soil orders where the influence of soil or drainage supersedes that of climate and vegetation.

Intrusive rock Igneous rock formed within Earth's crust from molten materials called magma (e.g., granite, gabbro, serpentine).

Inuit A group of people who live in the far north of Canada and who have inhabited this area and other polar areas for at least 5000 years.

Intertropical Convergence Zone of low atmospheric pressure and ascending air located at or near the equator. Rising air currents are due to global wind convergence and convection from thermal heating. The zone of convergence "migrates" with the seasons.

Isobar A line on a map joining points with the same atmospheric pressure – this is generally reduced to sea-level equivalents.

Isoline A line on a map joining points with the same numerical value (e.g., isobar, isotherm).

Isotherm A line on a map joining points with the same temperature.

Jet stream A narrow current of high-velocity wind found in the upper atmosphere. The polar jet stream exists in the mid-latitudes at an altitude of approximately 10 kilometres. This jet stream flows from west to east at speeds of 110 to 185 kilometres per hour. The subtropical jet stream occurs above the sub-tropical highs at an altitude of 13 kilometres.

Joule (J) A metric unit of energy defined as the work done by the force of one Newton when it moves its point of application a distance of one metre.

Labour force The number of people working or looking for paid work.

Land claims The cases presented by First Nations for ownership and/or control of lands on which they live or have lived. Some claims have been settled but many more are still in negotiation between First Nations peoples and the federal government, or are before the courts for settlement.

Landsat Series of satellites launched by NASA for the purpose of remotely monitoring resources on Earth. The first Landsat satellite was launched by the United States in 1972.

Land use The type of human activity that a given land area is used for (e.g., agriculture, commercial, residential, industrial).

Landed value The dollar value of fish caught, before marketing and processing.

Landform Any feature of Earth's surface formed by earth movements or by wearing down of the surface of Earth.

Latitude Distance north and south of the equator, measured in degrees. The north pole is at 90°N and the south pole is at 90°S. All lines of latitude are parallel to the equator.

Leaching The natural removal of soluble minerals in soil downward from the A to the B horizon by percolating water.

Life expectancy The average number of years that an individual is expected to live at the time of their birth. Good food and health-care services promote longer life expectancy.

Literacy The ability to read and write. There are no universal definitions and standards of literacy. The most common definition is the ability to read and write at 15 years of age. There are 22 countries that claim a literacy rate of 100%. While not a perfect measure of educational results, literacy is one of the most easily available and valid measures for international comparisons. Low levels of literacy and education in general, can impede the economic development of a country.

Lithosphere The solid outer layer of Earth including the top part of the mantle and Earth's crust.

Longitude Distance east and west of the prime meridian, measured in degrees. Lines of longitude, called meridians, join the north and south poles.

Mantle A concentric layer of Earth's interior, nearly 3000 kilometres thick, between the crust and the core.

Manufacturing Industry that changes raw materials into finished products.

Mass transit The movement of people, usually in an urban area by bus, streetcar, subway, or commuter train.

Meltwater Water produced by the thawing of ice or melting of snow. Meltwaters from the last glacial period covered large areas of Manitoba, southern Ontario and Québec, and the Clay Belts in northern Ontario.

Metallic mineral A mineral that yields a metal when processed (e.g., iron, gold, silver, copper).

Metamorphic rock A type of rock that results from changes – produced by heat and/or pressure – in other rock types (e.g., limestone becomes marble, granite becomes gneiss, and quartz sandstone becomes quartzite).

Métis People of mixed First Nations and European descent. The Métis have a unique culture that draws on their diverse ancestral origins such as Scottish, French, Ojibway, and Cree.

Migration The movement of people, birds, or animals from one location to another.

Mesozoic Geologic era that occurred from 245 to 65 million years ago.

Millibar (mb) A unit of atmospheric pressure. 1000 mb = 1 bar.

Mineral A naturally occurring crystalline substance with specific chemical composition and regular internal structure, composed of two or more elements. Examples of minerals are quartz and feldspar. Most rocks contain a combination of minerals.

Mineral fuel A fuel produced from minerals (e.g., uranium, coal, oil, natural gas).

Mixed farming A type of agriculture which involves the cultivation of crops and the raising of animals.

Moisture deficiency An amount of moisture needed for plant growth that is not produced by precipitation. When high temperatures increase evaporation, a moisture deficiency occurs. Irrigation is often used to reduce the deficiency and promote plant growth.

Monsoon A wind that changes with the seasonal changes in pressure systems resulting in distinctive wet and dry seasons (e.g., the summer monsoon of the Indian sub-continent).

Moraine Materials deposited by a glacier, often in the form of hills. End moraines are found at the farthest point of advance of the glacier.

Natural increase The difference between the number of births and deaths, usually based on 1000 people.

Nautical mile A unit of distance used in navigation, equal to 1.853 kilometres. The distance is one minute of an arc on a Great Circle drawn on a sphere the size of Earth.

Needleleaf A tree with needles rather than flat leaves. The needles fall and are replaced throughout the year (e.g., pine, spruce, fir).

Net migration The difference between immigration and emigration.

Nomadic Without permanent residence. Nomadic peoples may be hunters or herders, who move from place to place in search of food and pastures.

Non-porous rock A dense type of impermeable rock that prevents liquids from passing through its small number of pore spaces (e.g., shale and some forms of limestone).

Northwest Passage A sea route across northern Canada that is difficult to traverse due to ice conditions. Early explorers searched for this route to China (Cathay).

Nuclear power Electricity produced by using the heat from nuclear fission to produce steam to drive a generator.

Offshore fishery The sector of the fishing industry that usually operates more than 80 kilometres from shore using large ships that stay out at sea for several days.

Oil (or gas) field An area in which oil or gas has been discovered. New oil and gas fields have been found off the east coast of Canada and in the Beaufort Sea.

Oil sands Sands saturated with heavy crude oil. Large oil sands have been found near Fort McMurray on the Athabasca River in Alberta.

Organic materials Living materials, such as plants and animals.

Organic soil An incompletely developed soil containing more than 20% dead organic materials. This soil is often called "muck soil" or peat and is found in areas of poor drainage such as marshes and swamps.

Ozone layer A layer of the stratosphere where oxygen (O_2) is converted into ozone (O_3). Ozone absorbs much of the ultraviolet radiation. When the ozone layer is reduced in thickness, these harmful rays increase the likelihood of skin damage that can lead to skin cancer.

Pacific Rim The countries around the Pacific Ocean, from Chile to Alaska on the east side and from New Zealand to Japan and Russia on the west side.

Pack ice Seasonal ice formed by the joining of several ice floes.

Parkland A transitional vegetation zone between grassland and boreal forest containing differing combinations of both grassland and forest.

Percolation The downward movement of water through the soil and through joints in the bedrock.

Permafrost Ground that does not completely thaw in summer. The surface layer may thaw but the ground underneath remains frozen and does not permit meltwater to drain downward. Boggy conditions often result.

Permeable rock A porous type of rock with many pores or spaces that allow liquid to pass through.

Pesticide Chemical used to kill unwanted plants and animals. Some authorities include herbicides, insecticides, algaecides, and fungicides in the definition.

Plantation farming Using the land for a single commercial crop, usually on estates, especially in tropical countries where crops such as tea, rubber, coffee, sugar, and fruit are grown on a large scale.

Plate A section of Earth's crust that "floats" in Earth's mantle in much the same way as an iceberg floats in water. Plate movement (continental drift) can cause earthquakes, volcanoes, and tsunamis.

Plateau An upland area with a fairly flat surface and steep slopes. Rivers often dissect plateau surfaces.

Plate tectonics The theory suggesting that Earth's surface is composed of a number of oceanic and continental plates which move by the forces of convection currents. When these plates meet, one slides over or under the other, often producing earthquakes and volcanic activity.

Podzol A shallow, highly leached and acidic soil usually associated with coniferous forests.

Pollution The release of substances into the environment that harm living organisms and damage resources. A range of problems are created, such as an impairment of the quality of life (e.g., closed beaches) and hazards to human health (e.g., skin cancer).

Population density A figure determined by dividing the total population by the total area for a given region.

Population distribution The pattern of habitation in an area.

Population profile A diagram showing the structure of a population, usually by age and sex. Because of the general shape, the profile is often called a population pyramid.

Porous rock See permeable rock.

Post-glacial lake A body of water formed by the meltwaters of a receding glacier. Where ice blocked the normal drainage routes, ponding occurred. (e.g., Lake Agassiz in Manitoba and Lake Iroquois in Ontario).

Precambrian That period of Earth's prehistory dating from the formation of Earth (approximately 4.5 billion years ago) to approximately 600 million years ago.

Precipitation Moisture that accumulates in clouds and then falls to Earth as rain, snow, hail, sleet, or ice pellets.

Primary industry Industry that works directly with natural resources (e.g., fishing, forestry, mining, agriculture).

Prime meridian An imaginary line at zero degrees longitude, passing through Greenwich, England. All meridians are numbered east and west of this line to a maximum of 180°.

Quaternary The most recent period of the Cenozoic Era, also known as the Age of Humans.

Radarsat Satellites built by the Canadian Space Agency for the purpose of remotely sensing Earth's resources using a system that transmits microwaves.

Rainforest A thick luxuriant evergreen forest in areas of high precipitation, evenly distributed throughout the year. Tropical rainforests are found in such places as the Amazon and Congo basins. Temperate rainforests are found in China, Australia, New Zealand and the United States.

Rangeland Land used for grazing cattle.

Raw material Material that a manufacturing industry processes into a more finished state (e.g., iron to steel, crude oil to gasoline).

Reef A ridge of rock, sand, or coral whose top lies close to the ocean's surface.

Refinery A processing plant for raw materials (e.g., oil, sugar, copper).

Refugee An individual who has been compelled to move to another region or country because of political, economic, or environmental crises.

Relief The general physical variations of the land.

Remote sensing The gathering of information by the use of electronic or other sensing devices in satellites.

Reserve Land belonging to the federal government upon which First Nations peoples (and others) have the right to occupy and use.

Retail Business that sells products or provides services for consumers.

Ridge An area of higher elevation, usually long and narrow, with steep-sloped sides. Ridges are found both on land and in the ocean.

Rift Zone between two diverging tectonic plates. The mid-oceanic ridge is an area where such plate divergence is occurring.

Rift valley Steep-sided valley created by the downward displacement of land between two parallel faults as a result of tectonic movement (e.g., the Great Rift Valley in Africa).

Rock A compact and consolidated mass of mineral matter subdivided into three basic types — igneous, sedimentary and metamorphic.

Run-off Moisture, either from precipitation or from melting snow, that flows over the surface and eventually joins or creates streams and rivers. Excess water occurs often as part of the "spring thaw" and becomes run-off.

Rural Concerning the area outside towns and cities.

Satellite image Similar to a photograph, but recorded on bands of electro-magnetic spectrum, taken from a satellite.

Sea ice A covering of thick ice over a large area of water. Sea ice is common in the Arctic Ocean.

Sedimentary rock A type of rock formed by the compression of deposits from water wind and ice (e.g., shale, sandstone, limestone).

Seismic zone An area of Earth's crust that experiences horizontal or vertical movement, often associated with earthquakes and volcanoes. Areas of high seismic activity are found along fault lines and on the edges of tectonic plates.

Services Economic activities by people in which no goods are produced (e.g., sales personnel, bank employees, teachers, doctors, bus drivers, accountants).

Sewage treatment Methods of dealing with raw human wastes before being returned to bodies of water. Methods may be physical, chemical, or biological, or a combination of these.

Softwood Wood produced by most coniferous trees (e.g., pine).

Soil Layer of unconsolidated material found at the Earth's surface that has been influenced by climate, relief, parent material, time, and organisms. Soil normally consists of weathered mineral particles, dead and living organic matter, and air spaces.

Soil capability A classification system for soils based on characteristics of the soil as determined by soil surveys. There are 7 classes, each of which indicates the degree of limitation imposed by the soil in its use for mechanized agriculture. They are used for making decisions on land improvement, for developing land-use plans, and for preparing equitable land assessments.

Solar energy Energy produced directly or indirectly from the sun.

Solar radiation Radiant heat from the sun, emitted in the form of short waves. It is measured in megajoules per square metre.

Soluble Able to be dissolved. Certain minerals are soluble in water and are carried down through the soil from one horizon to the next.

Stratosphere The layer of the atmosphere from 10 to 50 kilometres above Earth's surface.

Subduction The downward movement of an oceanic plate into the asthenosphere along converging plate boundaries. Eventually the plate melts into the molten mass.

Subsistence farming A type of agriculture in which livestock is raised and crops are cultivated for consumption rather than for sale.

Sustainable development A level of development that ensures potential for future generations whereby the environment and its resources are not overwhelmed by human activity.

Tectonics The internal forces that form the features of Earth's crust.

Temperate Refers to the "middle" zones of Earth's surface, between the tropics and the polar regions.

Tertiary period The first period of the Cenozoic Era (65 million years ago to the beginning of the glacial periods about one million years ago), during which mammals developed.

Thermal energy Electricity produced by burning fossil fuels, such as coal, oil, and natural gas.

Time zone A geographical area within which clocks are set to a standard time. Time zones occupy approximately 15 degrees of longitude.

Topographic map A map that displays the relief of the land through the use of contour lines. Base elevation is sea level. Canada has national coverage in topographic maps at scales ranging from 1: 25 000 to 1: 250 000.

Tropic of Cancer An imaginary line drawn 23°30' degrees north of the equator indicating the northernmost extent of the apparent seasonal movement of the sun.

Tropic of Capricorn An imaginary line drawn 23°30' south of the equator indicating the southernmost extent of the apparent seasonal movement of the sun.

Troposphere The layer of air directly above Earth's surface where most of the important weather phenomena take place. It contains more than 95% of Earth's air and extends an average of 10 kilometres upwards, although the range is from 7 to 17 kilometres, depending upon latitude. Temperatures decrease with altitude.

Tsunami A seismic wave caused by an earthquake.

Tundra The climate, vegetation, or soil of the arctic and sub-arctic regions between the forested areas and those with permanent snow and ice. Mosses, lichens, and permafrost are characteristics of the area.

Urban Referring to a city or town. In Canada, an area that contains at least 1000 people with a population density of at least 400 people per square kilometre.

Urbanization The process of change in an area from a rural to an urban landscape.

Water table The level beneath Earth's surface below which the rock and soil are saturated. The depth of the water table varies, depending upon type of rock, availability of water, slope and human influences.

Watt The power that produces energy at the rate of one joule per second.

Weather station A location equipped with instruments to record atmospheric conditions. In Canada, continuous data is relayed to Environment Canada for analysis and forecasting purposes.

Wetland Land whose water table is at or very near the surface (e.g., bogs, swamps, marshes, and areas of shallow water). These areas are valuable for migrating birds and act as "filters" for water before it enters rivers or streams.

Wholesale The business of selling products and services in large quantities, not to the final consumer, but to retail businesses that then sell them to consumers.

Wind chill factor A measurement that combines the effect of low temperature and the speed of the wind. A high wind chill factor can cause frostbite or hypothermia.

Wisconsin ice sheet The most recent continental ice sheet that began to recede about 15 000 years ago. It covered much of North America with ice up to 2000 metres thick.

Zonal soil The most predominant of the three major soil orders reflecting the influence of climate and natural vegetation (e.g., chernozem, podzol). Soils in this group are well developed and have distinct horizons.

ECONOMICS AND TRADE

Part of Pacific Rim Thematic map, pp.164-165

HISTORY AND SOCIAL STUDIES

Part of Colonization and Indepedence map, p.131

ENVIRONMENT

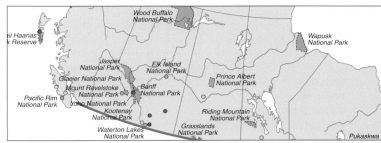

Part of Protecting the Environment map, p.55

TOURISM

Part of International Visitors map, p.49

WEATHER AND CLIMATE

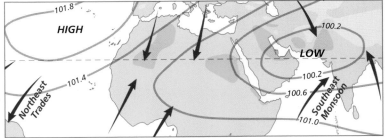

Part of July Temperature, Pressure and Winds map, p.82

How to use the Gazetteer

All the names on the maps in this atlas, except some of those on the special topics maps, are included in the gazetteer.
The names are arranged in alphabetical order. Where the name has more than one word, the separate words are considered as one word to decide the position of the name in the index:

White Bay
White Bear
Whitefish
White Hill
Whitehorse

Where there is more than one place with the same name, the country name is used to decide the order:

Los Angeles Chile
Los Angeles U.S.A.

If both places are in the same country, the county or state or province name is also used:

Fuzhou Fujian China
Fuzhou Jiangxi China

Each entry in the index starts with the name of the place or feature, followed by the name of the country, state, or territory in which it is located. This is followed by the number of the most appropriate page on which the name appears, usually the largest scale map. Next comes the alphanumeric reference, followed by the latitude and longitude.

Names of physical features, such as rivers, capes, and mountains, are followed by a description. The descriptions are usually shortened to one or two letters; these abbreviations are provided below. Town names are followed by a description only when the name may be confused with that of a physical feature:

Lake Louise *town*

To help distinguish the different parts of each entry, different styles of type are used:

place name / province /state name (if included) / page number / latitude/longitude
description (if any) / country name / alphanumeric gridreference

Deer Lake *town* Ont. Canada **64 B4** 52.37N 94.02W

The **alphanumeric grid reference** can be used to find the general location of a feature on a map. Page 170 in the atlas describes how to use the numbers and letters in the frame of the maps to locate a place or feature.

The **latitude and longitude reference** gives a more exact description of the position of the feature. Each name in the index has a different latitude and longitude reference, so the feature can be located accurately. Page 170 of the atlas describes lines of latitude and longitude, and explains how they are numbered and divided into degrees and minutes.

Abbreviations

Ala.	Alabama	Ind.	Indiana	*pen.*, **Pen.**	peninsula, Peninsula
Alta.	Alberta	*l.*, **L.**	lake, Lake	Phil.	Philippines
b., **B.**	bay, Bay	La.	Louisiana	P.N.G.	Papua New Guinea
B.C.	British Columbia	Liech.	Liechtenstein	*pt.*, **Pt.**	point, Point
Bosnia.	Bosnia-Herzegovina	Lux.	Luxembourg	Qué.	Québec
c., **C.**	cape, Cape	Man.	Manitoba	*r.*, **R.**	river, River
C.A.R.	Central African Republic	Mass.	Massachusetts	Rep. of Ire.	Republic of Ireland
Carib. Sea	Caribbean Sea	Med. Sea	Mediterranean Sea	*research stn.*	research station
Colo.	Colorado	Minn.	Minnesota	**Resr.**	Reservoir
Czech Rep.	Czech Republic	Miss.	Mississippi	R.S.A.	Republic of South Africa
d.	internal division e.g., state, province	**Mt.**	Mount	Russian Fed.	Russian Federation
		mtn., **Mtn.**	mountain, Mountain	Sask.	Saskatchewan
Del.	Delaware	*mtns.*, **Mtns.**	mountains, Mountains	Serb. and Mon.	Serbia and Montenegro
des.	Desert	N.B.	New Brunswick	**Sd.**	Sound
Dem. Rep. Congo	Democratic Republic of Congo	Neth. Ant.	Netherlands Antilles	S.C.	South Carolina
		Nev.	Nevada	S. Korea	South Korea
Dom. Rep.	Dominican Republic	Nfld. and Lab.	Newfoundland and Labrador	*str.*, **Str.**	strait, Strait
Equat. Guinea	Equatorial Guinea	N.C.	North Carolina	Tex.	Texas
est.	estuary	N. Korea	North Korea	U.A.E.	United Arab Emirates
f.	physical feature e.g., valley, plain, geographic district	N. Mex.	New Mexico	U.K.	United Kingdom
		N.S.	Nova Scotia	U.S.A.	United States of America
Fed. States of Micronesia	Federated States of Micronesia	N.Y.	New York	Va.	Virginia
		N.W.T.	Northwest Territories	Vt.	Vermont
Fla.	Florida	**Oc.**	Ocean	W. Va.	West Virginia
g., **G.**	Gulf	Ont.	Ontario	Wyo.	Wyoming
Ga.	Georgia	Oreg.	Oregon	Y.T.	Yukon Territory
i., **I.**, *is.*, **Is.**	island, Island, islands, Islands	Pa.	Pennsylvania		
Ill.	Illinois	P.E.I.	Prince Edward Island		

A

Aasiaat Greenland **75 M3** 68.42N 52.51W
Abadeh Iran **146 D4** 31.08N 52.36E
Abadla Algeria **128 C8** 31.00N 2.43W
Abakan Russian Fed. **143 L3** 53.43N 91.25E
Abaza Russian Fed. **152 G8** 52.44N 90.12E
Abbey Canada **60 B1** 50.44N 108.45W
Abbotsford Canada **57 Y3** 49.02N 122.18W
Abéché Chad **128 F6** 13.50N 20.49E
Aberdeen U.K. **138 C3** 57.09N 2.06W
Aberdeen U.S.A. **112 G6** 45.28N 98.30W
Abha Saudi Arabia **146 C2** 18.14N 42.27E
Abidjan Côte d'Ivoire **128 C5** 5.21N 4.02W
Abilene U.S.A. **112 G3** 32.27N 99.45W
Abitibi *r.* Canada **65 E3** 50.54N 81.01W
Abitibi, Lake Canada **65 E3** 48.55N 80.01W
Abu Dhabi U.A.E. **146 D3** 24.28N 54.20E
Abū Ḩallūfah, Jabal *hill* Jordan **150 B2** 31.24N 36.19E
Abu Hamed Sudan **146 B2** 19.30N 33.24E
Abuja Nigeria **128 D5** 9.06N 7.19E
Acadia National Park U.S.A. **72 A2** 44.20N 68.13W
Acapulco Mexico **116 E4** 16.51N 99.56W
Acarigua Venezuela **122 C7** 9.35N 69.12W
Accra Ghana **128 C5** 5.35N 0.14W
Achinsk Russian Fed. **143 L3** 56.10N 90.10E
Acklins I. The Bahamas **117 J5** 22.30N 74.10W
Aconcagua *mtn.* Argentina **123 B3** 32.37S 70.00W
A Coruña Spain **138 C2** 43.22N 8.23W
Acre Israel **150 A3** 32.56N 35.06E
Actéon, Groupe *is.* French Polynesia **163 R4** 22.00S 136.00W
Acton Canada **64 V2** 43.37N 80.05W
Adamawa Highlands *mts.* Nigeria/Cameroon **127 E5** 7.05N 12.00E
Adam's Peak Sri Lanka **147 G1** 6.49N 80.28E
Adana Turkey **139 G1** 36.59N 35.19E
Adare, Cape Antarctica **167 B2** 71.15S 170.18E
Ad Dahna *des.* Saudi Arabia **146 C3** 20.40N 46.52E
Addis Ababa Ethiopia **128 G5** 9.01N 38.45E
Adelaide Australia **158 C2** 34.56S 138.36E
Adélie Land *f.* Antarctica **167 A2** 69.21S 139.02E
Aden Yemen **146 C2** 12.49N 44.59E
Aden, Gulf of Somalia/Yemen **128 H6** 11.44N 45.16E
Adi *i.* Indonesia **155 I3** 4.10S 133.10E
Adirondack Mountains U.S.A. **65 G2** 44.01N 74.15W
Admiralty Is. P.N.G. **155 L3** 2.00S 147.00E
Admiralty Island U.S.A. **56 C4** 57.41N 134.18W
Admiralty Island National Monument - Kootznoowoo Wilderness U.S.A. **56 C4** 57.52N 134.28W
Adriatic Sea Europe **138 E2** 44.19N 13.24E
Advocate Harbour Canada **72 C2** 45.20N 64.47W
Ādwa Ethiopia **146 B2** 14.09N 38.52E
Aegean Sea Greece/Turkey **138 F1** 39.00N 24.51E
Afghanistan Asia **146 E4** 33.53N 65.52E
Africa 128-129
'Afula Israel **150 A3** 32.37N 35.17E
Agadez Niger **128 D6** 16.57N 7.59E
Agadir Morocco **128 C8** 30.27N 9.37W
Agana Guam **162 J8** 13.28N 144.45E
Agartala India **147 H3** 23.50N 91.16E
Agra India **147 F3** 27.09N 78.02E
Aguanus *r.* Canada **69 G3** 50.13N 62.07W
Aguascalientes Mexico **116 D5** 21.51N 102.18W
Agulhas, C. R.S.A. **129 F1** 34.50S 20.00E
Agulhas Negras *mtn.* Brazil **121 F4** 22.20S 44.43W
Ahmadabad India **147 F3** 23.03N 72.37E
Ahvaz Iran **146 C4** 31.15N 48.40E
Aigialousa Cyprus **150 A4** 35.31N 34.11E
Ailsa Craig Canada **66 C3** 43.09N 81.32W
Ainslie, Lake Canada **72 E3** 46.08N 61.10W
Aïr *mts.* Niger **128 D6** 18.46N 8.15E
Airdrie Canada **59 C1** 51.17N 114.01W
Aishihik Canada **56 B5** 61.36N 137.31W
Aitape P.N.G. **155 K3** 3.09S 142.22E
Aitkin U.S.A. **64 B2** 46.32N 93.43W
Aitutaki *i.* Cook Is. **163 P5** 18.52S 159.46W
Ajaccio France **138 D2** 41.55N 8.44E
Ajax Canada **64 X2** 43.50N 79.01W
Ajdabiya Libya **128 F8** 30.45N 20.13E
Akhdar, Jabal *mts.* Oman **146 D3** 23.22N 57.00E
Akimiski Island Canada **75 J2** 53.08N 81.17W
Akita Japan **153 Q5** 39.44N 140.05E
Aklavik Canada **74 E3** 68.17N 135.01W
Akobo *r.* Ethiopia/Sudan **128 G5** 7.47N 33.03E
Akordat Eritrea **146 B2** 15.31N 37.54E
Akpatok Island Canada **75 L3** 60.24N 67.45W
Akron U.S.A. **113 J5** 41.04N 81.31W
Aksai Chin Asia **147 F4** 35.08N 79.11E
Aksu China **152 E6** 42.10N 80.00E
Aktau Kazakhstan **139 I2** 43.39N 51.12E
Aktogay Kazakhstan **152 D7** 46.59N 79.42E
Aktyubinsk Kazakhstan **139 I3** 50.13N 57.10E
Akulivik Canada **68 C6** 60.49N 78.09W
Akureyri Iceland **138 B4** 65.41N 18.07W
Alabama *d.* U.S.A. **113 I3** 33.00N 87.00W
Alabama *r.* U.S.A. **113 I3** 31.05N 87.55W
Alagoinhas Brazil **122 F5** 12.09S 38.21W
Alakol', L. Kazakhstan **152 E7** 46.00N 81.40E
Åland *is.* Finland **138 E4** 60.28N 19.53E
Alaska *d.* U.S.A. **74 D3** 63.41N 143.45W
Alaska Range *mts.* U.S.A. **2 C4** 63.31N 148.02W
Alausí Ecuador **122 B6** 2.00S 78.50W
Albacete Spain **138 C1** 39.00N 1.50W
Albania Europe **138 E2** 41.56N 19.34E
Albany Australia **158 A2** 34.57S 117.54E
Albany *r.* Canada **65 E4** 52.08N 81.59W
Albany Ga. U.S.A. **113 J3** 31.37N 84.10W
Albany N.Y. U.S.A. **113 L5** 42.40N 73.49W
Al Basrah Iraq **146 C4** 30.29N 47.48E
Al Bayda' Libya **128 F8** 32.44N 21.44E
Albert, Lake Dem. Rep. Congo/Uganda **128 G5** 1.43N 30.52E
Alberta *d.* Canada **59 C2** 54.30N 114.00W
Albert Lea U.S.A. **113 H5** 43.39N 93.22W
Alberton Canada **72 C3** 46.49N 64.04W
Albion N.Y. U.S.A. **66 F3** 43.14N 78.11W
Albion Pa. U.S.A. **66 D1** 41.53N 80.22W
Ålborg Denmark **138 D3** 57.03N 9.55E
Albuquerque U.S.A. **112 E4** 35.05N 106.38W
Al Buraymī Oman **146 D3** 24.14N 55.46E
Albury Australia **158 D2** 36.03S 146.53E
Alcalá de Henares Spain **138 C2** 40.29N 3.21W
Aldabra Islands Seychelles **129 H4** 9.16S 46.30E
Aldan Russian Fed. **143 O3** 58.44N 125.22E
Aldan *r.* Russian Fed. **143 P4** 63.30N 130.00E
Aleksandrovsk-Sakhalinskiy Russian Fed. **143 Q3** 50.55N 142.12E
Aleppo Syria **146 B4** 36.12N 37.09E
Alert Canada **74 L5** 82.07N 62.23W
Ålesund Norway **138 D4** 62.28N 6.12E
Aleutian Is. U.S.A. **162 N12** 2.00N 52.00E
Aleutian Range *mts.* U.S.A. **166 B3** 58.00N 156.00W
Alexander Archipelago U.S.A. **74 E2** 57.59N 137.33W
Alexander Island Antarctica **167 F2** 71.13S 70.20W
Alexandria Canada **65 G2** 45.19N 74.38W
Alexandria Egypt **128 F8** 31.13N 29.56E
Alexandria U.S.A. **113 H3** 31.19N 92.29W
Aleysk Russian Fed. **152 E8** 52.32N 82.17E
Algeria Africa **128 D8** 30.15N 3.31E
Al Ghawr *f.* Jordan/West Bank **150 A2** 31.54N 35.30E
Algiers Algeria **128 D8** 36.46N 3.04E
Algona U.S.A. **64 B1** 43.04N 94.14W
Algonquin Park *town* Canada **66 F5** 45.33N 78.35W
Algonquin Provincial Park Canada **66 F5** 45.49N 78.21W
Al Ḩasā Jordan **150 A2** 30.48N 35.58E
Al Ḩuwayz Syria **150 B4** 35.30N 36.23E
Alicante Spain **138 C1** 38.21N 0.28W
Alice Springs *town* Australia **158 C3** 23.42S 133.52E
Al Jahrah Kuwait **146 C3** 29.20N 47.41E
Al Jawf Libya **128 F7** 24.12N 23.19E
Al Jawf Saudi Arabia **146 B3** 29.47N 39.55E
Al Jubayl Saudi Arabia **146 C3** 27.02N 49.38E
Al Khaşab Oman **146 D3** 26.11N 56.14E
Allahabad India **147 G3** 25.25N 81.52E
Allardville Canada **72 C3** 47.28N 65.30W
Allegheny *r.* U.S.A. **65 F1** 40.27N 79.59W
Allegheny Mts. U.S.A. **113 J4** 38.00N 81.00W
Allegheny Reservoir U.S.A. **66 F1** 41.56N 78.55W
Allemand, Lac *l.* Canada **68 D6** 61.02N 75.36W
Allenford Canada **66 C4** 44.32N 81.10W
Allentown U.S.A. **113 K5** 40.37N 75.30W
Alliance U.S.A. **112 F5** 42.08N 103.00W
Alliston Canada **64 W3** 44.09N 79.52W
Alma N.B. Canada **72 C2** 45.36N 64.57W
Alma Qué. Canada **68 E3** 48.33N 71.39W
Al Mafraq Jordan **150 B3** 32.20N 36.13E
Almaty Kazakhstan **152 D6** 43.19N 76.55E
Almería Spain **138 C1** 36.50N 2.27W
Almont U.S.A. **66 A2** 42.55N 83.03W
Alor *i.* Indonesia **155 G2** 8.20S 124.30E
Alor Setar Malaysia **154 C5** 6.06N 100.23E
Alouette Lake Canada **57 Y3** 49.21N 122.25W
Alpena U.S.A. **65 E2** 45.03N 83.27W
Alpine U.S.A. **112 F3** 30.22N 103.40W
Alps *mts.* Europe **138 D2** 45.24N 6.47E
Al Qa'amiyat *f.* Saudi Arabia **146 C2** 17.59N 47.47E
Al Qadmūs Syria **150 B4** 35.07N 36.09E
Al Qāmishlī Syria **146 C4** 37.03N 41.13E
Al Qaţrānah Jordan **150 B2** 31.14N 36.03E
Al Qunfidhah Saudi Arabia **146 C2** 19.09N 41.04E
Alsask Canada **60 B1** 51.23N 109.59W
Alsek *r.* U.S.A. **56 B4** 59.11N 138.26W
Altai Mts. Mongolia **152 G7** 46.30N 93.30E
Altamira Brazil **122 D6** 3.12S 52.12W
Altay China **152 F7** 47.48N 88.07E
Altay Mongolia **152 H7** 46.20N 97.00E
Altiplano *f.* Bolivia **122 C5** 18.00S 67.30W
Altiplano Mexicano *mts.* Mexico **109 I4** 24.00N 105.00W
Altona Canada **60 E1** 49.05N 97.34W
Altoona U.S.A. **113 K5** 40.32N 78.23W
Altun Shan *mts.* China **152 F5** 38.10N 87.50E
Alva U.S.A. **112 G4** 36.48N 98.40W
Al Wajh Saudi Arabia **146 B3** 26.17N 36.25E
Al Widyan *mts.* Iraq/Saudi Arabia **146 C4** 32.09N 40.22E
Amadeus, L. Australia **158 C3** 24.50S 130.45E
Amadjuak Lake Canada **75 K3** 64.57N 71.09W
Amamapare Indonesia **155 J3** 4.56S 136.43E
Amarillo U.S.A. **112 F4** 35.14N 101.50W
Amazon *r.* Brazil **122 D6** 2.00S 50.00W
Amazon Delta *f.* Brazil **122 E7** 0.50N 49.00W
Ambarchik Russian Fed. **143 S4** 69.39N 162.27E
Ambato Ecuador **122 B6** 1.18S 78.36W
Ambergris Cay *i.* Belize **116 G4** 18.00N 87.58W
Amberley Canada **66 C4** 44.03N 81.43W
Ambon Indonesia **155 H3** 3.50S 128.10E
Amdo China **152 G4** 32.15N 91.43E
American Samoa *is.* Pacific Oc. **162 O5** 14.20S 170.00W
Amery Canada **60 F3** 56.33N 94.05W
Amery Ice Shelf *f.* Antarctica **167 K2** 69.33S 70.52E
Ames U.S.A. **64 B1** 42.01N 93.37W
Amgun *r.* Russian Fed. **143 P3** 53.10N 139.47E
Amherst Canada **72 C2** 45.49N 64.11W
Amherstburg Canada **66 A2** 42.05N 83.06W
Amiens France **138 D2** 49.54N 2.18E
Amisk Lake Canada **60 D2** 54.33N 102.15W
Amman Jordan **150 A2** 31.57N 35.56E
Ammassalik Greenland **166 J2** 65.62N 37.70W
Amos Canada **68 C3** 48.34N 78.08W
Amqui Canada **68 F3** 48.28N 67.26W
Amravati India **147 F3** 20.56N 77.51E
Amritsar India **147 F4** 31.34N 74.56E
Amsterdam Netherlands **138 D3** 52.23N 4.54E
Amu Darya *r.* Asia **146 D5** 44.02N 59.39E
Amund Ringnes Island Canada **74 I4** 78.17N 96.35W
Amundsen Gulf Canada **74 F4** 70.25N 121.26W
Amundsen-Scott *research stn.* Antarctica **167 I1** 90.00S 0.00
Amundsen Sea Antarctica **167 E2** 72.33S 119.40W
Amuntai Indonesia **154 F3** 2.24S 115.14E
Amur *r.* Russian Fed. **143 P3** 53.17N 140.00E
Amursk Russian Fed. **143 P3** 50.16N 136.49E
Anabar *r.* Russian Fed. **143 N5** 72.40N 113.30E
Anacortes U.S.A. **57 X2** 48.30N 122.38W
Anadyr Russian Fed. **143 T4** 64.40N 177.32E
Anadyr *r.* Russian Fed. **143 T4** 65.00N 176.00E
Anadyr, G. of Russian Fed. **143 U4** 64.30N 177.50W
Anahim Lake *town* Canada **56 E3** 52.27N 125.18W
Anambas Is. Indonesia **154 D4** 3.00N 106.10E
Anápolis Brazil **122 E5** 16.19S 48.58W
Ancaster Canada **64 W1** 43.14N 79.58W
Anchorage U.S.A. **2 C4** 61.12N 149.52W
Andaman Islands India **154 A6** 12.46N 93.17E
Andaman Sea Indian Ocean **154 B6** 11.33N 95.20E
Anderson *r.* Canada **74 F3** 69.41N 128.56W
Andes *mts.* S. America **122 B5** 15.00S 74.00W
Andorra Europe **138 D2** 42.32N 1.35E
Andorra la Vella Andorra **138 D2** 42.31N 1.32E
Andros *i.* The Bahamas **117 I5** 24.30N 78.00W
Anegada *i.* Virgin Islands **117 L4** 18.46N 64.24W
Angara *r.* Russian Fed. **143 L3** 58.00N 93.00E
Angarsk Russian Fed. **143 M3** 52.24N 103.45E
Angel de la Guarda *i.* Mexico **116 B6** 29.10N 113.20W
Angers France **138 C2** 47.28N 0.33W
Angikuni Lake Canada **60 E4** 62.21N 99.42W
Angola Africa **129 E3** 11.40S 17.34E
Angren Uzbekistan **147 F5** 41.02N 70.07E
Anguilla *i.* Leeward Is. **117 L4** 18.14N 63.05W
Anguille, Cape Canada **72 F3** 47.55N 59.25W
Angus-Borden Canada **66 E4** 44.20N 79.53W
Ankara Turkey **139 G1** 39.56N 32.50E
Anmore Canada **57 X3** 49.19N 122.52W
Annaba Algeria **128 D8** 36.52N 7.48E
An Nabk Syria **150 B4** 34.01N 36.44E
An Nafud *des.* Saudi Arabia **146 C3** 28.28N 41.17E
An Najaf Iraq **146 C4** 31.59N 44.20E
Annapolis *r.* Canada **72 C2** 44.41N 65.46W
Annapolis U.S.A. **113 K4** 38.58N 76.30W
Annapolis Basin *b.* Canada **72 C2** 44.38N 65.44W
Annapolis Royal Canada **72 C2** 44.44N 65.31W
Annapurna I *mtn.* Nepal **147 G3** 28.34N 83.49E
Ann Arbor U.S.A. **113 J5** 42.18N 83.45W
An Naşirīyah Iraq **146 C4** 31.01N 46.14E
An Nu'ayrīyah Saudi Arabia **146 C3** 27.29N 48.26E
Anshan China **153 M6** 41.05N 122.58E
Anshun China **153 J3** 26.15N 105.51E
Antakya Turkey **139 G1** 36.11N 36.07E
Antalya Turkey **139 G1** 36.53N 30.41E
Antananarivo Madagascar **129 H3** 18.54S 47.33E
Antarctica 167
Antarctic Peninsula Antarctica **167 F2** 64.36S 68.38W
Anticosti, Île d' *i.* Canada **69 G3** 49.27N 62.59W
Antigonish Canada **72 E2** 45.37N 61.56W
Antigua *i.* Leeward Is. **117 L4** 17.09N 61.49W
Antigua and Barbuda Leeward Is. **117 L4** 17.30N 61.49W
Anti Lebanon *mts.* Lebanon/Syria **150 B3** 33.36N 35.54E
Antipodes Is. Pacific Oc. **162 M2** 49.42S 178.50E
Antofagasta Chile **123 B4** 23.40S 70.23W
Antsirañana Madagascar **129 H3** 12.19S 49.17E
Antwerpen Belgium **138 D3** 51.12N 4.26E
Anvil Range *mts.* Canada **56 C5** 62.36N 133.52W
Anxi China **152 H6** 40.32N 95.57E
Anyang China **153 K5** 36.04N 114.20E
Anzac Canada **56 F3** 54.46N 122.30W
Anzhero-Sudzhensk Russian Fed. **142 K3** 56.10N 86.10E
Aomori Japan **153 Q6** 40.50N 140.43E
Aoraki *mtn.* New Zealand **159 G1** 43.36S 170.09E
Apa *r.* Brazil/Paraguay **123 D4** 22.08S 57.55W
Apalachee B. U.S.A. **113 J2** 29.30N 84.00W
Aparri Philippines **155 G7** 18.22N 121.40E
Apennines *mts.* Italy **138 D2** 44.37N 9.47E
Apia Samoa **162 N5** 13.48S 171.45W
Apostle Islands U.S.A. **65 C2** 46.57N 90.25W
Appalachian Mts. U.S.A. **113 K4** 39.30N 78.00W
Appleton U.S.A. **113 I5** 44.16N 88.25W
Apsley Canada **66 F4** 44.45N 78.05W
'Aqaba Jordan **150 A1** 29.31N 35.01E
Aqaba, Gulf of Asia **146 B3** 29.19N 34.54E
'Arabah, Wādī al *r.* Israel/Jordan **150 A1** 29.56N 35.09E
Arabian Pen. Asia **134 G5** 25.00N 45.00E
Arabian Sea Indian Ocean **146 E2** 18.08N 66.38E
Aracaju Brazil **122 F5** 10.54S 37.07W
Aracatuba Brazil **123 D4** 21.12S 50.24W
'Arad Israel **150 A2** 31.15N 35.15E
Arafura Sea Australia/Indonesia **155 I2** 9.00S 135.00E
Araguaia *r.* Brazil **122 E6** 5.30S 48.05W
Araguaína Brazil **122 E6** 7.16S 48.18W
Araguari Brazil **122 E5** 18.38S 48.13W
Arak Iran **146 C4** 34.05N 49.42E
Arakan Yoma *mts.* Myanmar **147 A8** 20.18N 94.07E
Aral Sea Asia **142 H2** 45.00N 60.00E
Aralsk Kazakhstan **142 I2** 46.56N 61.43E
Araraquara Brazil **123 E4** 21.46S 48.08W
Ararat, Mt Turkey **139 H1** 39.42N 44.18E
Arbīl Iraq **146 C4** 36.11N 44.01E
Arborg Canada **60 E1** 50.54N 97.14W
Archangel Russian Fed. **139 H4** 64.33N 40.33E
Archipélago de Mingan, Réserve du Parc National de l' Canada **69 G3** 50.12N 63.37W
Arctic Bay *town* Canada **74 J4** 72.55N 85.10W
Arctic Ocean 166
Arctic Red *r.* Canada **74 E3** 67.27N 133.44W
Arctowski *research stn.* Antarctica **167 G2** 62.10S 58.29W
Ardabīl Iran **146 C4** 38.14N 48.15E
Ardbeg Canada **66 D5** 45.38N 80.04W
Arena, Pt. U.S.A. **112 B4** 38.58N 123.44W
Arequipa Peru **122 B5** 16.25S 71.32W
Argentia Canada **69 I2** 47.18N 54.00W
Argentina S. America **123 C3** 35.00S 65.00W
Argentino, L. Argentina **123 B1** 50.15S 72.25W
Argun *r.* Russian Fed. **153 M8** 53.30N 121.48E
Argyle Canada **72 C1** 43.48N 65.51W
Argyle, L. Australia **158 B4** 16.20S 128.14E
Århus Denmark **138 E3** 56.09N 10.12E
Arica Chile **122 B5** 18.30S 70.20W
Arichat Canada **72 E2** 45.31N 61.01W
Arinos *r.* Brazil **122 D5** 10.20S 57.35W
Aripuanā *r.* Brazil **122 C6** 5.05S 60.30W
Ariquemes Brazil **122 C5** 9.56S 63.04W
Arizona *d.* U.S.A. **112 D3** 34.00N 112.00W
Arkansas *d.* U.S.A. **113 H3** 35.00N 92.00W
Arkansas *r.* U.S.A. **113 H3** 33.50N 91.00W
Arkansas City U.S.A. **112 G4** 37.03N 97.02W
Arkona Canada **66 C3** 43.04N 81.50W
Arlington U.S.A. **57 Y1** 48.11N 122.08W
Arlit Niger **128 D6** 18.42N 7.21E
Arm *r.* Canada **60 C1** 50.47N 105.00W
Armavir Russian Fed. **139 H2** 45.01N 41.06E
Armenia Asia **139 H2** 40.26N 44.30E
Armenia Colombia **122 B7** 4.32N 75.40W
Armidale Australia **159 E2** 30.32S 151.40E
Armstrong B.C. Canada **56 G2** 50.27N 119.11W
Armstrong Ont. Canada **65 C3** 50.18N 89.03W
Arnaud *r.* Canada **68 E5** 59.59N 69.57W
Arnhem, C. Australia **158 C4** 12.10S 137.00E
Arnhem Land *f.* Australia **158 C4** 13.00S 132.30E
Arnold's Cove *town* Canada **69 I2** 47.46N 53.59W
Arnprior Canada **65 F2** 45.26N 76.22W
Arnstein Canada **66 E5** 45.55N 79.59W
Aroland Canada **65 D3** 50.13N 86.58W
Aroostook *r.* U.S.A. **72 B3** 46.46N 67.45W
Ar Ramthā Jordan **150 B3** 32.34N 36.01E
Ar Raqqah Syria **146 B4** 35.57N 39.01E
Ar Rimal *f.* Saudi Arabia **146 D3** 21.43N 52.53E
Arthur Canada **66 D3** 43.50N 80.32W
Artigas *research stn.* Antarctica **167 G2** 62.11S 58.55W
Aruba *i.* Netherlands Ant. **117 J3** 12.30N 70.00W
Aru Is. Indonesia **155 I2** 6.00S 134.30E
Arusha Tanzania **128 G4** 3.22S 36.37E
Aruwimi *r.* Dem. Rep. Congo **128 F5** 1.14N 23.38E
Arviat Canada **74 I3** 61.12N 94.09W
Arvidsjaur Sweden **138 E4** 65.35N 19.12E
Arzamas Russian Fed. **139 H3** 55.23N 43.49E
Asahi-dake *mtn.* Japan **153 Q6** 43.42N 142.54E
Asahikawa Japan **153 Q6** 43.46N 142.23E
Asansol India **147 G3** 23.41N 87.01E
Ascension *i.* S. Atlantic Ocean **128 B4** 7.50S 14.17W
Ashburton *r.* Australia **158 A3** 21.15S 115.00E
Ashcroft Canada **56 F2** 50.43N 121.17W
Ashdod Israel **150 A2** 31.48N 34.37E
Ashern Canada **60 E1** 51.11N 98.21W
Ashgabat Turkmenistan **146 D4** 37.53N 58.21E
Ashland U.S.A. **113 H6** 46.34N 90.45W
Ashqelon Israel **150 A2** 31.41N 34.34E
Ashtabula U.S.A. **66 D1** 41.52N 80.48W
Ashuanipi Lake Canada **68 F4** 52.48N 66.10W
'Āşī *r.* Lebanon/Syria **150 B4** 34.24N 36.26E
Asia 80 E5 52.00N 105.00E
Asir *f.* Saudi Arabia **146 C3** 20.53N 40.14E
Asmara Eritrea **128 G6** 15.20N 38.56E
Assab Eritrea **128 H6** 12.59N 42.43E
Aş Şāfī Jordan **150 A2** 31.02N 35.28E
As Salţ Jordan **150 A3** 32.03N 35.44E
Assiniboia Canada **60 C1** 49.38N 105.59W
Assiniboine *r.* Canada **60 E1** 49.53N 97.09W
Assiniboine, Mount Canada **59 C1** 50.57N 115.34W
As Suwaydā' Syria **150 B3** 32.43N 36.34E
Astana Kazakhstan **142 J3** 51.10N 71.28E
Astara Iran **146 C4** 38.27N 48.52E
Astoria U.S.A. **112 B6** 46.12N 123.50W
Astrakhan' Russian Fed. **139 H2** 46.20N 48.03E
Asunción Paraguay **123 D4** 25.15S 57.40W
Aswān Egypt **128 G7** 24.02N 32.56E
Asyūt Egypt **128 G7** 27.07N 31.08E
Atacama Desert S. America **123 B4** 20.00S 69.00W
Atafu *i.* Pacific Oc. **162 N6** 8.40S 172.40W
Atâr Mauritania **128 B7** 20.32N 13.03W
Atbara Sudan **128 G6** 17.43N 33.55E
Atbara *r.* Sudan **128 G6** 17.40N 33.58E
Athabasca Canada **59 C2** 54.43N 113.17W
Athabasca *r.* Canada **59 D3** 58.28N 111.09W
Athabasca, Lake Canada **60 B3** 59.17N 109.24W

C

Crow, North Fork *r.* U.S.A. **64 B2** 45.05N 93.46W
Crowsnest Pass Canada **59 C1** 49.38N 114.41W
Crowsnest Pass *town* Canada **59 C1** 49.38N 114.28W
Crow Wing *r.* U.S.A. **64 B2** 46.17N 94.20W
Crozet Islands Indian Ocean **80 C2** 47.00S 52.00E
Cruz, Cabo *c.* Cuba **117 I4** 19.52N 77.44W
Crystal Falls *town* U.S.A. **65 C2** 46.06N 88.20W
Cuanza *r.* Angola **129 E4** 9.21S 13.08E
Cuba C. America **117 I5** 22.00N 79.00W
Cuba U.S.A. **66 F2** 42.13N 78.17W
Cubango *r.* Angola/Namibia **129 F3** 18.01S 21.26E
Cub Hills Canada **60 C2** 54.22N 104.48W
Cúcuta Colombia **122 B7** 7.55N 72.31W
Cuddalore India **147 F2** 11.42N 79.43E
Cuddapah India **147 F2** 14.29N 78.48E
Cuenca Ecuador **122 B6** 2.54S 79.00W
Cuernavaca Mexico **116 E4** 18.57N 99.15W
Cuiabá Brazil **122 D5** 15.32S 56.05W
Culiacán Mexico **116 C5** 24.50N 107.23W
Cultus Lake Canada **57 Z3** 49.03N 121.59W
Cultus Lake *town* Canada **57 Z3** 49.04N 121.59W
Culuene *r.* Brazil **122 D5** 12.56S 52.51W
Cumaná Venezuela **122 C8** 10.29N 64.12W
Cumberland House *town* Canada **60 D2** 53.57N 102.16W
Cumberland Lake Canada **60 D2** 54.02N 102.18W
Cumberland Peninsula Canada **75 L3** 66.34N 64.34W
Cumberland Sound Canada **75 L3** 65.00N 65.00W
Cunene *r.* Angola **129 E3** 17.15S 11.46E
Cupica, G. of Colombia **117 I2** 6.35N 77.25W
Curaçao *i.* Netherlands Ant. **117 K3** 12.15N 69.00W
Curitiba Brazil **123 E4** 25.24S 49.16W
Cut Bank U.S.A. **60 A1** 48.37N 112.18W
Cuttack India **147 G3** 20.27N 85.55E
Cuzco Peru **122 B5** 13.32S 72.10W
Cypress Hills Canada **59 D1** 49.28N 109.40W
Cyprus Asia **139 G1** 35.38N 33.17E
Czar Canada **59 D2** 52.27N 110.49W
Czech Republic Europe **138 E2** 49.38N 15.37E

D

Dafoe *r.* Canada **60 F2** 55.54N 94.37W
Dagupan Philippines **154 G7** 16.02N 120.21E
Da Hinggan Ling *mts.* China **153 M7** 50.00N 122.10E
Dahlak Archipelago Eritrea **146 C2** 15.58N 40.04E
Dakar Senegal **128 B6** 14.43N 17.28W
Da Lat Vietnam **154 D6** 11.56N 108.25E
Dalhousie Canada **72 B4** 48.03N 66.23W
Dali China **152 I3** 25.42N 100.11E
Dalian China **153 M5** 38.53N 121.37E
Dallas U.S.A. **112 G3** 32.47N 96.48W
Dall Island U.S.A. **56 C3** 54.57N 133.09W
Dalmeny Canada **60 C2** 52.20N 106.47W
Daloa Côte d'Ivoire **128 C5** 6.54N 6.28W
Dalrymple, Mt. Australia **158 D3** 21.02S 148.38E
Dalton Canada **65 D3** 48.09N 84.03W
Daly *r.* Australia **158 C4** 13.20S 130.19E
Damar *i.* Indonesia **155 H2** 7.10S 128.30E
Damascus Syria **150 B3** 33.30N 36.20E
Dammam Saudi Arabia **146 D3** 26.24N 50.10E
Dampier Australia **158 A3** 20.40S 116.42E
Dampir Str. Pacific Oc. **155 I3** 0.30N 130.50E
Da Nang Vietnam **154 D7** 16.04N 108.14E
Dandong China **153 M6** 40.06N 124.25E
Daneborg Greenland **166 I2** 74.33N 20.22W
Danger Is. Cook Is. **162 O5** 10.53S 165.49W
Daniel's Harbour Canada **69 H3** 50.14N 57.35W
Danube *r.* Europe **138 F2** 45.26N 29.38E
Danville U.S.A. **113 K4** 36.34N 79.25W
Da Qaidam Zhen China **152 H5** 37.44N 95.08E
Daqing China **153 N7** 46.40N 125.00E
Dar'ā Syria **150 B3** 32.38N 36.07E
Dar es Salaam Tanzania **128 G4** 6.48S 39.16E
Darfur *f.* Sudan **128 F6** 14.55N 25.09E
Darhan Mongolia **153 J7** 49.34N 106.23E
Darién, G. of Colombia **122 B7** 9.20N 77.00W
Darjiling India **147 G3** 27.02N 88.19E
Darling *r.* Australia **158 D2** 34.05S 141.57E
Darling Downs *f.* Australia **159 D3** 28.00S 149.45E
Darnley Canada **72 D3** 46.32N 63.39W
Darnley, Cape Antarctica **167 K2** 67.26S 69.19E
Dartmouth Canada **72 D2** 44.41N 63.35W
Daru P.N.G. **155 K2** 9.03S 143.12E
Darwin Australia **158 C4** 12.23S 130.44E
Dashkhovuz Turkmenistan **146 D5** 41.49N 59.59E
Datong China **153 K5** 40.12N 113.12E
Daugavpils Latvia **138 F3** 55.53N 26.31E
Dauphin Canada **60 D1** 51.09N 100.02W
Dauphin Lake Canada **60 E1** 51.14N 99.48W
Davao Philippines **155 H5** 7.05N 125.38E
Davao G. Philippines **155 H5** 6.30N 126.00E
Davenport Iowa U.S.A. **113 H5** 41.40N 90.36W
Davenport Wash. U.S.A. **56 G1** 47.43N 118.12W
David Panama **117 H2** 8.26N 82.26W
Davidson Canada **60 C1** 51.16N 105.59W
Davis *research stn.* Antarctica **167 K2** 68.34S 77.57E
Davis Inlet *town* Canada **69 G4** 55.53N 60.45W
Davis Sea Antarctica **167 L2** 66.04S 91.45E
Davis Strait Canada/Greenland **75 M3** 66.00N 57.00W
Dawqah Oman **146 D2** 18.37N 54.04E
Dawson Canada **74 E3** 64.04N 139.24W
Dawson Creek *town* Canada **56 F3** 55.46N 120.17W
Dawson Range *mts.* Canada **56 B5** 62.00N 138.00W
Dawsons Landing Canada **56 E2** 51.34N 127.37W
Daxian China **153 J4** 31.10N 107.28E
Dayr az Zawr Syria **146 C4** 35.19N 40.06E
Dayton U.S.A. **113 J4** 39.45N 84.10W
Daytona Beach *town* U.S.A. **113 J2** 29.11N 81.01W
Dead Sea Asia **150 A2** 31.25N 35.30E
Dease *r.* Canada **56 D4** 59.55N 128.30W
Dease Lake *town* Canada **56 D4** 58.24N 129.59W
Dease Strait Canada **74 H3** 68.35N 108.56W
Death Valley *f.* U.S.A. **112 C4** 36.00N 116.45W
Debak Malaysia **154 E4** 1.30N 111.28E
Debden Canada **60 C2** 53.32N 106.53W
Debert Canada **72 D2** 45.26N 63.30W
Debrecen Hungary **138 F2** 47.32N 21.37E
Decatur U.S.A. **113 I4** 39.44N 88.57W
Deccan *f.* India **147 F2** 18.40N 77.05E
Deep River *town* Canada **65 F2** 46.05N 77.28W
Deer Lake Nfld. and Lab. Canada **73 G4** 49.07N 57.34W
Deer Lake Ont. Canada **64 B4** 52.41N 94.26W
Deer Lake *town* Nfld. and Lab. Canada **69 H3** 49.07N 57.14W
Deer Lake *town* Ont. Canada **64 B4** 52.37N 94.02W
Deer Pond *l.* Canada **73 H4** 48.30N 54.45W
Defiance U.S.A. **65 D1** 41.17N 84.22W
Dégelis Canada **68 E2** 47.33N 68.39W
De Grey *r.* Australia **158 A3** 20.12S 119.11E
Dehra Dun India **147 F4** 30.20N 78.05E
De Kalb U.S.A. **65 C1** 41.56N 88.44W
Delano Peak *mtn.* U.S.A. **112 D4** 38.23N 112.22W
Delap-Uliga-Djarrit Marshall Is. **162 M7** 7.07N 171.22E
Delaware *d.* U.S.A. **113 K4** 39.00N 75.30W
Delay *r.* Canada **68 E5** 56.57N 71.24W
Delevan U.S.A. **66 F2** 42.29N 78.29W
Delhi Canada **66 D2** 42.51N 80.29W
Delhi India **147 F3** 28.38N 77.17E
Déljne Canada **74 F3** 65.14N 123.20W
Delisle Canada **60 C1** 51.55N 107.08W
De Longa Str. Russian Fed. **143 T5** 70.00N 178.00E
De Long Mountains U.S.A. **74 B3** 68.40N 162.02W
Deloraine Canada **60 D1** 49.11N 100.30W
Del Rio U.S.A. **112 F2** 29.23N 100.56W
Delta *town* Canada **57 W3** 49.05N 123.06W
Deming U.S.A. **57 Y2** 48.50N 122.13W
Dempo *mtn.* Indonesia **154 C3** 4.02S 103.07E
Denakil *f.* Africa **128 H6** 14.27N 40.44E
Denali National Park and Preserve U.S.A. **74 C3** 63.16N 151.17W
Denizli Turkey **138 F1** 37.45N 29.05E
Denmark Europe **138 E3** 56.13N 10.09E
Denpasar Indonesia **154 F2** 8.40S 115.14E
D'Entrecasteaux Is. P.N.G. **155 M2** 9.30S 150.40E
Denver U.S.A. **112 F4** 39.45N 104.58W
De Pas, Rivière *r.* Canada **68 F4** 55.54N 64.39W
Deputatskiy Russian Fed. **143 P4** 69.17N 139.56E
Dêqên China **152 H3** 28.45N 98.58E
Dera Ghazi Khan Pakistan **147 F4** 30.05N 70.44E
Derby Australia **158 B4** 17.19S 123.38E
Desaguadero *r.* Argentina **123 C3** 34.00S 66.40W
Désappointement, Îles du Pacific Oc. **163 R5** 14.02S 141.24W
Deschambault Lake Canada **60 D2** 54.39N 103.34W
Deschambault Lake *town* Canada **60 D2** 54.55N 103.21W
Deseado Argentina **123 C2** 47.44S 65.56W
Des Moines U.S.A. **113 H5** 41.35N 93.35W
Des Moines *r.* U.S.A. **64 C1** 40.23N 91.28W
Des Moines, East Fork *r.* U.S.A. **64 B1** 42.41N 94.12W
Detroit U.S.A. **113 J5** 42.23N 83.05W
Detroit Lakes *town* U.S.A. **64 B2** 46.50N 95.51W
Deux-Rivières *town* Canada **66 F6** 46.15N 78.17W
Devils Lake *town* U.S.A. **112 G6** 48.08N 98.50W
Devil's Paw *mtn.* U.S.A. **56 C4** 58.43N 133.53W
Devon Island Canada **74 J4** 75.20N 85.00W
Devonport Australia **158 D1** 41.09S 146.16E
Dewdney Canada **57 Y3** 49.10N 122.12W
Dezadeash Canada **56 B5** 60.22N 137.03W
Dezful Iran **146 C4** 32.22N 48.24E
Dezhou China **153 L5** 37.29N 116.11E
Dhaka Bangladesh **147 H3** 23.43N 90.24E
Dhanbad India **147 G3** 23.47N 86.25E
Dharwad India **147 F2** 15.27N 75.04E
Dhaulagiri *mtn.* Nepal **147 G3** 28.40N 83.28E
Dhībān Jordan **150 A2** 31.29N 35.48E
Dhule India **147 F3** 20.53N 74.52E
Diamantina *r.* Australia **158 C3** 26.45S 139.10E
Dibrugarh India **147 H3** 27.27N 94.55E
Dickinson U.S.A. **112 F6** 46.54N 102.48W
Didsbury Canada **59 C1** 51.39N 114.08W
Diefenbaker, Lake Canada **60 C1** 50.44N 107.00W
Digby Canada **72 C2** 44.37N 65.46W
Dijon France **138 D2** 47.20N 5.03E
Dili Indonesia **155 H2** 8.35S 125.35E
Dillon Canada **60 B2** 55.54N 108.55W
Dillon U.S.A. **112 D6** 45.14N 112.38W
Dimapur India **147 H3** 25.54N 93.47E
Dīmona Israel **150 A2** 31.04N 35.02E
Dinaric Alps *mts.* Bosnia/Croatia **138 E2** 44.13N 16.16E
Dindigul India **147 F2** 10.22N 77.59E
Dingwall Canada **72 E3** 46.54N 60.29W
Dipolog Philippines **155 G5** 8.34N 123.28E
Dire Dawa Ethiopia **128 H5** 9.34N 41.53E
Dirranbandi Australia **158 D3** 28.35S 148.10E
Disappointment, L. Australia **158 B3** 23.30S 122.55E
Disraëli Canada **65 H2** 45.54N 71.22W
District of Columbia *d.* U.S.A. **113 K4** 38.55N 77.00W
Dixon Entrance Canada/U.S.A. **56 C3** 54.18N 133.28W
Dixonville Canada **59 B3** 56.33N 117.41W
Diyarbakır Turkey **139 H1** 37.55N 40.14E
Djado Plateau Niger **128 E7** 21.30N 12.53E
Djibouti Africa **128 H6** 11.34N 42.25E
Djibouti Djibouti **128 H6** 11.32N 43.09E
Dnieper *r.* Europe **139 G2** 46.30N 32.19E
Dniester *r.* Ukraine **138 F2** 48.06N 28.30E
Dnipropetrovs'k Ukraine **139 G2** 48.30N 35.05E
Doaktown Canada **72 B3** 46.33N 66.09W
Doberai Pen. Indonesia **155 I3** 1.10S 132.30E
Dodecanese *is.* Greece **138 F1** 35.57N 27.47E
Dodge City U.S.A. **112 F4** 37.45N 100.02W
Dodoma Tanzania **128 G4** 6.10S 35.45E
Dog Creek *town* Canada **56 F2** 51.35N 122.15W
Doha Qatar **146 D3** 25.17N 51.33E
Dolbeau Canada **68 D3** 48.53N 72.14W
Dolphin and Union Strait Canada **74 G3** 68.32N 116.00W
Dome Argus *f.* Antarctica **167 K1** 80.02S 75.08E
Dome Charlie *f.* Antarctica **167 L2** 74.33S 119.58E
Dome Creek *town* Canada **56 F3** 53.44N 121.01W
Dominica Windward Is. **117 L4** 15.30N 61.30W
Dominican Republic C. America **117 J4** 18.00N 70.00W
Don *r.* Russian Fed. **139 G2** 47.09N 39.15E
Donets'k Ukraine **139 G2** 47.59N 37.47E
Dongfang China **153 J1** 19.04N 108.39E
Dong Hoi Vietnam **154 D7** 17.32N 106.35E
Dongting Hu *l.* China **153 K3** 29.40N 113.00E
Donostia - San Sebastián Spain **138 C2** 43.19N 1.59W
Dorchester Canada **72 C2** 45.54N 64.31W
Dordogne *r.* France **138 C2** 45.00N 0.29W
Dore, Mont France **138 D2** 45.28N 2.45E
Doré Lake Canada **60 C2** 54.47N 107.18W
Döröö Nuur *l.* Mongolia **152 G7** 47.40N 93.30E
Dorset Canada **66 F5** 45.14N 78.53W
Dothan U.S.A. **113 I3** 31.12N 85.25W
Douala Cameroon **128 D5** 4.03N 9.42E
Dourados Brazil **123 D4** 22.09S 54.52W
Douro *r.* Portugal **138 C2** 41.09N 8.34W
Dover U.S.A. **113 K4** 39.10N 75.32W
Doyles Canada **72 F3** 47.50N 59.12W
Drakensberg *mts.* Lesotho/R.S.A. **129 F2** 29.59S 28.56E
Drake Passage S. Atlantic Ocean **167 F3** 57.47S 64.25W
Drayton Valley *town* Canada **59 C2** 53.14N 114.59W
Dresden Canada **66 B2** 42.36N 82.11W
Dresden Germany **138 E3** 51.03N 13.45E
Drobeta - Turnu Severin Romania **138 F2** 44.37N 22.40E
Drowning *r.* Canada **65 D3** 50.54N 84.36W
Drumheller Canada **59 C1** 51.27N 112.42W
Drummondville Canada **68 D2** 45.53N 72.29W
Dryden Canada **64 B3** 49.47N 92.51W
Drysdale *r.* Australia **158 B4** 14.04S 126.57E
Duarte, Pico Dom. Rep. **117 J4** 19.02N 70.59W
Ḍubā Saudi Arabia **146 B3** 27.20N 35.45E
Dubai U.A.E. **146 D3** 25.14N 55.17E
Dubawnt *r.* Canada **60 D4** 62.00N 103.13W
Dubawnt Lake Canada **74 H3** 63.05N 101.38W
Dubbo Australia **158 D2** 32.16S 148.41E
Dublin Rep. of Ireland **138 C3** 53.20N 6.16W
Du Bois U.S.A. **65 F1** 41.07N 78.48W
Dubuque U.S.A. **64 C1** 42.30N 90.40W
Ducie I. Pacific Oc. **163 S4** 24.40S 124.48W
Duck Bay *town* Canada **60 D2** 52.10N 100.10W
Dudinka Russian Fed. **143 K4** 69.27N 86.13E
Duero *r.* Spain **138 C2** 41.02N 6.56W
Dufferin, Cape Canada **68 C5** 58.52N 78.32W
Dukou China **152 I3** 26.30N 101.40E
Duluth U.S.A. **113 H6** 46.50N 92.10W
Dūmā Syria **150 B3** 33.33N 36.22E
Ḍumayr Syria **150 B3** 33.38N 36.42E
Dumont d'Urville *research stn.* Antarctica **167 A2** 66.40S 140.01E
Dumont d'Urville Sea Antarctica **167 A2** 63.02S 134.41E
Duncan Canada **57 V2** 48.47N 123.41W
Dundalk Canada **66 D4** 44.09N 80.24W
Dundas Canada **64 W1** 43.16N 79.56W
Dunedin New Zealand **159 G1** 45.53S 170.31E
Dungun Malaysia **154 C4** 4.44N 103.26E
Dungunab Sudan **146 B3** 21.04N 37.04E
Dunhuang China **152 G6** 40.00N 94.40E
Dunkirk U.S.A. **66 E2** 42.29N 79.19W
Dunnville Canada **66 E2** 42.54N 79.37W
Dunville Canada **73 I3** 47.16N 53.55W
Durango Mexico **116 D5** 24.01N 104.00W
Durban R.S.A. **129 G2** 29.51S 31.02E
Durham Canada **66 D4** 44.10N 80.49W
Durham *d.* Canada **64 Y3** 44.02N 78.55W
Durham U.S.A. **113 K4** 36.00N 78.54W
Durrell Canada **73 H4** 49.39N 54.44W
Durūz, Jabal ad *mtn.* Syria **150 B3** 32.42N 36.43E
Dushanbe Tajikistan **147 E4** 38.37N 68.49E
Düsseldorf Germany **138 D3** 51.13N 6.47E
Dutton Canada **66 C2** 42.39N 81.30W
Duyun China **153 J3** 26.16N 107.29E
Dyer, Cape Canada **75 L3** 66.39N 61.16W
Dyer Bay *town* Canada **66 C5** 45.10N 81.20W
Dzerzhinsk Russian Fed. **139 H3** 56.14N 43.28E
Dzhigudzhak Russian Fed. **143 R4** 64.33N 157.19E
Dzhugdzhur Range *mts.* Russian Fed. **143 P3** 57.30N 138.00E
Dzungarian Basin *f.* Asia **152 F7** 45.20N 86.30E

E

Eagle *r.* Canada **69 H4** 53.34N 57.15W
Eagle Creek *r.* Canada **60 C2** 52.20N 107.24W
Eagle Mountain U.S.A. **65 C2** 47.54N 90.31W
Eagle Pass *town* U.S.A. **112 F2** 28.44N 100.31W
Ear Falls *town* Canada **64 B3** 50.37N 93.13W
East Antarctica *f.* Antarctica **167 L1** 79.16S 109.58E
East Aurora U.S.A. **66 F2** 42.46N 78.37W
East C. New Zealand **159 G2** 37.45S 178.30E
East China Sea Asia **153 N3** 29.00N 125.00E
Eastend Canada **60 B1** 49.30N 108.50W
Easter I. Pacific Oc. **163 U4** 27.08S 109.23W
Eastern Desert Egypt **146 B3** 26.39N 32.50E
Eastern Ghats *mts.* India **147 F2** 11.54N 77.22E
Eastern Sayan *mts.* Russian Fed. **143 L3** 53.30N 98.00E
Easterville Canada **60 E2** 53.06N 99.49W
East Falkland *i.* Falkland Is. **123 D1** 51.45S 58.50W
East Gwillimbury *d.* Canada **64 X3** 44.08N 79.24W
East London R.S.A. **129 F1** 33.01S 27.56E
Eastmain Canada **68 C4** 52.14N 78.30W
Eastmain *r.* Canada **68 C4** 52.14N 78.24W
East Millinocket U.S.A. **72 A2** 45.37N 68.35W
East Point Canada **72 E3** 46.28N 61.59W
Eastport Canada **69 I3** 48.39N 53.46W
Eastport U.S.A. **72 B2** 44.54N 66.59W
East Siberian Sea Russian Fed. **143 S5** 73.00N 160.00E
East Timor Asia **155 H2** 8.40S 125.40E
Eatonia Canada **60 B1** 51.13N 109.23W
Eau Claire U.S.A. **64 C2** 44.49N 91.30W
Eau Claire, Lac à l' *l.* Canada **68 D5** 56.13N 74.07W
Eauripik Atoll *i.* Fed. States of Micronesia **155 K5** 6.42N 143.04E
Ebinur Hu *l.* China **152 E6** 45.00N 83.00E
Ebro *r.* Spain **138 D2** 40.43N 0.51E
Echo Bay *town* Canada **74 G3** 66.01N 117.59W
Echoing *r.* Canada **61 F2** 55.51N 92.04W
Echuca Australia **158 D2** 36.10S 144.49E
Ecuador S. America **122 B6** 2.00S 78.00W
Ed Damazin Sudan **128 G6** 11.47N 34.20E
Eddies Cove *town* Canada **69 H3** 51.24N 56.27W
Edinburgh U.K. **138 C3** 55.57N 3.11W
Edmonton Canada **59 C2** 53.33N 113.33W
Edmundston Canada **72 A3** 47.23N 68.20W
Edom *f.* Israel/Jordan **150 A2** 30.28N 35.16E
Edson Canada **59 B2** 53.35N 116.25W
Edward, Lake Uganda/Dem. Rep. Congo **128 F4** 0.30S 29.30E
Edwards Plateau *f.* U.S.A. **112 F3** 30.30N 100.30W
Edziza, Mount Canada **56 D4** 57.45N 130.37W
Eétamamiou *r.* Canada **72 F5** 50.21N 59.59W
Egmont Bay Canada **72 C3** 46.33N 64.13W
Egypt Africa **128 G7** 25.00N 31.16E
Eighty Mile Beach *f.* Australia **158 B4** 19.00S 121.00E
Ekwan *r.* Canada **65 E4** 53.15N 82.18W
Elat Israel **150 A1** 29.33N 34.56E
Elazığ Turkey **139 G1** 38.39N 39.15E
Elba *i.* Italy **138 E2** 42.50N 10.16E
El'ban Russian Fed. **153 P8** 50.05N 136.35E
Elbe *r.* Germany **138 D3** 53.53N 9.05E
El Beqa'a *f.* Lebanon **150 B4** 34.04N 36.11E
Elbow Canada **60 C1** 51.08N 106.36W
Elbrus *mtn.* Russian Fed. **139 H2** 43.22N 42.25E
Elburz Mountains Iran **146 C4** 36.52N 49.43E
El Djouf *des.* Africa **128 C7** 21.00N 8.00W
Eleuthera *i.* The Bahamas **117 I6** 25.00N 76.00W
El Faiyūm Egypt **146 B3** 29.18N 30.51E
El Fasher Sudan **128 F6** 13.36N 25.20E
Elgin U.S.A. **113 I5** 42.03N 88.19W
El Giza Egypt **128 G7** 29.59N 31.12E
El Goléa Algeria **128 D8** 30.34N 2.58E
Elgon, Mount Kenya/Uganda **128 G5** 1.08N 34.34E
Elista Russian Fed. **139 H2** 46.19N 44.16E
Elkford Canada **57 H2** 50.01N 114.56W
Elk Island National Park Canada **59 C2** 53.36N 112.50W
Elk Lake Canada **57 W2** 48.31N 123.24W
Elk Lake *town* Canada **65 E2** 47.44N 80.20W
Elko U.S.A. **112 C5** 40.50N 115.46W
Elk Point *town* Canada **59 D2** 53.54N 110.53W
Elk River *town* U.S.A. **64 B2** 45.18N 93.35W
Ellef Ringnes Island Canada **74 H4** 78.38N 101.56W
Ellensburg U.S.A. **112 B6** 47.00N 120.34W
Ellesmere Island Canada **74 J4** 77.10N 83.03W
Ellice *r.* Canada **74 H3** 67.56N 103.59W
Elliot Lake *town* Canada **65 E2** 46.23N 82.39W
Ellsworth U.S.A. **72 A2** 44.32N 68.26W
Ellsworth Land *f.* Antarctica **167 E1** 75.01S 90.55W
Ellsworth Mountains Antarctica **167 F1** 76.30S 88.46W
El Minyā Egypt **146 B3** 28.05N 30.45E
Elmira Canada **66 D3** 43.37N 80.33W
Elmira U.S.A. **65 F1** 42.07N 76.49W
El Muglad Sudan **128 F6** 11.01N 27.44E
Elmvale Canada **66 E4** 44.35N 79.52W
El Obeid Sudan **128 G6** 13.10N 30.11E
Elora Canada **66 D3** 43.41N 80.27W
El Paso U.S.A. **112 E3** 31.45N 106.30W
Elrose Canada **60 B1** 51.12N 108.01W
Elsa Canada **74 E3** 63.55N 135.26W
El Salvador C. America **116 G3** 13.30N 89.00W
Ely U.S.A. **64 C2** 47.54N 91.51W
Emerald Australia **158 D3** 23.31S 148.08E
Emerson Canada **60 E1** 49.02N 97.11W
Emi Koussi *mtn.* Chad **128 E6** 19.46N 18.34E
Emo Canada **64 B3** 48.38N 93.50W
Emory Peak *mtn.* U.S.A. **112 F2** 29.15N 103.19W
Emporia U.S.A. **112 G4** 38.24N 96.10W
Empress Canada **59 D1** 50.58N 110.01W
Emsdale Canada **66 E5** 45.33N 79.20W
Encantada, Cerro de la *mtn.* Mexico **116 A7** 31.00N 115.23W
Encarnación Paraguay **123 D4** 27.20S 55.50W
Endeh Indonesia **155 G2** 8.51S 121.40E
Enderby Canada **59 B1** 50.33N 119.09W
Enderby Land *f.* Antarctica **167 J2** 71.47S 50.19E
Endicott U.S.A. **65 F1** 42.06N 76.00W
Endicott Mountains U.S.A. **74 C3** 67.50N 152.33W

M

The Pearson School Atlas represents another stage in my 25-year association with Prentice Hall/Pearson Publishers. I have been blessed with gifted editors and production personnel who have brought this resource to reality. In this current edition, the assistance, direction, and support of Kelly Ronan have been exemplary. I have been surrounded by individuals and organizations who have contributed to my personal and professional development as a geographer, teacher, consultant, and author – the ROGES, the (former) Professional Development Committee of OSSTF, the Geography Consultants of Ontario, especially George Thompson, the consultative staff of Ontario Agri-Food Education, and my Agriculture in the Classroom colleagues across Canada.

Robert Morrow

Topographic map extracts on pages 58, 62, 63, 67, 70, 71, 76, 77, 169 and 175
© Produced under licence from Her Majesty the Queen in Right of Canada, with permission of Natural Resources Canada.

Photographs on pages 6-7 and 14-15 *Masterfile*
Satellite images on pages 57 and 173 *Science Photo Library*
Satellite images on pages 61, 65, 69, 73, 75, 129, 139, and 159 *NASA Visible Earth*
Satellite images on pages 117, 122 and 123 *data courtesy of the U.S. Geological Survey, EROS Data Center, Sioux Falls, SD*
Data for the map at bottom right page 111 *Stockholm Environment Institute at the University of York, UK*

The following lists give the references and sources used in the preparation of the thematic maps, graphs and statistical tables in the atlas :

CANADA THEMATIC

pages 4-5 Canada and the World Atlas
pages 6-7 Canada and the World Atlas
pages 8-9 Canada and the World Atlas, Environment Canada
pages 10-11 Canada and the World Atlas
page 12 Environment Canada
page 13 Environment Canada, NASA (National Aeronautics and Space Administration)
pages 14-15 Canada and the World Atlas
pages 16-17 Canada and the World Atlas
pages 18-19 Canada and the World Atlas, Statistics Canada, Organization for Economic Co-operation and Development (OECD)
pages 20-21 Natural Resources Canada, Petroleum Economist, The Times Atlas of the World 10th Comprehensive edition
pages 22-23 Canada Electricity Association, National Energy Board, Natural Resources Canada, ATCO Power, BC Hydro, Columbia Power Corporation, Energy Ottawa, Great Lakes Power, Hydro Québec, Manitoba Hydro, Maritime Electric, New Brunswick Power, Newfoundland and Labrador Hydro, Nova Scotia Power, Ontario Power Generation, Sask Power, TransAlta, Yukon Energy
pages 24-25 Canada and the World Atlas, Statistics Canada, UNCTAD/WTO International Trade Centre
pages 26-27 Canada and the World Atlas, Fisheries and Oceans Canada, Statistics Canada, Food and Agricultural Organization of the United Nations (FAO)
pages 28-29 Canada and the World Atlas, Natural Resources Canada, FAO
pages 30-31 Statistics Canada
pages 32-33 Statistics Canada, BC Finance and Economic Review 2002, Alberta Economic Development, The Saskatchewan Economy, Manitoba Financial Report 2002,Ontario Ministry of Finance, Institut de la statistique Québec, Department of Finance New Brunswick, Ministry of Finance Nova Scotia, Prince Edward Island Statistics
pages 34-35 Canada and the World Atlas, Statistics Canada 2001 Census
pages 36-37 Canada and the World Atlas, Statistics Canada 2001 Census
pages 38-39 Canada and the World Atlas
pages 40-41 The National Atlas of Canada
pages 42-43 Statistics Canada 2001 Census, Clean Air Strategic Alliance, World Bank World Development Indicators(WDI) 2002, National Sewage Report Card
pages 44-45 Statistics Canada 2001 Census, Citizenship and Immigration Canada (CIC)
pages 46-47 Transport Canada, Statistics Canada
pages 48-49 Canada Tourism
pages 50-51 UN Statistics Division, World Trade Organization
pages 52-53 Environment Canada, Carbon Dioxide Information Analysis Center
pages 54-55 Environment Canada, National Parks Canada, UNESCO (United Nations Educational, Scientific and Cultural Organization)

CANADA REGIONAL

pages 56 to 77 All Physical and Political maps on these pages are created from databases © Collins Bartholomew Ltd.

WORLD THEMATIC

pages 82-83 United Nations Environment Programme (UNEP)
pages 84-85 National Oceanic and Atmospheric Administration (NOAA)
page 87 FAO
page 88 The Times Atlas of the World 10th Comprehensive Edition, United Nations Population Division (UNDP), World Urbanization Prospects 2001
page 89 UNICEF (United Nations Children's Fund), World Bank WDI 2002
pages 90-91 UNDP World Urbanization Prospects 2001
page 92 World Bank WDI 2002, UN Statistics Division
page 93 World Trade Organization
pages 94-95 International Energy Agency, BP Statistical Review 2002
pages 96-97 UN Statistics Division, United Nations Framework Convention on Climate Change (UNFCCC)
pages 98-99 UN Human Development Reports 2002, World Bank WDI 2002, FAO State of Food Insecurity 2002, UNAIDS Report 2002
page 100 UN Human Development Reports 2002, UN Statistics Division
page 101 UNHCR Yearbook 2001
page 102 World Bank WDI 2002
page 103 UN Human Development Reports 2002
page 104 International Labour Organization, IDBAmerica, Year Book of Australia 2002
page 106 UN Human Development Reports 2002

page 107 The Commonwealth, North Atlantic Treaty Organization, Organization of American States, League of Arab States, African Union, Association of Southeast Asian Nations, South Pacific Forum, Colombo Plan, Organization of the Oil Exporting Countries, Organisation for Economic Cooperation and Development, European Union, The Caribbean Community, Latin American Integration Association, Andean Community, Economic Community of West Africa, Economic and Monetary Community of Central Africa, Southern African Development Community, North American Free Trade Agreement

WORLD REGIONAL

pages 108 to 167 All Political, Physical and Physical and Political maps on these pages are created from databases © Collins Bartholomew Ltd.
page 108 UNPD Urbanization Prospects 2001, UN Demographic Yearbook 1999
page 110 Canada and the World Atlas
page 111 World Tourism Organization, US Census Bureau, World Trade Organization, SEI/SIDA
page 114 USGS Land Cover Data Base, World Climate Data
page 115 US Census Bureau, US Department of Commerce, World Trade Organization
page 116 UN Urbanization Prospects 2001, UN Demographic Yearbook
page 118 USGS Land Cover Data Base, World Climate Data
page 119 World Tourism Organization, Canada and the World Atlas, UN Statistics Division
page 120 UN Urbanization Prospects 2001, UN Demographic Yearbook 1999
pages 122-123 UN Urbanization Prospects 2001, UN Demographic Yearbook 1999
page 124 USGS Land Cover Data Base, World Climate Data
page 125 World Tourism Organization, The Times History of the World, UN Statistics Division
page 126 UN Urbanization Prospects 2001, UN Demographic Yearbook 1999
pages 128-129 UN Urbanization Prospects 2001, UN Demographic Yearbook 1999
page 130 USGS Land Cover Data Base, World Climate Data
page 131 World Tourism Organization, The Times History of the World, UN Statistics Division
pages 132-133 UN Urbanization Prospects 2001, UN Demographic Yearbook 1999
page 136 UN Urbanization Prospects 2001, UN Demographic Yearbook 1999
page 137 The Times Atlas of European History
pages 138-139 Urbanization Prospects 2001, UN Demographic Yearbook 1999
page 140 USGS Land Cover Data Base, World Climate Data
page 141 World Tourism Organization, UN Statistics Division
pages 142-143 UN Urbanization Prospects 2001, UN Demographic Yearbook 1999
page 144 USGS Land Cover Data Base, World Climate Data
page 145 Canada and the World Atlas, UN Statistics Division
pages 146-147 UN Urbanization Prospects 2001, UN Demographic Yearbook 1999
page 148 USGS Land Cover Data Base, World Climate Data
page 149 World Tourism Organization, UNHCR Yearbook 2001, UN Statistics Division
page 150 UN Urbanization Prospects 2001, UN Demographic Yearbook 1999, BP Statistical Review 2002
page 151 The Times History of the World, World Factbook 2002
pages 152-153 UN Urbanization Prospects 2001, UN Demographic Yearbook 1999
pages 154-155 UN Urbanization Prospects 2001, UN Demographic Yearbook 1999
page 156 USGS Land Cover Data Base, World Climate Data
page 157 World Tourism Organization, The Times History of the World, UN Statistics Division
pages 158-159 UN Urbanization Prospects 2001, UN Demographic Yearbook 1999
page 160 USGS Land Cover Data, World Climate Data
page 161 World Tourism Organization, The Times History of the World, UN Statistics Division, Australian Bureau of Statistics, Statistics New Zealand
pages 164-165 UN Statistics Division

CANADA STATISTICS

pages 176-185 Statistics Canada, CIC, Fisheries and Oceans Canada, Natural Resources Canada, Industry Canada, Elections Canada

WORLD STATISTICS

(In this section, the data is provided for the latest date in which meaningful comparisons among the largest number of countries is possible.)
pages 186-193 UN Statistical Division, World Bank WDI 2002, UNESCO, CIA Factbook 2002

National Library of Canada Cataloguing in Publication

Morrow, Robert, 1942-
    Pearson school atlas / Robert Morrow.

Includes index.
ISBN 0-13-039311-8 (bound).--ISBN 0-13-122506-5 (pbk.)

    1. Atlases, Canadian. I. Title.

G1021.M87 2003   912   C2003-901252-2

Compilation Copyright © 2004 Pearson Education Canada, Inc., Toronto, Ontario.
26 Prince Andrew Place, Toronto, Ontario, M3C 2T8

Individual maps and material © Collins Bartholomew Ltd 2003
Narrative text © Pearson Education Canada inc

ISBN 0-13-039311-8 (Hardcover)   ISBN 0-13-122506-5 (Paperback)

Publishers: Mark Cobham, Susan Cox
Product Managers: Melanie Trevelyan, David LeGallais
Managing Editor: Elynor Kagan
Developmental Editor: Kelly Ronan
Coordinating Editor: Angelie Kim
Production Coordinator: Zane Kaneps
Cover Design: Alex Li
Cartography: Collins Bartholomew Ltd- Moira Jones, Mark Steward, Neal Jordan-Caws
Reviewers: *Aboriginal content:* Shawn Bernard, Patrick Loyer; *Middle-East content:*
Martin Bunton, Christopher Friedrichs, Derek Penslar, James Whidden; *Geographic
content:* Bruce Clark, Dennis Desrivieres, Lloyd Greenham, John Wallace

1. Grand Prismatic Spring, Yellowstone © Charles O'Rear/CORBIS
2. Iceberg, Newfoundland – © Grant V. Faint/ImageBank/GettyImages
3. Sydney – © Romilly Lockyer/ImageBank/GettyImages
4. Alberta – Corel
5. Earth showing Western Hemisphere – PhotoDisc/GettyImages
6. Morocco – © Darrell Gulin/ImageBank/Gettyimages
7. Ottawa (satellite shot) – DigitalVision
8. New Brunswick Landscape – © Carl & Ann Purcell/CORBIS
9. Teenagers – © Vicky Kasala/ImageBank/GettyImages
10. Contour Strip Farmed Wheat Fields, Washington – © Joseph Sohm;
    ChromoSohm Inc./CORBIS
11. Vancouver – Corel
12. Nepal – Corel
13. Earth showing Western Hemisphere – PhotoDisc/GettyImages

5 RRD 09

Manufactured in the United States.

PEARSON
Education
Canada

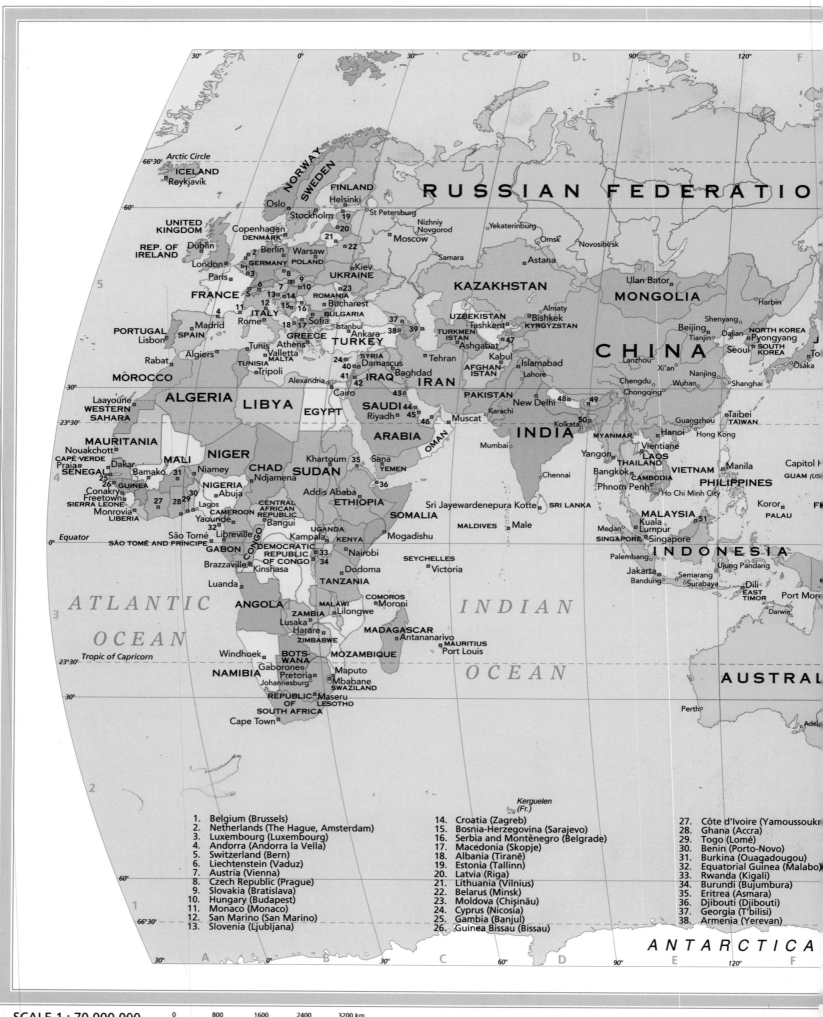

30° A 0° 30° C 60° D 90° E 120° F

66°30' Arctic Circle
ICELAND
Reykjavík
NORWAY
SWEDEN
FINLAND
RUSSIAN FEDERATIO

Oslo Helsinki St Petersburg
60° Stockholm 19
UNITED Copenhagen
KINGDOM DENMARK 20
REP. OF Dublin 21
IRELAND Berlin 22
Warsaw Kiev
London GERMANY POLAND
Paris 3 8 UKRAINE
FRANCE 6 7 9 10
13 14 23
12 15 16 ROMANIA
4 11 ITALY Bucharest
PORTUGAL Madrid Rome 18 17 BULGARIA
Lisbon SPAIN Sofia Istanbul
Tunis GREECE Ankara
Rabat Algiers Athens TURKEY
MOROCCO TUNISIA MALTA Tripoli 24 SYRIA Damascus
Alexandria 40 IRAQ Baghdad
WESTERN 41 42 43 Cairo
Laayoune SAHARA ALGERIA LIBYA EGYPT SAUDI 44
Riyadh 45
46 Muscat

Nizhniy Yekaterinburg
Novgorod Omsk Novosibirsk
Moscow
Samara Astana
KAZAKHSTAN Almaty Ulan Bator Harbin
Bishkek MONGOLIA
UZBEKISTAN Tashkent KYRGYZSTAN
TURKMEN- 47 Shenyang
ISTAN Ashgabat Beijing Dalian NORTH KOREA
Kabul CHINA Tianjin Pyongyang
Tehran AFGHAN- Islamabad SOUTH
ISTAN Lahore Xi'an Seoul KOREA
IRAN Karachi Chengdu Wuhan Shanghai
PAKISTAN Chongqing
New Delhi 48 49
Karachi 50 Guangzhou Taibei
INDIA Kolkata TAIWAN
ARABIA MYANMAR Hanoi Hong Kong
OMAN Yangon Vientiane
MAURITANIA Mumbai LAOS
Nouakchott CAPE VERDE Chennai Bangkok VIETNAM Manila
Praia NIGER Khartoum 35 Sana THAILAND CAMBODIA
SENEGAL MALI Niamey CHAD SUDAN YEMEN Phnom Penh PHILIPPINES
Bamako 31 CENTRAL Ndjamena 36 Ho Chi Minh City
Conakry 26 GUINEA NIGERIA Abuja AFRICAN Addis Ababa MALAYSIA 51
Freetown SIERRA LEONE 27 28 29 Lagos REPUBLIC ETHIOPIA Sri Jayewardenepura Kotte SRI LANKA
Monrovia CAMEROON Bangui SOMALIA Kuala
LIBERIA 32 Yaounde UGANDA MALDIVES Male Medan Lumpur
São Tomé Libreville Kampala KENYA SINGAPORE Singapore
SÃO TOMÉ AND PRÍNCIPE GABON 33 Nairobi SEYCHELLES
Equator DEMOCRATIC 34 Mogadishu Victoria
REPUBLIC Dodoma
OF CONGO TANZANIA
Brazzaville Kinshasa
Luanda COMOROS

ATLANTIC ANGOLA MALAWI Moroni INDIAN
ZAMBIA Lilongwe
OCEAN Lusaka MADAGASCAR
Harare Antananarivo MAURITIUS
Windhoek ZIMBABWE Port Louis OCEAN
Tropic of Capricorn BOTS- MOZAMBIQUE
NAMIBIA Gaborone WANA Maputo
Pretoria Mbabane
Johannesburg SWAZILAND
REPUBLIC Maseru LESOTHO
OF SOUTH AFRICA
Cape Town

INDONESIA
Palembang
Jakarta
Bandung Semarang Ujung Pandang
Surabaya Dili
EAST Port More
TIMOR Darwin

AUSTRAL

Perth

Kerguelen
(Fr.)

1. Belgium (Brussels)
2. Netherlands (The Hague, Amsterdam)
3. Luxembourg (Luxembourg)
4. Andorra (Andorra la Vella)
5. Switzerland (Bern)
6. Liechtenstein (Vaduz)
7. Austria (Vienna)
8. Czech Republic (Prague)
9. Slovakia (Bratislava)
10. Hungary (Budapest)
11. Monaco (Monaco)
12. San Marino (San Marino)
13. Slovenia (Ljubljana)

14. Croatia (Zagreb)
15. Bosnia-Herzegovina (Sarajevo)
16. Serbia and Montênegro (Belgrade)
17. Macedonia (Skopje)
18. Albania (Tiranë)
19. Estonia (Tallinn)
20. Latvia (Riga)
21. Lithuania (Vilnius)
22. Belarus (Minsk)
23. Moldova (Chişinău)
24. Cyprus (Nicosia)
25. Gambia (Banjul)
26. Guinea Bissau (Bissau)

27. Côte d'Ivoire (Yamoussoukr
28. Ghana (Accra)
29. Togo (Lomé)
30. Benin (Porto-Novo)
31. Burkina (Ouagadougou)
32. Equatorial Guinea (Malabo)
33. Rwanda (Kigali)
34. Burundi (Bujumbura)
35. Eritrea (Asmara)
36. Djibouti (Djibouti)
37. Georgia (T'bilisi)
38. Armenia (Yerevan)

ANTARCTICA

SCALE 1 : 70 000 000

0 800 1600 2400 3200 km